Elsa Morante's Politics of Writing

Elsa Morante's Politics of Writing

*Rethinking Subjectivity, History,
and the Power of Art*

Edited by Stefania Lucamante

FAIRLEIGH DICKINSON UNIVERSITY PRESS
Madison • Teaneck

Published by Fairleigh Dickinson University Press
Copublished by The Rowman & Littlefield Publishing Group, Inc.
4501 Forbes Boulevard, Suite 200, Lanham, Maryland 20706
www.rowman.com

Unit A, Whitacre Mews, 26-34 Stannary Street, London SE11 4AB

British Library Cataloguing in Publication Information Available

Library of Congress Cataloging-in-Publication Data

Elsa Morante's politics of writing : rethinking subjectivity, history, and the power of art / Stefania Lucamante.
pages cm
Includes bibliographical references and index.
ISBN 978-1-6114-7776-2 (pbk : alk. paper)
ISBN 978-1-61147-794-8 (cloth : alk. paper) — ISBN 978-1-61147-795-5 (electronic)
1. Morante, Elsa, approximately 1912-1985—Criticism and interpretation. I. Lucamante, Stefania, editor.
PQ4829.O615Z614 2015
858'.91209—dc23
                                    2014037506

♾™ The paper used in this publication meets the minimum requirements of American National Standard for Information Sciences Permanence of Paper for Printed Library Materials, ANSI/NISO Z39.48-1992.

Printed in the United States of America

Contents

Acknowledgments

As I always write in my acknowledgments, every book is the outcome of a collective effort. It is particularly true in the case of this volume, and my gratitude goes to all the contributors who have valiantly produced brilliant readings of Elsa Morante's works. In particular, and along with the Fairleigh Dickinson University Press evaluator Katja Lijmatta, I would like to thank those colleagues who have read and reviewed the essays that constitute the volume. Gabrielle Orsi, Nicoletta Marini-Maio, Gaetana Marrone, Kenise Lyons, and Sharon Wood have patiently noted points to be strengthened, and reviewed this volume with great attention. My editor, Noah Simon Jampol, has been invaluable in making sure the text is cohesive across the different essays—his attitude, and the precision with which he made comments and pointed out unclear parts, was priceless.

Research on Elsa Morante's manuscripts has been made possible by the kind assistance of Giuliana Zagra, director of the Fondo Elsa Morante of the National Library in Rome, as well as by Morante heirs Carlo Cecchi and Daniele Morante, who kindly agreed to let me examine Morante's documents and granted us permission for publishing excerpts from Elsa Morante's works.

I am extremely grateful to Anthony J. Tamburri, director of the series in which my book is published, for believing in the importance of my work. To Harry Keyishian, my warmest thanks for his queries on the project and for making sure that the volume would look at its best for publication. I would like to thank the Catholic University of America for the grant I received to pursue this project, and the then Dean of my School, Lawrence Poos, for believing in it. To my Italophile friend Peter Gribbin, all my thanks for offering such a wonderful and committed help through the process of the making of this volume.

Finally, I dedicate this volume to all scholars of Elsa Morante in hopes that it will contribute to the understanding of, and growing body of research on, this important voice in Italian literature.

All Italian excerpts from Elsa Morante's works by permission of the heirs, Carlo Cecchi and Daniele Morante. © Elsa Morante Estate. All rights handled by Agenzia Letteraria Internazionale, Milan, Italy.

Excerpts reprinted from *History: A Novel*, by Elsa Morante by permission of the publisher, Steerforth Press.

Excerpts reprinted from Aracoeli, by Elsa Morante, translated by William Weaver, translation copyright © 1985 by Random House. Used by permission of Random House, an imprint and division of Random House LLC. All rights reserved.

Every effort has been made to obtain permission to reproduce copyrighted material. If any proper acknowledgment has not been made, copyright holders are invited to inform the publisher of the oversight.

Introduction

Stefania Lucamante

It is difficult to overstate the value of Elsa Morante's contribution to contemporary Italian letters as a literary conduit that connected the novelistic tradition to a more international perspective, extended beyond modernism and the influence of American writers in postwar Italy. The idea of the present volume was born in 2012 at a conference on Morante. The chapters collected originated from this event and were later significantly expanded into rigorous analyses of the ways in which Morante's fictional and essayistic writings shape classical oppositions such as engagement and enchantment with the world, sin and repentance, self-reflection and corporality. Some of the chapters determine her ongoing engagement in the visual arts and theater, and study how cinematic adaptations of her works garner further perspectives to her stories and characters. All chapters focus on Elsa Morante's strategies to address her wide disinterest (and contempt) for the Italian intellectual status quo of her time, regardless of its political side, while showing at once her *own* kind of ideological engagement. In fact, if Morante actively contested bourgeoisie and its values (productivity, hard work, compensation, the arts as mercification of goods), she also exposed some of the gnawings of the rigid political thinking of leftist artists, as their denunciation "Piccolo Manifesto dei comunisti" aptly demonstrates. In all her considerations on class struggle, market capitalism, and commodification of culture, the body and its natural response to social conditioning remain, however, the author's fulcrum: it is through the heart and the mind that one can understand the world, always "more important than literature," as Morante wrote, for it is the world that creates relations between human beings. Rather than a strict dichotomy between Nature and Culture (see her oft-discussed leaning toward the former), Morante proposes that reality can be found only when individuals are aware that alienation, rigid thinking and powers (an erroneous idea of political thinking turned into violence against the Other) constitute the monsters of that very unreality that generates the ills of contemporary society. The very existentiality of Morante's work—her constant battle against the monsters of unreality—cannot be translated into mere critique or in expectations about society. Rather, it is revealed through the principles governing her aesthetic compositions, and it articulates the single contents that satisfy the logic of the writer's ideology and the theories in what Aby Warburg calls the *co-originariness* of form and content, time and space. In her analysis of the world, Morante consistently advances a poetics in which sexuality and sexual politics play a crucial role in the development of her characters and alienation from society. The laws governing Morante's writing are to be found in her own writing and only in that: the incidence of certain traits, of certain rhetorical strategies, the recurrence of certain themes, and particularly the ending she decides to give to the relations among the characters gives sense to, and shapes literarily, her thought. In short, the whole construct of her works makes us aware of what, according to Leo Spitzer, represents "the formal essence of an author." While her readers might believe their act of reading to be determined in complete freedom, Morante's scholars who contributed to this volume all share the belief that the process of reception has already been predetermined by the instruments Morante already predisposed within her texts for our careful reception of her message.

Her works—particularly the novels *Menzogna e sortilegio* (House of Liars, 1948), *La Storia: Romanzo* (History: A Novel, 1974), and more explicitly, *Aracoeli* (Aracoeli, 1982)—foreshadowed and advanced tenets and structures later affirmed by postmodernism, namely, the fragmentation of narrative cells, rhizomatic narratives, lack of a linear temporal consistency, and meta- and self-reflective processes. The mirrors and photographs that abound in Morante's first-person narrations lead the reader down a path of self-reflection, one of authentic investigation of the relation between the narrating protagonist and the author's prismatic personality. Particularly when deconstructed, Morante's ambitious aim at classicism reveals her uncanny ability to use her characters as fantastic alter egos for herself, her *alibis*. Characters can be considered a *pharmakon* against the lie of unreality that Morante consistently tries to expose in her works; only the truth of writing can constitute a safe refuge from the unhappiness of existence. Morante's assertion that the adolescent Arturo in her 1957 Strega Award–winning novel *L'isola di Arturo* (Arturo's Island) was, in fact, herself, hides a profound truth that justifies the author's self-dedication of her novel, that "to Remo N."[1] Anagrams (which, like charades and rebuses, represent one of Morante's ways of thinking about the human condition that she shares with her friend Carlo Levi) are steeped in the baroque, for they metaphorize the mutability of life. The author—as is her praxis—reflects herself in the image of Arturo; in all truth, however, she cannot reflect herself into this adolescent whose life is already embittered from sad events, not least his own father's disavowal, because her doting gaze over this boy is too motherly. If it is indisputable that Elsa Morante mirrors herself in every character that she presents to her readers as a restless Narcissus, it is also indisputable that, by virtue of the idea of mutability drawn from mirrors and pictures as integral parts of the narration, she also retains with each of them a dialectical relation, in which they appear to act more freely and spontaneously than usually stated. At times, Morante appears to be a sweet dictator to her personages, because she loves them more than herself. In other instances, she revolts against them like a Jungian devouring mother. From Elisa to Arturo, from Ida and Davide (these two united in a pairing that reflects the binary composition of Morante's Jewish descent), to Andrea and the unhappiest one of all, Manuele, Elsa is, in a way, one of *them*. As Franco Ferrucci notes, in Morante's *Menzogna e sortilegio* (House of Liars), characters "[. . .] represent the major and minor gods of a universe which concerns the childhood of a single character among all, that is, Elisa" (32). But Elisa has other peers: the Arturo of *L'isola di Arturo* and the Manuele of *Aracoeli*. Invariably, in Morante's universe, adults are the agents of "the future drama" (ibid.) in the child characters' lives. In turn, the children's curse is a cruel destiny because, in their mature age, they unmask their childhood myth while desperately loving it.

In Morante's world, everyone falls prey to his or her own idol, but every bewitchment follows a precise pattern that holds importance for the narrative. Love is the most desirable yet detested feeling, for it produces a deadly addiction: *Odi et amo, quare id faciam fortasse requiris, Nescio sed fieri sentio et excrucior* (I hate and love, you wonder why I do it. I don't know but I feel it and I suffer; Catullus 85). But Morante is not merely her characters' creator for, if she were just so, she would hold a different posture in the oscillating tension between the represented feelings of love and hate: this tension is perhaps the most baroque feature of her writing. This constant oscillation gives body to the chiaroscuro effects of her narratives of myths destroyed; her chiaroscuro effects reify monuments constantly razed and rebuilt to fictional heroes; it makes us understand the enclosed and shady spaces of Elisa's life and the deceivingly free and open existence of Arturo; it gives meaning to the shining presence of jewels in *Menzogna e sortilegio* and to the corals in *L'isola di Arturo*. Finally, the chiaroscuro effect lets us into the opaque and shapeless world (for different reasons) of Ida and Manuele, and the journey-quest to Andalusia of the latter only underscores the vanity of illusions. Morante shares the destiny of her characters like a great mythological mother who suffers for her children and yet, as previously stated, can also devour them. In the same way that the Spanish illiterate Aracoeli represents the embodiment of the entire maternal pantheon (all four of the Jungian mothers), Morante embodies an all-encompassing motherhood from which cruelty is not absent. This is particularly the case in *Aracoeli*, wherein Manuele, hoary Narcissus, reflects the author's own ruminations and existential despair in her aging years. The desperate tale of the *niñomadrero* (mother's boy) reveals such abysmal despair with and for life. Both manifestations of despair demand a life "come prima delle madri" (before the birth of the mothers) as the verses in her *Il mondo salvato dai ragazzini* (121) recite. Against devouring mothers there is no hope, for they are at once the object of our love and the reason for our disgrace. This is the paradox of mothers: they are the source of both our hope and disillusionment.

RETHINKING MORANTE AND HER POLITICS OF WRITING

August 18, 2012, marked the one hundredth anniversary of Elsa Morante's birth in Rome.[2] Other events also marked this important year: Morante's heirs bequeathed unpublished material by Elsa Morante to the Biblioteca Centrale Vittorio Emanuele II (National Library in Rome); this material was recently the subject of the exhibit "Santi, Sultani e Gran Capitani in camera mia. Inediti e ritrovati dall'Archivio di Elsa Morante," organized by Giuliana Zagra and Leonardo Lattarulo. This bequest greatly expanded the already existing Fondo Morante established by the author's will following her death in 1985. Additionally, this anniversary has offered young as well as more established Morante scholars the occasion and opportunity to rethink the significance of her works by looking at her writings—both published and unpublished—from multiple perspectives as well as the cinematic adaptations of some of her works. While some of these recent studies confirm more traditional readings of her work, others investigate the fluidity of borders and boundaries in relation to the genres and themes employed by Morante. To determine the importance of Morante today, to appreciate her theoretical and stylistic legacy, and to understand why and which elements of her work have interested Italian artists, we need to revisit the philosophy and aesthetic Morante outlined in her literary writings, essays, articles, reviews, and poetry, committing to a fresh outlook on her work.

Reflecting the proliferation of diverse critical perspectives on the life and works of Elsa Morante, even in our time a proper Morantian "school," that is, if such a thing exists at all, is still difficult to define. Unlike the intellectual legacy of her husband, Alberto Moravia, (whose literary progeny—from Antonio Debenedetti and Giorgio Montefoschi to Niccolò Ammaniti—are readily identifiable), Morante's direct influence on the Italian arts is not easily documented. Yet, she pioneered dramatic changes in rhetoric and style observable in the work of many contemporary writers including Fabrizia Ramondino, Patrizia Cavalli, Carmelo Samonà, Simona Vinci, and Elena Ferrante (Lucamante and Wood; Lucamante). Morante's echo permeates the pages of many contemporary Italian novels. The influence of her baroque and even anachronistic writing style has shaped films, as in the case of Cristina Comencini's and Francesca Archibugi's cinematic texts in which Morante's novels are openly cited as a source of inspiration for the filmmakers' subjects and characters. In this light, Morante's prophecies—her ideology, hopes, and dreams for a younger generation—need to be analyzed and reconsidered against the backdrop of our time. What is their validity today? In a thoughtful excursus on Morante criticism, Elena Porciani[3] touches on several issues that may potentially frustrate the would-be critic, not least of which is the overbearing voice of Cesare Garboli, the great essayist who became the voice for much of Morante criticism (a role he has similarly occupied for Natalia Ginzburg and, to some extent, Rosetta Loy).

While Garboli's authoritative assessments dissuaded some scholars from entering the conversation, these same writings inspired others to challenge his theories on Morante's writing and authorial intentions. In the 2006 documentary on Elsa Morante directed by Francesca Comencini (analyzed in one of this volume's chapters), Garboli offers theses on the corporeality of Morante's more intense writing, insisting that she did not love women and women did not love her. Is this really true? Garboli considers Morante's corporeal matter to represent her unsatisfied wish to have a child, a wish that she, in turn, sublimated in her prose and made manifest in her male characters (a known refrain drawn from Umberto Saba's well-known statements on the topic). Comencini's documentary relies almost exclusively on male testimony, with Patrizia Cavalli providing the lone female voice. Thirty years after Morante's death, there seems to be almost a tacit agreement with Biancamaria Frabotta's thesis (as well as Garboli's): Morante was a misogynist. While Garboli treats gender performance, sex, social conditioning, and instinctual behavior as if they were just one single construct, one cannot help but wonder whether Italian literary criticism would benefit from an unpacking of these features, subsequently expanding the field's theoretical borders, incorporating gender and queer studies as well as female narrative identity and the implications therein.

Like many artists, Morante loathed the application of potentially limiting labels to her work. However, she looked at and discussed everything from a profoundly gendered position: the problem of the atomic bomb as well as its true meaning (as presented in her 1965 Turin speech at the Carignano theater), the postwar rise of an Italian lower-middle bourgeoisie unwittingly complacent with capitalism because they were fundamentally unfit to do otherwise, the fate of the youth, and the idea of intellectual and esthetic commitment as political engagement. With striking prescience, Morante lent her prophetic voice to many contemporary issues that remain significant to modern Italian society, namely, those regarding the lives of outcasts: the disenfranchised, the powerless (like the *ghettaroli*, or Roman Jews, of the Roman roundup of 1943), children, animals, and most certainly women. While her women are underprivileged, poor, alone, ineffectual, but still endowed with a different kind of energy that does not pay homage to trends or conventions, she is also one of the first authors in Italian literature to openly address (and understand) the vexing situation of being homosexuals in Italian society, homophobia, and the disturbance her characters, like Wilhelm, like Manuele, would bring to stifling societal norms. She deals with incest, she talks about drug addiction, as in the case of Davide Segre of *La Storia* (History). She remains the most controversial female writer of her generation. Always challenging the establishment, Morante's writing needs to be queered, but not because it is fashionable to do so. Rather, her texts demand critical approaches that disturb a philological analysis because they inform obliquely queer readings of Italian society and its unrest. While the tendency in some critical works points toward normalization, reading, that is, into Morante's works the critic's own moral and ethical values, in Carla Kaplan's words: "prescriptive ethics" (33), her treatment of these themes far exceeds reductive interpretations and deserves problematization precisely because of her prophetic voice that still echoes in today's society.

The chapters in *Elsa Morante's Politics of Writing*: *Rethinking Subjectivity, History, and the Power of Art* point to different directions of contemporary criticism: confirmation that the works of a canonical author (such as we do not hesitate to label Elsa Morante) weather new rereadings well and lend themselves to confrontations with different and new contextualizations. While the order in which the chapters appear in this reader stands in accordance with the thematic lines of inquiry in Morantian criticism, they rethink conventional critical approaches and propound new perspectives that enhance the prophetic qualities of Morante's thought. The volume is divided into four parts: new approaches to Morante's oeuvre and previous criticism, interdisciplinary analyses of Morante and the visual arts and cinematic adaptations, queering readings, and considerations of her essays.

When revisiting Morante's literary spaces, unpublished materials, like the ones classified and present in the Fondo Morante, present a thorny issue. Since the invention of printing, countless artists have been distrustful of leaving behind writings that, for a variety of circumstances (considered by the author unworthy of publication, lack of publishers' interest), did not see publication. Similarly, personal correspondence can be considered a form of writing too private to be published. The notion that writings not edited by the author or pieces of unfinished fiction might end up haphazardly published just to meet dates and commemorations may be intolerable for some artists. Henry James's example tells us of an artist who, to prevent some irreparable damage to his fame, not only burned all his papers before dying but also immortalized this artistic nightmare into the subject of one of his most famous novellas, *The Aspern Papers*. Considering such a loss, we can readily appreciate the true gift that Morante and her heirs have bestowed upon us, both in 1985 and in 2012.

Morante's nonfictional work is invaluable. With few exceptions, most of her critical and essayistic writings were published only after her death. Reading her collected essays as well as the unpublished notebooks in which the author drafted her works is philologically illustrative, as this material demonstrates a trajectory that follows and develops a logical concretion of ideas; this approach is particularly informative in contrast to the critical vulgate, which instead divides Morante's work into two clear periods: before and after *Il mondo salvato dai ragazzini* (Bareil 5–13). Morante's archival materials, her unfinished and unpublished fiction and poems (written in her unmistakable longhand in beautiful notebooks she carefully chose for each work upon commencement), give the scholar insight into the intricacies of her artistic working process and creative flow. These texts are, perhaps, unfinished, but an invaluable compendium to the rest of her works nonetheless.

Morante was never an impassive bystander; rather, her writings and recorded actions speak to an unwavering dedication to the betterment of society and steadfast commitment to her system of logic. Intellectual consistency is thus revealed and reinforced by reading her essays and her unpublished papers collected at the National Library. Just like her alter ego Arturo, Morante wanted her papers to be kept: in *L'isola di Arturo*, the boy, already conscious to be an artist just like his author was at his age, warns his old nurse Silvestro, "I fogli scritti prendili *tutti,* non lasciarne nessuno, che quelli sono importanti, perché io sono uno scrittore" (Morante, *Opere* 1, 1360; "Bring *all* the paper that's written on. Don't leave any behind. It's important, because I'm a writer" [Morante, *Arturo's* 343]). These words resonate with Morante's consideration of her own work. The Fondo Morante provides scholars with the opportunity to pursue new directions in the understanding of one of the greatest twentieth-century European novelists. As Fofi notes, "Gli scritti di Elsa, tralasciandone per ora ogni valutazione, avrebbero dovuto servire e dovranno ancora servire a 'rendere più limpido il nostro progetto'" ("Elsa" 66; "Elsa's writings, not taking for the time being into consideration any evaluation, should serve and will still serve 'to make more limpid our project'"). Our project is to make Elsa Morante's legacy more "limpid."

The year 2012 also witnessed the publication of Elsa Morante's correspondence, which completes the recent expansion of the archive. Lovingly edited by her nephew Daniele Morante, with the invaluable consultation of Giuliana Zagra (director of the Fondo Morante), the epistolary *L'amata. Lettere di e a Elsa Morante* solidifies a multifaceted—at times even vulnerable—image of the artist. Her feelings, her dreams, her anxieties with respect to love and work, and her personal and public concerns all emerge from these letters such that we do not hesitate to consider these texts crucial to a new, holistic understanding of Morante's complex existence and choices she made in her artistic career. Letters to and by Morante demonstrate at once the degree of both her generosity and her capriciousness in amorous relations, her love for love and her insecurity of love. Yet, in reading these letters, the scholar never encounters any insecurity on Morante's behalf with respect to her art. Rather, she only fears the misunderstanding of her works and her creativity.

Of all the characters in her works, Elsa was the most baroque of all. She is the anthropomorphic version of the piazza Navona she so fondly describes in one of her writings: complex and rich in intellectual (as well as aesthetic) shadows. Carlo Levi, an artist Morante greatly admired, and to whom she is indebted for the concept of reality and unreality, wrote in "La solitudine di Roma" of a curious morphing of the square as of its noise. The initial quivering that fills the air of the popular square morphs, "as in an absurd spell," into an "immense, primitive prairie" (Levi 20). Crickets and fields take over the human crowd, the noise, everything. From the strata of civilization that piazza Navona conventionally evokes, for Levi it is the more natural landscape that will emerge. Elsa carries them both with herself throughout her literary work. Elsa can be Anna, the character of *Menzogna e sortilegio* who more than anyone else is enslaved by life's most beautiful whim: love. Anna is Capriccio's cousin and lover, she is capricious and faithful, she is the embodiment of what Elsa simultaneously does not want to be and yet is doomed to be all her life.

But aside from commenting upon the coincidences between Elsa and her characters, several of her collected letters render also full insight into her condition as a female artist whose name was forever connected to and oppressed by that of Alberto Moravia. Her rebellious attitude toward the stifling Roman artistic entourage, which confined the boundaries of her artistic voice into one exclusively capable of writing fiction, blazes through the pages of many a letter. In speaking of her essays and philosophical writings, Morante writes to her dear friend and companion of Carlo Levi, Linuccia Saba, in 1966: "Si, io lavoro, sebbene non sempre a romanzi; e quindi la maggior parte delle persone considerino [*sic*] questo mio lavoro un *non lavoro*. . . . Cioè: io per loro sono romanziere o novelliere. Il resto non è lavoro, né prodotto veramente utile" (D. Morante 398; emphasis original; "Yes, I am working, although not always to novels; and so most people consider this work of mine a *non-work*. . . . That is: for them I am either a novelist or a story writer. The rest is neither work nor a really useful work"). She feels bound to her condition of *romanziere* (novelist) and, unable to reply to her sarcastic detractors, she herself objects to the validity of her poetic work, particularly *Alibi*. But her power to divest current society of all its ideological gnawings goes unmatched. There is a form of Lutheran criticism in Morante.

She cannot escape from the idea that tolerance and forgiveness are powerful tools, but only for the subaltern. And even there, she realizes that these virtues are a benevolent form of condescension toward the unarmed citizens of the world.

Morante is implacable especially toward herself, like any Narcissus: tired of admiring and recognizing her virtues, she opens a monologue about her disastrous powers. Yet, her powers were great indeed. One of her favorite interlocutors, Linuccia Saba, in a previous letter, carefully chooses her words to describe her friend's uncanny ability to see the faults of society: "Tu sei il bambino che, solo, vede l'imperatore nudo e lo dice" (396; "You are the child who, alone, sees the emperor naked and says so"). As the child who alone can see the emperor for what he really is, Morante can continue predicating values that radically differ from the dominant lower middle-class values born out of the fascist epoch and sustained into postwar Italy. The testimony that emerges from the letters confirms Fofi's comments about his (difficult) friend Elsa Morante:

> *L'Elsa reale era piuttosto diversa da quella raccontata dai media, e da quella stessa che ci si immaginava prima di conoscerla. Era, per esempio, una persona estremamente sicura del proprio dono di poeta e narratrice ma anche della propria lucidità nel vedere e giudicare l'Italia del suo tempo e noi, suoi miseri cittadini delle ultime generazioni, nella cui capacità di operare un cambiamento di rotta ella sperava.* ("All'analfabeta" 11)

> The true Elsa was rather different from the one narrated by the media, as from the very one fancied before knowing her. She was, for instance, a person extremely sure about her gift as a poet and storyteller as well as of her own lucidity in looking at and judging contemporary Italy and us, its poor citizens of the latest generations, in which ability of making a difference she was hopeful.

In our volume, in "Elsa Morante's Correspondence: A New Source for the Artist's Biography," Daniele Morante explains his rationale for the compilation of his volume *L'amata* (The Beloved), a collection of correspondence both penned by and addressed to her. In this vigorous writing, Morante justifies the criteria that led to his editorial work as curator of his aunt's correspondence. Most importantly, he establishes a new mode for understanding a more vulnerable—however, loved—"Elsa," different from the one that surfaces in previous writings on the author's life. "Writing: A Lifelong Affair. Notes from the Elsa Morante Archives" by Giuliana Zagra tackles the notes, notebooks, and documents bequeathed to the National Library in Rome by Daniele Morante and Carlo Cecchi. Importantly, Zagra links what writing meant to Morante to what Morante made of writing in her life:

another life altogether in which frustrations, sorrows, and dreams could find a proper place.

PART I: NEW APPROACHES TO
MORANTE'S OEUVRE

In "In the Realm of the Lie: The Implosion of Thought and the Monsters of Reason in *Menzogna e sortilegio*," Francesco Chillemi reinterprets Elsa Morante's 1948 novel as the "performative mise en scène" of a philosophical aporia, the Epimenides Paradox. The subject matter of Morante's first novel is the irresistible power of the lie, and consequently the novel represents an implicit speculation on (meta)language. The narrator's paradoxical self-denunciation of being a liar triggers a metafictive impasse of difficult solution. In "Morante and Kafka: The Gothic Walking Dead and Talking Animals," Saskia Ziolkowski traces Kafka's appearances in Morante's authorial notes to *Diario 1938* and "Lo scialle andaluso." These appearances are notable because, while the first occurs well before Kafka's international fame was firmly established (after World War II), the second takes place while Dino Buzzati was hailed as the Italian Kafka. However, it is Kafka himself who plays a pivotal role in Morante's development, helping to reveal her sensitive, personal, and unique understanding of existence. The two authors' shared concern with oppressive spaces, ambiguous guilt, animals, and strained familial relationships warrant more exploration than they have so far been given.

"Elsa Morante: Envisioning History" by Sarah Carey examines the use of photography in Elsa Morante's 1974 novel *La Storia* and the work's ideological enterprise of conceiving of history as a "kind of art" (to use Hayden White's contentious distinction). The structure of *La Storia* shifts between reportage and the fictional rendering of a story of a half-Jewish mother, Ida. This dual approach to rendering history (at once objective and subjective) is an appropriate forum for both Morante's utilization of the photographic medium and an inquiry into photography's own ambiguous status between two poles of interpretation. In "Excursus as Narrative Technique in *La Storia*," Sharon Wood condemns Pier Paolo Pasolini's objection to the novel's narrative discourse stated in his now-famous review of *La Storia*. Wood claims that Pasolini once more de-historicizes the text, here diagnosing Morante's narrative ideological sin as a psychological as much as political disorder. The scholar reconsiders the narrative excursus of Morante's text as it appears in passages of apparent digression from the forward momentum of the plot. Their function is, largely, to recount the destiny of a character, not as a strategy of ideological evasion, but as a narratology of ethics. In "The World Must Be the Writer's Concern: Elsa Morante's Visions of History," Stefania

Lucamante shows the critical value of revisiting a controversial novel many years after its first publication. This study examines a path in Morante's writing that predates *La Storia* and draws concepts from her 1965 Turin lecture "Pro o contro la bomba atomica." Lucamante argues that rather than depicting only the disadvantaged, Morante was led to compose *La Storia* by an ethical and moral imperative that was at once intensely personal and public. *La Storia* is a narrative transfiguration of Morante coming to terms with the Shoah (the distruction of the European Jews) and marks then Morante's (re)discovery of her Jewish identity. Seen from this angle, *La Storia* is more than a fresco of WWII; it becomes one among the most emblematic texts for literary representations of the Italian Shoah.

In "In Marguerite Caetani's Literary Salon: A Study of Elsa Morante's Contributions to *Botteghe Oscure*," Lorenzo Salvagni investigates Morante's contributions to this literary journal—most notably "Lo scialle andaluso"—in the context of the literary review's editorial philosophy. Salvagni also looks at the writer's relations with the intellectuals who animated Marguerite Caetani's salon and/or published in her magazine, like Pier Paolo Pasolini and Morante's husband, Alberto Moravia. Salvagni's comprehensive study of the postwar Roman intellectual milieu at the outset of Neorealism allows for a better understanding of Morante's development as a writer and provides insight on less-known aspects of her personality.

PART II: THEATER, VISUAL ARTS, AND CINEMA

Following Salvagni's chapter on the publication of "Lo scialle andaluso," "*Lo Scialle Andaluso*: Performance, Performativity, and the Creativity of Elsa Morante " by Gabrielle Orsi examines Morante's use of theater and theatricality in her best-known novella. Though it has been often observed that allusions to theater pervade Morante's writing, only with "Lo scialle andaluso" does an actual theater figure centrally. In Orsi's view, theater in Morante bridges, however temporarily, the gap between imagined fantasy and embodied reality, thereby enabling the dreams of her often self-deluding characters. Theater also is associated with the enclosed spaces necessary for the upwelling of fantasy and creativity; such spaces host the creation of fiction and important events throughout Morante's oeuvre.

In "Elsa Morante's Pictorial References and Ekphrasis in *Alibi*: from Vittore Carpaccio to Silvestro Lega," Gandolfo Cascio expands the notion of literary influence to the realm of the visual arts. Elsa Morante had a strong and prolonged relationship with the visual arts: some of the most appreciated artists of the time—Carlo Levi, Renato Guttuso, Mario Schifano—befriended and loved her. More intense and extremely personal was her relation with the American painter Bill Morrow. It must be said, moreover, that—

although sporadically—Morante also wrote about painting. All these experiences, coupled with her natural attraction to the artistic expressions, provided Morante with some images she reused to create personal, strong "pictures" hidden into the diegesis and the structure of her poems in *Alibi*, creating a kind of ekphrasis devoid of the postmodernist game of quotations; it adopts, instead, some sophisticated intertextual dynamics.

Contemporaneously with her work on "Lo scialle andaluso," Morante was writing a novel that remained unfinished, *Senza i conforti della religione* (Without the Comfort of Religion). In "*Senza i conforti della religione*: An Interrupted Path between Cinema and Poetic Creation," Claude Cazalé Bérard illuminates the relevance Morante attributed to this unfinished novel. Despite the tormented course of her writing and the patent problems at an editorial level, Morante called this novel a "work in progress" for many years. One of the most important elements of Cazalé Bérard's analysis considers the characters and situations Morante drew on in *Il mondo salvato dai ragazzini*, *La Storia*, and *Aracoeli*. Cazalé Bérard deals also with the complex connection between filmmaking and poetic creation as embodied in the unfinished novel by the two main characters, brothers Alfio and Giuseppe. Their profound relationship of affection and friendship is the very foundation of the novel, both structurally and thematically.

Hanna Serkowska's "Arturo in the World of the 'Pharisees Fathers': The Cinematic Adaptation of *Arturo's Island*," pays special attention to how director Damiano Damiani utilizes, while revisiting, by-then timeworn neorealist techniques (Cesare Zavattini signed the script for this film). Here the cinematic adaptation appears to respect the deep intentions of the literary text, for the director even enriches it with meanings that involve Morante's Weltanschauung. Damiani translates, however, even the novel's most dreamlike scenes into questionable realism. The most striking shift from the novel's development regards the "happy ending" moral: Damiani turns *L'isola di Arturo* into a parable on the return of the prodigal son (or the father, for that matter), and a bourgeois "crime and punishment" tale. Damiani's *L'isola di Arturo* challenges spectators by simultaneously presenting both the loss of illusions and the possibility of keeping them. In the second analysis of the cinematic adaption of *L'isola di Arturo*, "No Novel Is an Island," Thomas Harrison examines the cinematic adaptation of Morante's novel by Damiano Damiani, shedding new light on both the latent content of the narrative and the generic differences between the two mediatic treatments of the story. In Damiani's first full-length feature, Morante's novel is rendered considerably more melodramatic than it was in written form. The film's director changes key elements of the plot, allowing the homosexual motif to be softened, and even abolished, with the return of Arturo's father to the family fold at the end of the film, embracing him in a gesture of dutiful love. In "The Myth of Childhood: Luigi Comencini's Adaptation of *La Storia*," Giovanna De Luca investigates major approaches to film adaptation, considering how Luigi Comencini's style borrows from Morante's text and molds the character of Useppe into a figure that is at once realistic and mythical. Comencini provides a cohesive portrait of an innocent and impetuous childhood (preferring to portray the peculiar character of Useppe within the parameters of a realistic style), showing that it is through the child's gaze upon history that the spectator can observe the limits of humanity. In "Staging a Writer's Journey: *Elsa Morante* by Francesca Comencini," Gaetana Marrone tackles the visual biography of the writer as represented by Comencini's documentary. *Elsa Morante* is her most intimate and poetic documentary, set within the format of a French television biographical series, "Un siècle d'ecrivains." With a style in between the documentary and feature film genres, Comencini propounds a poetic image of the author (albeit one marred by the lack of family testimonies).

PART III: QUEERING MORANTE: BODIES THAT MATTER FROM *DIARIO 1938* TO *ARACOELI*

In the chapters devoted to Morante's last novel, different approaches are used to reread *Aracoeli* in light of the contributions of post-deconstructionist and queer studies to theory and literary criticism. "Troubling *Aracoeli*" could thereby serve as an umbrella term for the interest in dissonance and resistance to any prescriptive readings evidenced by all three scholars in this section. Analytical trajectories, however, differ. In "'Tuo scandalo tuo splendore': The Split Mother in Morante's Works from *Diario 1938* to *Aracoeli*," Katrin Wehling-Giorgi investigates the portrayal of the mother-child dyad in "Lo scialle andaluso," *La Storia*, and *Aracoeli*. In this textual trajectory, the maternal figure expresses increasingly complex notions of fractured subjectivity. While Andrea and Manuele's relationship with the mother is characterized by both nostalgia and accusations of emotional neglect, Useppe remains anchored in a pre-symbolic form of symbiosis with the mother, which prevents him from forming an independent sense of selfhood. Contrary to the dominant critical consensus that *Aracoeli* provides us with a destructive notion of maternity, which is unprecedented in the author's previous texts, Wehling-Giorgi identifies a clear continuity and progression in Morante's discourse on motherhood as a distinctly disruptive function on the child's emerging sense of subjectivity.

In "Differently Queer: Sexuality and Aesthetics in Pier Paolo Pasolini's *Petrolio* and Elsa Morante's *Aracoeli*," Manuele Gragnolati proposes an aesthetic parallel between *Petrolio* and *Aracoeli*. He argues that both novels mobilize a complex sense of linear and teleological development, thus allowing for the articulation of queer desires and pleasures that cannot be inscribed in the normative logics of progression or productivity. Dissimilarities in the process of linking content and form in the two novels are the focus of his chapter. In "Kaleidoscopic Sexualities: Defying Normative Resistance and Maternal Melancholia in *Aracoeli*," Maria Morelli confronts the accusations levied against *Aracoeli*, namely, that the work was obscure and cryptic (as in Fortini's case) or a parody of everything she had previously written (Garboli). Morelli instead suggests a reading of the novel that is informed by more recent theoretical perspectives on gender and sexuality. Drawing on Judith Butler's interrogating notions of "performativity" and "undoing" gender, Morelli reveals Morante's queer feminism as made explicit in the text under scrutiny.

PART IV: MORANTE'S ESSAYS: THE SELF, SOCIETY, AND ART

In "Between Perception and Prophecy: Elsa Morante's Reflections for the Present," Flavia Cartoni proposes new reflections on Morante's *Piccolo Manifesto dei Comunisti (senza classe né partito)* in light of subsequent historical events and a consideration of the writer's world of reveries, made possible by the publication of Morante's private diary, *Diario 1938*. Cartoni threads the two texts together to create a new understanding of the author's inner world. From the concept of grace and disgrace, to the liberating function of art, the position of the writer has consistently been against the "sleep of reason." Such consistency makes Morante's philosophical approach all the more valid in our new century. Drawing from Pasolini's and Morante's divergences regarding the atom bomb, in "'Pro o Contro *La rabbia*': Elsa Morante, Pier Paolo Pasolini, and the Work of Art in the Atomic Age," Kenise Lyons shows how the image of the bomb unites Morante and Pasolini in a common critique of the neo-avant-garde's betrayal of reality and how such imagery betrays their diverging attitudes toward the enactment, and outcomes, of the postwar poetic mandate and its correlative ethics of reality. Lyons expounds upon the modalities of this nuclear point of contact through close readings of Morante's "Pro o contro la bomba atomica" (1965) and Pasolini's *La rabbia* (1962), focusing specifically on the authors' respective deployment of the material and metaphorical meanings attached to the atomic bomb.

In "Timely Anachronisms: Elsa Morante, Adriana Cavarero, and Roberto Esposito on Power, Violence, and Subjectivity" Claudia Karagoz considers a selection of Elsa Morante's critical writings in the context of recent theoretical responses to violence and war. Karagoz argues that, notwithstanding their numerous differences, both Morante and contemporary philosopher Adriana Cavarero foreground the perspective of defenseless children (as the figures of utmost human vulnerability), and focus on the corporal. Morante's stance on these issues, however, complements Cavarero's theorization of horrorism by highlighting the ability of the artist/poet to overcome the paralyzing effect of horror—as experienced by Hungarian poet Miklós Radnóti in a Nazi lager, for example, in "Pro o contro la bomba atomica"—and challenge unreality with art/poetry. Morante's influence thereby extends beyond the realm of literature to encompass contemporary philosophy and critical theory.

Our work on Morante by no means aims to be a final point in criticism. By looking at the blind spots other readings inevitably have left, our own discussion of Morante's works garners new ways of looking at her voice and her prophecies. We hope that our analysis of Morante's corpus will indeed open new hermeneutic paths for generations of scholars to come.

NOTES

Unless otherwise noted, English translations are mine.

1. See Zagra's important findings in the manuscript of the novel in the Fondo Morante. In addition to the autobiographic intent of the dedication (Remo Natales is the anagram of Elsa Morante), Zagra notes a "[. . .] structural thrust, internal to the novel, whereas, changing the epilogue into the prologue, she is almost forced [. . .] to find a different addressee external to the narrative [. . .]" ("I nomi nascosti," 155).

2. Considerable output (Splendorini; Bernabò; Giuntoli Liverani; Cazalé Bérard; Sofri and Fofi) preceded the anniversary, while other publications followed shortly afterward (*Nuovi Argomenti*'s special issue "Morante. Un secolo"; *Il Giannone*'s special issue on Elsa Morante; the proceedings of the *Seminar on* La Storia, edited by Siriana Sgavicchia).

3. Porciani laments with reason the almost exclusive use and commentary of Garboli's essays: "It's a fact: the essays and the attention of Garboli have been, and continue to be, paramount in the history of Morante criticism. Some of his assessments, however, regarding 'this author, literarily speaking, we don't know her provenance,' 'her late originality' despite the precocious beginnings, the division of her work in a 'phase of beatitude' to be extended up until *Il mondo salvato dai ragazzini* and in a later one marked by the *pesanteur*, must be rethought in the light of the same metamorphic cultural wealth of Morante's oeuvre. Such wealth is palpable whether it is placed in the relationship she entertained with her predilected authors or when looking to the internal dynamics of her thematic 'metastasis,' as Giuseppe Nava metaphorizes the process of constant expansion of her themes." Further, Morante's letters are particularly important because her correspondence with Renata Debenedetti, Linuccia Saba, and other female friends easily dismantles some of Garboli's statements of Morante's presumed loathing for women, especially if cultured and educated, i.e., "nessuno dei messaggi della Morante ha per destinatarie le donne" ("Elsa come Rousseau" 223; "[n]one of Morante's messages addresses women") or that "Morante non ama le donne. Le disprezza" (224; "Morante does not love women. She loathes them").

WORKS CITED

Bareil, Jean-Philippe. "Ricomposizione e ridistribuzione nell'opera di Elsa Morante: Svolgimento e concrezione." *Narrativa. Elsa Morante.* 17 (2000): 5–13.

Bernabò, Graziella. *La fiaba estrema: Elsa Morante tra vita e scrittura.* Rome: Carocci, 2012.

Cazalé Bérard, Claude. *Donne tra memoria e scrittura: Fuller, Weil, Sachs, Morante.* Rome: Carocci, 2009.

Fofi, Goffredo. "All'analfabeta per cui scrisse." Fofi and Sotri, 11–15.

————. "Elsa e il '68." Fofi and Sofri 62–66.

————, and Adriano Sofri, eds. *Festa per Elsa.* Palermo: Sellerio, 2011.

Fortini, Franco. *"Aracoeli."* Nuovi saggi italiani. Milan: Garzanti, 1987. 240–41.

Garboli, Cesare. "Elsa come Rousseau." *Il gioco segreto: Nove immagini di Elsa Morante.* Milan: Adelphi, 1995. 221–26.

Giuntoli Liverani, Francesca. *Elsa Morante. L'ultimo romanzo possibile.* Naples: Liguori, 2008.

Kaplan, Carla. *The Erotics of Talk: Women's Writing and Feminist Paradigms.* Oxford: Oxford University Press, 1996.

Levi, Carlo. "La solitudine di Roma." *Roma fuggitiva: Una città e i suoi dintorni.* Ed. Gigliola De Donato. Intro. Giulio Ferroni. Rome: Donzelli, 2002.

Lucamante, Stefania. *A Multitude of Women: The Challenges of the Contemporary Italian Novel.* Toronto: Toronto University Press, 2008.

————, and Sharon Wood, eds. *Under Arturo's Star: The Cultural Legacies of Elsa Morante.* West Lafayette, IN: Purdue University Press, 2006.

Morante, Daniele, ed. *L'amata. Lettere di e a Elsa Morante.* Turin: Einaudi, 2012.

Morante, Elsa. *Arturo's Island.* Trans. Isabel Quigly. South Royalton, VT: Steerforth Italia, 2002.

————. *Il mondo salvato dai ragazzini.* Morante, *Opere* 2:2–254.

————. *L'isola di Arturo.* Morante, *Opere* 1:945–1370.

————. *Opere.* Cesare Garboli and Carlo Cecchi, eds. 2 vols. Milan: Meridiani Mondadori, 1988 and 1990.

————. "Sul romanzo." Morante, *Opere* 2:1495–520.

Porciani, Elena. "Uscire dalla camera dei cliché. La critica su Elsa Morante nel centenario dell'autrice." *Le parole e le cose,* 19 Sept. 2012. Web. 12 July 2013.

Sgavicchia, Siriana, ed. *MOD-Seminar on La Storia. Proceedings.* Pisa: ETS, 2012.

Sofri, Adriano. "Anima e corpo." Fofi and Sofri 96–111.

Splendorini, Ilaria. *Menzogna e sortilegio di Elsa Morante. Una scrittura delle origini.* Florence: Le Lettere, 2010.

Zagra, Giuliana, ed. *Santi, Sultani e Gran Capitani in camera mia. Inediti e ritrovati dall'Archivio di Elsa Morante.* Rome: Biblioteca Nazionale Centrale, 2012.

————. "I nomi nascosti nella dedica de *L'isola di Arturo."* *L'ellisse. Studi storici di letteratura italiana,* Anno III (2008): 153–60.

I

New Approaches to
Morante's Oeuvre

Chapter One

Elsa Morante's Correspondence

A New Source for the Artist's Biography

Daniele Morante

Editing any writing not sent to the press during the lifetime of the author poses problems both of a deontological and of a literary order: all the more so when the relevant author is known to have repeatedly stated that all she had to say to others is contained in her published work, or rather in the specific canon of her books that she herself singled out by never allowing her other writings to be republished during her lifetime, and having been consistent with her purpose to the point that the catalog of her literary work may appear somewhat meager, and that her biography itself can be said to be, to this day, one of the less known among those of contemporary artists.

Nevertheless many posthumous writings of hers have been published in these last twenty-seven years: among them a book of her dreams and a *journal in time*, ostensibly not meant for publication, in addition to juvenile short stories not included in the collections she published in later years—as well as unfinished essays. Needless to say, an epistolary book is a different sort of literary object—if it is one at all—that involves different and perhaps still more arduous deontological and literary problems. A letter is by its very nature not meant for the public, but for the particular individual to whom it's addressed. Even laying aside the problem of the involvement of the recipient, publishing a letter is a risky affair: from a deontological point of view, because it makes public a private relationship—that is, it could be considered a violation of privacy; from a literary point of view, because it can alter—quite unduly—the perception of the writer in the eyes of her readers. In spite of that, many epistolary books have been published whenever enough material was available, focusing on renown personalities in every field of human creativity—some already during the lifetime of the author and others several generations or even centuries later. This is not to say that precedents can lift per se the problematic nature of such literary operations. As far as I am concerned, my doubts were so acute that, after having spent two years of hard work cataloging, filing, and mostly transcribing the *received* correspondence (over five thousand items) that Elsa Morante had left in a state of almost complete disorder, I did hesitate almost two more years before actually beginning to search for and contact prospective correspondents of hers and make myself acquainted with her extant letters to them.

In making up my mind to undertake this hard task, I found helpful the thought that, while we owe the dead exactly the same wholehearted respect we owe to the living, we must not imagine them nailed verbatim to the words we remember they used to utter in their worldly existence. Rather, we should imagine them as continuing to evolve over time and history. We the living should not think to how they would have replied based on their actual existence and deeds. Rather, we should think of the ways in which they would react in their present state of evolution, and from their present place wherever it may be. And indeed, as I went forward into the world of her correspondence, it was as if a "voice" of sorts was saying, "Go on," "Do it," "Let me speak again," "Don't let me rot alone"; or else, "Do you *really* think I have something to conceal?" "Do you think I really *care* about that?" To be sure, I believe that no harm can be done to the reputation of an artist from the knowledge of any petty—or even dramatic—circumstances of her biography and that, should such a circumstance risk jeopardizing her status as an artist, one is liable to find it as a flaw in her art itself.

But just as there are peculiarities—specific to the case of the artist Elsa Morante—that seem to argue against this undertaking, there are others that seem to argue for it. For one thing, the generation that was personally acquainted with the writer is slowly but inexorably passing away: while the fact of being personally acquainted with the writer is well known, on the one hand, to represent a potential handicap, there are, on the other hand, certain connections and references that only a firsthand knowledge of the writer can account for—and pass on to a younger generations of scholars.

More to the point, Elsa Morante was an artist of a very peculiar kind. Alongside her written legacy there was her conversation, or even her living presence, as sharp and memorable as her writings. Listening to her meant always being reminded of her literary work, that she hardly ever mentioned; and people who met her without knowing beforehand anything about her books (as was often the case with the youth she was surrounded by, especially in the last period of her life) soon felt hopelessly charmed, whether compelled to go and read her writings or not. She was, even before being a great writer, a guru of sorts, without anything of the asceticism and the sententiousness we tend to associate with this character. She, like Socrates, could have passed all her life without writing a single line, and yet remain forever in the memory of the people who had enjoyed her company (and indeed in the memory of coming generations, had there been a Plato in her presence!). That originated, in my opinion, in her never departing from her meditation of life, from her fundamental Weltanschauung, and from her sentiment of the beautiful for the sake of pleasing her table companions and winking at the "low" or "vulgar" dimension inherent in all of us. Although she seldom spoke of literature, if not by flashing judgments thrown out en passant, she was not the kind of intellectual who would say, or imply, in the middle of a dinner: "Well, now we have played the intellectual enough. Let us relax, and speak sport, or small talk, just like the common people! Let us confront the *real* things!" The fact is that to her small talk was really the *unreal* thing, the hideous adversary to reality, that is, to life; that *common people* speaking *commonplaces* is, too, the deceitful enemy of freedom, of attention, of beauty; and that, far from relaxing, such a voluntary debasement would sink one into the dreadful abysm of unreality, of nothingness, of death. Nonetheless her companionship was to everybody par excellence stimulating, exciting, even exhilarating in the most serious sense of the word; it was not at all devoid of lightness, of *légèreté*, the opposite of the *pesanteur* she abhorred. She would soon, with bitter irony, reprimand a friend who, out of light-mindedness, would say some commonplace, a triviality, or, worse, something *volgare* (vulgar); even in a restaurant or other public venue she wouldn't refrain from interfering, straightforward and in a loud, angry voice, in the conversation of the nearby table if she overheard statements that she could suspect, say, of racism, of fascism, or simply of vulgarity.

So it might seem unfair to take verbatim, if not out of modesty or paradox, what she often repeated, that *all she had to say was in her books*: one proof whereof is in the numerous letters she received from common readers, mostly admiring or enthusiastic but reflecting an image of her as a saint of sorts, or a motherly Madonna—that she was not. We had better say that there was no separation between her "colloquial speech" and her essays, and between these latter and her artistic work in the proper sense of the word. Among the three, a continuum of sorts could be established. If it's easy to perceive the continuity between the first two degrees of her expressiveness, it can be harder to detect the connection between these and the world of her artistic creation, often apprehended as fabulistic or fantastic, or more aptly according to the formula of "magical realism." The connection is readily made if one conceives of her more "profane" expression as of a poetics in which all her art is deeply and consistently rooted: this is most explicitly expressed in her political essay "Pro o contro la bomba atomica" (For or Against the Atomic Bomb), whose motto could be *beauty will save the world*—or foulness will damn it. In this perspective the universes evoked by her word, oral or written, no longer appear as worlds apart, but rather as different registers of a same language, more or less adapted to the extent of the audience and to the intimacy of the discourse. Her letters show this way a unique and precious middle point between registers, giving somehow the clue to the upper and the lower ones: a written medium but a kind of tête-à-tête, a spontaneous but meditated one. It seems to me that the best reward and the fairest vindication of my early scruples is in fact the sensation of having somehow cooperated in the editing of Elsa's last, posthumous book, a unique and unrepeatable one, one for which I can feel, *here and now*, her *gratitude* toward her editor.

The clue to the choices I made in composing this book, first of all of the title I gave to it, *L'amata* (The Beloved One), lies in the consistency and in the straightforwardness of her word, toward her correspondents and interlocutors even before toward her readers. In it lies the root of the extraordinary charm and charisma—to the extent of becoming a cult of personality—she exerted upon her audience. And yet anyone who happened to be acquainted with her can't help but immediately perceive the bitterly ironical antiphrastic value of such an expression, *L'amata*, because one of the everlasting and most profound leitmotifs of her interaction with friends and correspondents was that *no one ever loved her*. Can we say, when confronted with the testimony of the innumerable letters from her readers witnessing the fondest admiration and devotion (especially by women), that she was, in this connection, sort of unfair or ungrateful? My reply would be yes and no. *No*, if by this one would mean to question the sincerity of her deep feeling of loneliness, or even her intimation that under the cover of homage and flattery mostly hides a deep-rooted envy and ill will. Yes, if one considers that love of glory, or simply of attainment in one's skill, often proves antagonistic with that side of love—a part and parcel of it—demanding care, concern, not to say protection—a contradiction Morante, like many others, couldn't escape; and if one realizes that the very main prerequisite of *being loved, amata*, for which she was longing, is namely one's own capability of loving, which Morante should have questioned in herself because of the same contradiction we underscored earlier. There are certain excerpts of the letters of Morante and of her correspondents—put as epigraphs to the various chapters and the introduction—that seem to express at best the extremes of this contradiction. In a 1953 letter to Luchino Visconti, Morante writes, "Io non so bastare a me stessa in questo modo. Anche se ho scritto un libro, non sono una vera scrittrice. Adesso dico a tutti che lavoro sempre, [xxx xxx] e loro mi credono. Ma non è la verità. [xxx xxx xxx xxx] Lo dico [xxx] per evitare dei cocktails" (Morante 252; emphasis original; "I can't suffice to myself this way. Even if I did write a book, I'm not a real writer. Nowadays I'm telling everybody that I'm working all the time, and they do believe me. But that's not true. I say it just to avoid cocktails"). But in that same 1953, following the publication of *Lo scialle andaluso*, poet Umberto Saba replies to her this way:

La tua nostalgia di essere un ragazzo è—in realtà—la nostalgia di non aver messo al mondo un ragazzo: lo cerchi nell'arte perché [xxx xxx] non l'hai voluto nella sua fisicità. Non [xxx] vuol dire, cara amica: tutte le vite sono, in un senso o nell'altro, delle vite mancate: l'arte è lì per soccorrere a queste mancanze. Se non ci fossero, l'arte non avrebbe senso: non corrisponderebbe più ad un bisogno.[1] (127–28; emphasis original)

Your regretting of not being a boy is—actually—a regret for not having given birth to a boy: you seek after him in art because [xxx xxx] you didn't want him in his physicality. This does not [xxx] mean anything, my dear friend: every life is a failed life, in a sense: art is there to make up for these failings. Were they not there, art would be meaningless: it wouldn't match anymore a need.[2]

Alberto Moravia seems to provide the synthesis of Morante's contradiction by saying in a 1961 letter addressed to his estranged wife: "Tu vorresti imprigionare ciò che non dura e passa, e questo tutti l'hanno fatto prima di te e lo faranno dopo di te. Quello che ti fa quasi impazzire nei tuoi rapporti con B. M. non è altro che l'impossibilità di quei sentimenti assoluti che invece sono possibili nell'arte ossia in una superiore realtà" (336–37; "You would like to lock up what doesn't last and passes by—something everyone attempted before you and will attempt after you. What drives you nearly mad in your affair with B. M. is just the impossibility of those absolute feelings that, on the other hand, are possible in art—that is to say, in a superior realm of reality"). But Morante herself—and here we want to find the profound explication of her unhappiness with no healing—gives a different synthesis: in the grim days of her last hospitalization, according to a testimony of Adriano Sofri, "Una volta che le dissi che le volevo bene, e in tanti gliene volevano, domandò: 'Davvero?' e poi disse piangendo: 'Per tutta la vita non ho desiderato che questo'" ("Anima e corpo" 98; "Once as I told her that I loved her, and that many people did, she asked: 'Really?,' and at that, bursting into tears, she said: 'In all my life I didn't desire anything else'"). Another testimony, also by Sofri: "A un certo punto dice quasi singhiozzando di essere sempre vissuta, e aver scritto, solo perché qualcuno l'amasse" ("Gli ombrelli sono bellissimi quando si aprono" 162; "At a certain point she says, about to cry, that she ever lived—and wrote—only so that someone could love her"). At least, we now know for sure that she was offered—albeit in a rather "extreme" form—*even* that kind of love not arising at all from admiration, charisma or "cult," that she rightly doubted as ambiguous; and that she turned down or gave up it, out of what she "owed to her destiny" of artistic attainment. At any rate, "my own reply" is pointless. What I meant, by formulating it, is setting the "criterion" I actually used to include or exclude a letter or an exchange of correspondence.

In one word, this criterion is "love," to the extent that one takes this polysemous term in its widest meaning. By this yardstick, a letter from a sympathetic critic to the artist, and vice versa, would be "in," as well as an exchange of love letters (while a mere review of one of her books, although "positive," would obviously be "out"); by the same token the epistolary exchange between two fellow-writers appreciating one another and sharing akin sensibilities would be "in," but not an interchange of courtesies or information between two fellow-writers, even celebrated and respecting one another, *for the sake of fellowship*.[3] Moreover, since the phenomenology of "love" is also antonomastically ambiguous and contradictory, each and every "pathology" such as jealousy, possessiveness, envy, resentment, even *hatred*, had to be included.

One can see that, if knowledge—as Morante often repeated—can arise only from *simpatia*, sympathy (a soberer synonym for "love"), and if one acknowledges, at the same time, that she used to speak of "what she knew," her correspondence eligible for inclusion in the book matches nearly the whole of her correspondence: which doesn't mean that everything she wrote is *equally* representative of her "knowledge" and of her Weltanschauung![4]

One can wonder how I can freely expound upon the writer's Weltanschauung and biography, and speak of Elsa's "last, posthumous work," when one of the most prominent features of my book of correspondence, and indeed one of its main peculiarities, is the vast representation—actually preponderance—of letters *written to her by her correspondents*. I won't pretend that the actual ratio between letters *from her* and letters *to her* is entirely my choice. Much was due to the lack of time in the last stage of my work and also to the unavailability of Morante's letters to her correspondents and to my inability to find, approach, and deal with some of them in due time. . . . Whereas I originally envisaged a ratio of 1:1, the actual result was less than 1:2. The most prolific and significant epistolary exchanges of Morante, for example, her letters to Alberto Moravia (himself the author of 115 letters to her in our archives), couldn't be found anywhere, so that a handful of her drafts or copies had to suffice, along with two messages returned to the sender by chance;[5] we find ourselves in a similar situation with regard to William Edwards, the young English vagabond (author of over one hundred letters to Morante) that we find often escorting her after the tragic death of her last beloved one, the youthful American painter Bill Morrow. Both Tonino Ricchezza (130 messages, mostly postcards) and Adriano Sofri (twenty messages) were very close to Elsa in the last period of her life, especially during her last hospitalization, yet they state they didn't receive any letters from her, which seems altogether likely given her growing repugnance to write letters, bound to become a physical impossibility in the hospitalization days; the fate of Morante's letters to Luchino Visconti, with whom Elsa had fallen in love, is equally unknown, even if in this case we could luckily avail ourselves to numerous preparatory drafts; while the opposite situation also occurs in some instances, for example, for Pier Paolo Pasolini, whose twenty-five letters to Elsa we could read in her papers but whose heirs denied us the permission to publish: therefore we had to get along solely with her letters to him.

At any rate, we conceived of our book of letters, from the beginning, as a "polyphonic" and not a "monophonic" one. Elsa Morante would for sure have been its sole focus, its "protagonist" so to say, but she would be outlined by way of "dialogue," not of "monologue." Whatever the eventual ratio of her writings to others' should have been, we would have had perhaps to regret the "loss" of many a beautiful page of "epistolography," of which she proved doubtless a "master" of sorts; nonetheless we never wanted a "gallery" of beautiful pages of hers—not *that kind* of Morante's "posthumous book." So our "regret" happened to be offset by the realization that, far from being diminished or marginalized from the voice of others, her voice found itself *enhanced* by it: whereas she speaks / is spoken to / is spoken of, through every letter of the book, the other correspondents speak / are spoken to / are spoken of, only to or by her.

The structure of the book is, roughly, chronological. I identified four periods in Morante's life: the first one goes from her first known epistolary document (1930) to the separation from her English lover "Richard" (R. T. M.) following the entry of Italy into the war (1940); the second one from 1941 to 1957, year of publication of *L'isola di Arturo* (Arturo's Island); the third one from 1958 to 1974, publishing date of *La Storia: Romanzo* (History: A Novel); the fourth one, finally, from 1975 to the writer's death (1985). This general scheme notwithstanding, I often took ample liberties from it: the one-to-one epistolary exchanges (*carteggi* in Italian) wouldn't usually be interrupted, and the reconstruction of specific events could prompt me to gather groups of documents independent of temporal sequence. Each one of the periods outlined above corresponds to a chapter in the book, whose internal structure is made up of anthologies of "miscellaneous correspondence" and one-to-one *carteggi*. Sections devoted to letters from her readers, both renowned and "unknown," are added, naturally condensing around the publishing of her major books.

We couldn't warn enough against the danger of reading a book of correspondence like a biography. To such a conception stands opposed a series of obvious arguments, both "external" and "internal": among the former, the likelihood of the loss or destruction of specific letters and of whole *carteggi*, or the unwillingness of certain correspondents to get their papers or parts of them published; among the latter, the possible *under*representation—in the epistolary papers—of certain relationships, either because of the dislike of one or other of the interlocutors for the use of this particular communication medium[6] or simply because of the daily contact *de visu* between the two; as well as—vice versa—the *over*representation of other relationships due to motives of formality, of sheer kinship, or of business. That said, correspondence remains of course, with due circumspection, a first-rate *source for* biography!

NOTES

1. With regard to *L'isola di Arturo*, Elsa writes to Giacomo Debenedetti in her letter dated February 18, 1957: " [nel 1952] la sola ragione che io ho avuto (di cui fossi consapevole) nel mettermi a raccontare [xxx xxx] la vita di Arturo, è stata (non rida) il mio antico e inguaribile desiderio di essere un ragazzo. [. . .] di ritornare a [xxx xxx xxx] una mia rimpianta condizione di ragazzo che mi sembrava di ricordare" (D. Morante 190; "the only reason I had [at least consciously] for telling [xxx xxx] the life-history of Arturo, was [please don't laugh] my ancient, incurable longing for being a boy [. . .] of going back to [xxx xxx xxx] a regretted condition of mine as a boy, which I thought I could remember"). Actually, the writer put in exergue to *L'isola di Arturo* a line from one of Umberto Saba's known poems, "Il fanciullo appassionato": "Io, se in lui mi ricordo, ben mi pare."

2. All translations mine, unless otherwise noted.

3. For the sake of consistency, one wouldn't find in our book the extant (epistolary) "autographs" of such "celebrities" as, e.g., Ernest Hemingway, Michelangelo Antonioni, Oriana Fallaci, Curzio Malaparte, Sophia Loren, or Simone de Beauvoir, whose relationship with Morante, judging from correspondence, never rose above the level of formal "fellowship."

4. I must mention here that there is a whole component of her correspondence that I excluded from my anthology not because of its extraneity to the phenomenology of "love," but merely because its inclusion would have enormously inflated a theme, as we have seen, already all-encompassing (not to mention the very particular bias it could involve!): namely, the *lettres familiales*. As for the acceptation of *simpatia* in Morante, one can see her 1972 letter to Goffredo Fofi, "la vera 'intelligenza' (nel senso proprio della parola, cioè: capire) [. . .] nasce solo dalla simpatia. Per me, io potrei sopportare qualsiasi difficoltà dei rapporti, fuorché l'assenza di simpatia. [. . .] Negare a un altro la simpatia, significa rifiutarlo come prossimo" (Morante 565–66; "the actual 'intelligence' (in the proper sense of the word, i.e., understanding) [. . .] arises only from sympathy. As for me, I could stand any difficulties in relationships, except the lack of sympathy. [. . .] To deny to another person empathy, means to refuse him as our fellow creature"). See also the passage in the 1969 letter addressed to Dario Bellezza, "[. . .]solo la simpatia a me può dare ancora qualche contentezza, [*sic*] E io cerco la contentezza, come la gente comune" (539; "[. . .] only sympathy can still give me some enjoyment, And I'm looking for enjoyment, just like common people").

5. In one of her letters to him "returned to sender," Morante excuses herself for writing to him so seldom and so concisely because of his *spensieratezza* ("light-mindedness"), driving him to forget her letters "open on the tables of hotels and restaurants."

6. A circumstance that has become nowadays so prevalent as to portend the disappearance of the whole genre.

WORKS CITED

Fofi, Goffredo, and Adriano Sofri, eds. *Festa per Elsa*. Palermo: Sellerio, 2011.
Morante, Daniele, ed. *L'amata . Lettere di e a Elsa Morante.* Turin: Einaudi, 2012.
Sofri, Adriano. "Anima e corpo." Fofi and Sofri 96–111.
———. "Gli ombrelli sono bellissimi quando si aprono." Fofi and Sofri 155–89.

Chapter Two

Writing: A Lifelong Affair

Notes from the Elsa Morante Archives

Giuliana Zagra

A Morantian title, "Il poeta di tutta una vita" (the poet of an entire life) inspired the title of this chapter. Elsa Morante chose it for her essay on Trieste poet Umberto Saba, published in the April 1957 Einaudi newsletter. [1] In Morante's title, a double meaning is played around the concept of writing, for it comprises at once the whole of the author's existence as well as that of writing that encompasses the artist's entire life. It is worth remembering, in fact, that for Morante the writer/poet represents she who takes everything outside literature into great concern. The poet is also she whose task is finding answers for herself as for all living human beings.

Just like it does for her favorite living author, Umberto Saba, poetry represents a lifelong affair for Elsa Morante—writing, for her, is a vocation that begins at a very early age and never ceases. Immediately aware of such exclusive vocation, Morante devotes herself completely to it. By Morante's expressed wish, all manuscripts relative to her main works were donated to the Biblioteca Nazionale Centrale Vittorio Emanuele II of Rome (National Library) soon after her death and have been cataloged with a classification system numbered from 1618 to 1622 (Fondo V.E. 1618–1622). The bequest of a remaining part of her papers, relative to published writings or not, took place soon after the 2006 exhibit "Le stanze di Elsa, dentro la scrittura di Elsa Morante." Thanks to the generosity of heirs Carlo Cecchi and Daniele Morante, we now have a specific archival fund with cataloging number system ARC.52. The two have not yet been integrated into a single fund.

The first autographed documents present in the archive probably date to 1917–1919 and were written when Morante was between five and seven years old. The documents are two elementary school notebooks whose con-

27

tent deals with stories in verses and children's rhymes, written with the clear purpose of being recited in front of friends and family. Morante often spoke of her talented and precocious childhood, particularly in the anecdotes published in the column she held from 1939 in the weekly *Oggi*, entitled "Giardino d'infanzia" (Kindergarten):

> *Fui una bimbetta precoce. Cominciai a guadagnare a dodici anni scrivendo favole. Le illustravo da me e le inviavo al* Corriere dei piccoli *e ad altri giornalini del tempo. Era straordinario per me che per quelle storie mi venissero inviati dei soldi. Mi pareva una favola nella favola. Comunque andavo molto orgogliosa dei miei successi. Ho ancora vivo il ricordo di quando, aprendo il* Corriere dei Piccoli *vi trovai l'annuncio di un mio romanzo. Presentandomi ai miei lettori il direttore diceva che ero una bambina più piccola di tanti di loro.* (Grieco 51)

> I was a precocious little girl. I began making money at twelve writing fairy tales. I would also illustrate them, and then I would send them to the *Corriere dei piccoli* and other juvenile publications of the time. I still remember when upon opening the *Corriere dei piccoli* I found the notice for one of my novels. As a way of introduction the director wrote his little readers I was even younger than many of them. [2]

Morante's way of being a writer is thus quite different from that of other authors. Her early start and her having been a child prodigy make it possible to argue that her familiarization with the fairy tale signifies also her complete adherence, devoid of mediation and distance, to this genre. Her writing for children does not require yielding in their direction or looking at the world through their lens. Rather, what becomes a story for young Morante amounts to the reality as seen and described directly by a girl who has become adolescent along with other peers a little younger than she. As one of her young readers stated in her letter to Morante after reading *Le Bellissime avventure di Caterì*, "Gli altri libri per bambini sono tutti inventati, il suo invece è tutto vero" (Grieco 51; "All other children's books are made up, while yours is all true").

Unlike other Morante documents of that period, now lost, the writer kept the two notebooks with evident care. They let us into the world of Morante's childhood and also into her memories:

> *La mia intenzione di fare la scrittrice nacque, si può dire insieme a me; e fu attraverso i miei primi tentativi letterari che imparai in casa l'alfabeto. Nello scrivere mi rivolgevo naturalmente alle persone mie simili; e perciò fino all'età di quindici anni scrissi esclusivamente favole e poesie per bambini.* (Garboli and Cecchi, "Cronologia" XX)

My intention of becoming a writer was born—one might say—along with me; and it was through my first literary experiments that I learned the alphabet at home. In my writing I would naturally address people like me: that is the reason why until age fifteen I wrote exclusively fairy tales and children's rhymes.

The second notebook, dated 1919, *Storia di una bambola* (A Doll's Story), bears a price of 2,20 lire and opens with the words "Questo è il mio primo libro" (1; "This is my first book"). These extra-literary elements suggest Morante's very precocious attitude to fictional writing as well as her awareness and determination to become a writer. In a way, both the statement and the price marking the notebook compose a paratextual declaration of intents to which the writer proclaimed lifelong fidelity. The notebook *Storia di una bambola* opens with a story whose backdrop is graced by the descriptions of the Renaissance garden; the receiving rooms and the butlers evoke the fabulous residence of Marchesa Maria Maraini Guerrieri Gonzaga. The story foreshadows what the young writer feels will be her own destiny:

> *Era Natale. Il bell'albero di Natale preparato per Ida e Marcella era pronto, rifulgente di luce e pieno di splendidi giocattoli. C'era fra i balocchi una bella bambola vestita di raso celeste coi capelli biondi e da una parte all'altra dei capelli era legato un nastrino azzurro. Ida e Marcella entrarono nel salone. Marcella carezzò la bambola e fece per sollevarla e con gioia vide un biglietti-no con sopra scritte a lettere d'oro queste due parole: «Per Marcella». Fig-uratevi la gioia della bimba! Prese la bambola, se la strinse al seno, l'abbracciò e la baciò più volte e poi pensò per qualche istante e disse «Ti chiamerò Alba, sei contenta?»*
>
> *Ida la guardò un momento e poi vedendo il bigliettino che essa teneva in mano disse: «E non ò niente io?» «Si, - rispose Marcella, - hai quello la; - e indicò un grande pacco - . Io ho la bambola e tu il teatrino». Ida prese il pacco, lo slegò, levò l'involto e poi disse: «Come si chiama la tua bambola?» «Si chiama Alba» Rispose l'interrogata. «Allora, disse Ida, tu sarai la mamma di Alba, vi siederete nella poltrona che è vicina a quel tavolino. Io sarò la burattinaia e farò il teatro».* (Morante, *Bambola* 1v–2r)

It was Christmas. The beautiful Christmas tree set up for Ida and Marcella was ready, shining with light and full of splendid toys. Among the toys there was a beautiful doll dressed in light blue satin with blond hair whose head was adorned with a blue ribbon from one side to the other. Ida and Marcella entered in the salon. Marcella hugged the doll and was about to lift her and with joy saw a note with gilded characters forming two words: "Per Marcella." You can imagine the little girl's happiness! She took the doll, brought her close to her chest, hugged her and kissed her several times and then thought for a while and said, "I will call you Alba, are you happy?"

Ida looked at her for a second and then, looking at the note Marcella was holding in her hands, said: "Is there anything for me?" "Yes," Marcella answered, "you have that," and pointed at a big package. "I have the doll and you have the little theater." Ida took the parcel, unwrapped it, took the content out, and then said: "What is your doll's name?" "Her name is Alba" the girl answered. "Then," Ida said, "you will be Alba's mother, you will sit in the chair next to the little table. I will be the puppeteer and will make the theater."

The two protagonists, Ida and Marcella, appear in the story as the doubles of the two girls who were actually guests of Donna Maria in the same period: Giacinta and Elsa, one rich the other poor, one blonde the other with jet-black locks, one docile and passive victim of her friend's tyranny, the other with a soul like "una cosa grossa e nera" (Morante, "Patrizi" 244; "a big and black thing"),[3] however, endowed with a "mente pronta alle invenzioni" (244; "a quick and inventive mind"). In the story readers experience a sort of progressive multiplication of the theme of the double that, like in a mirror game, shifts from the actual little girls to the protagonists of the story, to the dolls. This mirror game, however, retains always the initial binary opposition, blond/dark, rich/poor, beautiful/ugly. As in a projection of their respective destinies, the gifts under the Christmas tree are of such different nature to direct the two girls toward opposite games: the typically maternal/feminine for Marcella/Giacinta, expressed through the doll, and that of the artist for Ida/Elsa through the puppet theater.

As a puppeteer, Ida can move the strings of the characters, and by virtue of the theater she holds the power of animating the dolls, a power supremely superior to that of owning them: she can give them a story and construct a fantasy world in which they can act. For instance, she can choose the ugliest and most forgotten doll in Marcella's collection and rescue her from her destiny by placing her at the center of her representation. In fact, *Storia di una bambola* narrates the story of Nannina, a rag doll who was relegated in a shabby cellar after her owner had undressed her and transformed her into a horrific ogre in a past home recital. Instead, Ida rescues Nannina from her destiny and casts her to play in a beautiful show with Alba. When the two girls are summoned to lunch, the two dolls, sitting down next to each other, strike up a conversation. It is in this way that Nannina begins to tell Alba of her past, all the way up until her fall to the Hades. Her narration is composed of sad and nice anecdotes, like the death of doll Ugolina, the excesses of a jealous lover (Aldo), the marriage to Marcellino, and even the birth of a little doll. The happy ending to the story of her doll is provided by a kind of appendix named "continuazione scritta dall'autrice" (author's written follow-up) in which the writer reassures readers about Nannina's destiny. Brought to the dolls' clinic, Nannina's lost beauty is finally restored.

Just like young Elsa's notebooks represent the starting point of the writer's collection of papers, we also have access to her final note, penned just a few months before her death. It is a fragment written on the first page of a notebook, otherwise completely blank:

Roma, 1 gennaio 1985. Soltanto oggi mi si risveglia nella memoria quell'incanto che pure lasciò qualche segno sulla mia vita. C'è stato di mezzo un intervallo di tenebre e oblio totale, come se il fiume Lete mi avesse inghiottito dopo. (Morante, ARC.52 XC)

Rome, January 1, 1985. Only today that enchantment that left some marks in my life seems to be reawakened. There has been an interval of complete darkness and oblivion, as if the River Lete had swallowed me after.

These ending points then, moving from the child's stories to the last poetic image of a marvelous mind in the process of turning itself off, mark the borders of an extraordinary patrimony of manuscripts recently bequeathed to the National Library. This archive spans seventy years, successfully representing the different shades and gradations of intensity across all phases of the writer's life. The breadth of the archive as well as its documentary wealth only reinforce the fact that Morante wrote incessantly during her life because writing *was* her way of being, because it *was* an attitude born with her.

The division of the archive as it is currently organized locates at least six sections and twenty subsections in which papers are divided: Works—Critical writings—Translations by Morante—Journals and other biographical documents—Letters—Criticism by and on Morante. The archive comprises of both the V.E. 1618–1622 papers and the ARC.52 ones. Distinction is always made between published and unpublished material.

Morante's essay on Umberto Saba is useful, once again, for a second aspect that further illuminates the importance of her papers. Through Saba's figure, Morante describes her own concept of poetry, the very same one that pervades the manuscript of *Menzogna e sortilegio* that we find explicitly declared on the inside back cover of notebook 12:

È compito dei poeti di rinnovare continuamente il mondo agli occhi degli uomini, che l'abitudine rende ciechi e distratti davanti alle cose, di rispiegare loro le cose con sempre nuove immagini, questo è il compito dato ai poeti quel sabato in cui Egli, finita la creazione si riposò. Io ho creato il mondo—disse— voi dovete far sì che esso sia giovane e nuovo per gli uomini in eterno—Da qui l'immortale necessità della poesia, senza poesia l'uomo muore di inedia. 22 maggio 1945. (XII, c. I)

It is the poets' duty to constantly renew the world before men's eyes, for habit blinds them and distracts them from things. Poets re-explain things with new images, this is the duty given to them that Saturday in which, He, finished with creation, finally rested. I created the world—He said—you must make sure to keep it eternally young and new for human beings—From this the immortal necessity of poetry for without it man dies from starvation. May 22, 1945.

More than any other artist, Saba embodies for Morante the figure of the poet capable of giving through his poetry, as in life, "una forma e un ordine assoluti agli oggetti dell'universo, traendoli dall'informe e dal disordine, e cioè dalla morte" (*Opere* 1, 1490; "an absolute form and order to objects of the universe, drawing them from the amorphous and chaos, that is, from death"). In "Il poeta di tutta la vita" Morante summarizes Saba's poetics by pointing out the three most important elements:

> *Fra le poesie del* Canzoniere *ce n'è una che per così dire, spiega la poetica di Saba. Ed è quella fuga, specie di religioso idillio, che si intitola* Canto a tre voci. *Si riconoscono in questo trio le stesse persone in cui lo stesso unico poeta è diviso, e che dialogano in lui. E fra i multipli significati dei loro temi, si potrebbero forse scegliere, per la poetica di Saba, questi tre, per cui le tre voci si distinguono: la simpatia con la realtà (come dire il realismo, che è la sostanza necessaria di ogni romanzo, anche del più favoloso); la solitudine della mente, che si matura in se stessa; e la poesia (o, diciamola: ispirazione!). (Opere* 1, 1492)

> Among the poems of the *Canzoniere*, there is one that so to speak, explains Saba's poetics: that fugue, a sort of religious idyll titled *Canto a tre voci*. We recognize in this trio the same people into which the very one poet is divided and dialogue within him. For Saba's poetics, and among the multiple meanings of their themes, one could perhaps choose these three for which the three voices can be singled out: empathy for reality (which is to say realism, the necessary substance to any novel, even the most fantastic); the solitude of the mind that matures by herself; and poetry (or let's say: inspiration!)

Realism, solitude of the mind, and poetry (that is, inspiration) compose in broad lines the three categories by which we outline the Saba/Morante poetics. These categories are useful in understanding the complexity of Morante papers. The Morante manuscripts embody and reify that enmeshing of realism, "sostanza di ogni romanzo, anche il più favoloso" ("Sul romanzo" 50; "substance of any novel, even the most fantastic") with the invention that is so integral to her art. In them, the narrative text appears enriched by a vast paratext of notes, bibliographical references, notes on characters, lists of words and jargon entries, literary citations, comments, and poetic expressions that constantly refer to the process of construction and express an incessant desire for coherence, accuracy, and truthfulness to facts ("Per la Storia cfr. Tutte le date!/ e rivedere tutti gli appunti sulla versione precedente/NB. Raccontare tutti i fatti storici con le date e scientificamente" [Morante, *La Storia* 1.I, c.1]; "For History check all dates!/ and review all the notes of the former draft/NB. Tell all historical facts with dates and scientifically").

In more than one instance, Morante underscored in fact how all her literary and poetic production contains a strongly autobiographical trait, as if all her characters had a root in the lived experience even when they were made unrecognizable in their fictional transformation. "Sono più autobiografici i romanzi di qualsiasi altra cosa si possa raccontare di sé" ("Novels are the most autobiographical thing to tell about oneself"), Morante explains in her 1972 interview to Enzo Siciliano, "perché nei romanzi avviene come nei sogni: una magica trasposizione della nostra vita, forse anche più significativa della vita stessa, perché arricchita dalla forza dell'immaginazione. La mia vita sta in *Menzogna e sortilegio*, nell'*Isola di Arturo*" (21; "because in the novels the same process of dreams intervenes: a magic transposition of our life, perhaps even more meaningful of life itself because enriched by the force of imagination. My life is in *Menzogna e sortilegio*, in *L'isola di Arturo*"). The substantial quantitative volume of Morante's manuscripts hereby reflects historical and linguistic contexts, the settings for the daily existence of her characters, the breadth of psychological motivations of these characters (even secondary ones), as well as the meticulous precision by which these motivations are construed, and results in an enormous quantity of work, which translates to the quantitative expansion of her novels' manuscripts. Without even mentioning the loose papers, notes, material predating and following the handwritten drafts, the forty notebooks of *Menzogna e sortilegio*, the sixteen of *L'isola di Arturo*, the eighteen of *La Storia* resemble monumental narrative cathedrals, built piece by piece, brick by brick. Not everything will end up on the printed page; much will be deleted during the revisions.

The psychology of Morante's characters is constructed so that in the novel they can live and act according with a coherence that takes into full account their personality and their "lived" life, even when it is a "lived" life that (as in the case of Arturo's prison) is left untold in an incipit rewritten many times and never incorporated in the body of the novel. In the end, Morante deemed it unnecessary to tell her readers of that period (Bardini 87 93).

"Non bisogna dire ogni cosa!" (Morante, *Menzogna* XIX; "Not everything must be said!") is a recurring statement in Morante's papers revealing her deep concern about burdening characters as well as their stories with too many details. "Quando imparerò il distacco da se stessi, raccontarsi senza quella partecipazione affannosa: la misura, la cronaca?" (Garboli and Cecchi, *Cronologia* LIX–LX; "When will I learn to be enough detached to tell without that frantic empathy: measure, chronicle?") Morante deemed it necessary for her characters to be free to lead their existences, to let feelings and moods transpire through their actions rather than being narrated by an omniscient narrator, as notebook IX of *L'isola di Arturo* states: "Importante! Togliere questi sentimenti e pensieri espressi: lasciare che i fatti parlino da sé" (*La Storia* XI 385; "Essential! Eliminate all these manifested feelings and thoughts: let events speak for themselves"). This concern, however, merely exemplifies the balance with which Morante is constantly struggling: the necessity to never leave out any detail or condense through revisions by which the text becomes contracted and more svelte.

Critics have often dwelt over Morante's secretive way of working, her inescapable compositional mode as well as the secret places where she would retire in monastic segregation to nourish the solitude of the mind. But the isolation and closure to the world necessary in order to write with quotidian dedication was a suffered conquest; the writer achieved this only after long periods of precariousness in rented rooms. The writing of *Menzogna e sortilegio* was rather adventurous, for the manuscript went lost and was found again after Morante went to Fondi to hide from the German roundups and deportations of the Italian Jews. As Alberto Moravia tells, the novel finally saw its completion in the little apartment of via Sgambati: "Avevamo due stanze. In una io scrivevo La *Romana*, nell'altra Elsa finiva *Menzogna e sortilegio*" (Siciliano 71; "We had two rooms. In one I was writing *The Woman of Rome*, in the other Elsa was completing *House of Liars*").

In 1949, once she achieved economic stability, Morante took up the habit of working in an office in the Parioli district. In this apartment, she would write most of *L'isola di Arturo* and begin to draft two unfinished novels, *Nerina* and *Senza i conforti della religione*. In addition, she wrote many essays and articles for newspapers and weekly magazines: this is one of best periods of her creative career. One description of the setting in which Morante writes in this fertile decade between the publication of *Menzogna e sortilegio* and the drafting of *L'isola di Arturo* can be read in an article from that period:

> *Non si capisce bene dove lavori Elsa Morante, se in via dell' Oca 27, dove ha alcune stanze sopra l'appartamento del marito Alberto Moravia o in via Archimede 161 dove ha uno studio più complicato e ancora più personale. Gli amici dicono che Elsa Morante pensi in via dell'Oca quello che poi scrive nel pomeriggio in via Archimede. Per ora comunque Elsa Morante passa quasi tutta la sua vita in questi due appartamenti, tra dischi di Mozart, Verdi, Pergolesi, e gatti siamesi e persiani.* (Saviane 11)

> We don't know exactly where Elsa Morante works, whether in via dell'Oca 27, whereshe has few rooms above her husband Alberto Moravia's apartment or in via Archimede 161 where she keeps a more complex and even more personal study. Her friends maintain that Elsa Morante thinks in via dell'Oca what she then writes in the afternoon in via Archimede. For the time being, however, Elsa Morante spends her time in these two apartments surrounded by music albums by Mozart, Verdi, and Pergolesi and Siamese and Persian cats.

In the solitude of her study, Morante develops a most personal, secret way of opening herself up to writing. The draft of the text, transmitted by the ordered series of notebooks, seems to be already an intermediate moment in the creation of the novel. First—although it is a difficult temporal stage to identify with "first,"—there is an elaboration expressed in fragments annotated everywhere: even on the cigarette paper, in scraps, in ideas jotted down on the calendar papers. Her authors, Mozart, Beethoven, Stendhal, Rimbaud, Saba, Simone Weil, along with Morante's ever-present cats assist, substantiate, sometimes even suggest ideas and form. Their presence can be found in the quotes on the covers of the notebooks of *Menzogna e sortilegio* and *Il mondo salvato dai ragazzini* (The world saved by the children) as well as in the epigraphs of *L'isola di Arturo*'s chapters. A close observation of the manuscripts allows one to argue that Morante's works could be borne out of an "illumination" obtained through an incessant search for the *mot juste*:

> *Dio mio grazie a te le parole diventano illuminanti, da una sola parola nascono immagini viventi, meravigliose storie. La ricerca suscita una vista improvvisa, di un mondo inaspettato, non mio, ma in te sorda, stupida sempre e in questo momento. Grazie tu mi scegli come piccolo strumento.* (*Menzogna* IV)

> My God, thanks to you my words become illuminating, from one only word living images arise, wonderful stories. My search produces a sudden view of an unexpected world, not mine, but in you always deaf, stupid and in this moment. Thank you, you choose me as a little tool.

We can perhaps trace in these words the countless lists of words traversing the notebooks in the process of composing the final draft before typing of all her novels. Similarly, one can trace to a poetic fragment the nucleus for the story of the novel, as we can hypothesize for *L'isola di Arturo*. In the first notebook, on the frontispiece, the epigraph of the novel states "Io se in lui mi ricordo ben mi pare" (*L'isola* 7; "If I see myself in him, I am content"). (This epigraph will stay in the final edition of the novel.) Morante had already underlined Saba's very same verse in a 1951 Garzanti edition of the *Canzoniere* volume in her property. On the other hand, Morante's novelistic drafts always carry a poetic incipit whose task is to connect the draft with real people in the author's life. Two poetic dedications, to F. L. M (Francesco Lo Monaco) and R. T. M., open the first notebook of *Menzogna e sortilegio*, although both would later be expunged from the manuscript. These are two central figures in Morante's life, for the first is her biological father and the second a lost British lover. Other poems, "Alla favola" and "Al gatto Alvaro," are also to be found in the Narcissus notebook, written between 1943 and 1945 and now partly published in *Cronologia*. So is the dedication to Remo N. opening *L'Isola di Arturo* (5).

Morante's work method is strictly tied to the writing materials she used: the materiality of the text takes on a key importance and is at times crucial to reconstruct the position of a given work within the archive. Morante always writes longhand the first draft of her novels and utilizes for this purpose a series of notebooks all alike for each single work. While all the same for each novel, the notebooks always differ from the series used for the earlier ones. Indeed, each novel has its own series of notebooks. In the typewritten transposition, Morante intervenes directly on the text, at times even heavily. For this reason, we consider the typewritten draft as an intermediate text between the first and the definitive one for Einaudi:

> *Scrivo sempre a mano—spiega Elsa in una intervista—e procedo molto lentamente, e solo quando il periodo mi è venuto ben chiuso e calettato e le parole sono quelle che devono essere e non altre suggerite dalla fretta, solo allora passo ad altro periodo. E lo stesso faccio con i capitoli.* (Monelli 118)

> I always write longhand—Elsa explains in an interview—and I move very slowly, and only when the sentence is really well closed and jointed and the words are those that must be and not others suggested by rush, only then do I move onto another paragraph. I do the same with the chapters.

In the notebooks, the text of the novels is written only on the front of the page while the back is left blank to be eventually utilized for revisions, corrections, notes, further insertions. Pages are numbered only on the front, and numbering does not restart but progresses to the next notebook. Before each novel's draft, it seems as if Morante would purposefully select the kind of notebook on which to work, always careful to look for the most congenial tool to her way of writing. The notebooks' typology varies over the years, and their external characteristics are invariably linked to the novel for which they are utilized. This tie between the work and the object is so strong that in the Morante archive one can not only immediately separate the manuscript of one novel from the notebooks, but the hand-made artifact in itself becomes a precious instrument to interpret the different writing phases, to correctly date them, locate the eventual temporal lapses of the project, the interruptions, even the hybrids that, at times, interlace one novel with another.

The first two notebooks of *Menzogna e sortilegio*, of the classic school type with black cover and red cut, are different from the remaining thirty-eight, of a more elaborate manufacture, and they all came from the Zampini paper store of via Frattina. These first two notebooks could indicate the initial nucleus of the novel, dating to 1943, lost and then found in the house of Anton Giulio Bragaglia. Between the 1950s and 1960s, Morante uses, for instance, a particular kind of notebook, a rectangular album, with a marbleized, plasticized hardcover, with moveable sheets, assembled with awkward copper screws. On this kind of album, Morante will write *Senza i conforti della religione*. Their presence in other manuscripts series attests to the transmigration of some parts of this unfinished novel into the *Mondo salvato dai ragazzini* and *La Storia*. It is precisely the evidence produced by four albums of this type contained in the manuscripts series of *La Storia* that has allowed scholars to date the beginning of its composition to the second half of the 1960s (Morante indicates its year as being 1971) and to establish strong ties between *Senza i conforti della religione* and *La Storia*.

What makes the Morante papers an exciting document, even besides their benefit to philological and scholarly research, lies in the fact that they appear to be—particularly in the case of *Menzogna e sortilegio*—like a kind of hypertext, the place in which the various moments that nourished and ingenerated the text conflate and converge: memory, chronicle, literary tradition, linguistic investigation, lived experience, poetry. In the same page poetics and poetry, writerly process and finished composition coexist.

The archive is testimony to the fact that writing for Morante amounts to a totalizing experience, constantly overlapping to life itself. In her writing one finds, as Cesare Garboli states:

> the wild and physiological connection Morante entertained with her work. Novels, stories, poems, any text coming out of her pen was an incarnation. [. . .] In Elsa Morante's creative experience there is no fissure between what is real and what is invention. This dialectic is removed. Fiction and artifice are part, like a dress, of the body: they are the body, for the needle is scorching even when the canvas is smoke. (*Alibi* XIX, XX)

NOTES

1. The essay was then republished in *Pro o contro la bomba atomica e altri scritti* (Morante, "Il poeta," 31–40) and in *Opere* 2 (1489–1493).
2. All translations mine.
3. This story, "Patrizi e plebei," is now collected in the volume *Racconti dimenticati* heavily drawn on *Storia di una bambola*, hence I allow myself to quote some of its passages to underscore the effective use of childhood memories in the construction of the story.

WORKS CITED

Bardini, Marco. *Morante, Elsa. Italiana. Di professione poeta*. Pisa: Nistri Lischi, 1999.
Garboli, Cesare. Introduzione. *Elsa Morante. Alibi: in appendice: quaderno inedito di Narciso*. Turin: Einaudi, 2004. I–XXII.
———, and Carlo Cecchi. *Cronologia*. Morante Elsa. Morante, *Opere* vol. 1. XVII–XC.
Grieco, Giuseppe. "Elsa Morante." *Grazia* (24 September 1961): 50–52.
Monelli, Paolo. "Elsa Morante." *Il successo* (February 1962): 118–20.
Morante, Elsa. "Il poeta di tutta una vita." Morante, *Pro o contro la bomba atomica*. 31–40.
———. *La Storia*. Nd. MS. V.E. 1618/1.I, c.1. Biblioteca nazionale centrale di Roma, Rome.
———. *L'isola di Arturo*. Turin: Einaudi, 1957.
———. *Menzogna e sortilegio*. 1943–1948. MS. V.E. 1619. Biblioteca nazionale centrale di Roma, Rome.
———. *Opere*. Cesare Garboli and Carlo Cecchi, eds. 2 Vols. Milan: Meridiani Mondadori, 1988 and 1990.
———. "Patrizi e plebei." *Racconti dimenticati*. Turin: Einaudi, 2002. 243–48.
——— . *Pro o contro la bomba atomica*. Milan: Adelphi, 1987.

————. *Storia di una bambola.* Nd. MS. A.R.C. 52 IV. 2/2, cc. 1 v-2r. Biblioteca nazionale centrale di Roma, Rome.

————."Sul romanzo." *Pro o contro la bomba atomica.* 41–73.

————. Untitled Fragment. Nd. MS. A.R.C. 52 XC. Biblioteca nazionale centrale di Roma, Rome.

Saviane, Giorgio. "Elsa Morante e *L'isola di Arturo*." *L'espresso* (2 October 1955): 11.

Siciliano, Enzo. "La guerra di Elsa." *Il mondo* (7 August 1972): 21.

Chapter Three

In the Realm of the Lie

The Implosion of Thought and the Monsters of Reason in Menzogna e sortilegio

Francesco Chillemi

The literary mode to which the novel *Menzogna e sortilegio* (1948; *House of Liars* 1951) belongs is still a matter of debate. Is it pure fiction, autobiographical fiction, or a hybrid of a fantasy narrative and a realistic novel? In conventional terms, Elsa Morante's notion of autobiography and its problematic relation to literary texts cause all her novels to elude rigid genre categorization (Bardini, *Morante* 18–20, 29–33, 50, 51). Moreover, the conceptual issues that *Menzogna e sortilegio* deals with further add to the complexity of a possible classification.

The subject matter of Morante's first published novel is the irresistible power of the lie and, I maintain, its bearing on faculties of mind such as imagination and reason. I reread *Menzogna e sortilegio* as the performative mise en scène of a pertinent philosophical aporia, namely, the ancient liar paradox. As a matter of fact, the nexus between philosophy and literature is inscribed in Morante's thought, as expounded in her essay "Pro o contro la bomba atomica" (For or Against the Atomic Bomb). In her opinion, literary works embody theoretical conceptions and frameworks:

> *il romanziere, al pari di un filosofo-psicologo, presenta nella sua opera un proprio e completo sistema del mondo e delle relazioni umane. Solo che, invece di esporre il proprio sistema in termini di ragionamento, è tratto, per sua natura, a configurarlo in una finzione poetica, per mezzo di simboli narrativi. Ogni romanzo, perciò, potrebbe, da parte di un lettore attento e intelligente [. . .], essere tradotto in termini di saggio, e di "opera di pensiero."*
> (Morante, "Sul romanzo" 1499–1500)

a novelist, like a philosopher-psychologist, conveys through her or his work a
personal and fully developed conception of the world and human relationships.
However, the novelist, instead of elaborating such a conception in rational
terms, is predisposed to represent it in fictional form by employing a set of
narrative symbols. Therefore, an attentive and intelligent reader [. . .], could
translate every novel into a theoretical essay. [1]

Starting with this premise, I argue that *Menzogna e sortilegio* exposes the
limits of imagination and reason if conceived of only as epistemological
tools. While imagination is explicitly described as a source of false representation of the real events, reason is implicitly put into question. Indeed, not
only does the novel show the interrelation between the imaginative faculty
and deception, but by embedding in the text a pertinent philosophical aporia,
namely, the ancient liar paradox, it also discloses the self-referential and
enigmatic aspects of logical reasoning. To elucidate the extent to which these
philosophical cruxes affect the narrative of *Menzogna e sortilegio*, I investigate both the development of the narrating protagonist's struggle against her
tendency toward pathological lying and, at a deeper level, the impact of the
aforementioned paradox on the relationships between the narrator Elisa and
her own narrative's protagonist, a younger Elisa, the narrator and the other
characters, and the narrator and the reader.

In the prologue of the novel (comprising the opening poem and the first
three chapters), the first person narrator Elisa, now a twenty-five-year-old
woman, recounts her unhappy childhood. She depicts herself as a victim of
her family's cruelty, bad faith, and indifference, who was then forced to take
refuge in solitude, despising reality and people to the point of segregating
herself in the solipsistic world of her mind. In Ilaria Splendorini's words,
"[Elisa's] continuous search for isolation and her tendency to retreat into
herself" has involved "a progressive loss of contact with reality" and "an
increasingly manifest indifference to the world surrounding her" (38). Elisa
now realizes that she has "developed defense mechanisms that [. . .] have
overlapped and even repressed the most authentic and spontaneous aspects of
her being" (31). The prologue concludes with Elisa's declaration of intent:
she will write about her past to trace the history of her family in search of her
lost identity.

From the first chapter of the prologue, Elisa establishes a special relationship with the reader. After a few pages, she engages her or him in the novel:
"Qui, il mio lettore vorrà sapere che sorta di casi m'abbia condotta a trovar
rifugio fra queste mura: e a ciò si darà risposta nel corso della presente
storia" (Morante, *Menzogna* 12; "My reader must want to know what
circumstances could have led me to find refuge in such a house—a question
that will be answered as my story progresses" [Morante, *House* 5]). The
reader is challenged by the fact that the line of demarcation that usually

separates the extradiegetic and diegetic levels here is blurred. In fact, the involvement of the narratee causes the narration to proceed on two levels: one concerning the act of conceiving and narrating the story (a "behind the scenes" dimension where the narrator weaves the story line and addresses the reader) and the other consisting of the narrated story.[2]

In narratological terms, Elisa's status as a narrator is subjected to an oscillatory motion. On the discourse-time level, she is an autodiegetic narrator; that is, she is identical to the protagonist (Genette 245). On the contrary, on the story-time level, she is a "pseudodiegetic" narrator (236–37).[3] Elisa—who aims to recollect her traumatic life events—cannot remember her own early childhood. She needs, therefore, to rely on the subtle whispers of her ancestors' spirits. As a result, this "reduced metadiegetic" narrative perpetually crosses the conventional boundaries of narratological levels (236–37).[4]

Additionally, as the characters are introduced in the story, their individual perspectives, secret obsessions, and ill-concealed perversions arise. The reader is compelled to continually review his or her interpretation according to the new revelations. Both the narrator and the narratee are challenged by this problematic narrative-level overlapping and forced to deal with the characters' unreliable ambivalence. Conni-Kay Jørgensen concludes that "[all the characters] create and perpetuate a false image of themselves and the world" (30). Undoubtedly, lying is not simply related to the concept of fallacy but, rather, originates from an intentional mixture of true and false. A liar is the one who adulterates truth with falsehood, and the Devil ($\delta\iota\acute{\alpha}\beta o\lambda o\varsigma$ [diàbolos]—the slanderer, according to the etymology)—who takes pleasure in altering things and deceiving his victims—is the most repugnant and aggravated version. While Edoardo plays the role of the sadistic slanderer, the compulsive tendency to lie affects every character, each of whom shows devilish traits with varying degrees of intensity.

One could be tempted to draw a parallel between the two narratological figures—the narrator and the narratee—by maintaining that they have the same limited point of view on the story in terms of knowledge and information. However, such an argument would be erroneous. Elisa, who belongs to both diegetic levels, shares the duplicity of her obscure characters. She is a victim of the spirits' lies, but at the same time, she cannot help falsifying reality. While *Menzogna e sortilegio* may initially appear to be an autobiographical novel—a self-analytical and therapeutic writing path, one in which Elisa's ancestors' spirits would just be a metaphor for the emergence of the unconscious—as early as in the second of forty chapters, this assumption is proven wrong. Strikingly, Elisa alerts the reader by denouncing herself as a deceptive narrator: "E sebbene voi dobbiate aspettarvi, o lettori, di conoscere attraverso questo libro più d'un personaggio contagiato dal nostro morbo fantastico, sappiate che il malato più grave di tutti lo avete già conosciuto. Esso non è altri se non colei che qui scrive: son io, Elisa." (Morante, *Menzog-*

na 23; "And while you must expect to meet in the course of my story more than one person contaminated by our family disease of illusion, you must realize that you have already met the sickest of all. And that is of course the person who writes this book: I, Elisa" [Morante, *House* 11]). Such a warning powerfully resonates within the text, undermining the foundations of the novel: it revives—albeit shrewdly concealed in an imaginary form—the liar paradox. The aporistic dilemma can be summarized as follows: "I'm lying" or "this sentence is false." This kind of self-referential sentence causes a circular reasoning pattern that defies logic: if one assumes that the statement is true, such reasoning is immediately contradicted by the content of the sentence itself. Conversely, if the statement "this sentence is false" is assumed to be false, it implies that the sentence is true. Nonetheless, since the content of the sentence denounces the sentence itself as false, a contradiction arises again.

Accordingly, Elisa's declaration casts a sinister doubt on her story. As the aporia impacts the text, a disturbing ambiguity (or "undecidability," in Derridean terms) invades the novel.[5] In this regard, Stefania Lucamante points out that "the doubt, or better the neurosis it provokes, prevents the narrator from developing a monologic narrative: she is forced to accept her alienating and alienated condition" (*Elsa* 52). Elisa's confession severely affects the structure of *Menzogna e sortilegio*. The linguistic puzzle in which she has entangled herself is impossible to solve, so the lie contaminates both the narrative and metanarrative levels like a virus: the lie is the "last and most important of her inheritances" (Morante *House* 10).[6] She professes to aim solely to her "propria sincerità" (Morante, *Menzogna* 13; "the truth of [her] spirit"; [Morante, *House* 5]), without asking for the readers' sympathy. Indeed, the narrator's paradoxical self-denunciation results in a metafictive block: the reader comes to realize that not only is the diegetic world represented in the secondary story delusive but even the primary story (the level of narration) is intrinsically misleading. As Sharon Wood observes, "[Elisa] warns us that, while she is a character in her own story—and therefore, as witness and participant, some sort of guarantor of the text—she is nonetheless a romancer, afflicted by the same *menzogne* as her family" (102). Lucamante also clarifies that "from the very beginning of the story, the reader should distrust Elisa's account about her past, simply because it is a tale by a sick person, who is [still] on the way of recovery" (*Elsa* 68).

As the plot develops, it both provides selection criteria for the information that Elisa is constantly offering her readers while also affecting the emotional impact of events on the readers. Uncertainty dominates the novel, becoming its stylistic trait while "the discourse enhances the ambiguous forms of the 'insolvable duplicity'[7] that shapes human behaviors" (Rosa 64). The ambivalence is the paradigm that allows the narrative to unfold smoothly by absorbing the contradictions that it continually creates. In an endless accumulation of different interpretations, the reported events are distorted by the spirits' untruthful whispers and filtered by the unreliable narrator.

Moreover, the text is disseminated with analepses and prolepses. Far from assisting the reader, they manage to blur the chronological order of the events. The text appears to superimpose "temporal planes whose diachronic flow is interrupted by analepsis, gaps, ellipsis, a kind of stitching together reminiscent of spatial rather than merely temporal organization" (Wood 101). As a consequence, such an "interpolated narration"[8] amplifies the reader's discomfort and disorientation, since "[it] lacks the teleology and story configuration that are frequently considered to be necessary constituents of narrativity" (Fludernik 610).

A way to escape the condemnation to deception and misunderstanding, to which Elisa and the reader would seem inevitably destined, arises at the end of the fourth part. With an unpredictable twist, Elisa stuns her reader by announcing that she will not be a spectator of a "comedy of ghosts" any longer. "From now on" she will rely on her "true memory":

> *Le figure dei miei, che m'avevano circondato* fin qui, *[. . .] diventavano via via più frettolose e roche, dileguavano una dopo l'altra. Onde finito è* d'ora innanzi *il mio privilegio d'assistere, sola spettatrice, a una commedia di spiriti. Non udirete più da me la voce molteplice della dormiente. Una lucida insonnia s'impadronisce di me e io, nella camera taciturna e spopolata, altro non potrò interrogare* d'ora innanzi *che la mia vera memoria.* (Morante, *Menzogna* 578–79; emphasis added)

> The faces of my people who have surrounded me *until now* [. . .] have become little by little more hurried and hoarse and one after another has faded away. *From now on* it is over, my privilege of witnessing, as a solitary spectator, a comedy of ghosts. You will no longer hear from me the many voices of sleep. A lucid insomnia has taken hold of me and, in my silent, deserted room, I can turn to nothing *from now on* but my own true memory. (Morante, *House* 348–49; italics added)

As Lucio Lugnani suggests, "the disjunctive grid 'until now/from now on'" emphasizes the imminence of a narrative shift from story to chronicle of events of which Elisa's ideal reader should be aware (9). This way, having confirmed her status as a pseudodiegetic narrator, Elisa changes to an auto-diegetic narrator, becoming the protagonist of the secondary story. Consequently, in the second half of the novel, the discrepancy between the two different roles that Elisa has played so far is finally solved. Notwithstanding the change, the new narratological status of Elisa does not determine the expected shift to a truly autobiographical novel. Her claim is just an illusion. Since the true/false dichotomy is nullified by the liar paradox previously triggered, the validity of any assertion is totally compromised. This evidence discredits the act of writing itself, by which the protagonist vainly hopes to heal from sickness. Not by chance, in the autographic manuscript of the novel, among the possible titles considered by Morante were "Confessioni bugiarde" (Deceitful Confessions) and "Falsa autobiografia" (False Autobiography) (Morante, *Menzogna* MS 1).

As a result, the novel deconstructs itself: the diegetic story, the narration, and the literary work are not simply imaginary but mystifying and self-referential.[9] Nothing can evade the realm of the lie, whose opacity also pertains to the temporal dimension. As Elisa states:

> *Il passato e il futuro, infatti, sono due campi di nebbia e di vertigine, che i vivi non possono esplorare se non con la fantasia e con la memoria; ma forse fantasia e memoria sono soltanto strumenti d'illusione, e soltanto per un gioco ingannevole l'uomo crede di avere il passato alle spalle e il futuro innanzi a sé. In realtà egli si muove sopra una sfera immobile, conchiusa fin da principio, e il passato e il futuro sono tutt'uno. A che serve esplorare questa reggia della morte? Il solo tentativo di sondarla produce angoscia e nausea, come quando ci si affaccia su un precipizio.* (Morante, *Menzogna* 307)

> Past and future are two foggy, indistinct regions that the living can explore only in imagination or in memory; but perhaps memory and imagination are only instruments of illusion, perhaps it is only a misleading game for man to believe that the past stands at his shoulder, that the future lies before him. In reality, he moves over an immobile sphere, complete from the beginning, in which the past and the future are one. What use is there in exploring this realm of death? The mere effort to sound its depths causes anxiety and nausea, as if one leaned too far over a precipice. (Morante, *House* 195)

By echoing in her words Henri Bergson's notion of time as continuous duration,[10] the narrator herself criticizes and dismantles the conventional conception of linear temporality according to the measurable categories of past-present-future, further unmasking the deception perpetuated by memory.

Not only does the perception of time as a succession of "distinct states"[11] vanish, but the dissolution of the spatial barriers is also exposed, uncovering "a spatial dynamic that seems to be another manifestation of the characteristic ambiguity of Morante's work" (Siddell 23). For instance, Edoardo's room "becomes the site of the conceptualisation about elsewhere, which may incorporate map space or emblematic settings associated with epics or fairy-tales. All these possibilities coexist in the imagination, not clearly distinguished one from another, in a state of mergence" (39). Similarly, Elisa's room is the occult place where she manipulates the story, "a place which has all the apparent coherence of the Map, which seems to contain itself and many other places as well, but reveals itself, on a closer examination, to be nothing but *Menzogna e sortilegio*" (42–43).

Afterward, some crucial pages attest to the impossibility of destroying the seed of the lie, showing instead the emergence of a spectral obsession, the metaphor of duplicity. In many passages, the supposed recovery of true memories still bears the indelible trace of falsehood. For example, in the third chapter of the sixth section, the ghost of the perfidious cousin Edoardo assumes the form of an enchanting thought provoked by his "false letters" and capable of seducing Elisa, her mother Anna, and his mother Concetta:

> *Qual virtù avevano mai dunque le finte lettere per conquistare tre donne? Appena appena mia madre ne aveva mormorato il principio, che già ogni forma sgraziata o pesante, ogni colore brutto o funerario dileguava dalla camera. E vi abitava invece, pieno di festa e di fuoco, un Pensiero (non so trovare altro nome più adatto alla sua volatile natura), del quale m'è impossibile enumerarvi, né, tanto meno, descrivervi una ad una, tutte le grazie. [. . .] Ma la più singolare, la più preziosa delle sue grazie era l'ambiguità, senza la quale nulla piace.* (Morante, *Menzogna* 778)

> What strange powers were in these letters that they could so entrance three women? Mother had no sooner begun to read the first few words that every awkward object, every ugly or funereal color faded away in the room. And there entered, full of fire and gaiety, a Thought (I don't know any better name for so volatile a thing), the charms of which I cannot begin to list much less describe for you. . . . (Morante, *House* 470) But the most singular, the most precious of its charms was ambiguity, without which nothing is attractive. [12]

The long description not only pulls the narrative again into the abyss of falsifying imagery but also makes the nexus between thought and deception apparent. Page by page, the inconsistency of the allegedly true memories dramatically increases so that the fragmentation of Elisa's self emerges more openly.

From this, it is evident that the protagonist's attempts to free herself from her proneness to fantasy—the "morbo fantastico" (Morante, *Menzogna* 23; "disease of illusion" [Morante, *House* 11])—are doomed to failure. This awareness marks the conclusion of the novel. The narrator dedicates the epilogue—the poem "Canto per il gatto Alvaro"—to her cat, which symbolizes her diabolic fascination with the manipulative power of mind. [13] She praises Alvaro as the only fellow in her arcane deliria. As Elisa confesses, she owns nothing but "prigione peccato e morte" (943; "prison, sin, and death" [*House* 564]). The belief in being able to redeem herself from the sin of lying by rationally overcoming her traumatic experiences was illusory. The salvific path meant to recover her mental integrity has collapsed.

After all, Elisa's inner experience is a journey from the hope of redemption to hopelessness and apathy. In this sense, the first part of the novel—where Elisa regards imagination as a dangerous faculty capable of blurring the boundaries between the fantastic and the real—can be read as the ekphrasis of the famous Francisco De Goya's aquatint *El sueño de la razón produce monstruos* (The Sleep of Reason Produces Monsters). The *Capricho 43* (see fig. 1) depicts the artist himself dreaming on a table. A dark flock of bats and owls flutters about his head, as if they are infesting his dreams with frightening nightmares and terrible visions. On the right, crouched on the floor, a haughty-looking cat stands vigil over him. According to the eighteenth-century iconography, each of these kinds of animals has a symbolic meaning: bats stand for ignorance, owls for folly, and cats for witchcraft. As the aphoristic title proclaims, the etching exhorts the viewer not to abandon reason in favor of pure imagination. Otherwise, man falls prey to the horrifying monsters of fantasy.

The theoretical position that Goya's etching conveys perfectly reflects Elisa's naïve explanation for her alienation—which she thought she could emancipate herself from through the intended rational path. Interestingly enough, a sketch included in *Menzogna e sortilegio*'s manuscript may confirm the hypothesis that *El sueño de la razón produce monstruos* was a visual reference for Morante's novel. The sketch (see fig. 3.1) imitates Goya's aquatint in terms of both symbolic representation and spatial organization: a cat-bodied female figure—indisputably a metaphorical Morante self-portrait—is surrounded by flying dark cat heads, while a demonic feline stands on the right side of the drawing.

With regard to Morante's interest in Goya's thought-provoking art, while it is worth mentioning that she decided to use his etching El caballo raptor (1816–1824) as the new cover for the 1975 edition of *Menzogna e sortilegio*, it is even more significant to recall the argument made by Morante in the interview "Nove domande sul romanzo" (1959). Here, after quoting the title of the aforementioned Goya's work, she states: "*El sueño de la razón produce monstruos. E in poche epoche, come nella presente, il sonno della ragione è stato assecondato, cullato, lusingato. Perfino le macchine prodotte dalla scienza, che dovrebbero rappresentare i monumenti della ragione, si riducono, invece, a dispensieri inerti di questo sonno senile*" ("Sul romanzo," 1518; "*El sueño de la razón produce monstruos*. Only in a few other historical periods the sleep of reason has been as favored, cherished, and pleased as it is now. Even the machines that the sciences have invented, which should be a monument to reason, prove instead to be lifeless devices dispensing this senile sleep").

In this regard, Elio Gioanola speaks of "[a] reversal of the famous motto of the Enlightenment—according to which the sleep of reason produces monsters—because [here] it is the rational insomnia to cause the 'senile sleep,' which produces nightmares" (360). Accordingly, in *Menzogna e sortilegio* a new realization subverts Elisa's initial assumption. As Lugnani illustrates (92–93), one of the last lines of the aforementioned concluding poem catches and summarizes Elisa's final achievement: "Si ripiega la memoria ombrosa / d'ogni domanda io voglio riposarmi" (Morante, *Menzogna* 943; "The shadowy memory fades / I want to rest from all my questions").[14] This assertion

Figure 3.1. *El sueño de la razón produce monstruos* and an untitled Morante sketching. The Metropolitan Museum of Art; *riproduzioni della Biblioteca Nazionale Centrale di Roma* (reproductions of the National Gallery of Rome).

illuminates the other side of the claustrophobic circle in which human existence is inscribed. If the sleep of reason produces monsters, the monsters of reason produce a deadly sleep—that is, the hypertrophy of thought eventually raises an irrepressible desire for self-annihilation. Elisa cannot avoid acknowledging her miserable, hopeless state. She is chained to insanity, imprisoned in her "mente stregata" (Morante, *Menzogna* 590; "bewitched mind" [*House* 358]), where reason is powerless in front of the sorcery of the lie, which paralyzes action and inhibits any possibility of interaction with the outside world.

At the end, the protagonist seems to give herself up to θάνατος (Thànatos), the daemon of death. In this respect, it would be misleading to recall the psychoanalytic concept of the "death drive"—that is, "a primitive urge towards death" (Gay 402)—for Elisa is not driven by primary instincts. While there is no denying the influence of psychoanalysis on the novel,[15] a substantial distance from the psychoanalytic model remains. Far from any form of psychic determinism,[16] the novel presents Elisa's choice as a free, fully conscious one. Exhausted from the furious battle she has waged against the decaying world of her psyche, she gives up: the attempt to cure her madness is unsuccessful. Her audacious presumption has been punished, and by the law of *contrappasso*, every effort has had the opposite effect. Most importantly, the act of writing has not led to healing. On the contrary, it has caused Elisa to get lost in the tricks of memory illusion and the "black holes" of reasoning, which finally trigger the implosion of thought. It is because of this realization that the protagonist comes to her final decision. Thus, Elisa's capitulation cannot be explained in terms of Freudian death drives. Ensnared in the intricate labyrinth of thought, she denies the will to live through a deliberate act of Schopenhauerian *unwillingness*.[17]

In other words, to use Morante's typology of literary characters ("I personaggi" 1468), we witness Elisa's allegoric metamorphosis from Don Quixote to Hamlet. On the one hand, during the novel, the protagonist struggles to overcome her Don Quixotic attitude to life—that is, the attitude of a character disgusted by real life and seeking his or her salvation in the fictional world. On the other hand, the conclusion of *Menzogna e sortilegio* attests to Elisa's change. She now identifies with Hamlet, the one who rejects the disguises of reality, embraces the absence, and contemplates death.

However, behind the figure of Hamlet-Elisa, another double lurks. According to Donatella Ravanello, by frequently addressing the reader, the author "never hides behind the stories of her characters, but constantly tends to make her presence felt through a narrator who describes and shares characters' experiences" (25–26). More specifically, it is Elisa's lack of credibility as a narrator that evokes the "implied author," in the terminology of Wayne Booth.[18] Besides, her name itself is almost homophonous with Elsa. Although the letter "i" that differentiates the two names can be interpreted as a symbolic bar marking the distance between reality and fiction, in the unveiled mirror of self-reflection, creator and creature imply each other. In the novel, the real self—the writer Elsa—disappears behind the imaginary one—the narrator Elisa, who is, therefore, an "Elsa *elisa*" (i.e., an *elided* Elsa). She is a fantastic double, an invisible shadow, a grim omen of death. From this perspective, one can read the illuminating side note in the autographic manuscript. It is a written soliloquy, a sort of farewell speech from Morante to the novel and its protagonist El(i)sa: "Cara Elsa / siamo intesi: copiare il libro e poi basta, morire. Quel che ti resterebbe da fare dopo non sarebbe che mortificazione e scherno. Allora promesso eh? Affettuosamente Elsa" (Morante, *Menzogna* XXXVI; "Dear Elsa, then we agree: just copy the book and this is it, to die. What would remain to you afterward would be nothing but mortification and derision. You promise me, don't you? Fondly, Elsa").

NOTES

1. Unless otherwise noted, all translations are my own.
2. Gérard Genette defines this kind of narration as "interpolated" (217).

3. Genette calls "pseudodiegetic" or "reduced metadiegetic" narratives "[those] forms of narrating where the metadiegetic way station, mentioned or not, is immediately ousted in favor of the first narrator, which to some extent economizes on one (or sometimes several) narrative level(s)" (236–37).

4. See note 3.

5. In criticizing the idea of language as a system of dichotomous oppositions in which one of the two terms is (arbitrarily) assumed to be dominant, Derrida examines some particular words, the "undecidables." They are "unities of simulacrum, 'false' verbal properties (nominal or semantic) that can no longer be included within philosophical (binary) opposition, but which, however, inhabit philosophical opposition, resisting and disorganizing it, without ever constituting a third term, without ever leaving room for a solution in the form of speculative dialectics (the gram is neither a signifier nor a signified, neither a sign nor a thing, neither presence nor an absence, neither a position nor a negation. . . . Neither/nor, that is, *simultaneously* either *or*)" (*Positions* 23). However, such an irreducible duplicity does not simply pertain to semantically peculiar words; rather, it operates at the very basis of language by affecting formal properties such as syntax: "'undecidability' is not caused here by some enigmatic equivocality, some inexhaustible ambivalence of a word in a 'natural' language. . . . What counts here is the formal or syntactical *praxis* that composes and decomposes it" (*Dissemination* 220).

6. In the English translation, *menzogna* is rendered with "illusion" rather than "lie."

7. See Morante, "Una duplicità senza soluzione" (126).

8. See note 2.

9. By performatively exposing the undermining consequences of a self-referential aporia such as the liar paradox, Morante's novel seems to anticipate Derrida's deconstructive procedures. They aim at questioning Western notions of truth and meaning by disclosing the systemic contradictions and arbitrary hierarchies that every text contains. In this respect, *Menzogna e sortilegio* shows the potential of literature not only to question its own structures but also, in Derrida's words, to "neutralize[s] the [metaphysical] 'assumptions' which it carries" ("This Strange Institution" 49).

10. In his essay, "The Perception of Change," French philosopher Bergson argues that "there is neither a rigid, immovable substratum nor distinct states passing over it like actors on a stage. There is simply the continuous melody of our interior life, a melody that runs and will run, indivisible, from the beginning to the end of our conscious existence. . . . It is precisely the indivisible continuity of change that constitutes true duration" (124). He concludes that "[t]he distinction we make between our present and past is therefore, if not arbitrary, at least relative to the extent of the field which our attention to life can embrace. . . . What we have is a present which endures" (126–27).

11. See note 10.

12. Since the final part of the quoted excerpt is omitted in the English version, the translation of the last sentence is mine.

13. Although Alvaro has often been seen as a positive figure (Bardini considers it a divine creature [*Morante* 297]), Angelo Pupino describes the final poem as "a sort of Mephistophelean hymn" (79). Similarly, I maintain that the cat incarnates the sinister allure of mystification. As a matter of fact, characters such as Edoardo, Anna, Francesco, and Cesira are compared to cats throughout the novel to allude to their weird attitudes and insane behaviors.

14. English translation is mine. The official translation of this passage—"The memory of all my questions fades, / Grows shadowy, and I would rest" (Morante, *House* 565)—misreads the real meaning of the original lines.

15. The psychoanalytic subtext of the novel has been extensively explored: see Scarano, "La 'fatua veste' del vero" (114–32), and Marco Bardini, "Dei 'fantastici doppi'" (173–205), to name a few. For example, the relationships between the characters are dominated by sadism, masochism, repetition, compulsion, heightened self-punitive tendencies, and paranoid behaviors.

16. Freud's biographer A. E. Jones states that "Freud believed in the thorough-going meaningfulness and determinism of even the apparently most obscure and arbitrary mental phenomena" (366).

17. The influence of Schopenhauer's philosophy on Morante's thought is particularly manifest in her early works, such as the essay "Mille città in una" (1938) and the diary *Lettere ad Antonio* (1938; published in 1989 with the title *Diario 1938*). Significantly, the latter is widely considered to be the main source of *Menzogna e sortilegio* (Wood, "Models of Narrative" 72–74; Gambaro, "Strategies of Affabulation in Elsa Morante's *Diario 1938*" 21–44; and Tuck 36–38; among others).

18. Wayne Booth defines the "implied author" as one who "chooses, consciously or unconsciously, what we read; we infer him as an ideal, literary, created version of the real man; he is the sum of his own choices" (74–75).

WORKS CITED

Bardini, Marco. "Dei 'fantastici doppi,' ovvero la mimesi narrativa dello spostamento psichico." Lugnani and Scarano 173–299.

———. *Morante Elsa. Italiana. Di professione, poeta.* Pisa: Nistri-Lischi, 1999.

———. "Scheda sugli esordi editoriali di Elsa Morante." *Italianistica* 3 (1999): 461–67.

Beall, J. C., and Michael Glanzberg. "Liar Paradox." *The Stanford Encyclopedia of Philosophy.* Ed. Edward N. Zalta. Spring 2013 Edition. Web. 29 March 2013.

Bergson, Henri. *The Creative Mind: An Introduction to Metaphysics.* 1934. Trans. Mabelle L. Andison. Mineola: Dover Publications, 2012.

Booth, Wayne. *The Rhetoric of Fiction.* Chicago: University of Chicago Press, 1982.

Dell'Orca, Alessia. "Le illustrazioni di copertina dei romanzi di Elsa Morante." Zagra and Buttò 87–100.

Derrida, Jacques. *Dissemination.* 1970. Trans. Barbara Johnson. Chicago: University of Chicago Press, 1981.

———. *Positions.* 1972. Trans. Alan Bass. Chicago: University of Chicago Press, 1981.

———. "This Strange Institution Called Literature." *Acts of Literature.* Ed. Derek Attridge. New York: Routledge, 1992. 33–75.

Fludernik, Monika. "In Time Narrative." Ed. David Herman, Manfred Jahn, and Marie-Laure Ryan. *The Routledge Encyclopedia of Narrative Theory.* New York: Routledge, 2005.

Gambaro, Elisa. "Strategies of Affabulation in Elsa Morante's *Diario 1938*." Lucamante and Wood 21–44.

Gay, Peter. *Freud: A life for our time.* London: W. W. Norton & Co Inc., 1989.

Genette, Gérard. *Narrative Discourse: An Essay in Method.* 1972. Trans. Jane E. Lewin. Ithaca: Cornell University Press, 1980.

Gioanola, Elio. *Psicanalisi e interpretazione letteraria: Leopardi, Pascoli, D'Annunzio, Saba, Montale, Penna, Quasimodo, Caproni, Sanguineti, Mussapi, Viviani, Morante, Primo Levi, Soldati, Biamonti.* Milan: Jaka Book, 2005.

Goya, Francisco. *El sueño de la razón produce monstruos.* 1797–99. The Metropolitan Museum of Art, New York. Web. 27 March 2013.

Jones, Alfred Ernest. *Sigmund Freud: Life and Work. Vol. 1: The Young Freud 1856–1900.* London: Hogarth Press, 1953.

Jørgensen, Conni-Kay. *La visione esistenziale nei romanzi di Elsa Morante.* Rome: L'Erma, 1999.

Lucamante, Stefania. *Elsa Morante e l'eredità proustiana.* Fiesole: Cadmo, 1998.

———, and Sharon Wood, eds. *Under Arturo's Star: The Cultural Legacies of Elsa Morante.* West Lafayette: Purdue University Press, 2006.

Lugnani, Lucio. "Logos kai Ananke." Lugnani and Scarano 9–93.

———, and Emanuella Scarano, eds. *Per Elisa: studi su "Menzogna e sortilegio."* Pisa: Nistri-Lischi, 1990.

Morante, Elsa. *House of Liars.* Trans. Adrienne Foulke. Ed. Andrew Chiappe. New York: Harcourt, Brace & Company, 1951.

———. "I personaggi." Morante, *Opere* 2, 1467–69.

———. *Menzogna e sortilegio.* 1943–1948. MS. V.E. 1619. Biblioteca nazionale centrale di Roma, Rome.

———. *Menzogna e sortilegio. Opere* 1, 1–943.

———. "Mille città in una." *Prospettive* 4–5 (February 1938): 14–15. In Bardini, "Scheda sugli esordi editoriali di Elsa Morante."

———. *Opere*. Cesare Garboli and Carlo Cecchi, eds. 2 vols. Milan: Meridiani Mondadori, 1988 and 1990.

———. "Sul romanzo." Morante, *Opere* 2, 1495–520.

———. "Una duplicità senza soluzione." *L'Europa letteraria* 27 (1964): 126.

———. Untitled drawing. In *Menzogna e sortilegio* MS.

Pupino, Angelo. *Strutture e stile della narrativa di Elsa Morante*. Ravenna: Longo, 1968.

Ravanello, Donatella. *Scrittura e follia nei romanzi di Elsa Morante*. Padova: Marsilio, 1980.

Rosa, Giovanna. *Cattedrali di carta*. Milan: Il Saggiatore, 1995.

Scarano, Emanuella. "La 'fatua veste' del vero." Lugnani and Scarano 95–171.

Siddell, Felix. *Death or Deception. Sense of Place in Buzzati and Morante*. Leicester: Troubador, 2006.

Splendorini, Ilaria. *Menzogna e sortilegio: Una scrittura delle origini*. Florence: Le Lettere, 2012.

Tuck, Lily. *Woman of Rome: A Life of Elsa Morante*. New York: Harper Collins, 2008. Print.

Wood, Sharon. "Models of Narrative in *Menzogna e sortilegio*." Lucamante and Wood 94–111.

Zagra, Giuliana and Simonetta Buttò, eds. *Le stanze di Elsa. Dentro la scrittura di Elsa Morante*. Rome: Colombo, 2006.

Chapter Four

Morante and Kafka

The Gothic Walking Dead and Talking Animals

Saskia Ziolkowski

Although the conjunction of Elsa Morante and Franz Kafka may initially seem surprising, Morante asserts that Kafka was the only author to influence her (*Lo scialle* 215). Morante's own claim notwithstanding, relatively few studies compare in detail the author of *La Storia* (History) and that of *Der Process* (The Trial).[1] In contrast to Morante, who openly appreciates Kafka but is infrequently examined with him, Dino Buzzati is often associated with Kafka, despite Buzzati's protests. Referring to Kafka as the "cross" he had to bear (54), Buzzati lamented that critics called everything he wrote Kafka-esque. Whereas Buzzati insists that he had not even read Kafka before writing *Il deserto dei Tartari* (*The Tartar Steppe*, 1940), which was labeled a mere imitation of Kafka's work,[2] Morante mentions Kafka repeatedly, particularly in the 1930s. Clarifying that Morante later turned from Kafka to Stendhal and other writers, Moravia also remarked upon Kafka's significance to Morante in this period, referring to the author as Morante's "master" and "religion."[3] While Morante may be less obviously Kafkan than Buzzati, an exploration of her work and her "master's" sheds new light on Morante.

Like Marcel Proust, whose importance to Morante has been shown by Stefania Lucamante, Kafka offers Morante an important reference point, especially in the years in which she was establishing herself as an author. Showing the productive affinities between Morante and Kafka, a German-language author from Prague, complements studies on Morante and French authors. Non-Italianists often overlook Morante, and by engaging Morante in conversation with Kafka, Morante is drawn into new critical discussions, adding to her growing revaluation as not just an Italian author but also a world author. This chapter provides two examples of productive ways to analyze Morante with Kafka: one explores Morante's reading of Kafka as Gothic, and another focuses on how associating Kafka and Morante calls attention to unnoted elements of Morante's animal representations.

Kafka and Kafkan themes make significant appearances in Morante's *Diario 1938* and her stories of the 1930s, works that provide insight into Morante's development as a writer. Indicating an intensely personal sense of the author from Prague, Morante dreams of Kafka's death and associates herself and Moravia with the figure of Kafka in the *Diario* (40). Morante also dreams of Odradek, a bizarre Kafkan creature who looks like "eine flache sternartige Zwirnspule" (Kafka, *Erzählungen* 343; "a flat, star-shaped spool for thread" [*Transformation* 176]). According to Morante's self-analysis, her dream was shaped by Max Ernst's picture of Odradek in the surrealist journal *Minotaure* ("Odradek" 17; Morante, *Diario* 32).[4] In Ernst's drawing, the threads of this strange creature, whose problematic existence raises questions about life, form his name. Trying to explain Odradek the narrator asks, "Kann er denn sterben?" (Kafka, *Erzählungen* 344; "Can he possibly die?" [Kafka, *Complete* 344]), and Ernst's Odradek evokes this confusion, since he is part creature, part word, maybe alive, maybe dead, maybe object.

Ernst's unusual picture has been identified as one of the earliest visual representations of Kafka's works, revealing that Morante was at the forefront of Kafka appreciation. The same issue of *Minotaure* that includes this depiction also contains a short description of Kafka by André Breton, who viewed Kafka as sharing a great deal with surrealism (Breton 7, Whitlark 151). Kafka was not indisputably famous until after World War II and readers of the 1920s, 1930s, and 1940s often stressed different aspects of Kafka's work than later critics did. While French intellectuals tended to focus on Kafka's surrealism and existentialism, many Italians highlighted Kafka's realism and Jewishness.[5] From the 1920s to today, Italian critics cite Kafka as emblematic of someone who had a complex relationship to his Jewishness in discussions of Jewish authors.[6] This early Italian emphasis on Kafka's Jewishness is worth briefly noting, since it adds to the complicated picture of Morante's relationship to her Jewish origins.[7]

Morante characterizes Kafka not as surreal or Jewish, but Gothic in her note to the collection *Lo scialle andaluso* (1963): "'L'uomo dagli occhiali,' il quale risente poi, nel suo goticismo, di qualche influsso kafkiano (questa però fu la prima e l'ultima che E.M.—sia detto a sua giustizia—risentí l'influsso di un qualsiasi altro autore al mondo)" (*Lo scialle* 215; "'The Man with the Glasses,' which betrays, in its Gothicism, some Kafkan influence [this however was the first and last time that E. M.—it is to be said in all fairness—was influenced by any other author in the world]").[8] Carlo Sgorlon discounted Morante's description of "L'uomo dagli occhiali" as Gothic, in part because the idea of a Gothic Kafka seemed implausible to him (35).[9] Indeed Mark Anderson observes that, "Kafka's work generally, has not been read in terms of the Gothic" (384), a remarkable fact given both the abundance of criticism on Kafka and that Kafka's work and Gothic ones are often described using similar terms such as *nightmarish*, *weird*, *eerie*, and *uncanny*, in addition to containing unsettling transformations and expressing desires of the unconscious. Only in the twenty-first century have Kafka scholars explored in detail the relationship between Kafka and the Gothic (see Anderson and Bridgwater, written in 2002 and 2003, respectively). Morante's unusual interpretation of Kafka as Gothic is due to both her individual perspective and the fact that she came to Kafka at an early point, in her own development as well as in Kafka's reception. Her appreciation of Kafka was neither helped nor hindered by later criticism and commonplaces about the author from Prague. Given the unusual nature of her description, this chapter now explores what Morante might have meant by calling Kafka "Gothic."

One of the few critics to explore Kafka and Morante together in detail, Angelo Pupino concentrates primarily on Kafka's *The Castle*, "L'uomo dagli occhiali," and "Il ladro dei lumi," in order to flesh out Morante's characterization of her own and Kafka's works as Gothic. While Pupino finds several intriguing connections between the two authors, such as damnation, the restriction of space, and the unreal (17–38), Morante's Kafka can be distinguished from Pupino's Kafka of the 1960s, not only because of her understanding of him but also because of which translations existed at the time that she wrote "L'uomo dagli occhiali." *The Castle* was only published in Italian in 1948, over a decade after the first publication of "L'uomo dagli occhiali" in 1937. Although Morante could have read it in, for instance, English, I propose that Morante's idea of the Gothic may have been informed by a story that she definitely read in the 1930s, "Der Jäger Gracchus." Based on the evidence we have, Morante's Kafka is shaped less by many of the works he is famous for today, such as *The Castle*, and more by short stories of Kafka's published in the collection *Il messaggio dell'imperatore* (1935), like "Il cacciatore Gracco" (The Hunter Gracchus) and the story about Odradek, "Il cruccio del padre di famiglia" (The Cares of a Family Man). These two Kafka stories, which Morante directly mentions, explore the boundary between life and death, as does "L'uomo dagli occhiali."

In "Der Jäger Gracchus," a hunter pulls into the port of Riva and discusses his situation—he is dead and roams the earth unable to find peace—with the mayor of Riva: "'Seitdem bin ich tot.' 'Aber Sie leben doch auch?' sagte der Bürgermeister. 'Gewissermaßen'" (Kafka, *Erzählungen* 268–69; "'Since then I have been dead.' 'But you are alive, too,' said the mayor. 'In a certain sense'"; [Kafka, *Complete* 228]). Like Odradek, the hunter exists but cannot die. The less fantastical elements of Kafka's story could have been based on actual experience, since Kafka traveled twice to Riva, in 1909 and 1913. The story's unusual location in an Italian city, "the only geographically specific setting in any of Kafka's short fiction" (Gross 249), may make the fragmented tale of particular interest to an Italian author. Revealing how present the story was in Morante's imaginary, Morante refers to "Der Jäger Gracchus" during a trip to Cefalù in 1937: "Finestre chiuse, fa pensare alla morte. Sembra una barca di un morto pagano, stanca di errare e approdata a questa riva ('Il cacciatore gracco' di Kafka). Certo disabitata, d'inverno" (*Opere* xxix; "Windows closed, it makes one think about death. It seems like the boat of a dead pagan, tired of wandering and come ashore [Kafka's 'The Hunter Gracchus']. Certainly uninhabited in winter"). The closed windows of this Hunter Gracchus-esque port remind Morante of death. I will return to these windows since they play an analogously symbolic role in "L'uomo dagli occhiali" and "Der Jäger Gracchus."

Although by no means the best known of Kafka's works, "Der Jäger Gracchus" has influenced other authors, like W. G. Sebald. Lionel Trilling chose the fragmented story for his *The Experience of Literature* reader. Wilhelm Emrich claims that "Der Jäger Gracchus" represents a model for Kafka's work more generally, since it depicts "two worlds that cannot make themselves understood by one another" (7). The living and dead characters of the stories can be read as embodying different perspectives. Many of Morante's early stories, like "L'uomo dagli occhiali," can similarly be described as juxtaposing two worlds or genres to create a sense of unease or alienation. Morante's Kafkan story is focalized through two different characters, the man with glasses and Clara, whose points of view are foreign to each other.

Patrick Bridgwater argues that the Gothic alienation in Kafka's works originates from the author's life experiences: "Kafka's Gothic is a reflection of his identity problem. However he looked at his genetic inheritance and position, and therefore at his own identity, he could not get away from a sense of alienation" (32). While Morante's self-proclaimed Gothic story depicts a solitude that reflects an analogous alienation, the story refers to a different set of identity issues, with a particular focus on sexuality. This notable distinction between the stories relates to Elisa Gambaro's sensitive exploration of how Morante's transforms Kafka's male Odradek into a female character in her dream (26). In "L'uomo dagli occhiali," the man with glasses wakes up, looking forward to seeing the object of his obsession, a girl named Maria. He hurries to the school yard where Clara informs him that Maria died. The story's focus then switches to Clara who speaks to and holds hands with her dead friend Maria, who confesses that the man killed her. The story ends with the two friends examining Maria's budding breasts.

"L'uomo dagli occhiali" explores several transitions, including the one from childhood to adulthood, made obvious in the last few moments of the story, and between life and death. In Morante's story, the reflection of Clara on the windows of her school could easily be on the strangeness of death: "le finestre erano chiuse; anche la cancellata era chiusa, ed ella si meravigliò che la scuola, già così animate, si fosse in pochi minuti fatti deserta" (*Lo scialle*

25; "the windows were closed, the gate was also closed, and she marveled that the school, so animated before, had been deserted in just a few minutes"). These closed windows, signifying barriers between two realities, emphasize loneliness. At the same time, although viewers cannot see inside the buildings, the windows also represent possibility, offering a potential space of transition. Guy Davenport has emphasized the particular focus on the transition from life to death in Kafka's story (14). The dead Hunter Gracchus laments, "ware als Aufgabe gesetzt mir zu helfen, so blieben alle Türen aller Häuser geschlossen, alle Fenster geschlossen, alle lägen in den Betten" (Kafka, *Erzählungen* 270; "even if all the people were commanded to help me, every door and window would remain shut, everybody would take to bed" [Kafka, *Complete* 230]). While the closed windows block the dead man from entering the buildings of the living, they also draw attention to a potential opening between life and death. Indeed, the dead continue to exist in both stories.

The two stories also contain dialogues between a living and dead person, Clara and Maria in Morante's work, and the major of Riva and the hunter in Kafka's. The content of these conversations suggests that the dead person's continued presence relates to how they died. In "L'uomo dagli occhiali," the man's potential crime constitutes the main subject of Maria's conversation, linking it to Maria's return. The mayor of Riva, meanwhile, hints that the Hunter Gracchus cannot leave the land of the living because of his own actions before his death: "'Ein schlimmes Schicksal,' sagte der Bürgermeister mit abwehrend erhobener Hand. 'Und Sie tragen gar keine Shuld daran?'" (Kafka, *Erzählungen* 269; "'A terrible fate,' said the mayor, raising his hand defensively, 'And you bear no blame for it?'" [Kafka, *Complete* 229]). Both stories insinuate that crimes have been committed, indicating another potential reason that Morante called "L'uomo dagli occhiali" a Gothic-Kafkan tale, since Gothic works often "manifest unresolved crimes or conflicts that can no longer be successfully buried from view" (Hogle 2). The man with glasses, the original point of focalization in Morante's story, may actually be, unbeknownst to himself, a murderer. At the same time, his guilt may be primarily based on his thoughts, his desire for a young girl, not his behavior. The reader cannot be sure what the man with glasses or the hunter did because of the narratives' ambiguities and openness. Interpretations that focus on guilt because of one's mental state or actions, the guilt of not knowing what one's sin was, or a general guilt of being human are all possible for both stories.

"The Hunter Gracchus," composed of fragments and unpublished in Kafka's lifetime, contains unsettling shifts in perspective. As mentioned, Morante's work also changes from concentrating on the man's point of view, to following Maria and her conversation with her dead friend about the man. The extent of the strangeness of this conversation depends in large part on if the reader interprets the dialogue as a fantasy or "reality," within the context of the story. Nicoletta Di Ciolla McGowan, for instance, reads it as imagined: "Clara wants to see Maria, her dead friend, and her resolution is so strong that Maria materialises in front of her" (249). Because of how bizarre they are, several of Kafka's stories have also been interpreted as psychological hallucinations, but viewing the events in Kafka's work and Morante's story as actually happening makes the description of them as "Gothic" more convincing. Just as with Kafka, an interpretation of the events as a dream rests in large part on the eeriness of what occurs, not necessarily on textual evidence. The fact that Clara relates details, like the timing of her death in relationship to the days the man does not remember, that Maria could not have known and that link the two parts of "L'uomo dagli occhiali" together, supports a non-visionary reading of the story.

Morante's story starts with a realistic scene of the man waking up, confused, and beginning his daily routine: "Il tre dicembre (era un giovedì) l'uomo uscí dal suo studio squallido posto alla periferia della città" (*Lo scialle* 21; "The third of December (it was a Thursday) the man exited his squalid studio located in the periphery of the city"). The seemingly banal detail that it was a Thursday gains importance as the man discovers that his sense of time is distorted, that it is not Sunday as he had thought.[10] Like Morante's story, Kafka's "Der Jäger Gracchus" begins with a description of seemingly mundane activities (*Erzählungen* 266, *Complete* 248), which juxtaposes with the bizarre arrival of a dead man. A sense of the uncanny pervades the works in part because of the contrast between realistic openings and the later appearance of the dead. Freud discusses this combination of realism and the impossible as significant for literary evocations of the uncanny, "das Unheimliche" (156–67). Both Kafka and Morante found reading Freud fruitful for their own writing, and "L'uomo dagli occhiali" and "Der Jäger Gracchus" can both be productively read with a Freudian lens. For the purposes of my analysis, the importance of Freud's work on the uncanny in discussions of the Gothic supports further Morante's unusual description of Kafka as Gothic.

Although Kafka and Morante are not the only authors to share the Gothic qualities discussed, Morante's claim that Kafka was the "first and last" author to influence her suggests that Kafka prompted her to experiment with her content and style. While Morante's statement on Kafka's overwhelming influence cannot be accepted without qualification, both because of the potential problems with any author's self-commentary and because of Morante's noted tendency to embellish the truth, Morante's characterization of her work reveals that she considered Kafka particularly significant for her development as an author. The importance of Kafka to Morante reveals that even though she was perhaps, as has often been stated, out-of-step with her contemporaries' artistic interests, she did look to other authors for inspiration. This analysis of Morante's encounter with Kafka includes Morante in a genealogy of Italian authors who looked to foreign, Gothic tales that offered "alternative narrative models to the ethos and closed linear structure prescribed by realism" (Billiani 15).[11] Comparing Kafka and Morante also provides another way to discuss Morante's early work that does not relegate it to mere thematic fodder, a source of themes expanded upon in her later novels.

While the exploration of "L'uomo dagli occhiali" and "Der Jäger Gracchus" as Gothic Kafkan works draws on Morante's explicit mentions of Kafka, I now want to suggest how a comparison with Kafka based on the relevance of Kafka criticism to Morante can bring her work into broader discussions. The unnoted significance of Morante to what is called "Animal Studies" contrasts with the place Kafka holds in the growing field. While Italianists have called attention to some of the complexity of Morante's animal imagery and Giorgio Agamben has discussed the intersection of Morante and Kafka's thoughts on animals and Paradise (102–8), many moments in Morante's texts that are relevant to current debates in Animal Studies remain overlooked.[12] By concentrating on the importance of Morante's talking animals to discussions that include Kafka's "Ein Bericht für eine Akademie" (A Report to an Academy), I aim to add to the body of criticism that considers Morante's numerous animals and animal imagery and call attention to the potential significance of Morante to Animal Studies. Like Kafka, Morante portrays a number of realistically communicating animals in her fiction, and I argue that the representation of animals in *La Storia* (History) and *L'isola di Arturo* (Arturo's Island) contributes to and often anticipates the debates on the human-animal boundary.

Kafka's work figures prominently in debates on the human-animal boundary, making significant appearances in *The Lives of Animals* (1999), *Animal Acts: Configuring the Human in Western History* (1997), *Savages and Beasts: The Birth of the Modern Zoo* (2002), *Melancholia's Dog: Reflections on our Animal Kinship* (2006), and *Thinking Animals: Why Animal Studies Now?* (2012). Critics view Kafka as a rare author whose literature questions humans' attempt to separate themselves from other animals:

> In a post-Darwinian world, *all* stories are stories about apes told by other apes—or at least primates. Implicitly, all stories are about the struggle of a particular species of ape to invent and preserve a nonanimal identity for itself. Only a few writers consciously incorporate that struggle into the bodies of their texts. (Scholtmeijer 139)

Portrayal of this struggle is a large part of why Kafka's "Ein Bericht für eine Akademie," a story of an ape who supposedly becomes a man, plays a central role in discussions on the human animal boundary. Distinguishing "Ein Bericht für eine Akademie" from the many stories in which animals and humans communicate thanks to magic or unexplained circumstances, critics highlight the story's realistic focus on interspecial communication.

Like Kafka, the narrator of *La Storia* often blurs the line between human and animal characters. Davide, for instance, confuses himself not only with the human boy Giuseppe but also with the dog Bella:

> *E Davide, frattanto, rincorreva le sue proprie meditazioni a voce alta, quasi ragionasse in sogno con qualche gran Dottore, senza piú accorgersi di parlare a due poveri analfabeti . Quasi non rammentava piú, anzi, chi fra i tre, là dentro, fosse lo studente colto, e chi il pischelletto e chi il cane.* (Morante, *La Storia* 524)

> And Davide, meanwhile, pursued his own meditations aloud, as if he were disputing in a dream with some great Doctor, no longer realizing he was speaking to two poor illiterates. As if, indeed, he no longer remembered who, among the three there in the room, was the cultivated student, and who the kid and who the dog. (Morante, *History* 589)

In this passage the narrator complicates the categories of human and nonhuman animals, associating the two together as "illiterates." This identification of humans and animals as illiterates suggests that *La Storia* itself can be seen as addressing animals, since Morante dedicates her work to the "illiterate," with a quote from César Vallejo: "Por el analfabeto a quien escribo." By including a dog and therefore other nonhuman animals in this category of illiterates, Morante aims to reach and portray even more than the "history of humanity," as Cesare Garboli characterized it ("Elsa Morante"). This wider perspective is confirmed by the way *La Storia* also includes animals, like Bella and Blitz, that are treated as characters, given their own history, and shown interacting with others even when they are not with their human companions in the novel. In other words, *La Storia* often presents animals as subjects and protagonists, as Concetta D'Angeli has observed (104).

Morante's representation of animals anticipates more recent views in Animal Studies that discuss how historical studies have neglected to include animals and could, in fact, be rewritten focusing on them. For instance, John Simons describes his project, *Animal Rights and the Politics of Literary Representation* (2002): "In this book I am proposing that there is yet another way of rewriting Marx: 'The history of all hitherto existing society is the history of the struggle between humans and non-humans'" (7). For critics like Simons, the inclusion of animals naturally follows other rewritings of history, with more focus on women, children, the poor, and so on. Morante had already made this move in her novel published in 1974.[13] Morante presents a worldview that includes animals, in a portrayal that partially attempts to balance more official histories that concentrate on the powerful.

La Storia also represents animals that are able to communicate with one of the human protagonists of the work. Unlike in works in which there is no explanation for how humans can understand animals, Giuseppe's comprehension abilities are described as growing partially out of isolation: "Quelle erano fortune indimenticabili, per Giuseppe: e forse fu in quei suoi duetti primitivi con Blitz, che imparò il linguaggio dei cani" (Morante, *La Storia*, 110; "These were unforgettable strokes of luck for Giuseppe; and perhaps it was in those primitive duets with Blitz that he learned the language of dogs" [Morante, *History* 121]). The narrator's "perhaps" highlights the complexities of understanding how interspecial communication can occur. Although this aspect of Morante's work has been pointed to as an odd moment of magical realism in an otherwise realistic historical fiction, isolation from one's species is examined as a realistic element of Kafka's "Ein Bericht für eine Akademie," showing that often what is credible in stories of animal-human communication has more to do with preconceived notions on the part of the human reader than on animals' abilities. Morante's narrative pushes up against the barrier of what humans conceive of as possible when it comes to human-animal communication.

Animals are not only treated as subjects in *La Storia* and understood by one of the human protagonists, but their noises, or language, are also transcribed and translated into human terms, anticipating current attempts made to understand animals' expressions. Although a more lighthearted and brief examination of animal speech than the scientific experiments conducted today, Morante's work similarly raises questions about what animal speech is and how humans can try to understand it. *La Storia* includes a description and gloss of how a particular cat's various sounds can be interpreted: "Per chiedere, diceva míu o mèu; per chiamare, mau, per minacciare, mbroooh, ecc. ecc." (Morante, *La Storia* 189; "To ask for something, she said: *myew* or *mayeu*; to call, she said *mau*, to threaten *mbrooooh*, etc. etc." [Morante, *History* 208]). The question of whether cats' mews are words is debatable, but *La Storia* reveals that they do communicate translatable ideas that can be represented with letters. While the description is playful, the narrator also takes the cat's noises seriously, as one would a foreign, human language.

Morante's cat who mews with meaning is an instance of an animal whose expressions can be represented verbally, but communication does not necessarily have to be verbal, an idea explored in *L'isola di Arturo*. Just as Giuseppe has intimate relationships with his dogs in *La Storia*, Arturo develops a special bond with his, which leads to understanding another species:

> *Si dirà: parlare tanto d'una cagna! Ma io, quand'ero un ragazzino, non avevo altri compagni che lei, e non si può negare ch'era straordinaria. Per conversare con me, aveva inventato una specie di linguaggio dei muti: con la coda,*

con gli occhi, con le sue pose, e molte note diverse della sua voce, sapeva dirmi ogni suo pensiero; e io la capivo. (Morante, *L'isola* 46)

What a lot of fuss about a dog, you'll say. But when I was a boy I'd no other friend, and you can't deny she was extraordinary. We'd invented a kind of deaf-and-dumb language between us: tail, eyes, movements, the pitch of her voice—all of them told me every thought of hers, and I understood. (Morante, *Arturo's* 3)

The passage suggests that the primarily nonverbal communication of Arturo and his dog companion may be clearer than the spoken language most humans use with each other, similar to how Giuseppe's communication with dogs often seems to be the most the profound of any depicted in Morante's *La Storia.* In both novels, again as in "Ein Bericht für eine Akademie," isolation from other humans contributes to the intense communication between a human and an animal.

Like Kafka, Morante's depiction of animals reveals the complexities of interspecial communication. Morante's animal depictions are multifaceted and can provide the starting points for conversations that continue to be of interest to critics, philosophers, and animal rights advocates. Although Morante's representations of various modes of potential human-animal communication are nuanced, realistic, and striking, they have been basically ignored by Animal Studies' scholars. Animal Studies scholarship can provide a new lens on some of Morante's work, and Morante's depictions of animals and animal-human communication have a great deal to offer Animal Studies. This chapter is not comprehensive but offers a few suggestions of how Kafka and Morante can be productively read together.[14] Comparison with Kafka may help underscore unusual elements of Morante's work, put her into conversation with other Kafkan authors, and draw the attention of non-Italianists to the power of Morante's literary representations.

NOTES

1. For notable exceptions of critics who discuss Kafka and Morante in detail, see Gambaro and Pupino.

2. "Buzzati's book enjoyed a popularity precisely because the success of Kafka, a true writer, had prepared the ground for the work of his imitator" (Moravia and Elkann 269).

3. See Moravia's "master" comment (*Life of Moravia* 190) and "religion" comment in Paris (50).

4. For more on Kafka and Ernst, see Spies 214–22.

5. Kafka's European reception is more complex than this but is beyond the scope of this article. See, for instance, Caputo-Mayr and Herz.

6. See, for instance, Debenedetti (68) and De Angelis (27) on Svevo.

7. For more on Kafka's reception as a Jewish author in Italy, see Ziolkowski. For more on Morante's Jewishness, see, for instance, Popoff.

8. Translation mine unless otherwise indicated. Morante esteemed the story enough to republish "L'uomo dagli occhiali" in her collections *Il gioco segreto* and *Lo scialle andaluso.*

9. Cesare Garboli, meanwhile, claims that Kafka is the only author to have clearly left his mark on Morante's work (*Il gioco segreto* 130–31).

10. Giovanna Rosa focuses on the importance of time in the story (170).

11. Although Morante is not cited in the collection, much of the analysis in *The Italian Gothic and Fantastic: Encounters and Rewritings of Narrative Traditions* could also be used to engage Morante's early work.

12. For work on Morante and animals, see D'Angeli 104–18, Porciani 230–33, Splendorini 319–41.

13. Morante's friends remember her as ahead of her time in terms of animal rights (Fontana 20).

14. Other critics have referred to interesting similarities between the two authors that deserve further attention. Enrica Puggioni for instance calls Davide Segre a "Kafkaesque hero" (V) and mentions that *History* clearly references Kafkaesque power structures (43).

WORKS CITED

Agamben, Giorgio. "The Celebration of the Hidden Treasure." *The End of the Poem: Studies in Poetics.* Trans. Daniel Heller-Roazen. Stanford, CA: Stanford University Press, 1999. 102–8.

Anderson, Mark M. "The Shadow of the Modern: Gothic Ghosts in Stoker's Dracula and Kafka's *Amerika.*" *Literary Paternity, Literary Friendship: Essays in Honor of Stanley Corngold.* Ed. Gerhard Richter. Chapel Hill: University of North Carolina Press, 2002.

Billiani, Francesca. "The Italian Gothic and Fantastic: An Inquiry into the Notions of Literary and Cultural Traditions (1869–1997)." *The Italian Gothic and Fantastic: Encounters and Rewritings of Narrative Traditions.* Ed. Francesca Billiani and Gigliola Sulis. Cranbury, NJ: Farleigh Dickinson University Press, 2007. 15–31.

Breton, André. "Franz Kafka." *Minotaure* (Winter 1937): 7.

Bridgwater, Patrick. *Kafka, Gothic and Fairytale.* Amsterdam: Rodopi, 2003.

Buzzati, Dino. "Le case di Kafka." *Corriere della Sera.* March 31, 1965. In *Buzzati e il Corriere. Corriere della Sera 1876/1986 Dieci anni e un secolo.* Ed. Vittorio Feltri and Bruno Rossi. Milan: Corriere della Sera, 1986. 54–56.

Caputo-Mayr, Marie Luise. "Kafka and Romance Languages. A Preliminary Survey." *Journal of the Kafka Society of America: New International Series* 27, no.1–2 (2003): 5–6.

Caputo-Mayr, Marie Luise and Julius M. Herz. *Franz Kafka: International Bibliography of Primary and Secondary Literature. 1908–1997 (Primary Literature); 1995–1997 (Secondary Literature).* Second Enlarged Edition. Munich: Saur, 2000.

Coetzee J. M. *The Lives of Animals.* Ed. Amy Gutmann. Princeton, NJ: Princeton University Press, 1999.

D'Angeli, Concetta. "'Soltanto l'animale è veramente innocente.' Gli animali nella Storia di Elsa Morante." *Leggere Elsa Morante: Aracoeli, La storia e Il mondo salvato dei ragazzini.* Rome: Carocci, 2003. 104–18.

Davenport, Guy. *The Hunter Gracchus and Other Papers on Literature and Art.* Washington D.C.: Counterpoint, 1997.

De Angelis, Luca. *Qualcosa di più intimo. Aspetti della scrittura ebraica del Novecento italiano: da Svevo a Bassani.* Florence: Giuntina, 2006.

Debenedetti, Giacomo. *Saggi critici: seconda serie.* Venice: Marsilio, 1990.

Emrich, Wilhelm. *Franz Kafka: A Critical Study of His Writings.* Trans. Sheema Zeben Buehne. New York: Frederick Ungar, 1968.

Ernst, Max. *Odradek. Minotaure* (Winter 1937): 17.

Fontana, Luca. "Elsa Morante: A Personal Remembrance." *PN Review* 14.6, 62 (1988): 18–22.

Freud, Sigmund. *The Uncanny.* Trans. David McLintock. New York: Penguin, 2003.

Gambaro, Elisa. "Strategies of Affabulation in *Diario 1938.*" *Under Arturo's Star: The Cultural Legacies of Elsa Morante.* Stefania Lucamante and Sharon Wood, eds. West Lafayette: Purdue University Press, 2006.

Garboli, Cesare. "Elsa Morante: la storia e le sue vittime." *Il grillo.* 23 April 2002. Web. 10 Jun. 2013.

———. *Il gioco segreto.* Milan: Adelphi, 1994.

Gross, Ruth V. "Hunting Kafka Out of Season: Enigmatics in the Short Fictions." *A Companion to the Works of Franz Kafka.* Ed. James Rolleston. Rochester, NY: Camden House, 2002.

Ham, Jennifer, and Matthew Senior, eds. *Animal Acts: Configuring the Human in Western History.* New York & London: Routledge, 1997.

Hogle, Jerrold E. "Introduction: the Gothic in Western Culture." *The Cambridge Companion to Gothic Fiction.* Ed. Jerrold E. Hogle. Cambridge: Cambridge University Press, 2002.

Kafka, Franz. *The Complete Stories.* Trans. Willa and Edwin Muir. New York: Schocken Books, 1971. Print.

———. *Die Erzählungen und andere ausgewählte Prosa.* Ed. Roger Hermes. Frankfurt am Main: Fischer, 1998.

———. *The Transformation ("Metamorphosis") and Other Stories.* Trans. Malcolm Pasley. New York: Penguin Books, 1992.

Kuzniar, Alice. *Melancholia's Dog.* Chicago: University of Chicago Press, 2005.

Lucamante, Stefania. *Elsa Morante e l'eredità proustiana.* Fiesole: Cadmo, 1998.

McGowan, Nicoletta Di Ciolla. "A Child with a View: Childhood and Self-Discovery in Mansfield and Morante." *New Comparison: A Journal of Comparative and General Literary Studies. "Legenda": Reading and Writing Myth* 27/28 (Spring–Autumn 1999): 239–58.

Morante, Elsa. *Arturo's Island.* Trans. Isabel Quigly. South Royalton, VT: Steerforth Italia, 2002.

———. *Diario 1938.* Ed. Alba Andreini. Turin: Einaudi, 1989.

———. *History.* Trans. William Weaver. Hanover, New Hampshire: Steerforth Press, 2000. Print.

———. *L'isola di Arturo.* Turin: Einaudi, 1995.

———. *La Storia.* Turin: Einaudi, 1995.

———. *Lo scialle andaluso.* Turin: Einaudi, 1963.

———. *Opere.* Cesare Garboli and Carlo Cecchi, eds. 2 vols. Milan: Meridiani Mondadori, 1988 and 1990.

Moravia, Alberto, and Alain Elkann. *Life of Moravia.* South Royalton, VT: Steerforth Italia, 2000.

Paris, Renzo. *Ritratto dell'artista da vecchio. Conversazioni con Alberto Moravia.* Rome: minimum fax, 2001.

Popoff, Gabrielle Elissa. "'Once upon a time there was an S.S. officer': The Holocaust between History and Fiction in Elsa Morante's *La Storia.*" *Journal of Modern Jewish Studies* 11.1 (2012): 25–38.

Porciani, Elena. *L'alibi del sogno nella scrittura giovanile di Elsa Morante.* Calabria: Iride, 2006.

Puggioni, Enrica. *Davide Segre, un eroe al confine della modernità.* Alessandria: Edizioni dell'Orso, 2006.

Pupino, Angelo Maria. *Strutture e stile della narrativa di Elsa Morante.* Ravenna: Longo, 1968.

Rosa, Giovanna. *Cattedrali di carta: Elsa Morante romanziere.* Milan: Il saggiatore, 1995. Print.

Rothfels, Nigel. *Savages and Beasts: The Birth of the Modern Zoo.* Baltimore, MD: Johns Hopkins University Press, 2002.

Scholtmeijer, Marian. "What is 'human'? Metaphysics and Zoontology in Flaubert and Kafka." *Animal Acts: Configuring the Human in Western History.* Ham and Senior 127–44.

Sgorlon, Carlo. *Invito alla lettura di Elsa Morante.* Milan: Mursia, 1988.

Simons, John. *Animal Rights and the Politics of Literary Representation.* New York: Palgrave, 2002.

Spies, Werner. *Kunstgeschichten von Bildern und Kunstlern im 20. Jahrhundert.* Vol. 1. Cologne: DuMont, 1998.

Splendorini, Ilaria."'Grâce' et 'pesanteur': Les metaphors animalières dans *La Storia* et *Aracoeli* d'Elsa Morante." *Italies* 12 (2008): 319–41.

Weil, Kari. *Thinking Animals: Why Animal Studies Now?* New York: Columbia University Press, 2012. Print.

Whitlark, James. *Behind the Great Wall: A Post-Jungian Approach to Kafkaesque Literature.* Cranbury, NJ: Associated University Press, 1991.

Ziolkowski, Saskia. "Primo Levi and Jewish Kafka in Italy." *Journal of the Kafka Society of America* 35/36 (2010–2011): 76–89.

Chapter Five

Elsa Morante

Envisioning History

Sarah Carey

The epigraph to Elsa Morante's 1974 novel *La Storia* reads: "Por el analfabe-to a quien escribo" (To the illiterate for whom I write), a line from the Peruvian poet César Vallejo. It sets up Morante's work as one meant to reach everyone, even those who are incapable of reading. Through its chronicling of the events leading up to and surrounding World War II, the novel aims to transcend this obstacle by making history accessible to all. In an attempt to reach a larger audience, in fact, the novel was published immediately in paperback (rather than the traditional hardcover). The original cover featured a Robert Capa photograph called "The Fallen Partisan," taken during the Spanish Civil War.[1] Many of Capa's photographs have been found to be less than objective reporting; even his most famous photograph, "The Falling Soldier," was supposedly staged. While Morante may not have been aware of the controversy surrounding Capa's work, the constructed nature of his his-torical images underscores Morante's own polemical take on history.

The particular image used on the paperback cover of *La Storia* is not simply a war photograph; however, it is a photo-montage, tinted a garish red and depicting a lifeless body sprawled on a pile of rubble. The cover image's stylized nature and its provocative caption suggest the work will be less a witness to history than a self-conscious interpretation of it. The structure of the novel is, in fact, a back-and-forth between reportage (the beginning of each chapter straightforwardly lists relevant dates and developments sur-rounding World War II) and the fictional story of a Jewish mother. This dual interpretation of history (both objective and subjective at the same time) also makes it an appropriate forum for Morante's own consideration of the power of photography. The photographs that later appear in the main plot of *La*

Storia reveal themselves to be texts whose interpretations allow the characters to come to terms with their wartime experience.

The interpretation of photographs is a subject that a number of twentieth-
century thinkers have taken up—from Walter Benjamin to Roland Barthes to
Susan Sontag. There is general consensus that photographs are "read" much
like pages of traditional text.[2] More recently, critic Geoffrey Batchen has
used the term *photogrammatology* to describe the language of photographic
objects, situating them instead in the realm of the textual (79). The sort of
exegesis at work in photographic interpretation thus is amplified further
when photographs appear in literary or cinematic texts that already invite
their own interpretation. The presence of these objects within other narratives
sets up if not an outright ekphrastic enterprise then, at the very least, a nod to
the ability of a photograph to tell "a story."[3]

La Storia's cover image is just the first photographic operation that Morante undertakes in the ideological enterprise of conceiving of history as (to
use Hayden White's contentious distinction) a "kind of art" (111). The title
of the work—while echoing White's use of the paradigm of the nineteenth-
century novel for thinking about historical artifice—directly equates a form
of fiction with "fact," positing history as a constructed narrative.[4] Morante's
type of history embodies a truth that so-called official accounts often distort
or even entirely repress. In Gramscian terms, she highlights how these types
of accounts tend to be particularly biased in favor of the powerful to the
detriment of the weak. Such is the operation at work when Morante fore-
grounds a widowed Jewish mother and her sons as the central characters in a
chronicle of World War II. Hers is not a "spiritualized" version of history,
however, but rather a reevaluation of the past that calls into question the
cultural politics of both religiously rooted and gender-based visions of Italian
society.

It is critical to note that Morante's subaltern protagonists engage with the
personal past and historical present vis-à-vis the photographic object. Photographic images and their interpretations serve as true "mediums" through
which the characters try to cope with the world changing around them. In one
of the work's most harrowing scenes, a German soldier (who, as we will
soon find out, will rape and impregnate Ida) investigates her home and sees a
photograph of her eldest son Nino on the wall:

> *Ma per l'ingrandimento eccessivo operato su quello che era stato, all'origine,*
> *il volgare prodotto di un fotografo ambulante, l'intera scena risultava piuttos-*
> *to pallida e sfocata. Il militare, scrutato il quadro nel suo insieme, lo collegò,*
> *di sua propria supposizione, col culto familiare dei defunti [. . .].*
>   *"Tot?" (morto?)*
>   *[. . .]*

No! no! Rispose [. . .]. E di fatto, secondo la verità, quella non era il ricordo di un morto, ma una foto recente di suo figlio Ninnuzzu. (Morante, *La Storia* 65)

But the excessive enlargement, blown up from what had been originally the cheap products of a street photographer, had made the whole scene somewhat faint and blurred. Having examined the picture thoroughly, the soldier connected it, in his own supposition, with the family cult of the dead [. . .].
   "*Tot?*" (dead?)
   [. . .]
   No! no! she answered [. . .]. And, in fact, that was truly not the memorial of a dead person, but a recent photo of her son, Ninnuzzu. (Morante, *History* 55)

In this description—with its vague echoes of the photographic enlargements featured in Michelangelo Antonioni's 1966 film *Blow-Up*—Morante continues to explore how the photographic apparatus can alter personal appearance and, in this case, to cause confusion in the image's interpretation. The fact that the soldier assumes that the boy depicted has joined the "cult of the dead" also speaks to photography as a locus of remembrance. As if to connect their familial situations, the soldier, in turn, shows Ida an innocent family photograph—pointing out himself among five or six of his siblings and then explaining the location of the image's background landscape (Dachau, in an eerie allusion to the Nazi death camps of which Ida, at this point, is unaware) (Morante, *La Storia* 68; Morante, *History* 57). This feigned moment of benevolence, unfortunately, is merely a way to get closer to the apprehensive woman before raping her—resulting in the birth of her younger son Useppe.

The traumatic experience of war is likewise evidenced through the identification card of the character Carlo Vivaldi/Davide Segre. As Ida compares the younger image in the photograph to the emaciated frame of the young man in real life when he returns home from the front, she sees the ravages of wartime through a corporeal change:

Adesso invece la sua fisionomia era segnata da qualcosa di corrotto, che ne pervertiva i lineamenti dall'interno. E questi segni, ancora intrisi di uno stupore terribile, parevano prodotto non da una maturazione graduale; ma da una violenza fulminea, simile a uno stupro. (Morante, *La Storia* 198–99)

Now instead his features were marked by something corrupt, which perverted them from within. And these marks, filled with a terrible stupor, seemed to have been produced not by a gradual development, but by a lightning violence, like a rape. (Morante, *History* 169–70)

Here, though the photograph is proof of Vivaldi's identity, it is the physical body that is more the document of history. Not coincidentally, his physical deterioration is likened to a rape, much like Ida's own photographic encounter, and is further emphasized by Morante's word choice (*stupore/stupro*). What Ida is able to glean from the photograph, on the other hand, is an aura of innocence that is now decidedly gone.

Even less fortunate, however, is one of the missing inhabitants of the shared living space in which Ida and her family are ultimately forced to reside. Ida and the young Useppe come to know the young man's story through two photographs of him that his mother has kept faithfully in the home.

> [La] seconda, portata da un reduce che lo aveva incontrato in Russia, era una piccola istantanea [. . .]. [In] secondo piano, si vedevano delle sagome scure, tutte in un mucchio e infagottate, così che non si riconosceva nemmeno che fossero militari e non civili, né se in testa portassero degli elmetti, o non, piuttosto, delle specie di cappellucci mosci. Fra quelli là, c'era lui; ma veramente, non era possibile individuarlo, e nemmeno indicarlo, dentro al mucchio, in un punto preciso. (Morante, *La Storia* 314)

> [The] second picture, brought back by a soldier who had met him in Russia, was a little snapshot [. . .]. [Farther] to the rear, you could see some dark forms, all in a huddled mass, so you couldn't even say whether they were soldiers or civilians, or if there were helmets on their heads, or rather, some kind of limp little hat. Among them was Giovannino; but really it was impossible to distinguish him, or even to indicate him at a precise point within the pile. (Morante, *History* 268–69)

What is striking about this passage is that Giovannino has become just one of the masses, just another indiscernible casualty of war. Unlike Carlo, he seems to have lost his identity entirely.

Perhaps the most important use of photography in *La Storia*, however, occurs just after the aforementioned descriptions of Carlo and Giovannino. In keeping with a non-hegemonic take on history, Morante segues into a unique description of some very famous, actual photographs through the point of view of a child—a reinterpretation of history through a naïve and thus subaltern point of view that is the antithesis of hegemonic historical discourse. In the spring of 1945, two photographs manage to capture Useppe's attention, both of hanged people. The narrator, though she indicates that it is Useppe who is looking at these images, describes the first one for the reader with an attention to its formal composition and the shapes of the bodies (some of them labeled with signs reading "PARTIGIANO"). Such a description goes beyond what the young boy could have actually made of the scene, revealing a more complex hermeneutical operation at work. The description of the second image is far simpler but nonetheless loaded with signification. "Nella seconda fotografia dello stesso foglio, si vedeva un uomo vecchio, dalla testa grassa e calva, appiccato per i piedi con le braccia spalancate, sopra una folla fitta e imprecisa" (Morante, *La Storia* 314; "In the second photograph on the same page, an old man was seen, with a fat, bald head, hanging by his feet, his arms wide, over a large, blurred crowd" [Morante, *History* 269]). The fact that the body is hung upside down would have had little meaning for the child, but a knowledgeable reader cannot help but surmise that this is an image of Benito Mussolini's demise. Furthermore, the two images together are "reverse" images of wartime retribution in Italy: the partisans slaughtered by fascists and then their leader killed and held up for public display. This is a distinction that figures little, however, in young Useppe's mind.

Useppe's encounter with the photographic medium does not end here, however. It is taken up again later as part of the narrator's description of his visual education, the way in which he comes to learn how to "read" photographs. This takes place when he accidentally finds images of concentration camps in Nazi Germany on the pages of a popular magazine that have been used to cover up a basket of fruit at home.[5] The narrator, again acting as a secondary point of view, clarifies that these images, however, do not even begin to tell the whole story: "A causa del carattere divulgativo e poco scientifico della rivista, le foto stampate in quella pagina non erano nemmeno delle piú terribili fra quante se ne vedevano allora" (Morante, *La Storia* 372; "Because of the magazine's popularizing, unscholarly nature, the photographs printed on that page weren't even among the most terrible of those to be seen at that time" [Morante, *History* 317]). Rather than provide Useppe's interpretation of the images, the narrator gives the "grown-up version" first in a systematic rendering of their content:

1) un cumulo di prigionieri assassinati, nudi e scomposti, c già in parte disfatti – 2) una grossa quantità di scarpe ammonticchiate, appartenute a quelli o altri prigionieri – 3) un gruppo di internati, ancora vivi, ritratti dietro una rete metallica – 4) la 'scala della morte' di 186 gradini altissimi e irregolari [. . .] – 5) un condannato in ginocchio davanti alla fossa che lui stesso ha dovuto scavarsi [. . .] – 6) e una piccola serie di fotogrammi (quattro in tutto) che presentano fasi successive di un esperimento in camera di decompressione, eseguito su una cavia umana (Morante, *La Storia* 372)

1) a heap of murdered prisoners, naked and sprawling, and already partly decomposed; 2) a huge quantity of piled-up shoes, which had belonged to those or other prisoners; 3) a group of prisoners, still alive, seen behind a metal fence; 4) the "death stairway" of 186 very high and irregular steps [. . .] 5) a sentenced man on his knees before the ditch he himself had been made to dig [. . .] 6) and a little series of frames (four in all) which show successive stages of a decompression-chamber experiment, performed on a human guinea pig (Morante, *History* 317)

All of the images were explained by the accompanying text: "Tutto ciò era spiegato, a quanto io ricordo ancora oggi, da brevi didascalie poste al basso di ciascuna foto" (Morante, *La Storia* 372; "All this was explained, as far as I can recall today, by brief captions underneath each picture" Morante, *History* 317). At precisely this moment of description, the narrator inserts herself into history, drawing now (in the present) upon her own memory of these images of the past in order to explain Useppe's fictional encounter with them.

The experience for Useppe is only a visual one, however, since he does not know how to read yet and must interpret the ambiguous and indistinct images based purely on their visual content. Morante uses an interesting narrative technique that again describes the photographic images, though from the point of view of Useppe. Useppe's interpretation of the image naturally centers on what is most significant to the eyes of a child, and therefore differs in important respects from that of the narrator. He emphasizes the forms and colors of the visual images rather than the deeper (and more frightening) meaning of their content. Some of Useppe's observations are less detailed than the descriptions the reader has encountered through the narrator, while others contain emotional reactions to the images, a quality that is absent from the real captions.

> *Ci si vede un cumulo caotico di materie biancastre e stecchite, di cui non si discernano le forme, e, altrove, un enorme sfasciume di scarpacce ammonticchiate che, a vista, si lascerebbe scambiare per un cumulo di morti [. . .]. E dall'altra parte della pagina, delle figure di ometti scheletrici, occhieggianti dietro una rete, con addosso certe casacche a strisce, flosce e cascanti, che li fanno somigliare a burattini. Alcuni di costoro hanno la testa nuda e rapata, altri portano una scopoletta; e le loro facce si atteggiano a un sorrisetto agonizzante, misero come una depravazione definitiva.* (Morante, *La Storia* 372–73)

> You see there a chaotic heap of whitish, stick-like objects, whose forms cannot be distinguished, and, elsewhere, an enormous waste of piled shoes which, at first sight, could be mistaken for a pile of dead bodies [. . .]. And on the other side of the page, some little skeletal human shapes, staring behind a fence, wearing striped tunics loose and sagging, which make them look like puppets. Some of them have bare, shaven heads; others wear caps; and their faces show an agonizing smile, a wretched, definitive depravity (Morante, *History* 317–18)

Useppe's observation of the second photograph is compelling since he mistakes the pile of shoes for a pile of bodies, which was something that he could not make out with the first photograph, which actually *was* a heap of bodies. Though he does not realize it, of course, the effect of this description is one of a very meaningful synecdoche. The passage is also revelatory in its portrayal of the young boy's textualization of the visual material: he reads the images and their variations, puts them in a sort of order, and interprets them as part of a short narrative. The narrator admits, however, that it is impossible to know what the young boy could have truly understood from the photographs; they may easily remain just visual nonsense to him.

When Ida finds him looking at these photographs, she forces him to throw away the ugly images, helping him avoid the sort of visual trauma for which he is not yet prepared. Morante's use of descriptions of photographs in this section of the novel is pivotal in shaping Useppe as a character who—through a visual education—begins to encounter for the first time the frightening world that lies beyond childhood. In fact, photographs in the novel, as a whole, come to represent a certain loss of innocence that is a consequence of wartime. Furthermore, Morante shows just how subjectively each individual might perceive images that are perhaps meant to be objective. The result is a multifaceted, visual view of wartime that challenges the hegemonic discourse of history and, paradoxically perhaps, reads as more truthful through its very fiction.

NOTES

1. See Fumi and Oram for a study of visual elements in *La Stori*a. Neither critic, however, notes the presence of photographs as an integral part of the novel's plot.

2. On the subject of visual textuality, see Melville and Readings; Bryant; Schwenger; Eugeni; Basso Fossali and Dondero.

3. On ekphrasis and photography, see Krieger; W. J. T. Mitchell; Hermange and Barnett; and Cheeke.

4. At issue here is the polemical discourse surrounding White's 1973 publication of *Metahistory* with its likening of historical discourse to fictional narrative, a comparison that is also outlined in the aforementioned essay "The Burden of History" from several years earlier. On Morante and the historical novel, see Della Coletta and Re, both of whom engage with the cultural hegemony surrounding historical discourse.

5. Sontag herself reiterates her own young encounter with these images: "For me, it was photographs of Bergen-Belsen and Dachau which I came across by chance in a bookstore in Santa Monica in July 1945. Nothing I have seen—in photographs or in real life—ever cut me as sharply, deeply, instantaneously. Indeed it seems plausible to me to divide my life into two parts, before I saw those photographs (I was twelve) and after, though it was several years before I understood fully what they were about" (*On Photography* 20).

WORKS CITED

Barthes, Roland. *Camera lucida—Reflections on Photography*. Trans. Richard Howard. New York: Hill and Wang, 1981.
———. "The Photographic Message." *Image-Music-Text*. Trans. Stephen Heath. New York: Hill and Wang, 1977. 15–31.
———. "Rhetoric of the Image." *Image-Music-Text* . Trans. Stephen Heath. New York: Hill and Wang, 1977. 32–51.
Batchen, Geoffrey. *Each Wild Idea—Writing, Photography, History*. Cambridge, MA: MIT Press, 2001.

Bazin, André. "The Ontology of the Photographic Image." *What is Cinema?* Vol. 1. Berkeley: University of California Press, 1967. 9–16.

Benjamin, Walter. "A Short History of Photography." Trachtenberg 199–216.

———. "The Work of Art in the Age of Mechanical Reproduction." *Illuminations—Essays and Reflections.* Trans. Harry Zohn. New York: Schocken Books, 1968. 218–51.

Berger, John. "Understanding a Photograph." Trachtenberg 291–94.

Bryant, Marsha, ed. *Photo-Textualities—Reading Photographs and Literature.* Newark: University of Delaware Press, 1996.

Cheeke, Stephen. *Writing for Art: The Aesthetics of Ekphrasis.* Manchester, England: Manchester University Press, 2008.

Della Coletta, Cristina. *Plotting the Past: Metamorphoses of Historical Narrative in Modern Italian Fiction.* West Lafayette, IN: Purdue University Press, 1996.

Eugeni, Ruggero. *Analisi semiotica dell'immagine—Pittura, illustrazione, fotografia.* Milan: Università Cattolica, 1999.

Fossali, Pierluigi Basso, and Maria Giulia Dondero. *Semiotica della fotografia: Investigazioni teoriche e pratiche d'analisi.* Rimini: Guaraldi, 2006.

Fumi, Elena. "La Storia negli occhi." *Studi Novecenteschi: Rivista Semestrale di Storia della Letteratura Italiana Contemporanea* 21.47–48 (1994): 237–50.

Hermange, Emmanuel, and Tracy Barnett. "Aspects and Uses of Ekphrasis in Relation to Photography, 1816–1860." *Journal of European Studies* 30.1 (2000): 5–18.

Krieger, Murray. *Ekphrasis: The Illusion of the Natural Sign.* Baltimore: Johns Hopkins University Press, 1992.

Melville, Stephen, and Bill Readings, eds. *Vision & Textuality.* Durham: Duke University Press, 1995.

Mitchell, W. J. T. *Iconology—Image, Text, Ideology.* Chicago: University of Chicago Press, 1986.

Morante, Elsa. *History: A Novel.* Trans. William Weaver. New York: Knopf, 1977.

———. *La Storia: Romanzo.* Turin: Einaudi, 1974.

Oram, Lydia M. "Rape, Rapture and Revision: Visionary Imagery and Historical Reconstruction in Elsa Morante's *La Storia.*" *Forum Italicum* 37.2 (2003): 409–35.

Re, Lucia. "Utopian Longing and the Constraints of Racial and Sexual Difference in Elsa Morante's *La Storia.*" *Italica* 70.3 (Autumn 1993): 361–75.

Schwenger, Peter. *Fantasm and Fiction—On Textual Envisioning.* Stanford: Stanford University Press, 1999.

Sontag, Susan. *On Photography.* New York: Picador, 1973.

———. *Regarding the Pain of Others.* New York: Picador, 2004. Print.

Trachtenberg, Alan, ed. *Classic Essays on Photography.* New Haven: Leete's Island Books, 1980.

White, Hayden. "The Burden of History." *History and Theory* 5.2 (1966): 111–34.

Chapter Six

Excursus as Narrative Technique in *La Storia*

Sharon Wood

One of the many criticisms leveled against Morante's *La Storia* was its failure to align itself with an identifiable political Left, its perceived refusal to engage directly and openly in the struggle against contemporary capitalist structures of power in the late 1960s and 1970s that sought to exploit the working class in the pursuit of profit:

> *A noi* La Storia *non sembra altro che una scontata rassegnazione, un nuovo discorso delle beatitudini, che l'ideologia della classe sfruttatrice trova del tutto funzionale al proprio attuale progetto economico [. . .] una mediocre scrittrice. [. . .] Allora, compagni: oltre che dai decretoni, cominciamo a difenderci anche dai romanzoni.* (Balestrini 3)

> *History* seems to us nothing other than an act of inevitable resignation, a modern discourse of the Beatitudes, which the exploiting class finds completely functional to their current economic plans [. . .] a mediocre writer. [. . .] So, comrades, as well as defending ourselves from big fat decrees, let us start to defend ourselves from big fat novels. [1]

Leaving aside the tangible sidelining of Morante's historicizing subtitle, "uno scandalo che dura da diecimila anni" ("a scandal lasting ten thousand years," though this has intriguingly vanished also from the published translation), the *Manifesto* article accuses Morante of collusion with established hierarchy and power through the sanctification of poverty and destitution. The simultaneous conferment and deferment of transcendental value (in itself another way of ignoring the present) equates to the acceptance of an outdated, servile order that subsumes ideology in the name of the status quo. Morante is dismissed unceremoniously as a "mediocre scrittrice" (a "mediocre writer"though the feminine inflection is inevitably also lost in translation), condemned by the very size of her novel; the delight of the "romanzone" in digressive "histoire" (or "histories"), its largesse of plot and character, is inimical to a teleological Marxist view of history, even more than is its depiction of failed ideological revolutionaries such as Davide Segre. Narrative discourse, the very expansive discursiveness of the novel, has itself become the enemy.

Pier Paolo Pasolini states the problem only slightly differently. In his notoriously hostile review he decants the novel from "history" into "fable" stating that "la Morante, che accetta la convenzione della 'favola,' e quindi la necessaria funzionalità di ogni sua parte, non è fatta per gli *excursus*. . ." (77; "Morante, who accepts the convention of the 'fable' and thus the necessary functionality of all of its parts, is not cut out for excursus. . ."), pursuing characters and destinies with "una diligenza che rasenta l'ossessione" (78; "a diligence that verges on obsession"). Pasolini's objection to the novel's narrative discourse once more dehistoricises the text, here diagnosing Morante's narrative ideological sin as a psychological as much as a political disorder. It is my purpose here to reconsider the narrative excursus of Morante's text as it appears in passages of apparent digression from the forward momentum of the plot. Their function is, largely, to recount the destiny of a character, not as a strategy of ideological evasion, but as a narratology of ethics.

Temporal markers in the novel, beginning with ". . . 19**" and ending with ". . . e la Storia continua" (. . . and History goes on) locate the "histoire" in a continual becoming, a brief horizontal snapshot within a dizzying, vertical ontological historical sweep. The story of Ida and Useppe is just a brief flicker in this vast onslaught of official historical occlusion. The narrative excursus, deeply implicated and imbricated with discursive and narrative time, becomes thus an effort at restoration, a philosophical rather than party political refusal of official history that negates individual experience in favor of the political narrative. Just as Primo Levi, in *Se questo è un uomo*, seeks to recall the name, place of origin, and language of his fellow prisoners as act of restitution against the anonymizing and homologizing brutalism of life in Auschwitz, so Morante's text seeks to offer narrative space, a moment of being, to those characters cancelled and obliterated by wider events. The excursus interacts with and illuminates contingent text, just as the "plot" of Ida and Useppe's tale interacts and interleaves with the broader historical sweep of each chapter's introduction. This interaction offers a brief, poetic, grieving, transcendental refuge from the onward rush of power, melancholy in its inevitable transitoriness.

History itself then, or perhaps linear time, is itself the "scandalo," the scandal. Lucia Re attributes to the narrator a "voce femminile" (271; "a female voice"), in other words "a strategic way of positioning the writer's discourse to address the question of history, gender, and their narrative representation" and aligns Morante's text with Kristeva's concept of "women's time," which is: ". . . not the linear time of history and politics, nor is it time as project, progression, and arrival; rather it is time as the repetition of natural cycles based on the period of gestation and other phenomena linked to biological processes and rhythms" (362).

The excursus as practiced by Morante in *La Storia* is also, however, marked by the differentiated and calibrated cognitive and affective positions assumed by the narrator. Common to each excursus, to each of the several passages that accompany a character usually toward tragedy or death, is a sense of solidarity and, as with Primo Levi, a moment of witness, a rejection of the solitude of violent death, and through description, a simultaneous holding of the character within the gaze of the narrator and therefore the reader; we experience a halting of narrative time, a moment of contemplation before the character is returned to the maelstrom of "history." The narrator's declaration of homodiegesis, that she is personally known to many of the characters directly or indirectly, through photograph, gossip, personal contact, offers a variegated depiction of emotional and cognitive response. The narrator is simultaneously extra- and intradiegetic to the narrative, and it is in the excursus that her witnessing presence is most strongly felt.[2]

An early example of the excursus is the largely unnoted passage of the death of Nora.[3] This episode is placed between an impassioned denunciation of power within Italy and the diabolic alliance between Mussolini and Hitler, and the shock of the consequent imposition of racial laws that were to have such tragic consequences for Ida and Useppe. Ida's classroom displays the obligatory representations of Mussolini and the king, whose failure to resist the subjugation of Italy to Nazi Germany was to lead to the abolition of the Italian monarchy. Power is personalized by these two photographs on the classroom wall of a teacher whose smallness and fragility are further underlined in the diminutive form of her name:

> *Agli occhi di Iduzza, le immagini dei due personaggi (non meno, si può dire, del Crocefisso, che e lei significava soltanto il potere della Chiesa) rappresentavano esclusivamente il simbolo dell'Autorità, ossia dell'astrazione occulta che fa la legge e incute la soggezione.* (Morante, *La Storia* 44)

> In Iduzza's eyes, the images of the two figures (no less, you might say, than the Crucifix, which to her meant only the power of the Church) represented the absolute symbol of Authority, that occult and awe-inspiring abstraction which makes laws. (Morante, *History* 55)

Mussolini, we read, "era succube semi-cosciente di un sogno tuttora informe" (Morante, *La Storia* 45; "was the half-conscious minion of a still formless dream" [Morante, *History* 55]). The price of alliance was the replacement of "Romanness" with "race": "e fu così che sui primi mesi del

1938, anche in Italia, attraverso i giornali, nei circoli locali e alla radio, ebbe inizio una campagna preparatoria contro gli Ebrei" (Morante, *La Storia* 45; "and so it was that in the first months of 1938, in Italy too, the newspapers, the local clubs, the radio, began the preparatory campaign against the Jews" [Morante, *History* 56]). The horror of the racial laws and the delusions and deceptions of the Jewish population are reposited and rearticulated immediately following the episode of Nora's death. The narrator sharply and ironically underlines the vanity of hopeful trust in those looming presences in Ida's classroom:

> *Esse confidavano nelle amicizie importanti (o anche nelle benemerenze fasciste) dei Capi della Comunità e del Rabbino; nella benevolenza di Mussolini verso gli Ebrei; e addirittura nella protezione del Papa (mentre i papa, in realtà, nel corso dei secoli, erano stati fra i loro peggio persecutori).* (Morante, *La Storia* 59)

> They trusted in the important friendships (or also in the fascist merits) of the heads of the Community or of the Rabbi; In Mussolini's benevolence towards the Jews; and even in the protection of the Pope (whereas Popes, in reality, over the centuries, had been among their worst enemies). (Morante, *History* 71)

Nora's grief, madness, and death shift the narrative into a different dimension of space and time. A melancholy innocence is underlined by the childlike hair, tiny shoes, and Nora's intact body, so unlike the ravaged flesh encountered later in the text, while the lingering, detailed description of the dead woman gives a painterly quality, as of a Pre-Raphaelite Ophelia:

> *Essa giaceva dentro il limite della battigia, ancora bagnato della marea recente, in una posa rilasciata e naturale, come chi viene sorpreso dalla morte in uno stato d'incoscienza o di sonno. La testa le poggiava sulla sabbia, che il lieve deflusso aveva lasciato liscia e nitida, senza alghe né detriti; e il resto della persona le stava adagiato per intero sul grande mantello da uomo. . . [l]'unica violenza del mare, era stata di toglierle via le scarpette e di sciogliere i capelli che, nonostante l'età, le rimanevano lunghi e abbondanti, e solo in parte incanutiti: così che adesso, zuppi d'acqua, parevano tornati neri, e le si erano disposti tutti su un lato, quasi con grazia.* (Morante, *La Storia* 51)

> She was lying below the waterline, on sand still wet from the recent tide, in a relaxed and natural attitude, like someone surprised by death in a state of unconsciousness or in sleep. Her head was on the sand, which the light flux had made even and clean, without seaweed or flotsam; and the rest of her body was on the great man's cloak. [. . .] The sea's only violence had been to tear off her little shoes and undo her hair which, despite her age, had remained long and abundant, and only partly graying, so that now, wet, it seemed black again, and had fallen all down one side, almost gracefully. (Morante, *History* 63)

Nora occupies a liminal space between land and water, text and digression. The melancholic solitude of the scene emphasizes an innocence, a discursive space that serves as counterpoint to the threatening whirlwind of macropolitics all around her, both historically and textually. "Conosco Nora solo da una fotografia" (Morante, *La Storia* 53; "I know Nora only from a photograph" [Morante, *History* 64]) comments the narrator. Morante's narrative strategy counterposes the single photograph of Nora with the ubiquitous images of Mussolini, Hitler, and the king, and makes a direct textual as well as historical and political connection between them. Nora's dress and clothes mark her as a bourgeois woman of the early twentieth century, already a part of "history," while her face, "di fattura delicate ma commune" (Morante, *La Storia* 53; "delicately made but ordinary" [Morante, *History* 64]) metonymizes both her typicality and her youthful, sentimental innocence (the photograph is dedicated to her fiancé). The implicit narrative structural opposition of the ordinary, almost banal photograph of Nora to the aggrandizing photographs in every classroom, via the depiction of Nora's dead body, offers an alternative visual narrative that subtly confronts official historical discourse.

As she follows the final destiny of her characters Morante emphasizes the physicality, fragility, and vulnerability of human flesh caught up in the violence of "history." Eppetondo, murdered as partisan by the invading German military, is depicted at the moment of death, hallucinating as to the nature of the strange helmeted figures before him. The butchering of Mariulina, Nino's girlfriend, is preceded by a walk through the woods accompanied by German soldiers whom she is leading to the partisans' hut. The youthful Mariulina is testament to both the powerful presence and the fragility of the body: she is oblivious to herself as object of another's gaze, aware only of the pleasure of the corporeal, even in the spurt of menstrual blood from a vagina that will shortly be obscenely desecrated:

> *Avvezza com'era a quei cammini, essa procedeva sciatta e incurante come una bestiola, e anzi, in qualche punto, seguendo la sua prontezza naturale, saltava avanti ai soldati. La vergogna, la paura, e anche la noia della sua sporcizia fisica le si scioglievano nell'unico piacere sventato del corpo in movimento, come andasse ballando. E non si accorgeva che i capelli pesti e scarmigliati le cadevano in faccia, né che la maglietta strappata le lasciava il petto mezzo scoperto; perfino la sensazione del sangue fra le gambe o della saliva in bocca le davano un senso di calore.* (Morante, *La Storia* 306)

> Accustomed as she was to those hikes, she walked on, limber and heedless as a little animal; and indeed, at some points, in her natural readiness, she jumped ahead of the soldiers. The shame, the fear, and even the nuisance of her physical filth were dissolved in the sole carefree pleasure of her body in movement, as if she were dancing along. And she didn't notice her damp,

disheveled hair falling in her face or her torn jersey that left her bosom half revealed; even the sensation of blood between her legs or the saliva in her mouth gave her an affectionate feeling of warmth. (Morante, *History* 343)

The political and ethical valence of language and register, speech and silence, is foregrounded in these moments of excursus. The utterances of Giovannino, the young soldier who freezes to death in the Russian campaign shift from standard Italian to dialect, in contrast with the bureaucratic language of war, to a failure of linguistic expression, an enforced helplessness at odds with the articulated clarity of his desire and will. Hallucinated scenes from his rural childhood in Ciociaria with its unsentimental but vibrantly colorful family interaction, contrast his current desperate solitude; the loosening of his bowels translates into a scolding from his mother. Carpet bombing, the Final Solution, the violence of bureaucratic and industrial language contrast with the furiously innocent scatology of Giovannino, cut off by silence and death:

> *Al posto dei piedi e delle gambe, dal ginocchio in giù, gli sembra di portare due sacchi di sabbia. [. . .] Le raffiche lo sbattono e lo schiaffeggiano fischiando, e lui borbotta contro di loro: 'va affà inculo a nònneta' 'fregna fottuta' e altre simili proteste di casa, familiari a lui fin da bambino. . . In realtà, come avesse la lingua mozza, di fra i labbri gli esce appena un gorgoglio di sillabe confuse [. . .] Che ti pòzzi dannare, nonno! tanto, io fra un po' me ne vado a Roma a fare il carabiniere.* (Morante, *La Storia* 383–84)

> Instead of his feet and legs, from the knee down, he seems to be carrying two sandbags. [. . .] The gusts jolt him and slap him, whistling, and he grumbles against them: "go fuck yourself," "goddam cunt," and other such homely protests, familiar to him since childhood. . . . In reality, from his lips, a gurgle of confused syllables barely emerges, as if his tongue had been cut off [. . .]. Damn you, Granddad! I'm going to leave home soon anyway, and go to Rome, to be a carabiniere. (Morante, *History* 429–30)

The extensive episode of Giovannino, recounted in the present tense to mark a continuing sense of devastating loss, ends the section on 1945 and thus the account of wartime experience. The valedictory farewell from the narrator, "Buonanotte biondino" (Morante, *La Storia* 387; "Good night, Giovannino" [Morante, *History* 432]) laments the ending of a man alone, but of a community whose way of life has been destroyed by events played out elsewhere and also, perhaps, a direct correlation between word and world lost in the language of bureaucratic politics and totalizing ideologies.

Inarticulacy and silence mark similarly the utterances of Vilma, the apparently mentally disturbed ghetto mystic, the one person who foresees the day before, unheeded, the dramatic and traumatic clearing of the ghetto on 16 October 1943. Glimpsed again at the end of the war, the narrator describes her as a mythical creature with neither age nor sex, her few clumps of white hair tied in a bow with blue ribbon, her legs bare in the winter cold:

> *Rideva clamorosamente, con entusiasmo, quasi che da gran tempo attendesse questo incontro con Ida; e le faceva dei grandi gesti febbrili e scoordinati, che assumevano l'aria, di volta in volta, di danze ieratiche, o bacchiche. Sembrava smaniosa di comunicarle qualche notizia o annuncio gaudioso; ma dalla bocca non le uscivano che certi suoni grossi e inarticolati [. . .] La sua bocca era sdentata, ma lo splendore dei suoi occhi, già da sempre anormale, si era fatto quasi insostenibile.* (Morante, *La Storia* 480)

> She laughed loudly, with enthusiasm, as if she had been waiting a long time for this meeting with Ida; and she made great feverish and disjointed gestures to her, assuming the poses, from time to time, of hieratic or bacchic dances. She seemed eager to tell some news or some joyous announcement; but from her mouth came only certain thick and inarticulate sounds. [. . .] Her mouth was toothless, but the splendor of her eyes, abnormal before, had now become almost unbearable. (Morante, *History* 531)

Vilma, whom the narrator has reason to suppose lives long after the end of the war, is tentatively placed among the dismissed and the dispossessed, one of the many elderly women who feed the myriad stray cats of Rome, a final act of generous if unacknowledged mercy in such vivid contrast with the violent greed visited upon the Jewish population of Rome during the war.

Those few Jews who did survive war and concentration camps also discover their own tales to be unwelcome, not so much unspeakable as inaudible and unreadable. Their stories are dismissed as unwelcome diversion and digression from the day-to-day business of getting on with life after the end of the war. This perceived excursus is, for them, disallowed, an illegible script that contains, as Vilma's chaotic sounds, what is beyond human imagination and comprehension:

> *È curioso come certi occhi serbino visibilmente l'ombra di chi sa quali immagini, già impresse, chi sa quando e dove, nella rètina, a modo di una scrittura incancellabile che gli altri non sanno leggere—e spesso non vogliono. Quest'ultimo era il caso per i giudeii. Presto essi impararono che nessuno voleva ascoltare i loro racconti [. . .]. La gente voleva rimuoverli dalle proprie giornate come dalle famiglie normali si rimuove la presenza dei pazzi, o dei morti.* (Morante, *La Storia* 376)

> It's odd how some eyes visibly retain the shadow of who-knows-what images, impressed on them before, no telling when and where, in the retina, like an indelible writing that others cannot read—and often don't want to. This was the case with the Jews. Soon they learned that nobody wanted to listen to their stories [. . .]. People wanted to censor them from their days as normal families remove the mad or the dead. (Morante, *History* 421)

One of the few to pay heed to the Jews' traumatized behavior is Useppe himself. Deeply disturbed on witnessing the train full of Jews about to be transported to Auschwitz from the Stazione Tiburtina, he is similarly shocked by the photographs of hanged partisans that he sees in a magazine, bodies in the process of being commodifed by a news-hungry press. The extensive final scenes of the novel that take place between the child Useppe and the ex-partisan, bourgeois, would-be revolutionary Davide Segre offer an excursus into the realm of cultural formations and language, art, and culture as well as politics, while with Useppe's death, Ida's final lingering madness mutely articulates a grief and protest definitively marginalized.

The brutal pathological violence of Davide in his partisan guise as Piotr and Carlo Vivaldi finds echoes in his speeches against the restoration and reinvigoration of capitalism with its destructive exploitation of the factory worker, and his own final self-destruction.[4] Davide's abhorrence of the refusal to address and analyze the recent past, his denunciation of the continuing of age-old systems of oppression, and his own problematic position, the shame of his body's refusal to embody a proletarian existence on the factory floor, find expression in an idiolect that interweaves standard Italian and dialect, a linguistic marker of both individualism and localism. He belongs, however unwilling or reluctantly, to a place and culture rather than an ideology:

> *Come si trattasse di un affare liquidato, nessuno più voleva parlarne [. . .]*
> Nisún . . . nisún. . . . *però il sistema in quanto tale è in atto sempre e dovunque*
> *(sotto aspetti e nomi diversi, e magari contrarii. . .)* sèmpar e departút *dall'*
> inissio *della Storia umana. . . [. . .] Il sistema non cambia mai. . .* se ciamàva
> *religione, diritto divino, gloria, onore, spirito, avvenire . . .* tuti *pseudonimi,*
> tute *maschere. [. . .] questa povera materia de servissio e de fatica, se rende*
> *una pasta de sterminio e* disintegrassione . . . Campi di sterminio . . . *il nuovo*
> *nome della terra l'hanno già trovato . . .* Industria dello sterminio, *questo è il*
> *vero nome odierno del sistema!* (Morante, *La Storia* 566)

As if it was something over and done with, nobody wanted to talk about it anymore [. . .] however, the system as such is still functioning everywhere (under different, even contradictory names and aspects. . .), always, everywhere, since the beginning of human History. . . . The system never changes. . .it was called religion, divine right, glory, honor, spirit, future, all pseudonyms . . . all masks [. . .] this poor matter, material for work and labor, becomes fodder for extermination and destruction. (Morante, *History* 624)

Davide's multilayered use of language, once again lost in translation, in which dialect erupts and disrupts, both semantically and visually, an orthodox political commentary from the Left, begins and ends in linguistic dislocation. His conviction that each individual contains both a bourgeois or SS and a (secular) Christ signals a fragmentation that seeps into his discourse.

While Giovannino's use of dialect signified his adherence to a past, in Davide's case it marks a past that adheres, rather, to him. Davide recites his own poem to an eager Useppe, and the very title of *Ombre luminose* once more suggests contradiction, opposition, and frustrated desire. The emphasis on poetry and music in this final part of the novel recalls the lengthy excursus in the early pages into Ida's family history, between her encounter with Gunther and the moment of rape in her kitchen. Recollections of jostling popular and scabrous songs on the radio form a soundscape that is not mere background but an affirmation of a vibrant popular culture transmitted down the generations, the same songs obscenely and grotesquely appropriated played at top volume to cover Nazi atrocities in local apartments converted to torture chambers.

> *Useppe's use of language, on the other hand, is at once both metaphor and metonym: Giuseppe era ammaliato dalle parole. Si capiva che le parole, per lui, avevano un valore sicuro, come fossero tutt'uno con le cose [. . .] I mobili e le masserizie erano case, treni. Gli asciugamani, gli stracci e anche le nubi erano dandèle (bandiere). Le luci delle stelle erano erba, e le stelle medesime erano formiche intorno a una mollichella (la luna.)* (Morante, *La Storia* 131)

> Giuseppe was bewitched by words. Obviously words, for him, had a sure value, as if they were one with objects. [. . .] Articles of furniture and domestic objects became for him houses, trains. Towels, rags, even clouds were lags (flags). The lights of the stars were grass, and the stars themselves were ants around a crumb (the moon.) (Morante, *History* 151)

Davide quotes Dante's exquisite passage from *Paradiso*: "E vidi lume in forma di rivera / Fluvido di fulgore intra due rive / Dipinte di mirabil primavera / Di tal fiumana uscian faville vive!" ("And I saw light in the form of a river pouring its splendour between two banks painted with marvellous spring!" [Dante 433]).[5] Useppe's final poem on the other hand, composed on the day of his death, closer perhaps to haiku than to traditional Italianate poetic forms, transforms the syntagms of Davide's own poetry through simile and metaphor to create a linguistic universe of light that is whole and undivided, which heals the split between signifier and signified, masculine and feminine, heaven and earth: "Il sole è come un albero grande / che dentro tiene i nidi. / E suona come una cicala maschio e come il mare / e con l'ombra ci scherza come una gatta piccolo" (Morante, *La Storia* 632; "The sun is like a big tree / that has nests inside. / And it sounds like a male cicada and like the sea / and it plays with the shadow like a little cat" [Morante, *History* 697]).

Useppe's understanding of his world is affective, inclusive, an implicit rejection of the fractures that inhabit Davide's discourse: "Giganti o nani, straccioni o paíni, decrepitudine o gioventù, per lui non faceva differenza.

[. . .] solo che fossero tutti amici pari e sorridessero" (Morante, *La Storia*
557; "Giants or dwarfs, beggars or dandies, decrepitude or youth, nothing
made any difference to him. And neither the twisted nor the hunchback, the
paunchy nor the scrawny: to him none was less lovely than the world's
Paragon, provided all were friends equally and smiling" [Morante, *History*
615]).

Davide's death is, ironically, reported by the local newspaper in the language of bland standardization not far removed from the desensitizing discourse of warfare and modern industrialization. The narrator steps in to challenge the idea of suicide, but the language of bureaucracy, so hated by
Davide, has the final word: "La mia opinione sarebbe che Davide Segre, di
sua natura, amava troppo la vita per disfarsene consapevolmente da un giorno all'altro. A ogni modo, lui 'del suo gesto non ha lasciato nessuna spiegazione" (Morante, *La Storia* 612; "My opinion would be that Davide Segre, by
nature, loved life too much to rid himself of it knowingly from one day to the
next. In any case, he 'left no explanation of his act'" [Morante, *History* 686]).

The final few days and death of Useppe, on the other hand, his conversations with Bella, his fantasy childhood of adventure and excitement in the
liminal space of the "forest" where he meets Scimò and fights pirates, followed by his fatal attack of epilepsy, are offered, in an oblique reference to
Dante's *Paradiso*, as a final excursus that encapsulates and articulates the
ethical and emotive thrust of Morante's narrative. The narrator is unapologet-
ic in her desire to watch over her character in his "passione," his "passion," a
term in which religious connotation gives way to philosophical *reverie*:

> *A qualcuno parrà inutile raccontare la restante vita di Useppe, durata ancora*
> *poco più di due giorni, e già sapendone la fine. Ma a me non pare inutile.*
> *Tutte le vite, invero, hanno la medesima fine: e due giorni, nella piccola*
> *passione di un pischelluccio come Useppe, non valgono meno di anni. Che mi*
> *si lasci, dunque, restare ancora un poco in compagnia del mio pischelluccio,*
> *prima di tornarmene sola al secolo degli altri.* (Morante, *La Storia* 625)

> So, some may think it now useless to narrate the rest of Useppe's life, which
> lasted a little over two days more, since the end is already well known. But it
> doesn't seem useless to me. All lives, really, have the same end: and two days,
> in the brief passion of a kid like Useppe, are not worth less than years. Allow
> me, then, to stay a bit longer in the company of my little kid, before coming
> back alone to the secular life of the others. (Morante, *History* 689)

With his death and Ida's refusal to give up his body, the language of media
and bureaucracy dominate once more: "Pietoso dramma al quartiere Testaccio—Madre impazzita vegliando il corpo del figlioletto" (Morante, *La Storia*
647; "Pathetic drama in the Testaccio quarter—Crazed mother watching over
little son's corpse" [Morante, *History* 714]). Ida, too, falls prey to the epilep-

sy, which marks the vulnerability of each successive generation. Her further years of life, in a mental institution, provide perhaps the final narrative excursus of the novel, into empty, endless, wordless grief.

NOTES

1. English translations are my own, unless otherwise indicated.
2. For a discussion of the varied positions of "incompetent" and "knowing" narrator, see Serkowska.
3. See, however, Lucamante, for a consideration of this part of the novel.
4. Re comments in the conclusion to her article that Davide is "the symbolic representation of the powerlessness of any totalizing theory or system of thought to explain or rationalize this scandal that has gone on for ten thousand years, History itself" (Re 372). For a lengthy discussion of the figure of Davide Segre, see Puggioni.
5. For a study of Dante as intertext for Morante, see Gragnolati, et al.

WORKS CITED

Balestrini, Nanni, Elisabetta Rasy, Letizia Paolozzi, and Umberto Silva. "Contro il romanzone della Morante." *Il Manifesto* (18 July 1974): 3.

Dante. *The Divine Comedy 3: Paradiso.* Trans. and ed. John D. Sinclair. Oxford: Oxford University Press, 1971. 433.

Gragnolati, Manuele et al., eds. *Metamorphosing Dante: Appropriations, Manipulations and Rewritings in the Twentieth and Twenty First Centuries.* Berlin: Turia and Kant, 2012.

Levi, Primo. *Se questo è un uomo.* Turin: De Silva, 1947.

Lucamante, Stefania. *Quella difficile identità. Ebraismo e rappresentazioni letterarie della Shoah.* Rome: Iacobelli, 2012.

Lucente, Gregory. "Scrivere o fare. . .o altro. Social commitment and ideologies of representation in the debates over Lampedusa's *Il gattopardo* and Morante's *La Storia.*" *Italica* 61.3 (Autumn 1984): 220–51.

Morante, Elsa. *La Storia.* Turin: Einaudi, 1974.

———. *History: A Novel.* Trans. William Weaver. London: Penguin, 1980.

Pasolini, Pier Paolo. "La gioia della vita la violenza della storia." *Il Tempo* (26 July 1974): 77–78

Puggioni. Enrica. *Davide Segre, un eroe al confine della modernità.* Alessandria: Edizioni dell'Orso, 2006.

Re, Lucia. "Utopian longing and the constraints of racial and sexual difference." *Italica* 70.1 (Autumn 1993): 361–75.

Serkowska, Hannah. *Uscire da una camera delle favole: I romanzi di Elsa Morante.* Krakow: Rabid, 2002.

Sgavicchia, Siriana, ed. *La Storia di Elsa Morante.* Pisa: ETS, 2012.

Chapter Seven

"The World Must Be the Writer's Concern"

Elsa Morante's Visions of History

Stefania Lucamante

In her "Introduction *into* Politics," Hannah Arendt examines the essential conditions for politics to exist. Since there is no political action in isolation, the first element is a world in which human affairs can take place. They "are the result of the fact that human beings produce what they themselves are not—that is, things—and that even the so-called psychological or intellectual realms become permanent realities in which people can live and move only to the extent that these realms are present as things, as a world of things" (Arendt, "Introduction" 106–7). When Elsa Morante argues that the writer's concern must be the world and not literature, because the writer is *"an individual whose concern must be everything that happens, except because literature"* ("Pro o contro la bomba" 97; emphasis original), she extols the necessity for the writer to gain a holistic understanding of human interaction. As a consequence, I take Morante's statement as a profoundly political one. Her humanism concerns the world as the space into which human beings come to interact and produce things.

"The world must be the writer's concern," words that I quote in the title of the present chapter, characterizes one of Elsa Morante's most profound statements in the inquiry by *Nuovi Argomenti* entitled "Nove domande sul romanzo" ("Nine Questions on the Novel" 53). Such a statement, in fact, lies at the core of the composition of her 1974 anti-illusionist historical novel *La Storia*. A canonical retelling of all horrors of the twentieth century, the one Bernard Brunetau dubbed as "the century of genocides," *La Storia* exemplifies in many ways, this is my argument, the ideal literary work whose programmatic content never prevails over form. Morante's 1974 *La Storia* organizes in its novelistic format ideas, themes, and linguistic images related to the topic of social exclusion by the means of power and becomes an emblematic container for the private story of powerless characters to whom Elsa Morante lends her (rather authoritative) voice. She is convinced that "il valore, anche storico, di un romanzo non dipende dai suoi pretesti narrativi, ma dalle sue verità."[1] By juxtaposing its powerful novelistic structure to such important authorial intentions, *La Storia* illustrates the artist's unease for a lasting history that tantalizes the subaltern and justifies the use of war as instrument for prevarication. It also sets a precedent in describing what until then had not quite been a frequent task for Italian writers usually preoccupied with our own totalitarianism: making Hitler and Nazism integral parts of the novel, as Adriano Prosperi noted in a conversation with Cesare Garboli (*Il gioco* 237–39). The unbelievable was retold in great detail and precision while the plot endowed readers with the ability to provide their own conclusions to the story of violence and love presented to them. In its awareness of commenting upon a century that is the site of a "passaggio drammatico" ("Sul romanzo" 64; dramatic passage), *La Storia* sets a precedent in Italian literature that is still today difficult to parallel.

Elsa Morante consistently expressed her humanistic concern regarding the destiny of the disenfranchised, the underprivileged, and minorities—be they racial, gender, or religious. In her view, oppressive politics—disguised as historical forces masked by words like *progress*—determines the destiny of such minorities. Morante utilizes the term *Power* as a linguistic signifier— a sort of umbrella term—encompassing all the disastrous consequences of progressive history, this last to be intended according to Arendt as a byproduct of politics. The word *Power* projects the image of a perverse totalitarian and self-destructive aspect of humankind: an aberration of Nature, that is. In Morante's writing, the word *Power* functions as a lexical *fil rouge*, a rather negative tantric word enveloping all of humanity's ills. *La Storia* divulges the writer's message about the artist's ethical duty more explicitly than the rest of her fictional works in that her reflections are reified into characters and situations that readers can easily appreciate and understand. Morante's use of anthropomorphism (in the sense André Bazin gives to this term) proves crucial to our identification and understanding of her characters and garners several perspectives at once. We become Useppe, Ida, Ninnuzzu, Bella as the novel proceeds in its story. Animals speak because they all belong to this world of human affairs where realms become permanent realities without which people could not act.

AN IMPORTANT ANTECEDENT:
CRITICISM OF *LA STORIA*

In 1974, critics' overreaction to the newly published *La Storia* was laden with political implications. While ridiculing it for its use of neorealist elements and presumed melodramatic tones, such violent critique did not affect *La Storia*'s reception by the general public. Almost forty years later, the political and artistic sensitivities for which critics like Renato Barilli took a strong position against Morante's "anachronistic" novel ("Lacrime" 10; "La Storia" 105–10), even stronger than the one taken by Nanni Balestrini, Elisabetta Rasy, Letizia Paolozzi, and Umberto Silva in their infamous letter in *Il Manifesto* "Contro il romanzone della Morante," luckily for us, no longer exist. Actually, *La Storia*'s authorial intentions can be better grasped now than forty years ago, for, aside from the effect time always affords to sincere and unbiased appreciation of artistic works, deconstructionism and postcolonial studies have each opened new paths of looking at literature and granted more subtlety to the interpretation of the author's adoption of techniques. Morante's essayistic and fictional writings predating and molding *La Storia* constitute the novel's philosophical backbone. Contrary to what was stated by its detractors, these writings fully justify *La Storia*'s physical structure as its stylistic choices and precede the exposition of her philosophical tenets on history.[2]

I argue that an overarching ethical and moral imperative *led* Elsa Morante to compose this complex and searing novel. In "Il test della 'Storia'" Camon considers Morante's work among one of the most emblematic literary representations of the *Shoah*. Camon's genuine and disinterested analysis of Morante's novel has informed much of my own reading.[3] She conceived the novel in order to lend a voice to the subaltern. In addition to this ethical and political necessity, I argue that there lies another one. Morante wrote the novel in an effort to come to terms with her own, at least until then, buried Jewish extraction—her "intimate" *Hebräitude*—and to assess how oppressive politics such as totalitarian regimes can lead to astounding examples of antihumanistic aberration. Morante's voice emerges powerful and crystalline from the pages of *La Storia* in her intense effort to make sense of the atrocity and beauty that paradoxically coexist and make up the world as we know it. By utilizing the tool of fictional writing, Morante elucidates how there can be nothing less political than a tyrant insofar as his eventual domination marks the dissolution of action, which is what constitutes the true political sphere. Totalitarianism and its byproducts in the terms discussed by Arendt represent the closest form to Morante's concept of *male assoluto* (absolute evil). Useppe, Ida's second child, the illiterate happy young boy, fruit of a war rape, will not survive to it.

As I unfold my argument I discuss chiefly three points: The first deals with the coherence of Morante's discourse with respect to the role of the artist/poet. Whether in her introduction to the catalog of Beato Angelico, "Il beato propagandista dell'universo" (The Blessed Promoter of the Universe), her answers in the interview "Nove domande sul romanzo" (Nine Questions on the Novel), her "Piccolo manifesto dei comunisti (senza classe e senza partito)" (Little Manifesto of the Communists [with no class or party]), or her "Intervention" following the Spanish publication and censorship of *La Storia*, Morante never deviates from her original take on history, power, and subaltern classes and the role of the artist/poet who must explain the world to himself and for the others who cannot. The second point is Morante's notion of "Progress": the tragic outcomes of the word *progress* date in the author's essayistic writing at the very least to 1965, when she delivered in Turin at the Carignano Theater "Pro o contro la bomba atomica," a seminal lecture on the atomic bomb and its detriment to humanity. Finally, I argue for the consistency of Morante's ideological thinking about Power, war, and human evil. The unreality of evil is elaborated and expressed in all her literary works (short stories, novels, poems).

Love for anarchy as extoled by Francesco De Salvi's inebriated tirades in the inn in Morante's 1948 *Menzogna e sortilegio* (The House of Liars) and as the threat of a useless war as advanced in her 1957 *L'isola di Arturo* (Arturo's Island) are instances that point at a precise ideological path for the writer that she will never renounce but rather will culminate in the successful paperback publication of *La Storia*. Also some parts of her 1968 *pastiche*, *Il mondo salvato dai ragazzini* (The World Saved by the Boys), to be yet translated into English, present in poetic form the preparatory and complex discourse rendered through *La Storia*'s prose (though interspersed with some poetic texts and songs of the period). Morante's unending project aimed at raising consciousness about the underprivileged finds its climax in *La Storia*: it is hard to challenge the fact that this work of fiction underscores the author's understanding of the unpredictable, yet often observed, paths by which individuals prefer stories about power to any kind of happiness that comes from a life without any power intended as violence.

ON THE FUTILITY OF WAR: ABATING NEOREALISM

Deconstruction of the neorealist matrix is already present in her 1957 *L'isola di Arturo* (Arturos' Island). The novel's chronotope is no longer unfocused as the tenuous one sustaining the over seven hundred pages of her 1948 *Menzogna e sortilegio* (House of Liars). In Arturo's bitter fairy tale, the moment of his departure from Eden is temporally marked by the outset of the colonial wars. We follow his life from 1938 to December 1940. To reach adulthood means leaving the island: the only honorable way to do so for a sixteen-year-old boy like Arturo is to enroll in the army and go to war. Knowledge of sex and knowledge of war remain the key distance to determine the end of childhood and the beginning of adult age. The kind of war taking place is not the one dreamed of by Arturo in his long afternoon readings of Norman cavaliers and myths, but the one concretely real and paradoxically produced by the unreality of Powers. A war whose only positive consequence will be that of leading Arturo to the African prison camp from where he is most likely now writing his memoirs. His childhood is written while Death, something of which Arturo has always been afraid of, lurks in its grueling shadows. Only in death can we escape the prosthetics of subjectivity (Wolfe 187). War is a mechanism that tears man away from the desire for humanism to be intended as *pietas* and epitomized by the search of the good and the beautiful. Instead, war throws man into an "imbroglio demoniaco" (hellish business): because war is the daughter of history (Morante, *L'isola* 1356; *Arturo's Island* 340). As Hannah Arendt states,

> The West's solution for escaping from the impossibility of politics within the Western creation myth is to transform politics into history, or to substitute history for politics. In the idea of world history, the multiplicity of men is melted into *one* human individual, which is then also called humanity. This is the source of the monstrous and inhuman aspect of history, which first accomplishes its full and brutal end in politics. (Arendt, "Introduction" 95).

Silvestro, Arturo's old nurse, comes back on Arturo's sixteenth's birthday. Although happy to see Arturo abandoning the island of Procida and the haunted Casa de' Guaglioni, Silvestro regrets the boy's decision to go to war and warns him against the mystique intrinsic to the rhetoric of war. Silvestro explains to him the difference between "le guerre antiche" e "le guerre moderne" (1356; 340). The old war stories they shared when Arturo was little, prompt Silvestro to revert to his original role of guide for the poor orphan. Silvestro distinguishes the reasons leading to war between the noble ones, the sort of which books often romanticize, and the more utilitarian ones. The difference between myth and reality, between dream and destruction looms large:

> *Egli m'andava spiegando che, nonostante una recente intesa di pace firmata con cerimonie grandiose dalle Potenze (dovevano essere stati questi, ora lo capivo, i famosi* eventi internazionali *cui Stella alludeva, origine dell'amnistia, e della sua libertà), la guerra mondiale, in realtà, era imminente, senza rimedio. Poteva prorompere da un mese all'altro, forse da un giorno all'altro. E anche chi era contrario, come lui, ci andava di mezzo, in questo imbroglio demoniaco!* (Morante, *L'isola* 1356; emphasis original)

> He went on explaining to me that in spite of a recent peace pact, grandly
> signed by the Powers (these must be, I now realized, the famous *international
> events* that Stella had meant, which had brought about the amnesty and his
> freedom), the World War was properly and hopelessly upon us. It might break
> out from one month to the next, even from one day to the next. And even those
> who were against it, like him, were going to get involved in the whole hellish
> business. (Morante, *Arturo's* 340; emphasis original)

Modern war, according to Silvestro, "era tutta un macchinario di macelleria, e un orrendo formicaio di sfaceli, senza nessun merito di valore autenti-
co" (Morante, *L'isola* 1357; "was nothing but mechanized butchery, a loath-
some ant heap of destruction and not a matter of courage" [Morante, *Arturo's*
340–41]). In short, war intended in contemporary terms "era come cantare
gratuito con una spina in gola. *Un disastro senza nessun compenso*" (Morante, *L'isola* 1357; emphasis added; "was like singing with a thorn in your
throat, a disaster, *with nothing to be said for it*" [Morante, *Arturo's* 340–41]).
The images offered by Silvestro to his beloved Arturo: "imbroglio demoniaco" (hellish business), "macchinario di macelleria" (mechanized butchery),
"formicaio di sfaceli" (ant heap) define the terms in which powers and their
politics take human beings into consideration: they simply do not. War, the
state of war, "suspends morality," because, as Lévinas states,

> [i]t divests the eternal institutions and eternal obligations of their eternity and
> rescinds ad interim the unconditional imperatives. In advance its shadow falls
> over the actions of men. The art of foreseeing war and of winning it by every
> means—politics—is henceforth enjoined as the very exercise of reason. Poli-
> tics is opposed to morality, as philosophy to naïveté. (*Totality* 21)

Further, when the expression "multiplicity of men" is lexically substituted
("melted" Arendt writes) with the clustering word "humanity," we face the
hard fact that humanistic values—distinct fates of the individual—cease to
exist when one uses a collective noun, that is, humanity. As a consequence,
semantics makes us realize the hypocrisy inherent in society through its very
practice. By explaining to Arturo the differences between the kinds of wars,
Silvestro voices what Lévinas considers as the "hypocrisy inherent in society" (21). There is no such thing as a noble war, no matter the reasons that
propelled it.

As the above quoted excerpt reveals, already *L'isola di Arturo* introduces
a public aspect of society—war—into the very intimate private story of its
protagonist, an orphan. In "Pro o contro la bomba atomica" (For or Against
the Atomic Bomb), Morante declares that although "Civil society lives in the
era of the atomic bomb" (98), the adjective "atomic" is misleadingly still tied
to its original meaning indicating a minuscule element. The adjective appears, therefore, to be underestimated and misunderstood in its cataclysmic

importance, in what its actual significance, that is, has come to be in the course of the twentieth century. The motivations leading science to invent the atomic bomb, its birth right in that historical period appears to not be dictated by sheer happenstance of the progress of science but because such discovery complies with the needs of the Powers:

> *No: tutti sanno ormai che nella vicenda collettiva (come in quella individuale) anche gli apparenti casi sono invece quasi sempre delle volontà inconsapevoli (che, se si vuole, si potranno pure chiamare* destino*) e, insomma, delle scelte. La nostra bomba è* il fiore, ossia la espressione naturale della nostra società contemporanea, *così come i dialoghi di Platone lo sono della città greca; il Colosseo, dei Romani imperiali; le Madonne di Raffaello, dell'Umanesimo italiano; le gondole, della nobiltà veneziana; la tarantella, di certe popolazioni rustiche meridionali; e* i campi di sterminio, *della cultura piccolo-borghese burocratica già infetta da* una rabbia di suicidio atomico. *Non occorre, ovviamente, spiegare, che per* cultura piccolo-borghese *s'intende la cultura delle attuali classi predominanti, rappresentate dalla borghesia (o spirito borghese) in tutti i suoi gradi. Concludendo, in poche, e oramai, del resto, abusate parole: si direbbe che l'umanità contemporanea prova la occulta tentazione di disintegrarsi.* (Morante, *Pro o contro* 98–99; emphasis added, except for *"destino"* and *"cultura piccolo-borghese"*)

> No: everybody knows by now that in the collective history (as in the individual one) even the seeming chances are almost invariably unconscious wills (which, if one wants, they can be called *destiny*), in short, choices. Our bomb *is the flower, the natural expression of our contemporary society*, just like Plato's dialogues are an expression of the Greek city; the Coliseum of Roman imperials; Raphael's Madonnas of Italian Humanism; gondolas of Venetian aristocracy; tarantella of some Southern rural populaces; and *the extermination camps* of the petit-bourgeois bureaucratic culture already infected by *a rage of atomic suicide*. We don't need to explain, of course, that by *petit-bourgeois culture* we signify the culture of the leading classes, represented by bourgeoisie (or bourgeois spirit) in all its degrees. In conclusion, in few and by now abused words: one could say that contemporary human beings feel *the hidden temptation of disintegrating themselves*.

In this lecture, Morante formulates a clear equation between the Nazi extermination camps and the atomic bomb; she describes them as the Baudelairian "negative flowers"—natural expressions—of humanity (a semantic cluster devoid of meaning as far as she is concerned) and progress (other term used in a negative acception that we will discuss later). Arendt makes a distinction between the two terms Morante brings together, the extermination camps and the nuclear bomb. According to Arendt, twentieth-century totalitarian governments and the manifest "emergence within politics of the possibility of absolute physical annihilation" have managed to "threaten the very thing that, according to modern opinion, provides its ultimate justification—that is,

the basic possibility of life for all of humanity" (Arendt, "Introduction"110).
In theory, politics would not give way to human self-annihilation. And yet,
this it what appears to have happened. Looking closely at Morante's statement, the artist reveals the existence of an undeniable process: a not so
"hidden temptation of disintegrating themselves" is what humanity has done
with the progressive elimination of politics intended as freedom but understood, rather, in terms of an administrative machine whose only tasks are
bureaucracy and exercise of force against the Other. The state of Nirvana that
petit-bourgeoisies manage to reach is achieved by that very process that
Morante calls a "disintegrazione della coscienza" ("Pro o contro" 100), a
disintegration of our conscience that, as Lévinas notes, takes inevitably place
at the expense of the Other, since "[t]he fear of each himself, in his own
mortality, does not succeed in absorbing the scandal of indifference toward
the suffering of the other" (Lévinas, *On Thinking* 192). The path toward our
conscience's disintegration—the one that allows for "things" to destroy human beings, is defined "per mezzo della ingiustizia e demenza organizzate,
dei miti degradanti, della noia convulsa e feroce" (Morante, "Pro o contro"
100; "by organized injustice and dementia, by degrading myths, by ferocious
and convulsive boredom"). "Le bombe, le 'Orchesse balene' [. . .] non sono
la causa potenziale della disintegrazione, ma la manifestazione necessaria di
questo disastro, già attivo nella coscienza" (Morante, "Pro o contro" 100;
"the ogress whales [. . .] are not the potential cause of disintegration, but the
necessary manifestation of this disaster, already active in our conscience").[4]
In speaking of "things," Arendt brings up the atomic bomb, yet another
"thing" produced by human beings that brings catastrophe rather than betterment to the world:

> We can also imagine that nuclear war, if it leaves any human life at all in its
> wake, could precipitate such a catastrophe by destroying the entire world. The
> reason human beings will then perish, however, is not themselves, but, as
> always, the world, or better, the course of the world over which they no longer
> have mastery, from which they *are so alienated* that the automatic forces
> inherent in every process can proceed unchecked. (Arendt, "Introduction" 107;
> emphasis added)

If it is unquestionable that the process of disintegration takes place at the
expense of the Other, as Lévinas argues, one could suggest that it also happens at one's own expense, because human beings no longer hold a "mastery
of the world." What Arendt calls "the monstrous development of modern
means of destruction over which states have a monopoly" ("Introduction"
109) further defines Morante's distrust for Power and its monstrous productions. The world without human beings, Arendt states, would be a contradiction in terms ("Introduction" 108). The "thing" produced, the atomic bomb,
that is, for all the repercussions that yet this definitive annihilating tool can

produce, serves as the analysis of world and power by the means of which we intercept the seamless ideological transition to the author's philosophical reflections about human beings and their apparent desire for self-destruction. Circa 1970, Morante drafts her then posthumously published "Piccolo manifesto dei comunisti." The manifesto contains thirteen statements, each protesting against the historical situation of the time. Two of the points in particular help constitute, to paraphrase Arturo's youthful "Certezze Assolute" (Absolute Certainties), Morante's own absolute certainties: "3. The dishonor of Man is Power; 4. The honor of Man is the freedom of the spirit (. . .) [understood as] the complete, true and natural state of man" (*Il Piccolo* 7). These points further elicit the *fil rouge* that links the anti-illusionist novel *La Stori a* to Morante's previous writings with the word *Power*. *La Storia* opens with an epigraph in which concept and language are indissolubly tied together:

> *Non c'è parola, in nessun linguaggio umano,*
> *capace di consolare le cavie che non sanno il*
> *perché della loro morte.*
> *(Un sopravvissuto di Hiroscima).* (Morante, *La Storia* 257)

The first of two epigraphs of *La Storia*, "There is no word in the human language capable/ of consoling the guinea pigs who do not know/ the reason for their death"[5] points directly at the atomic bomb as the focus of much to come in the novel for the words belong to the oral testimony of a Hiroshima survivor. The epigraph, however, states also the impossibility of speaking— or explaining—in "any human language" (thus also eliminating the possibility of any linguistic supremacy over others) what constitutes the cause leading humans to destroy themselves and their conscience (self-annihilation) while simultaneously terminating the Other (adding one more layer to Lévinas's understanding of the problem). Powers and ideological forces dispose of individuals' destinies as if they were wordless and speechless—but this is not quite true. Someone finds their voice. It is the artists who speak for individuals because artists can unsay stated things,[6] say unstated ones, and finally grasp how every element around human beings is a prosthetic element of some sort, language being the first, according to Jacques Derrida. The epigraph synthesizes many of Morante's intentions, sets forth much of her projectuality in the writing of this novel. *La Storia* artfully juxtaposes parallel subnarratives that compose—in my view—a narrative transfiguration of her mature coming to terms with, and understanding of, the Holocaust; the experience of the racial laws; the 1943 deportation of the Roman Jews from the Ghetto; and, last but not least, the ultimate literal and metaphoric disintegration of human beings and their conscience via the atomic bomb. This is a novel in which Morante's personal vicissitudes during World War II become visible in their fundamental connection to those of the millions of victims of power games. She has lived in the *pragma* of all the historical events forming the backdrop of the novel. But only after thirty years—after a temporal hiatus—can she assume ethical and intellectual responsibility to give voice to the victims of infamous decisions made at the table of the super Powers. Rather than being authoritarian her voice is authoritative because she lived many of the facts narrated in her novel. *La Storia* is set in Rome and deals especially about Romans struggling during World War II: not far from her house, actually very close, why should Elsa pretend to be someone else just to ingratiate critics who talk about her work as one belonging to the "restaurazione" (restoration) (Barilli, "La Storia" 105)?

This is the era of self-destruction: posthuman bodies speak through Elsa's outrage already decreeing the death of humanism as we know it. In Cary Wolfe's words, "we attend to the specificity of the human . . . acknowledging that it is fundamentally a prosthetic creature that has coevolved with various forms of technicity and materiality, forms that are radically 'non human' and yet have nevertheless made the human what it is" (xxv). Already at the outset of the novel, in the part titled "19—," the omniscient narrator declares that in 1900–1905 "Le ultime scoperte scientifiche sulla struttura della materia segnano l'inizio del secolo atomico" (Morante, *La Storia* 263; "The latest scientific discoveries concerning the structure of matter mark the beginning of the atomic century" [Morante, *History* 3]). Halfway through the novel, harmless Ida will whisper to Signora Di Segni, "Io pure sono ebrea" (Morante, *La Storia* 539; "I am Jewish, too" [Morante, *History* 267]).

The coherence and consistency with which Morante formulated the parallel between the atomic bomb and the extermination camps as major elements of self-annihilation (and appropriate to totalitarian regimes) where the voice of the people could be forever silenced fully justifies the adoption of the very technical choices that Barilli and *Gruppo '63* so harshly criticized in 1974.[7] For the purpose of writing about this horror, Morante needed to shift from the narrating protagonist she used in her previous works to the quasi-omniscient narrator of *La Storia*. Morante experienced the war along with her characters Ida and Useppe; the narrator-Elsa claims to have actually seen them while walking through the streets of Rome. Elsa felt a surge of her Jewish blood at the advent of the racial laws or while hearing of the October 16 roundup and October 18 deportation of the harmless *ghettaroli*. Particularly because of their fate, Elsa tries to give a charitable voice to her doomed characters. Despite Alberto Asor Rosa's considerations on Morante's dictatorial intentions and effects on her readers, her presumed "monodirectionality of certain psychic reactions . . . whose only scope is that of moving the reader" (7), Morante's narrator is uncertain of many details she recounts to us. She is an unreliable witness in that the passage of time does not allow for precision. The empathic "mechanism leading to readers" reaction might prompt commotion, and not without reason. But "moving the reader" was not the empirical author's actual purpose. The personal involvement of Morante in the story of Ida, Useppe, Nino, and Davide is made palpable by remarks the narrator makes in some delicate passages like "if I remember correctly," "I am not sure," "it could be that . . ." *Elsa Ipse*, as Cesare Garboli defined the narrator of *La Storia* (*Il gioco* 188) is not afraid to express her own hesitation and insecurity, because these feelings—we know—are justified by reasons altogether different than the acidulous ones advanced by Asor Rosa. Morante is fully aware of her role as commentator and chronicler of her own time and of her own world. "Non si deve dimenticare che il romanziere, per sua natura, non è soltanto un termine sensibile nel rapporto fra l'uomo e il destino, ma è anche lo studioso e lo storico di questo rapporto sempre diverso" (Morante, "Sul romanzo" 68; "One should never forget that the novelist by his or her own nature is not only a sensitive term in the relationship between man and destiny but also the scholar and the historian of this everchanging relationship"). *Elsa ipse* experienced those events near her Ida and her Useppe, but, as Primo Levi reminds us in *The Drowned and the Saved*, memory can be fallacious. In a period in which victims voicing of their memories can finally contribute to the shaping of historiographic discourse and diminish the superiority of history's "winners"; right at a time in which the "drowned" appear paradoxically to be the ones who were actually saved and spared by the ignominy of returning to a so-called normal life, Morante writes a novel for which "romanzo delle vittime" (victims' novel) represents the most common label. Her characters are all victims of the tragic scandal called History, a scandal in which, far from representing life and its continuation, genealogical trees become sinister forebodings of disintegration and annihilation. A scandal in which a man called Davide, like the star and like the king, becomes a grotesque parody of what he could have become, had not the war, that tragic ordeal from which Silvestro was trying to prevent Arturo, swept his family away and, along with it, his very reason to exist.

If fascism represents a mere twenty years of history, the scandal of the pervasiveness of linear history compels Morante to create a voice for the voiceless. To official historiographic narratives, Morante opposes another type of discourse, attuned to the existence of her beloved characters, the unnamed "Thousand." To explain the impasse of having to defend individuals who never quite asked to be defended but that Morante felt needed to be, she chooses the point of view that belongs to herself as to the collectivity she represents. The most arduous task was to build a comprehensible plot out of an unjustifiable trauma. It was a subjective, personal *trauma* with respect to what the author saw before her eyes, offended like Useppe's by the sight of war pictures at the newsstand. An artist, a witness to the evil of the war years; a profound listener of human dramas, Morante could never be an *impartial* witness to the disaster, but brings testimony to it:

Trovandomi alle soglie della vecchiaia, sentivo di non potermene partire da questa vita senza lasciare agli altri una testimonianza dell'epoca cruciale nella quale il destino mi aveva fatto nascere. Prima ancora che un'opera di poesia (e questo, per grazia di Dio, lo è) il mio romanzo La Storia *vuol essere un atto di accusa contro tutti i fascismi del mondo. E insieme una domanda urgente e disperata, che si rivolge a tutti, per un possibile risveglio comune.* (Morante, "Intervento" 731)

Getting close to old age, I felt that I could not depart from this life without leaving to others a testimony of the crucial epoch in which fate chose to give me birth. More than a work of poetry (and thank God, this one is) my novel *La Storia* wanted to be an accusation against all fascisms. Also, it is a desperate and urgent request to everyone for a possible collective reawakening.

Keenly aware of the essence of evil, Morante now presents it without mediation. Evil is composed of a heap of elements made up of the same substance famously defined by Arendt in terms of banality of evil:

It is indeed my position that evil is never "radical," that is only extreme, and that it possesses neither depth nor any demonic dimension. It can overgrow and lay waste the whole world precisely because it spreads like a fungus on the surface. It is "thought-defying," as I said, because thought tries to reach some depth, to go to the roots, and the moment it concerns itself with evil, it is frustrated because there is nothing. That is its "banality." Only the good has depth and can be radical. (Arendt, Letter to Gershom Scholem 396)

"Evil expands like a fungus": Arendt's simile links lexically her reflections to Morante's when speaking about the bomb shaped like a mushroom. The imperative for Morante is to be radical in alerting us about the banality of evil. The inanity of evil imposed on the powerless Roman *ghettaroli* poisons even their return to a so-called normal life:

Erano figure spettrali come i numeri negativi, al di sotto di ogni veduta naturale, e impossibili perfino alla comune simpatia. La gente voleva rimuoverli dalle proprie giornate come dalle famiglie normali si rimuove la presenza dei pazzi, o dei morti. *E cosí, assieme alle figure illeggibili brulicanti nelle loro orbite nere, molte voci accompagnavano le solitarie passeggiatine dei giudii, riecheggiando enormi dentro i loro cervelli in una fuga a spirale, al di sotto della soglia comune dell'udibile.* (Morante, *La Storia*, 696–97; emphasis added)

They were spectral figures like negative numbers, beneath all natural sight, inconceivable even for common friendliness. People wanted to censor them from their days as normal families remove the mad or the dead. And so, along with the illegible visions swarming in their black eye sockets, many voices accompanied the lonely walks of the Jews, echoing vastly in their brains, in a fugue, below the ordinary threshold of the audible. (Morante, *History* 422; emphasis added)

Ferdinando Camon claims that, rather than dealing with history as a by-product of politics, Morante deals with history as if it were a "fenomeno extra-storico o, al limite, puramente biologico" (187; "an extra-historical or at the most, purely biological phenomenon"). Ida's story is emblematic of the assimilation of history to a biological realm. History is about living human beings' bio-history. The fundamental convergence between Simone Weil (a philosopher often quoted when discussing Morante's novel) and Hannah Arendt can be found in the shared concept of uprooting (*déracinement*). Deprived of a place in the world, human beings can be submitted to forced labor, deported, and treated as nonentities, as if they had never actually existed. Once uprooted from their *humus* as from their *habitat*, once elimi-nated the sense of what is real or not from them, oppression becomes a relatively simple job. In Arendt's theory, *déracinement* constitutes the indis-pensable foundation of every form of totalitarianism, and it is only in this way, that unreality takes over everything. Useppe's "orrore sterminato del suo sguardo" (Morante, *La Storia* 544; "endless horror of his gaze" [Mo-rante, *History* 272]) makes tangible, almost palpable what we should all feel when thinking of that train full of deportees from Rome emitting a deadly sound. Useppe's gaze merely transmits to the external world his physical response to such spectacle: the beat of his little heart becomes so strong that his mother Ida mistakes it for the noise of the train.

If history is a human path and it is also part of the very nature of human beings, one then needs to find the evidence of the innocence of Morante's characters. "[U]na riduzione al grado naturale di tutti i personaggi" (Camon 190; "a reduction to the natural degree of all characters") can be useful to prove their innocence in a newly found naïveté of humans. In this perspec-tive, if "naiveté is the opposite of philosophy" (as Lévinas states), we can safely assume that philosophical systems are enemies of Morante's charac-ters because they force human existence into a pattern that is not as natural as the "biological" one. When Italo Calvino explained in a letter to Morante what he meant by "la contemporaneità" of her "encyclopedic" *La Storia* (1246), the writer skillfully arranged the correct critical skills to contrast Barilli's accusations of anachronism. What Barilli found anachronistic, for Calvino, was Morante's ethical necessity to state the existence of something traumatic, perhaps unutterable, "unknown in our action and language" (Ca-ruth 4), and to express it in a gesture of profound charity, apt to comfort the others. This is what I call the characters' return to innocence: Morante presents them with such gift as she often does with her characters. She burdens herself with the weight of knowledge and saves them from it.

Puppets of Power, *poor 17-year old "soldatucci,"* harmless teachers, all easy preys of fascist *mediocritas*, her "pre–Animal Studies" speaking animals like Bella, are presented as powerless in front of quotidian horrors, a place in which the human is *one life* form among many. These are the innocent characters who seem to entirely conform with Walter Benjamin's idea of marginal history, that fleeting moment that risks "not to be seen depending on who constructs and directs the circulation of memory" (Boscagli 167). In his ninth thesis on the philosophy of history, Benjamin describes Paul Klee's angel with his face turned toward the past looking at the disaster for which he would like to make amends. The more the angel tries to repair the past, the stronger becomes the wind of the storm that prevents him in his effort: "This storm" Benjamin writes, "is what we call progress" (258). This is the storm that sweeps Morante's characters away. Historiography shows its inadequacy to reconstruct the sense of the past coupled with the problem of the existence of something we can safely call a "correct memory" (Robin 146). Such inadequacy resides in its own nature as in its scope: the writing of the *historia rerum gestarum* does not allow for the transmission of intimate sensations because it is a product of execrated Power.

The complex relationship between a historiographic text and a creative one, the latter still defined in terms of "fiction," is exacerbated by the creative writer's basic mistrust of the very sense of history as *historia res gestae*—upon which rests "the politician's stubborn faith in progress" (Benjamin 258) and hinders the possibility of alternative readings of the past. Gerard Génette reminds us that literature is chiefly art and art of language, but the mere use of words and phrases is not sufficient to produce what we consider to be literature (12). It is the literariness of the text—the writerly practice as its awareness of its ethical action that declares the esthetic essence of a work. Literary works deal with how historical events subvert the destiny of humans who are prone to construct a tense relationship with official history. This history proves its inability to tell of the human beings as such and not compact bodies into an indistinct mass ("humanity") to be examined all together.

An ethical conflict emerges between the need for a narrative of individuals being impacted by historical facts and the way in which facts are assembled a posteriori. The narrative significance of official historiographic discourse proves to be insufficient. As a consequence, it arises the need for a narrative that, although based on the very same facts that historiography deals with, stems from different ethical premises. This means coming to terms, in a theoretical sense, with the very values that have allowed the making of that kind of history, a product of Power.

In one of the theoretical parts of *La Storia*, those in which readers take a pause to reflect on the events narrated before them, the narrator ponders on the instinctive need of human beings to make sense of their surroundings:

L'umanità, per propria natura, tende a darsi una spiegazione del mondo, nel quale è nata. E questa è la sua distinzione dalle altre specie. Ogni individuo, pure il meno intelligente e l'infimo dei paria, fino da bambino si dà una qualche spiegazione del mondo. E in quella si adatta a vivere. E senza di quella, cadrebbe nella pazzia. (Morante, *La Storia* 758–59)

Man, by his very nature, tends to give himself an explanation of the world into which he is born. And this is what distinguishes him from the other species. Every individual, even the least intelligent, the lowest of outcasts, from childhood on gives himself some explanation of the world. And with it he manages to live. And without it, he would sink into madness. (Morante, *History* 482)

The need to understand the world and one's place inside it, is also what Morante has long considered to be the artist's duty. Literature constantly renews its innovative possibilities with respect to historiography because, while "[a]ll knowledge involves [. . .] a certain amount of molding and shaping of pre-existing material" (Korhonen 16), literature offers us patterns that makes us think in terms of "if only" we could have a role in the stories it depicts. Because of the relative freedom of the literary word, one should review the very use of the word fiction/*fictio*. The use of imagination in fiction as *fiction* does not mean invention out of nothing—illusion, lie—since "all fiction selects and combines elements coming from the real world, and the reader fills in" (17). As a consequence, "there is no fiction that cannot be interpreted as an allegory of the world" (17). The artist's duty—if he or she truly cares for humanity—lies in making the difference between fiction as a lie, as unreality, and fiction as poetry in the making about the world. Only this can save us from the negative flowers we ourselves produce. Morante's portrayal of the subalterns as the just ones and of the powerful as the bringers of injustice confirms her faith in the necessity of art for the betterment of society. As Morante demonstrates in her thinking about Power, war, and human evil as promoters of a wrong notion of Progress, we need to conceive a new notion of history. Far from being an anachronistic novel, *La Storia* demonstrates how Morante sublimated the original subconscious perception of herself as the persecuted outsider, the holder of secrets, the heir of lies through her narrators Elisa and Arturo, or Manuele, and made her most autobiographical narrating voice—*Elsa ipse*—an indispensable one in which her own story collapses into one as enduring as her characters.

NOTES

1. "The value, even historical, of a novel, does not rely on its narrative pretexts, but on its truths" (Morante, "Sul romanzo" 62). Unless otherwise noted, all translations mine.

2. "Ogni romanzo . . . potrebbe . . . essere tradotto in termini di saggio, e di 'opera di pensiero'" (Morante, "Sul romanzo" 47; "Every novel . . . could . . . be interpreted as an essay and 'work of thought'").

3. Ferdinando Camon is one of the "felici pochi" (happy few) who understood Morante's intentions for moving beyond the borders erroneously placed by Italian critics around the genre of the novel.

4. These statements echo those found in Benedetto Croce's famous essay "Di un equivoco storico: la borghesia." Croce denies the correlation between Italian bourgeoisie and its molding of a historic period. Italian bourgeoisie appears to the Neapolitan philosopher marked by a distinctive quality: mediocrity. They embody all the values of what "non è né troppo alto né troppo basso, il «mediocre» nel sentire, nel costume, nel pensare" (374; "neither too high nor too low, the "mediocre" in their sentiments, habits, thinking"). Middle class then is a more apposite expression for this class in Italian society, for the spirit that forms an entire class in a historic sense was never quite formed in the mind of Italians.

5. Strangely, in the Steerforth translation, this epigraph, as well as the one from Luke's Gospel, are physically distant from the beginning of the novel. The space taken by Barbara Grizzuti Harrison in between the two epigraphs and the novel itself is cumbersome for it severs Morante's work from its own epigraphs.

6. I am drawing from Emmanuel Levinas's idea of language's performative quality of "continually undoing its phrase by the foreword or the exegesis, in unsaying the said" (*Totality* 30).

7. It is worth remembering also Pier Paolo Pasolini's *stroncatura* to *La Storia*, first published in *Il tempo* (July 25 and August 1, 1974) then reprinted in *Descrizioni di descrizioni*, 353–62, and Pasolini, Pier Paolo, "Elsa Morante: *La storia*," in *Saggi sulla letteratura e sull'arte*, 2096–2107.

WORKS CITED

Arendt, Hannah. "Introduction *into* Politics." *The Promise of Politics.* Ed. Jerome Kohn. New York: Shocken Books, 2005. 93–200.
———. Letter to Gershom Scholem. July 24, 1963. *The Portable Arendt.* Ed. Peter Baehr. London: Penguin Books, 2000. 396–98.
Asor Rosa, Alberto. "Il linguaggio della pubblicità." *La fiera letteraria* (6 October 1974): 7. Print.
Balestrini, Nanni, Elisabetta Rasy, Letizia Paolozzi, and Umberto Silva. "Contro il romanzone della Morante." *Il Manifesto* (18 July 1974): 3.
Bardini, Marco. *Morante Elsa. Italiana. Di professione, poeta.* Pisa: Nistri Lischi, 1999.
Barilli, Renato. "Lacrime in superficie." *La fiera letteraria* (6 October 1974): 10.
———. Review to "La Storia," *Il Verri* (October 7, 1974): 105–10.
Benjamin, Walter. *Theses on the Philosophy of History. Illuminations: Essays and Reflections.* Ed. Hannah Arendt. Trans. Harry Zohn. New York: Shocken Books, 2007. 253–64.
Boscagli, Maurizia. "Brushing Benjamin against the Grain, Elsa Morante and the Jetztzeit of Marginal History." *Gendering Italian Fiction: Feminist Revisions of Italian History.* Maria Ornella Marotti and Gabriella Brooke, eds. Madison: Fairleigh Dickinson University Press, 1999. 163–77.
Calvino, Italo. *Lettere 1940–1985.* Ed. Luca Baranelli. Milan: Meridiani Mondadori, 2000.
Camon, Ferdinando. "Il test della 'Storia' (Letteratura di massa. Critica della critica)." *Nuovi Argomenti* 45–46 (1975): 186–239.
Caruth, Cathy. *Unclaimed Experience: Trauma, Narrative, and History.* Baltimore: Johns Hopkins University Press, 1995.
Croce, Benedetto. "Di un equivoco storico: la borghesia." *Etica e politica.* Ed. Benedetto Croce. Bari: Laterza, 1931.
Garboli, Cesare. *Il gioco segreto: nove immagini di Elsa Morante.* Milan: Adelphi, 1995.
Génette, Gerard. *Fiction et diction.* Paris: Editions du Seuil, 1991.
Korhonen, Kuisma. "History as Quasi-Fiction, Fiction as Quasi-History." *Tropes for the Past: Hayden White and the History-Literature Debate.* Ed. Kuisma Korhonen. Amsterdam: Rodopi, 2006. 16–20.

Lévinas, Emmanuel. *Totality and Infinity.* Trans. Alphonso Lingis. Pittsburgh: Duquesne University Press, 1969.

———. *On Thinking of the Other: Entre Nous.* Trans. Michael B. Smith and Barbara Harshaw. New York: Columbia University Press, 1998.

Morante, Elsa. *Arturo's Island.* Trans. Isabel Quigly. South Royalton: Steerforth Italia, 2002.

———. *History: A Novel.* Trans. William Weaver. South Royalton: Steerforth Italia, 2000.

———. "Intervento." Bardini 731.

———. *L'isola di Arturo.* Morante, *Opere* 1:945–1370.

———. *Opere.* Cesare Garboli and Carlo Cecchi, eds. 2 vols. Milan: Meridiani Mondadori, 1988 and 1990.

———. *Il Piccolo Manifesto dei Comunisti (senza classe né partito).* Rome: Nottetempo, 2004.

———. *Pro o contro la bomba atomica e altri scritti.* Milan: Adelphi, 1987.

———. "Pro o contro la bomba atomica." Morante, *Pro o contro* 95–118.

———. *La Storia: Romanzo.* Morante, *Opere* 2:255–1036.

———. "Sul romanzo." Morante, *Pro o contro* 41–74.

Pasolini Pier Paolo. *Descrizioni di descrizioni.* 1979. Pasolini, Pier Paolo. "Elsa Morante: *La storia.*" *Saggi sulla letteratura e sull'arte.* Vol. 2. Walter Siti and Silvia De Laude, eds. Milan: A. Mondadori, 1999. 2096–2107.

Robin, Régine. *I fantasmi della storia. Il passato europeo e le trappole della memoria.* Verona: Ombre corte, 2005.

Wolfe, Cary. *What Is Posthumanism (Posthumanities)?* Minneapolis: University of Minnesota Press, 2009.

Chapter Eight

In Marguerite Caetani's Literary Salon

A Study of Elsa Morante's Contributions to Botteghe Oscure

Lorenzo Salvagni

In this chapter I examine Elsa Morante's contributions to the international literary review *Botteghe Oscure*, printed in Rome from 1948 to 1960, as well as Morante's interaction with the journal's founder and editor, American-born Marguerite Chapin Caetani. I will focus on the years 1948–1959, a decade in which Morante's writing reached full maturity and obtained international acclaim. I will show how the two works published in *Botteghe Oscure* are particularly representative of Morante's stylistic development, and argue that, thanks to Marguerite Caetani, Morante could establish productive relations with her future translator, William Weaver, and with publisher Blanche Knopf.

Caetani's work as an editor and her role as *trait d'union* between European and American writers and intellectuals during the Cultural Cold War have only recently begun to garner scholarly attention; since her name may not be immediately familiar even to a specialized audience, it is necessary to share a few details about her life and work before *Botteghe Oscure*.

Marguerite Caetani was born Marguerite Chapin in New London, Connecticut, in 1880. She grew up in New York City and moved to Paris in 1902. Here she nurtured her passion for music and art, putting together a remarkable collection that included works by Bonnard, Vuillard, Picasso, Balthus, Braque, and many others. In 1911 she married the composer Roffredo Caetani, thus acquiring the titles of Duchess of Sermoneta and Princess of Bassiano. The couple lived in a beautiful villa in Versailles, where they hosted the

Parisian elite: Picasso, Debussy, Stravinsky, Valéry, Joyce, and many other writers, artists, and intellectuals were among their guests. Marguerite decided to finance the publication of a luxury review together with Paul Valéry, Valery Larbaud, and Leon-Paul Fargue; the magazine, named *Commerce* after the "commerce of ideas" of the Enlightenment, aimed to offer a selection of quality literature without being tied to a particular style, country, or age. It published the first French translations of Joyce's *Ulysses* and Woolf's *To the Lighthouse*, among many other masterpieces of early modernism. *Commerce* ran for nine years, from 1924 to 1932, until the stock market crash depleted Marguerite's funds and forced her to suspend publication. The Caetanis relocated to the family palace on via delle Botteghe Oscure, in Rome; here Marguerite had to cope with a regime that was becoming increasingly hostile toward her native country. After the war, in which she lost a son, Marguerite decided to resume her editorial activity. Following her friend Elena Croce's suggestion she hired a young Giorgio Bassani to help her set up a new magazine, which would be named after the street where she lived; the name *Botteghe Oscure* also hinted at the goal of promoting unknown, "obscure" works by authors who did not find space in other periodicals.

Despite its importance for the development of transatlantic modernism, relatively little is known of *Botteghe Oscure* besides its affiliation with chief editor Giorgio Bassani, Caetani's only stable collaborator for the entire run of the magazine. It will be useful then to briefly summarize the salient features of this magazine before addressing the main topic of my chapter.

Botteghe Oscure was a biannual anthology of new international literature. In twelve years it published writers from thirty countries in five languages: English, Italian, French, German, and Spanish. Most contributions appeared in the original, with no translation; the only exceptions were made for texts written in less common languages like Greek, Korean, or Dutch, which were translated into English. Each volume averaged four hundred and seventy-seven pages, which were entirely reserved to literary content; any advertising and criticism were excluded. Caetani wanted to create something different from the publications that populated the Italian literary scene in the 1940s, which she described as "historical, critical, political, dry as dust" in a letter to her half sister, poet Katherine Biddle, dated 12 January 1941 (Caetani). *Botteghe Oscure* was partly modeled on her first literary review, *Commerce*; unlike *Commerce*, however, *Botteghe Oscure* did not limit its scope to one language, and aspired to become a reference for students and budding writers in universities and public libraries on both sides of the Atlantic.

The repertoire published in each volume of *Botteghe Oscure* was not organized thematically, and it did not address any political or social issues. Its content, subdivided by language, was chosen by the editors, Marguerite Caetani and—for the Italian section—Giorgio Bassani, according to their personal taste and a few unwritten rules: an author could not appear in two consecutive numbers; all contributions had to be unpublished when they first appeared in *Botteghe Oscure* and could not be reprinted for six months after they did; most importantly, Caetani tended to favor young and little-known authors, who were often paid more generously and given more space than acclaimed writers. This last policy reflected Caetani's passion for discovering and promoting new talents, and explains why, for example, Elsa Morante found a place in *Botteghe Oscure* five years before Alberto Moravia.[1]

The editors of *Botteghe Oscure* assembled a unique and influential collection of contemporary literature, which included many unknown names that would later join the new literary canon. In this sense Marguerite's intuition was remarkable: she encouraged Bassani to write prose when he saw himself mostly as a poet; she hosted Guglielmo Petroni's first novel, *Il mondo è una prigione*, and the first chapter of Giuseppe Tomasi di Lampedusa's *Il Gattopardo*, both of which had been ignored or refused by other publishers. Dylan Thomas found in Marguerite Caetani a generous patron and a friend in times of hardship; *Botteghe Oscure* published the first part of his radio play *Under Milk Wood* and the villanelle "Do Not Go Gentle into that Good Night." Other authors who gained international visibility through the pages of *Botteghe Oscure* include Ingeborg Bachmann and Maria Zambrano, whom Morante met and befriended in Caetani's salon.

After an all-Italian first number, from the fall of 1948 *Botteghe Oscure* became multilingual with the addition of a section dedicated to British and American authors.[2] Finding good proof correctors for works written in foreign languages was no easy task in postwar Rome; therefore, Caetani was most happy when William Weaver, a young writer who had just moved to Rome from Naples and was looking for work, told her of his boarding-school experience as proof corrector. "The Italian printers," Weaver recalls, "excellent artisans, inevitably made gibberish of some of the magazine's English and French texts, and complaining authors drove Marguerite to despair" (Weaver, *Open City* 8). Weaver first met Marguerite Caetani through a common friend, Dario Cecchi, painter and son of the famous literary critic Emilio Cecchi; at that time Weaver had published a couple of articles on American reviews, was writing his first novel and badly in need of money. Thus he started working for Marguerite, which gave him access to her "inner circle" of friends and collaborators; this group included a young Giorgio Bassani, who performed a variety of editorial tasks including—but not limited to—the selection of Italian contributors; Elena Croce, daughter of Benedetto Croce, who had just ended her collaboration with Francesco Flora's *Aretusa* and codirected *Lo Spettatore Italiano* together with her husband, Raimondo Craveri; Ignazio Silone and his Irish wife, Darina; and many other American and European writers, artists, and intellectuals.

A few months before, during a visit to the island of Capri, Weaver had made the acquaintance of Alberto Moravia and Elsa Morante. Weaver had read Moravia's *La romana* but did not know that his wife also was a writer; he found out only after moving to Rome, when they all started going out for lunch or dinner in local trattorias with various groups of friends and acquaintances (Spiegelman). It is possible that Weaver acted as intermediary between Morante and Caetani, although Bassani was also a common friend of the couple. At any rate, Morante's poem "L'avventura" found its way to Marguerite's desk and was selected for inclusion in the spring issue of 1951. In the same year her first novel, *Menzogna e sortilegio*, was published in the States with the title *House of Liars*. Due to a mediocre translation and massive cuts, however, the book went largely ignored by the American readership. In Italy *Menzogna e sortilegio* won the Viareggio Prize in 1948, but here too the critics' praise was not unanimous, and the book did not sell well. Hence, when she submitted "L'avventura" to *Botteghe Oscure*, Elsa Morante still lacked the recognition she deserved in her country and abroad.

"L'avventura" appeared on the seventh issue of *Botteghe Oscure*. The poem bears a dedication to an unknown person of whom Morante indicates only the initials "W. T. M." At the end of the poem Morante wrote place and date of composition: London-Cambridge and April 1948, respectively. When "L'avventura" was included in the collection *Alibi*, published by Longanesi in 1958, the mysterious dedication had disappeared; the composition year, however, still figured as 1948.[3] Cesare Garboli, Lily Tuck, and Graziella Bernabò all pointed to Luchino Visconti as the person Morante was thinking of when she wrote "L'avventura." Her relationship with the famous movie director, however, according to Morante's own admission, did not begin until 1949; this led the above-mentioned authors to conclude that Elsa had back-dated "L'avventura" and added a fictitious dedicatee in order to divert suspicions.[4] Garboli described "L'avventura" as "uno spavaldo richiamo d'amore a Luchino Visconti" (102). The tone of the poem is jaunty and fantastic; its language evokes courtly romance and Ariosto's epic poems, but the traditional roles are inverted; it is Lisa, the female protagonist and narrator, who sets on a quest to conquer the heart of the man she desires.

Morante's identification with Lisa is revealed by the often-quoted triplet that indicates the time and date of her birth: "Invece, Lisa è il mio nome, / nacqui nell'ora amara / del meriggio, nel segno del Leone, / un giorno di festa cristiana" ("L'avventura" 1390; "Instead, Lisa is my name, I was born / at the noon's bitter hour, in the sign of the Lion / a day of Christian festival," Morante, "Adventure" 26). Morante was in fact born on a Sunday, a day of Christian feast, August 18, 1912. Lisa's quest, she declares, does not make her a hero: she only wants to play with her lover for a while, like a girl with her kitten, and then leave him heartbroken. This final twist reveals the mocking spirit that runs through the entire poem; Morante defuses Lisa's dramatic gestures, and pokes fun at her romantic self. In a review appearing in *Società* the piece was termed "contraffazione" (counterfeiting), while Pasolini called it "capriccio o pastiche" on *Il Popolo di Roma*, describing it as "ondeggiante tra un dubbio gusto e un gusto squisito" ("oscillating between questionable and exquisite taste," Pasolini, *Botteghe* 383). The lighter character of "L'avventura," however, seems to conceal a more somber, self-destructive side of Elsa's nature, which resurfaces when Lisa says, for example, "A difficili amori io nacqui" or "Le cose amare sono le più care" (1388–90; "For difficult loves was I born," "The bitterest things are the things most dear," Morante, "Adventure" 24–25). While quasi-oximoronic in nature, verses like these hint in many ways at the writer's tumultuous sentimental life.

Caetani's decision to publish "L'avventura" in *Botteghe Oscure* might have been influenced by William Weaver, but we cannot know it for sure. It is certain, however, that he greatly admired Morante's poem; two years later, in fact, he decided to translate it for the American review *Wake* (formerly known as *The Harvard Wake*), which was edited by a young Seymour Lawrence at Harvard University.[5] "The Adventure" appeared in the twelfth issue of *Wake* (Fall 1953), listed in the table of contents simply as "Poem." Morante came first in a short but impressive selection of Italian authors, introduced by Renato Poggioli, which included works by Corrado Alvaro, Giuseppe Ungaretti, Rocco Scotellaro, Eugenio Montale, Salvatore Quasimodo, and Luigi Pirandello. In the years that followed, William Weaver became one of the most respected translators of Italian literature. He continued to support Morante's work; he translated two of her novels, *La storia* (1974) and *Aracoeli* (1982).

Elsa Morante's second contribution to *Botteghe Oscure* is the short story "Lo scialle andaluso," which was published on the journal's eleventh issue in the spring of 1953. Morante's story closed the volume, preceded by Rolando Anzilotti's translation of an influential poem by Robert Lowell, "The Quaker Graveyard in Nantucket." Given her fascination with the sea, it is worth noting that both of Morante's contributions to *Botteghe Oscure* are preceded by works in which the sea features prominently. In particular, Raffaello Brignetti's story "Il destino," which came before "L'avventura" in *Botteghe Oscure* 7, takes place on an island shrouded in a veil of mystery and besieged by heaven and sea. This setting reminds us of Morante's second novel, *L'isola di Arturo*. Written between April and June 1951, "Lo scialle andaluso" was also meant to become a novel, to be published together with *L'isola di Arturo* in a volume entitled *Due amori impossibili* (Pallagrosi 9).

In 2001 the National Library of Rome acquired an autograph of "Lo scialle andaluso" that precedes and differs in numerous parts from the version published in *Botteghe Oscure*. In her analysis of the manuscript, Gioia Pallagrosi writes that the great number of corrections and additions seem to mark a new stage in Morante's creative process:

L'autrice abbandona i panni del feuilletonista a getto continuo, indossando quelli del puntiglioso romanziere attento e scrupoloso, revisore delle proprie bozze di stampa. . . . Questa sorta di riscatto sembra preludere ad una meta-morfosi: dai modi romanzeschi e famigliari di Menzogna e sortilegio *(1948) si passa a quelli simbolici e leggendari de* L'isola di Arturo. (1952, 13–14)

The author sheds the feuilleton writer clothes and becomes a meticulous nov-elist, attentive and conscientious, reviewer of her own proofs. . . . This sort of redemption seems to announce a metamorphosis: from the fantastic-familiar writing mode of *House of Liars* to the symbolic-legendary mode of *Arturo's Island*.

According to Pallagrosi, the long gestation of "Lo scialle andaluso" re-flects Morante's increased attention to the formal aspects of her writing; the story represents a transition between two distinct narrative modes, and em-bodies the combination of fantastic, psychological, and autobiographical ele-ments that will become a signature trait of Morante's style.

In Italy, "Lo scialle andaluso" was reprinted in several anthologies and gave the title to a collection of stories published by Einaudi in 1963, the same year it appeared in *Les Temps Modernes*.[6] The collection included a selection from *Il gioco segreto* (1941) and other stories written between 1935 and 1951 (Pallagrosi 7). In the United States, an English translation of "Lo scialle andaluso" ("The Andalusian Shawl") was included in the anthology *Modern Italian Stories*, edited by Walter John Strachan and published in New York in 1956.[7] In the preface to the volume, Strachan explicitly mentions "that excel-lent bi-annual *Botteghe Oscure*" in which he first read Morante's story (Stra-chan 7).

In the afterword to the Einaudi edition, Elsa Morante wrote that she had always had a particular fondness for "Lo scialle andaluso." She dedicated it to her faithful housemaid, Lucia Mansi, and added a short introductory poem in which Mansi is compared to a sea bird lovingly brooding eggs in her nest on a solitary and stormy cliff (Bernabò 284). Dedication and poem were absent in *Botteghe Oscure*; Morante added them later, as if she wanted to further emphasize the theme of motherhood that lies at the core of her work. Marguerite Caetani had lost both parents by the time she was fifteen; could this be one of the reasons that drew her attention to Morante's story? It seems safe to assume that Marguerite Caetani would not have published "Lo scialle andaluso" had she not felt some kind of affinity with the writer's aesthetic vision. Despite their obvious differences, both women were not in full sync with the cultural climate of their time; they refused to embrace the dominant cultural trends of Neorealism and Hermeticism, were skeptical of militant criticism and engaged literature, and rejected partisan readings of their work. Moreover, Marguerite Caetani appreciated the clarity, balance, and lightness that informed Morante's style. Hence, as she did for all the authors she admired, Caetani started sending out Morante's work to some of her influential friends in the publishing field.

In 1957, for example, she sent a copy of *L'isola di Arturo* to Jamie Hamilton, *Botteghe Oscure*'s distributor in the United Kingdom. He gave it to his wife for an opinion, but she was not impressed, as he recalls: "She knew that it was supposed to be having a success in Italy, but in spite of this is convinced that it is not worth another report and is prepared to bet large sums of money that no one will publish it here! Which only goes to show how different people's views can be" (Hamilton). It would take somebody more farsighted than Hamilton (who had previously rejected Caetani's precious pitches of works by Calvino, Char, and others) to introduce Morante to the English-speaking world.

The Anglo-American presence had always been strong in via delle Botteghe Oscure, home to the Caetani's historical residence; poet and Librarian of Congress Archibald MacLeish, poets Allen Tate and Robert Lowell, novelist Truman Capote, all were affectionate guests, collaborators, and supporters of Caetani's editorial enterprise. American editor Blanche Knopf was also well acquainted with Marguerite Caetani, and often listened to her advice for new Italian authors to follow and publish. Records from the Gotham Book Mart in New York City, an early distributor of *Botteghe Oscure* in the United States, reveal that Knopf had first subscribed to the magazine in 1952 (Knopf 1952). Three years later, in the spring of 1955, Knopf visited Marguerite Caetani at her flat in via delle Botteghe Oscure. Caetani was hoping that Knopf would take over the distribution of *Botteghe Oscure* for the United States, since she was not happy with Farrar and Straus, but Knopf had no intention of dealing with a "prestige magazine" that sold a few thousand copies at best and was difficult to handle. In the fall, in order to improve Knopf's disposition toward her review, Caetani published the short story "A Day in the Dark" by Elizabeth Bowen, another of Knopf's writers. Blanche did not change her opinion, although she did not exclude the possibility of a different form of collaboration, "perhaps through books" (Knopf 1955).

Knopf's visit, however, is important for another reason: she had the opportunity to meet Caetani's collaborators, including Bassani and Weaver, at a time when she was actively looking for new Italian authors to add to her catalog. It is likely that she read Morante's contributions to *Botteghe Oscure*, but we do not know if they actually met during this trip. Morante knew that Knopf had published Sigmund Freud, Katherine Mansfield, and Simone de Beauvoir, authors who were among her favorites. The American editor was well versed in French and German literature, as she spoke both languages fluently; her knowledge of Italian, however, was not as thorough, and she had to rely on the advice of others before making decisions. This set of circumstances, while it does not constitute proof, seems to indicate that Morante and Knopf became acquainted through Marguerite Caetani and her collaborators.

Besides Morante, Caetani signaled at least two more of "her" writers to Knopf and arranged meetings for them with the American publisher. The first was Giorgio Bassani, who wanted Knopf to publish an English translation of his *Cinque storie ferraresi*. The book, edited in Italy by Feltrinelli, had won the prestigious Premio Strega in 1956. The following year Knopf came to Italy accompanied by a well-known literary agent, Jenny Bradley; they stayed in Rome, at the Grand Hotel, from July 11 to 17. During this time, Knopf met Bassani several times. She expressed interest in the translation, authored by Macha Louis Rosenthal, and took it with her to Paris for further evaluation. On July 27 Bassani asked Caetani to gauge Knopf's intentions in regard to his novel, and to return to him the translation in case it did not meet with Knopf's approval. In the end, Rosenthal's effort did not satisfy Knopf, which brought the entire project to a sudden stop. An English version of *Cinque storie ferraresi* would only appear in 1971, edited by none other than William Weaver and published by Harcourt Brace Jovanovich in New York City.

The second writer Caetani introduced to Blanche Knopf was Guglielmo Petroni. His novels *Il mondo è una prigione*, *La casa si muove*, and *Noi dobbiamo parlare* had all appeared on *Botteghe Oscure* between 1948 and 1954. Knopf and Bradley met with Petroni at the Grand Hotel; Bassani, who was also present, thus described the scene to Marguerite Caetani: "Credo che l'incontro sia andato molto bene: la signora Knopf, ogni tanto, mi bisbigliava all'orecchio: 'mi sembra serio . . . sincero. . . . mi interessa molto'" [*sic*] ("I believe the meeting went very well: Mrs. Knopf, every now and then, whispered into my ear: 'He seems serious . . . sincere. . . . I am very interested in him,'" Valli 100–101). At the same meeting Bassani gave Knopf and Bradley a list of young Italian writers, per her request, and a copy of the latest issue (the 19th) of *Botteghe Oscure.* "Lo hanno ambedue ammirato moltissimo" ("They both admired it very much"), Bassani commented in the same letter quoted above. Later that evening Knopf and Bradley had dinner at Trattoria del Bolognese in Piazza del Popolo. At the event, organized by Bassani, were present several other writers and intellectuals including Rosenthal, Alberto Moravia, Elsa Morante, and Pier Paolo Pasolini.

Even though in 1955 Knopf had refused to take on the distribution of *Botteghe Oscure* in the United States, Caetani continued to play the role of literary agent and social mediator so that the writers in her network could reach an international readership. Nor did she give up hope that Knopf would one day change her mind and become *Botteghe Oscure*'s distributor in the States; she asked again in the spring of 1959, when the journal's twelve-year-long run was coming to an end, but this time, too, she received a negative answer.

In the meantime, Morante had published her second novel, *L'isola di Arturo*, which won the Strega Prize and enjoyed a positive reception from critics and readers alike. Blanche Knopf secured the rights for publication in the States and had the book translated by Isabel Quigly. In the summer she sent an advance copy to the American ambassador in Rome, encouraging him to meet Morante and "do something about her" (Knopf 19 June 1959). Morante had lunch at the embassy and later wrote Knopf that she wanted to visit the States in the fall. It is during this visit that she began her tormented love affair with the young painter Bill Morrow, an event that will influence her later production. Blanche Knopf came back to Italy in October, again visiting Caetani and a few other friends. To the cultural attaché at the American Embassy she expressed her will to "publish more Italian books and get more translated into Italian" (Knopf 9 Sep. 1959).

Caetani's declining health, the lack of funding, and the premature death of the journal's trusted printer, Luigi De Luca, were the concurring factors behind the decision to quit *Botteghe Oscure* one year later, in 1960. In the course of its life span, the magazine had published over twelve thousand pages of literature written by seven hundred authors. To these remarkable numbers one must add the volumes, booklets, and leaflets associated with but separated from *Botteghe Oscure*. For two years in a row, for example, in 1949 and 1950, the Italian translation of the journal's English section was published in separate booklets under the title "Poeti inglesi e americani" (British and American Poets). At the same time Caetani prepared a selection of *Botteghe Oscure*'s Italian contributions for the English-speaking audience; the anthology, entitled *New Italian Writers*, was received favorably and opened the way to a wider circulation of contemporary Italian literature in the Anglo-American markets. Not only did Caetani connect Italian authors to American and British publishers like Blanche Knopf and Jamie Hamilton; she also introduced the poetry of René Char to the American audience by promoting the publication of his first full-length anthology, *Hypnos Waking*, with Random House in 1956.

Despite such achievements, it would be hard to measure the actual extent of Marguerite Caetani's contribution to the development of Italian-American cultural and literary relations. Still, her continued efforts to establish connections among Italian writers and English-speaking translators, critics, publishers, and literary agents cannot be underestimated. Caetani never received credit for introducing William Weaver and later Blanche Knopf to some of Morante's early work; nor had she sought recognition for what she considered a duty toward an artist she clearly admired, and whose work resonated with her own aesthetic views. In this sense, one might argue that her ability to foster productive and extended relationships with the literary elite proved just as important as the craft of writing itself.

There is little doubt that, thanks to her cosmopolitan attitude and multiple connections on both sides of the Atlantic, Marguerite Caetani was able to act as intermediary between European and American writers at a time when ideological and cultural factors could represent insuperable barriers. In this chapter, by looking back to the relationships that developed in Caetani's salon, I focused my attention on the chain of events that resulted in Morante's international launch after the false start of *House of Liars*; the thread connecting Elsa Morante to William Weaver and Blanche Knopf, however, is only one of many unfolding from this animated and influential cultural center. Future investigations surrounding the "Dark Shops" of European literature may lead to other discoveries and shed light on less-known but influential figures of twentieth-century transatlantic modernism.

NOTES

1. Moravia's first submission to *Botteghe Oscure*—the story "Luna di miele, sole di fiele"—was rejected by the editors. Only in 1955 did the magazine publish his play *Beatrice Cenci*.
2. More sections in French, German, and Spanish began appearing, respectively, in *Botteghe Oscure* 3 (Spring 1949), 14 (Fall 1954), and 16 (Fall 1955).
3. Morante changed the title to "Avventura," without the article, for the Longanesi edition. The volume also included a selection of verse by Sandro Penna and Pier Paolo Pasolini, who both were close friends of Morante's.
4. Daniele Morante, Elsa's nephew, rejects this interpretation. He claims that the initials W. T. M. refer to a British young man who had a passionate affair with Elsa after the war; he has not been able to find out the man's name (from a private conversation with the author).
5. Seymour Lawrence later embarked on a successful career as an independent publisher and talent scout. He brought to the American readership masterpieces like Kurt Vonnegut's *Slaughterhouse-Five* (1969), as well as works by distinguished authors such as Thomas Berger, Katherine Anne Porter, Pablo Neruda, and George Seferis.
6. *Les Temps Modernes*, August–September 1963, 207–8.
7. British poet, editor, art critic, and translator Walter John Strachan (1903–1994) authored two volumes of poetry and translated a number of French and Italian writers including Julien Gracq, Albert Camus, Cesare Pavese, Elsa Morante, and Vera Cacciatore.

WORKS CITED

Bernabò, Graziella. *La Fiaba Estrema: Elsa Morante Tra Vita e Scrittura.* Rome: Carocci, 2012.
"Botteghe Oscure. Rivista semestrale di letteratura. Quaderno VII, maggio 1951, Roma." Rev. of *Botteghe Oscure* 7. *Società* 7.2 (1951): 383.
Caetani, Marguerite. Letter to Katherine Biddle. 12 Jan. 1941. MS. Katherine Biddle Papers. Special Collections, Georgetown University Library, Washington, DC.
Garboli, Cesare. *Il gioco segreto. Nove immagini di Elsa Morante.* Milan: Adelphi, 1995.
Hamilton, Jamie. Letter to Marguerite Caetani. 5 June 1957. TS. Archivio della Fondazione Camillo Caetani, Rome.
Knopf, Blanche. Letter to Marguerite Caetani. 25 Apr. 1955. TS. Alfred A. Knopf, Inc. Records. Harry Ransom Center, Austin, TX.
———. Letter to Gotham Book Mart. 13 June 1952. TS. Gotham Book Mart Records. Harry Ransom Center, Austin, TX.

―――. Letter to James Zellerbach. 19 June 1959. TS. Alfred A. Knopf, Inc. Records. Harry Ransom Center, Austin, TX.

―――. Letter to James Zellerbach. 9 Sep. 1959. TS. Alfred A. Knopf, Inc. Records. Harry Ransom Center, Austin, TX.

Lucamante, Stefania, and Sharon Wood, eds. *Under Arturo's Star: The Cultural Legacies of Elsa Morante*. West Lafayette, IN: Purdue University Press, 2006.

Morante, Elsa. "The Adventure." Trans. William Fense Weaver. *Wake* 12 (1953): 24–26.

―――. "Avventura*." Opere*. Carlo Cecchi and Cesare Garboli, eds. Vol. 1. Milan: Meridiani Mondadori, 1988. 1388–91.

―――. *Racconti Dimenticati*. Torino: Einaudi, 2002.

―――. "Lo scialle andaluso*." Opere*. Carlo Cecchi and Cesare Garboli, eds. Vol. 1. Milan: Meridiani Mondadori, 1988. 1407–578.

Pallagrosi, Gioia, ed. *Nell'officina di Elsa Morante: un'inedita redazione autografa de Lo scialle andaluso*. Rome: Spolia, 2009. *Torrossa Casalini*. Web. 15 October 2012.

Pasolini, Pier Paolo. Rev. of *Botteghe Oscure* 7. *Il Popolo di Roma* (15 September 1951): n. a.

Spiegelman, Willard. *William Weaver, The Art of Translation No. 3*. Interview with William Weaver. *The Paris Review* (Spring 2002). Web. 15 October 2012.

Strachan, W. J., ed. *Modern Italian Stories*. New York: Philosophical Library, 1956.

Tuck, Lily. *Woman of Rome: A Life of Elsa Morante*. New York: Harper Collins, 2008.

Valli, Stefania, ed. *La rivista Botteghe Oscure e Marguerite Caetani: La corrispondenza con gli autori italiani, 1948–1960*. Roma: L'Erma di Bretschneider, 1999.

Weaver, William, ed. *Open City: Seven Writers in Postwar Rome*. South Royalton: Steerforth Italia, 1999.

―――. *A Tent in This World*. Kingston, NY: McPherson & Co., 1999.

II

Theater, Visual Arts, and Cinema

Chapter Nine

"Lo Scialle Andaluso"

*Performance, Performativity, and the
Creativity of Elsa Morante*

Gabrielle Orsi

This chapter will examine how the important novella "Lo scialle andaluso" (The Andalusian Shawl) fits into Elsa Morante's corpus, and how it illustrates the evolution of her writing between and beyond her novels. Unusually, "Lo scialle andaluso" departs from the private, enclosed spaces favored by Morante, where fantasy and creativity typically burst forth for her characters. Such confined spaces appear throughout Morante's oeuvre; and while they often have theatrical aspects, only in "Lo scialle andaluso" does Morante make the setting of such fantasy an actual theater. Accordingly, this novella should be seen as a defining experiment for Morante: she plays with the limits of fantasy's power to transform reality— or in more theoretical terms, she pits performance against performativity. Finally, I see this novella as suggesting an approach for considering the difficult question of *Hebräitude* or the expression of her Jewish roots in her writing.

"Lo scialle andaluso" tells the story of the widow Giuditta Campese, who flees north from Palermo to pursue a career as a dancer, and her twin children, Laura and Andrea. Andrea is fiercely jealous of his mother's theatrical career and friends. After a religious awakening, he enters a seminary. Yet, after seeing a poster for a performance by his mother, he flees the seminary to watch his mother perform for the first time. Andrea is dazzled then shocked as Giuditta—a mediocre middle-aged dancer—is booed off the stage by the audience. After a brief mother-son rapprochement, during which Giuditta drapes an Andalusian shawl from her theatrical wardrobe over Andrea, their family life settles into a new uncertain pattern. Andrea abandons his religiosity (for, it's suggested, radical politics). Meanwhile, Giuditta, after quitting the stage, withers into a secluded old age akin to that of Cesira in *Menzogna e sortilegio*. Disillusion dawns for Andrea as he realizes that Giuditta did not give up the theater for his sake, but rather she has retired due to her age and lack of talent; the story closes with his musings about his future, haunted by the image of himself wrapped in the Andalusian shawl.

"Lo scialle andaluso" was composed in the spring of 1951 and first published in 1953 in the periodical *Botteghe Oscure*. The novella would later anchor a collection of stories in 1963, also titled *Lo scialle andaluso*. This important collection, by appearing in print after the publication of Morante's second novel, thus positions the novella between Morante's first and second novels—*Menzogna e sortilegio*[1] in 1948 and *L'isola di Arturo*[2] in 1957. I concur with Cesare Garboli's observation that Morante's decision to publish "Lo scialle andaluso" more prominently after her second novel suggests that she wished the story to be understood as stylistically belonging with *L'isola di Arturo* (Garboli 139).[3]

Yet in these same years Morante also was cultivating her image as a novelist above all, thus complicating the place of "Lo scialle andaluso" in her oeuvre. Indeed, in this self-portrait from 1960, Morante emphasizes her evolution toward writing novels:

> *La sua (per così dire) attività letteraria è cominciata fino dalla sua primissima età. Fino all'età di quindici anni, ha scritto soltanto poesie e fiabe. Alcune di queste fiabe apparvero stampate su periodici già ai loro tempi. Una,* Le avventure di Caterina, *è stata pubblicata,* postuma, *dall'Editore Einaudi nel 1941; e ristampata dallo stesso editore nel 1959.*
>
> *Dall'età di quindici anni in poi—abbandonate del tutto le fiabe e quasi del tutto le poesie—la scrittrice si è dedicata quasi esclusivamente all'arte del romanzo e del racconto.* ("La casa dei sette bambini" 47)

Her literary activity (to describe it thusly) began at a very early age. Until the age of fifteen, she only wrote poetry and fables. Some of these fables were published in periodicals at the time of their writing. One, *The Adventures of Caterina*, was published, *posthumously*, by Einaudi in 1941; and was reprinted in 1959 by that same publishing house.

From the age of fifteen on—abandoning the fables altogether and the poetry almost entirely—the writer has dedicated herself almost exclusively to the art of the novel and the short story.

Thus, in the same years "Lo scialle andaluso" received its most prominent placement as the cornerstone of that 1963 collection, Morante's desired authorial image was that of a *romanziere*, a novelist.

Yet "Lo scialle andaluso" in fact does exhibit continuity with the "fiabe" (fables) Morante dismisses above; though of course the length and complexity of "Lo scialle andaluso" does distinguish it from earlier Morantian tales.

There is a particular affinity between "Lo scialle andaluso" and the short story "La nonna" (The Grandmother)[4] from 1937. Like "Lo scialle andaluso," this story also features a widow, Elena, and her twin children; her husband has an obsessive relationship with his mother, the namesake "nonna."[5] The dominant figure in "La nonna" is Giuseppe's mother, a dangerous storyteller who eventually lures the twins to their death. She foreshadows the eroticism of other Morantian mothers such as Giuditta of "Lo scialle andaluso," whose relationship with Andrea has an oedipal quality— "I suoi piedi, molto piccoli, erano calzati con civetteria di stivalini lucidi. . . ." (Morante, *Opere* 1, 1429; "Her feet, very small, were shod coquettishly in shiny little boots. . . .").[6] The *nonna* also reiterates the connection between the maternal figure and narration, underscoring the equivocal nature of both for Morante. Giuditta in fact, particularly evokes Aracoeli, the elusive Andalusian mother of the novel *Aracoeli*, who stages for her son Manuele a parade of roles just as stereotyped as Giuditta's: "Pastora. Idalga. Santa. Meretrice. Morta. Immortale. Vittima. Tiranna. Bambola. Dea. Schiava. Madre. Figlia. Ballerina" (Morante, *Opere* 2, 1194; "Shepherdess. Hidalga. Saint. Sinner. Dead. Immortal. Victim. Tyrant. Doll. Goddess. Slave. Mother. Daughter. Ballerina").

I find the description of Elena's children in "La nonna" is worth citing at greater length: it illustrates the important Morantian theme of passionate family relationships, particularly between children and mothers. This description also links such relationships to language.

> *I due gemelli si rassomigliavano fra loro fino ad essere pressoché uguali. . . .*
> *Camminavano quasi sempre tenendosi per mano, con piccole corse attente, e,*
> *non parlando ancora bene il linguaggio degli uomini, avevano un particolare*
> *linguaggio comune, fatto di balbettii e di gridi, un che di mezzo fra l'idioma*
> *dei gatti e quello degli uccelli.* (Morante, "La nonna," *Opere* 1, 1440)

> The two twins resembled each other so as to be nearly identical. . . . They
> would walk almost always holding hands, in small careful runs, and, not yet
> able to speak well the language of humans, they had a special shared language,
> made of babblings and shouts, just a little between the language of cats and
> that of birds.

A similar animalistic unity and pairing appear in "Lo scialle andaluso" during Andrea and Giuditta's reunion as he sees "L'Orsa in cielo con le sue mille figlie," and two stones as "somigliante a una pecora col suo agnello" (Morante, *Opere* 1, 1570; "The Great Bear with his thousand children," "like a ewe with its lamb" [Morante, "Andalusian" 47]). Just as *Menzogna e sortilegio* concludes with the imagined constellation "Del Cugino" (The Cousin's) that offers a cosmic resolution to the unhappy triangle of Anna, Francesco, and Edoardo, so too does Andrea project his family's story skyward. Likewise, Giuditta becomes the heavenly creature "Febea" (a name akin to

"Phoebe") when onstage. And in a similar pattern of the domestic and famil-ial becoming writ large across a sympathetic cosmos, Arturo of *L'isola di Arturo* notes in the novel's very first paragraph that he is named after the star Arcturus in the constellation Boötes.

Importantly, as these animal pairs from "Lo scialle andaluso" demon-strate, in moving from "La nonna" to "Lo scialle andaluso," Morante merges the maternal and sibling roles. In fact, Andrea's twin sister Laura has a strikingly diminished role in comparison to the narrator-protagonist Elisa in *Menzogna e sortilegio*.

Additionally, "Lo scialle andaluso" highlights other efforts of Morante's that did not ultimately come to fruition, such as the unfinished *romanzo* or novel entitled *Nerina* of late 1950, a "romanzo-balletto mai stampato" ("a never-published novel-ballet"), which only would find partial expression in print in the 1950 story "Donna Amalia" (*Morante Opere* 1: LVIII). Indeed, "romanzo-balletto" is an apt label for "Lo scialle andaluso" as Giuditta is a ballet dancer. And Nerina, like Giuditta, hails from Palermo.

If "Lo scialle andaluso" is Morante's proto-*romanzo*, weaving together diverse strands of her writing, and is meant to occupy the place between her first and second novels, what is gestating in "Lo scialle andaluso"? What important developments or experiments does "Lo scialle andaluso" show us?

I find it very significant that "Lo scialle andaluso" is so specifically theatrical. It is the sole Morante work to feature a main character, Giuditta, as a performer who appears onstage. If, as Stefania Lucamante writes, "Teatro, passione, immaginazione, melodramma" ("Theater, passion, imagination, melodrama") comprise the most important elements of Morantian style, then "Lo scialle andaluso" must be taken as a serious attempt by Morante at tackling representational issues in the period between her first two novels (Lucamante 41–42). The theater and its denizens, particularly Giuditta, in "Lo scialle andaluso" are Morante's subsequent iteration of the female artist, post-Elisa. Thus the Andalusian shawl comes to symbolize, among other things, the female artist. Intriguingly, Giuditta's medium of ballet is word-less, not textual—unlike Elisa, Giuditta limits her writing to scrawling a few picture postcards, whose exotic images are as stereotyped as the roles she plays. The wandering Giuditta, touring with her ballet company, embodies a drastic change from *Menzogna e sortilegio*, in which Elisa leads a cloistered existence and the only voyages are the dazzling fictions concocted by Edoar-do and Anna, or Edoardo's own desperate sojourns in a sanatorium.

Moreover, to the best of my knowledge, one key point has not been made previously in the sparse critical literature on "Lo scialle andaluso": Morante thrusts her readers into the same position as Andrea, not Giuditta. Thus "Lo scialle andaluso" anticipates the dwindling narrative role of female charac-ters in Morante: her subsequent novels nearly all feature male narrators. Like Andrea, the reader remains apart from the theatrical world inhabited by Giuditta. We never see Giuditta wearing the gorgeous Andalusian shawl—instead, it is Andrea's jealousy of the theater, his imaginings of the stage, and his wearing of the shawl that is a synecdoche for the theater in "Lo scialle andaluso." Andrea's thoughts upon entering Teatro Gloria, whose name could be translated as Glory Theater, illustrate my point:

> *Ecco, dunque, le fatali porte che il suo proprio decreto gli aveva reso inaccessibili durante tutta la sua vita, fino ad oggi! A dispetto del suo odio, e della sua negazione, i loro misteri avevano dominato la sua infanzia. La sua fantasia disubbidiente gli aveva fatto intravvedere, al di là, dei miraggi straordinari; i quali, sebbene ricacciati mille volte con disdegno, si riaccendevano sempre alla parola teatro. Istoriato e sfavillante come un duomo orientale; popoloso come una piazza nella festa dell'Epifania; signorile come un feudo; e di nessuno dimora, mai, come l'Oceano! Ah, povero Andrea Campese! Così armato, invincibile ti appariva il teatro, che, davanti a un simile rivale, il cuore, provocato al grande combattimento, ricorse alla fortezza suprema del Paradiso!* (Morante, *Opere* 1, 1555)

> Here then were the fatal doors that he had intentionally shunned all his life up to the present moment! Despite his hatred and hostility, their mysteries had dominated his childhood. His imagination, in revolt, had conjured up the most extraordinary fancies ever since. However contemptuously he dismissed them, they invariably flashed back in his mind when the word "theater" came up. Painted and sparkling like some oriental pleasure-dome, thronged like a town square at the festival of Epiphany, aristocratic, situated nowhere in particular, vast as the Ocean. Poor Andrea Campese! So strongly, so invincibly armed did the theater appear to him that his heart, provoked to great combativeness in the face of this rival, had taken refuge in the supreme strength of Paradise. (Morante, "Andalusian" 34)

It is apparent that Andrea, like Giuditta, is governed by what Cesare Garboli terms the "fascinazione diabolica del teatro" (139; "the diabolical fascination of the theater"). The humble provincial theater whose threshold Andrea is about to cross is far from glamorous. Instead, it is so dilapidated that its sign reads "T ATR GLORIA." The manuscript of "Lo scialle andaluso" reveals that Morante clearly toiled over this sign's details, as she wrote the theater's full name capitalized with the letters E and A of "TEATRO" carefully scratched out, with a blot of ink covering the letter O (*Lo scialle* MS).[7] Yet she intentionally left the provocative word GLORIA intact, hinting at both Giuditta's dreams of stardom and Andrea's religious ecstasies.[8] Giuditta is in fact introduced by the narrator as "destinata alla gloria" (Morante, *Opere* 1, 1529; "destined for stardom" [Morante, "Andalusian" 11]) who lived in an apartment in which "regnava la certezza che lei fosse una *stella*" (Morante, *Opere* 1, 1529; "expressed the certainty that a 'star' dwelt there" [Morante, "Andalusian" 11]). The novella plays upon the "gloria" and stars sought by Giuditta and Andrea, not to mention the idea of Paradise each of them searches in different ways; they are illusions that eventually crumble for both characters. Their performances are not sustained or sustainable to successfully create their desired identities—there is a gap between the overt theatricality they embrace and the phenomenological, social reality that ultimately overwhelms their performances.

Likewise, absences and gaps are crucial to the structure of "Lo scialle andaluso": Giuditta's dancing and the theaters where she performs remain unseen throughout most of the novella, until Andrea enters a shabby theater in the novella's dénouement. Play between concealment or deception and revelation or truth is at the heart of "Lo scialle andaluso." Only with "Lo scialle andaluso" does Morante make the private ludic, creative spaces archetypal in her writing specifically creative by choosing the setting of a theater. Confined, private spaces in which fantasy and creativity can emerge are deeply rooted in Morante's writing, dating back to the key early story "Il gioco segreto" (The Secret Game)[9] in which three children escape a grim present by secretly staging chivalric romances in a frescoed room of a decrepit palazzo.

Throughout "Lo scialle andaluso," this tension between seen and unseen, private and public, performativity and performance is maintained by richly evocative doubling or mirroring—for example, Giuditta and Andrea, Andrea and his twin sister Laura, theater and home, ballet and religion. [10]

Yet after "Lo scialle andaluso," never again would a theater or performers figure as centrally in a Morantian work. Why not? And why is Giuditta such a grotesque failure onstage? Though Andrea at first perceives her as a "meravigliosa artista" clad in "un abito d'eleganza mai vista," truly a vision from painting or poetry (Morante, *Opere* 1, 1562; "wonderful artiste"; "in an elegant gown, but not of the kind that it is vouchsafed to the ladies—even the wealthiest—in this world to wear; it belonged rather to the fantastic domain of painting and poetry" [Morante "Andalusian" 40]), he realizes with shock that the audience is jeering at the middle-aged dancer. Disgraced, Giuditta flees offstage then quits the stage for good.

With "Lo scialle andaluso," I see Morante testing the limits of fantasy, of the illusions that sustain the characters and ultimately generate the text itself. Like her biblical namesake, Giuditta has been an "eroina" (heroine) in her rebellion and flight from Palermo; and though she is in fact only a member of the *corps de ballet*, she reigns as an unquestioned "primadonna" and "stella" (star) in her home for Laura and Andrea (Morante, *Opere* 1, 1529).

Judith Butler observes in regards to gender identity in her seminal essay "Performative Acts and Gender Constitution: An Essay in Phenomenology and Feminist Theory" that there must be an element of cooperation from the audience for a performative act—in her argument, an act constitutive of gender—to succeed (Butler 519).[11] And in her probing of the theatrical aspects of performative gender theory, Butler imagines what would happen if a theatrical performance were to be exposed in public: "On the street or in the bus, the act becomes dangerous, if it does, precisely because there are no theatrical conventions to delimit the purely imaginary character of the act, indeed, on the street or in the bus, there is no presumption that the act is distinct from a reality; the disquieting effect of the act is that there are no conventions that facilitate making this separation" (Butler 527). Morante imaginatively writes such transgressions into "Lo scialle andaluso" with Giuditta and Andrea; and additionally, with Giuditta onstage, she dramatically explores what happens to a would-be performative act when its audience denies its validity.

With Giuditta's disgrace, Morante finds the point where fantasy's power to transform reality ends, where for her, the border between performace and performativity is fixed. After "Lo scialle andaluso," Morante's experiment in dramatically exposing the secret, creative spaces harboring the fantasies central to her narrative from "Il gioco segreto" onward, ends and is not repeated. Even the emblem of the theater in "Lo scialle andaluso," the titular Andalusian shawl, turns out to be a costume that conceals.

On a related note, in his description of literary *ebraismo*, the Jewish roots of writers such as Morante, Luca De Angelis argues that one must explore "la cosmografia interiore dello scrittore ebreo occidentale, che si delinea essenzialmente come qualcosa di riposto, di celato con riserbo" ("Come un amore illecito" 15; "the interior cosmography of the Jewish writer of the West, that is defined essentially as something hidden, concealed with reserve"). De Angelis's insight evokes the cosmographic and heavenly aspects of "Lo scialle andaluso," from Andrea's embrace of religion to Giuditta's dreams of the stage, "che era stato sempre il suo Paradiso" (Morante, *Opere* 1, 1529; "which she had always regarded as her paradise" [Morante, "Andalusian" 11]).

I propose that this Morantian cosmography, in conjunction with the missing letters of "T ATR GLORIA," and the importance of private space, provide a framework for considering Morante's *ebraismo* (sometimes termed *ebraicità* or *ebraitudine* by critics). Apart from Morante's early story "Il ladro dei lumi" (The Thief of the Lights), *La Storia*'s Holocaust content,[12] and, as Sergio Parussa observes, some cabbalistic aspects of *Aracoeli*, it is quite difficult to pinpoint *ebraismo* in Morante's work. In other words, it is hard to determine how, if at all, Morante expresses her Jewish origins in her work. One might recall the elusiveness of Giorgio Bassani's phrase "qualcosa di più intimo" (something more intimate) in reference to this question of "Jewishness" in literature (341).[13] Gandolfo Cascio has attempted to define Morante's *ebraitudine*, proposing an aesthetics that he maps to Apollonian-Christian and saturnine-Jewish archetypes in the 1963 collection *Lo scialle andaluso*. Yet he reaches an ambivalent conclusion regarding Morante's characters nonetheless (Cascio 44–45). To me, "Lo scialle andaluso" suggests that Morante's *ebraismo* is characterized by reticence, complex play, ambiguity, and also recognition of one's self in others, as with Andrea's vision of the Ursa Major constellation. Whereas Arturo's star is among the brightest in the sky, Giuditta's star shines most brilliantly for herself, for Laura, and for Andrea—a private constellation, the last traces of a myth. Giuditta's failure to achieve glory anticipates *L'isola di Arturo*, in which the convict Stella (note the name) declares that Wilhelm Gerace, Arturo's father, is a parody (Morante, *L'isola* 339). Like Wilhelm, Giuditta is a parody of a star.

With these missing letters of "T ATR GLORIA" I conclude my observations on "Lo scialle andaluso." Esther Zago has argued that the word T ATR—while extremely important in revealing the contrast between illusion and reality with its dilapidated sign—is a mere jumble of letters that do not make sense and further Andrea's disappointment (35). In contrast, I see "T ATR GLORIA" as an enticing invitation to join in the fantastical yet fragile play of identities and desires that Giuditta embodies, as the reader must fill in the missing letters to fully understand the sign. The enchantment, the allure, and the deception of the theater are conveyed by this sign, whose meaning is not necessarily pejorative. The fragmentary sign sums up the experiment in Morantian poetics that "Lo scialle andaluso" represents: something more intimate must be conserved and withheld. Finally, this sign reminds us that in Morante's oeuvre, the question of *ebraismo* remains an intriguing riddle, undecipherable or bordering on illegible, like "T ATR GLORIA."

NOTES

1. Translated into English as *House of Liars*.
2. Translated into English as *Arturo's Island*.
3. More recently, Gandolfo Cascio has seconded Garboli, writing that the collection of *Lo scialle andaluso* "può considerarsi come l'anello di congiunzione" (40; "can be considered as the joining link") between *Menzogna e sortilegio* and *L'isola di Arturo*.
4. This story has not been published in English to the best of my knowledge.
5. Gisela Pankow has paralleled "La nonna" with "Lo scialle andaluso," noting in both what she terms a "fusion" between mother and child.
6. All translations are my own, unless otherwise noted.
7. These are my observations from examining the manuscript in 2007. For a thorough comparison of this manuscript to the published version of "Lo scialle andaluso," see Pallagrosi.
8. Esther Zago is quite correct to point out the importance of print characters and punctuation in "Lo scialle andaluso" as echoing the characters' grandiose dreams—she highlights the capitalization of T ATR GLORIA (35–39).
9. This story has not been published in English.
10. See Cale-Knezevic (135) for her discussion of these dichotomies.
11. Butler writes that gender identity is "tenuously constituted in time—an identity instituted through a stylized repetition of acts. Further, gender is instituted through the stylization of the body and, hence, must be understood as the mundane way in which bodily gestures, movements, and enactments of various kinds constitute the illusion of an abiding gendered self.

This formulation moves the conception of gender off the ground of a substantial model of identity to one that requires a conception of a constituted social temporality. Significantly, if gender is instituted through acts which are internally discontinuous, then the appearance of substance is precisely that, a constructed identity, a performative accomplishment which the mundane social audience, including the actors themselves, come to believe and to perform in the mode of belief."

12. See Popoff (now authoring as Orsi).

13. See also De Angelis's book *Qualcosa di più intimo*, whose title is inspired by Bassani's phrase.

WORKS CITED

Bassani, Giorgio. *Opere*. Ed. Roberto Cotroneo. Milan: Meridiani Mondadori, 2001.

Butler, Judith. "Performative Acts and Gender Constitution: An Essay in Phenomenology and Feminist Theory." *Theatre Journal* 40.4 (1988): 519–31.

Cale-Knezevic, Morana. "Scialle, velo e maschere varie della vanagloria: appunti di una lettura parallela de *Lo scialle andaluso* di E. Morante e della *Glorijav* di R. Marinkovic." *Studia Romanica et Anglica Zagrabiensia* 39 (1994): 135–54.

Cascio, Gandolfo. "L'estetica dell'ebreo e del cristiano nei racconti de *Lo scialle andaluso* di Elsa Morante." *Proceedings of the International Conference: Contemporary Jewish Writers in Italy: A Generational Approach*. Raniero Speelman, Monica Jansen, and Silvia Gaiga, eds. Utrecht: Igitur, 2007. 39–45.

De Angelis, Luca. "Come un amore illecito. Sulla *Teshuvah* di Zeno." *Proceedings of the International Conference: Contemporary Jewish Writers in Italy: A Generational Approach*. Raniero Speelman, Monica Jansen, and Silvia Gaiga, eds. Utrecht: Igitur, 2007. 13–26.

———. *Qualcosa di più intimo: aspetti della scrittura ebraica del Novecento italiano, da Svevo a Bassani*. Florence: Giuntina, 2006.

Garboli, Cesare. *Il gioco segreto: nove immagini di Elsa Morante*. Milan: Adelphi, 1995.

———, and Carlo Cecchi. Cronologia. Morante, *Opere* 1, XVII–XC.

Lucamante, Stefania. "La costruzione del romanzo morantiano." *Cristallo: Rassegna di Varia Umanità* 38.1 (1996): 39–48.

Morante, Elsa. *House of Liars*. Trans. Adrienne Foulke and Andrew Chiappe. New York: Harcourt, 1951.

———. "The Andalusian Shawl." *Modern Italian Stories*. Ed. W. J. Strachan. Trans. W. J. Strachan. London: Eyre & Spottiswoode, 1955. 11–54.

———. *L'isola di Arturo: romanzo*. 1957. Turin: Einaudi, 1995.

———. *Arturo's Island*. Trans. Isabel Quigly. 1st ed. New York: Knopf, 1959.

———. *Lo scialle andaluso*. Turin: Einaudi, 1963.

———. *Opere*. Cesare Garboli and Carlo Cecchi, eds. 2 vols. Milan: Meridiani Mondadori, 1988 and 1990.

———. "La casa dei sette bambini." *Linea d'ombra* 66 (1991): 45–47.

———. *Lo scialle andaluso*. Nd. MS. V.E. 1742. Biblioteca Nazionale Centrale di Roma, Rome.

Pallagrosi, Gioia. *Nell'officina di Elsa Morante: Un'inedita redazione autografa de Lo Scialle Andaluso*. Fregene (Rome): Spolia, 2009.

Pankow, Gisela. "Les dangers de la fusion: À propos de deux nouvelles d'Elsa Morante." *Esprit* 121 (1986): 37–45.

Parussa, Sergio. "The Womb of Dreams: Cabbalistic Themes and Images in Elsa Morante's *Aracoeli*." *The Power of Disturbance: Elsa Morante's Aracoeli*. Manuele Gragnolati and Sara Fortuna, eds. London: Legenda, 2009. 130–44.

Popoff, Gabrielle Elissa. "'Once Upon a Time There Was an S.S. Officer': The Holocaust between History and Fiction in Elsa Morante's *La Storia*." *Journal of Modern Jewish Studies* 11.1 (2012): 25–38. Web.

Zago, Esther. "Il carattere di stampa come segno ne *Lo scialle andaluso* di Elsa Morante." *Il Lettore di Provincia* 23 (1991): 33–40.

Chapter Ten

Elsa Morante's Pictorial References and Ekphrasis in *Alibi*

From Carpaccio to Silvestro Lega

Gandolfo Cascio

In this chapter, I explore Morante's appropriation of some pictorial references to demonstrate that, to some extent, the images have become integrated parts, that is to say subjects of their own, and belonging to a new literary context. This comparative study reveals the Morantian dialogue with the pictorial sources and aims to a more general objective: to contribute to the debate between literature and the fine arts. In this specific case study, I speak of ekphrasis, but in a *modus* that eludes the postmodernist game of quotations and adopts, instead, some sophisticated strategies of appropriation. The recognition of the ekphrasis does not solely illustrate these visual sources, but it also contributes to emancipating Morante from her aura of a "virgin writer." Elsa Morante fiercely refused any indebtedness or degree of kindred to any writer, nor could she bear to be associated with any school or organized and programmatic movement (Morante, *Opere* 1, LXXIV); instead she favored the creation of her own myth as genius (in the literary meaning of the term) and of her solitary autogenesis.

Even though her most influential critic, Cesare Garboli, encouraged this orientation (*La stanza* 105), in more recent years it has been established that even the "barbaric and divine"[1] writer had not been spared her part of anxiety of influence. My iconographic quest, still at an embryonic stage, focuses on Morante's first poetry collection, *Alibi*, leaving aside the other books with the single, and yet specular, detour toward *L'isola di Arturo* (Arturo's Island.[2] Elsa Morante attended the Liceo classico Virgilio—a strict and prestigious Roman grammar school—where she completed a curriculum of compulsory subjects such as Italian literature, classical languages, philoso-phy, and art history. She was given, thus, the essential critical instruments to recognize and understand works of art, their makers, and to place movements in the right historical context. Further, she lived in Rome, a city brimming with masterpieces: in museums, of course, but also in many public spaces where Morante certainly did familiarize with artistic works. A clarifying example of this self-awareness can surely be her reflections included in the prose dedicated to piazza Navona. In this text, as splendid as it is potent, she argues on some aesthetic categories such as Baroque and Romanticism. Her opinion on the matter is not just based on historical data, but defines them as "a real element of nature and fantasy" (Morante, *Navona* 48).[3] In saying so, she reemploys and resumes the Nietzschean idea on the subject (Nietzsche n. 144).

After this introductory education, the young writer was able to build up a network of connections and acquaintances with many artists, with whom, not sporadically, she maintained a close and prolonged friendship. Most of these personalities, though not exclusively, were leading representatives of the so-called art group *Scuola romana*: Renato Guttuso, Carlo Levi, Giuseppe Cap-ogrossi, Corrado Cagli, Mario Schifano, Toti Scialoja, Emanuele Cavalli, Bice Brichetto, Onofrio Martinelli, and Adriana Pincherle (the latter artists are, respectively, the brother-in-law and sister of Alberto Moravia). Of a different nature were the relations that she held with Luisa Fantini, a book illustrator and "Elsa's best friend" (D. Morante, *L'amata* XI) during her first years of independence, and then—and certainly even more importantly— with the American painter Bill Morrow. Their *liaison* is not a subject of the discourse that I am moving forward in this chapter; however, it can be rele-vant to the fact that Morante was interested in fostering contemporary art. The many volumes, especially of old masters, kept in the family library at via dell'Oca 27—the Roman apartment close to piazza Del Popolo that she shared with Moravia until 1962—provide more evidence of the continuous widening and intensification of her knowledge of artistic matters—and of these books she diligently reported all bibliographic data in her notebooks (Desideri 77–85); secondly, we know Morante drew the illustrations of her first book, *Le bellissime avventure di Caterì dalla Trecciolina* (1942), with which she shows an extremely skilled hand and the capacity to set up an organized iconographic cycle. At last, we can also mention her expertise and involvement, very often decisive, in choosing the covers of her own novels (Dell'Orca).

Although these pieces of evidence can be perceived, by some, as circum-stantial, more tangible ones must be considered her critical texts on art. As a matter of fact, Morante did not dedicate much effort to this activity: she only wrote a few essays, posthumously collected in *Pro o contro la bomba atomi-ca* (1987) and actually, from the moment that she became economically independent, she quit this task, which, in her opinion, would take her mind off her constant and supreme worry: writing literature. On the other hand, Morante has never been a prolific author, at least not when we compare the relatively scarce amount of titles in her œuvre to that of some other writers, and in particular to some novelists very close to her such as Moravia, Pasolini, Ginzburg, Siciliano.

However, she did write about art. An early example is her short comment included in a survey, in which she remarks the idea of art as a necessity and as a "natural human expression" (Morante, *Morte* 277). A few years later, in one preface—in her distinctive and uncompromised manner—she solemnly stated:

> *Per varie ragioni, che credo giuste, io da gran tempo ho promesso risolutamente a me stessa (quasi un voto) di non scrivere mai prefazioni per nessuna mostra di pittura al mondo. Solo nella presente occasione, ho sentito come, astenendoni, avrei peccato peggio che non infrangendo per una volta il mio voto. E questa sarà, però, la prima e l'ultima volta; alla prossima, non potrei perdonarmi più per nessun motivo, e finirei magari dannata.* (Morante, "Presentazione")

> Because of various reasons, which I believe to be right ones, since a long time and resolutely I have promised to myself (almost like a vow) that I would never write a preface to an art exibition, none whatsoever in the entire world. Only on this occasion I felt that my abstention would have been even a greater sin than this singular infringement of my vow. However, this will be my first and last time; indeed, if I would do it again, I could never forgive myself, and I might even be damned.

The "occasion" to which Elsa Morante refers to in the above quotation is represented by the foreword meant for the exibition catalog of her friend Bice Brichetto and *in nuce* it contains and confirms some of the writer's features, such as her hyperbolic linguistic register as well as her psychological disposition. This short introduction in fact was written in 1965, and the lie is easily discovered, since Morante had already, in 1955, introduced the catalog of another friend-painter, Renato Guttuso, and—unmindful of her solemn promise, or reckless—she will do so again a few yars later, in 1968, with an essay on Onofrio Martinelli.

A longer and more complex text is the one she dedicated to Beato Angelico in 1970: *Il beato propagandista del Paradiso* for the Rizzoli series called "Classici dell'arte" where some of the masters of Western canon would be presented by some of the best-known writers of the time, in order to have a "fresh" look at art and hoping to reach a broader audience thanks to the fame of the drafters.[4]

Alibi is Morante's first poetry collection, and it was released in 1958 by Longanesi as part of a project directed by Nico Naldini in the same series as

Pier Paolo Pasolini's *L'usignolo della Chiesa cattolica* and Sandro Penna's *Croce e delizia* after which the collection was suspended. The volume consists of some preliminary remarks by the author and only sixteen texts. Some of them had already been included in previously published novels (*Menzogna e sortilegio* 1948; *L'isola di Arturo* 1957). This aspect tells us how permeable her attitude was—almost proto-postmodern—toward some literary categories as genres and their dynamics within the text. In spite of such anomalies, the philosopher and critic Giorgio Agamben considered Morante's as "one of the great post-war poetry books" (22).

Elsa Morante—an obstinate believer in the identification between life and literature—used to say that if anybody wanted to know about her life, it would be enough to read her books (Schifano, *La divina* 6). Valery Larbaud was very much in line with Morante's belief and even, if possible, more extreme: "L'essentiel de la biographie d'un écrivain consiste dans la liste des livres qu'il a lus. Tout le reste est un amalgame de faits étrangers à la littérature, fait sociaux, biologiques" (Letter; "The essential information we need to know about a writer's biography is his list of books read. All the rest is a mixture of facts unrelated to literature: they are social or biological facts"). Larbaud's conviction that books form the main cultural and spiritual structure of any writer can be agreed upon; however, to this principle, I'd like to propose a corollary. I suppose that it must be possible to add to this list a repertory of motion pictures, theatrical pieces, musical fragments. The cultural package as a whole, indeed, has more influence than the singular disciplines, and if such perspective would be advantageous to interpret any author, it most certainly can be applied to Morante's production. To support my statement, it is worth remembering that a good two painters are placed on the Cross of the " Felici Pochi " (Happy Few): Giovanni Bellini and Rembrandt (Morante, *Opere* 2, 140), while in her own words Morante in an interview to Virduzzo (1961) refers to Mozart as her only and unique *Maître* (Morante, *Opere* 1, LXXIV). It also is interesting to mention that in 1937 Morante published a short story, *Due sposi molto giovani* (1937) which, as Dell'Orca suggests, is a portrait of Vincent van Gogh, an artist that Morante knew well (Dell'Orca 100). The Dutch painter and Beato Angelico belong, even with different artistic results, to a category of realistic painters. If this aesthetical concept can easily be understood regarding Van Gogh, in order to do so for the *Quattrocento* painter we have to quote Morante's commentary:

> *La proprietà sacrosanta e preziosa degli idioti—la loro cultura stupenda, la poesia popolare—è in quei giorni una creatura viva, respirante, piena di grazia e di salute. Le storie straordinare che essa fornisce al Beato (fortunato) riferiscono la perfetta realtà della natura, più vera di qualsiasi "realtà" storica* (Morante, *Opere* 2, 1566).

The sacrosanct and precious quality of the idiots, their marvelous culture, the folk poetry—is in those days a living creature, breathing, full of grace and welfare. The extraodinary tales that it provides to Beato Angelico (the lucky one) do report the perfect reality of nature, more authentic than any historical "reality."

Morante—reconciling her ideas with a Dostoevskian creed—underlines some peculiarities such as the deeper simplicity and complete moral tension between art and life: elements that suggest a *correspondance d'idées* and are to be found in full in her own poetics. For these reasons, I tend to disagree with Cesare Garboli, who, instead, stated that Morante's *Wahlverwandts-chaften* had to be found in "strong, dramatic, but sublime [painters]" (*Scritti* 162). Angelico is undoubtedly an artist we can include in this category, however his status is accomplished because of his seraphic translations of divine episodes, and not because of any applied *drâma* as Aristotelian precept. After all, within Beato Angelico's images, Morante's main interest and concern remain the linguistic aspect, not intended in its communicative role but as aesthetical (and thus ethical)[5] results and implications: "La povera mia (nostra) lingua materna è cresciuta nella fabbrica deformante delle città degradate. . . . Come potrà, dunque, una nel mio-nostro stato, non dico capire, ma perdonare quella lingua beata e angelica? (Morante, *Opere* 2, 1558; "My poor [our] mother-tongue has grown in the disforming factory of our degraded cities. . . . And if to understand such a blissful and angelic language is impossible, how can, therefore, one person in my-our state, at least forgive it?"). This kind of choice is more in line with Morante's poetics, exclusively based on the ideas of realism. Her poetics should be considered both as Auerbachian praxis, as well as—in its eschatologic concerns—the *"opposite to disintegration"* (Morante, *Opere* 2, 1542; emphasis original). In accordance with this stylistic methodology, I consider an even more complex hermeneutic interpretation of the phenomenology as an epiphany based on the hermeneutic circle where, eventually, the ideas expressed on Angelico can be experienced as a medium to an original exegesis of Morante's literary production. After all, coherence to realism can be experienced in all her work; in fact, in *Alibi*'s poems can be found pictorial references that are the result of ekphrasis based upon "un-dramatic" works of art, while some other examples can be experienced as suggestions or, in Leopardian terms, imitations. Both cases underscore the relevance of Morante's productive relation with the fine arts.

   A first example can be found in *Poesia per Saruzza* (Poem to Saruzza). It is the second poem of the collection, and in the first edition it is dated 1943. In verses 2–6 of the fourth stanza we can read this description:

> *Canaria bella volavi*
> *a questo nido.*

Dolce manina frugavi
fra queste foglie.
Gemma arancione t'accendevi
sul calcinato muro. (Morante, *Opere* 1, 1377)

Beautiful canary you used to fly
to this nest.
Sweet little hand you searched
amongst these leaves.
Orange gem, you kindled
on the calcined wall.

Consequently, while the "Orange gem" can be seen as an adequate embel-
lishment of the background (the "calcined wall" of Montalian and Pennian
authority),[6] a few elements devoid of a merely decorative purpose surround
the portrait of the girl. For instance, the hand and the female canary are
elements of a narrative sequence, since in both cases we have a verb denoting
movement that enables the scene to take action. I propose that, if the diegetic
description might be based on the memory of a personal experience, the stage
designing surely shows without any doubt a great debt to Silvestro Lega's
First Pain.[7]

Lettera (Letter), dated 1946, is the sixth poem of *Alibi*. Here, in the last
verse of the second stanza Morante refers to the "Gates of Paradise," which,
apart from being a popular expression, can be interpreted as a reference to
Ghiberti's masterpiece in the east door of the baptistery of the Santa Maria
del Fiore dome in Florence.

In *Canto per il gatto Alvaro* (Song to the Cat Called Alvaro) Morante
talks to the cat, and she describes him in action: "ma la camera tua là rimane,
/ e nella mia terrestre fugace passi / giocante pellegrino" (Morante, *Opere* 1,
1386, "but your room is over there, / and in my terrestrial you pass by
fleeting / playful pilgrim"). Unlike the latter poem, we cannot use the term
ekphrasis, as this is more a kind of echo or reminiscence of another fairly
popular image as is the *Recanati Annunciation* by Lorenzo Lotto.[8] The painting presents a cat fleeing from one side of the room to the other because it
has felt the presence of the supernatural (the archangel Gabriel). Morante,
who uses the *present* participle, "giocante," and the syntagm "fugace passi"
uses a strategy of identification between her and Alvaro (both have been
citizens of the "barbaric Paradise") just like Lotto makes Maria's fright coincide with the feeling experienced by her own and nameless cat.

Avventura (Adventure) is dated 1948 and, with the eponymous poem
Alibi, is positioned in the very middle of the collection. Together they consi-
tute a perfect pendant as far as themes and stylistic solutions are concerned
and establish a strong base to learn how to interpret the text as specimen of
Morante's poetics on Love. The poem has probably been written for R. T. M.
(a certain Richard), an English aristocrat who lived in Rome in the 1930s and

with whom Elsa had an intense love relation (D. Morante, *L'amata* 75). The two met again in 1948 during a trip Morante took with Moravia.

In my current research, I also study the possibility of the presence of Vittore Carpaccio as source in Morante's lyrical œuvre. Because of some biographical and iconographic references, a direct link can be outlined between the Venetian painter and the Roman writer. Particularly interesting in this respect are the *telèro Meeting of the Betrothed Couple and the Departure of the Pilgrims*,[9] the fifth panel of the *St. Orsola's Stories*, and the *Vision of St. Augustine in His Study*,[10] the first *telèro* describing the lives of George, Jerome, and Tryphon, made for the guild of the Dalmatians (i.e., *Schiavoni*). The iconographic interpretation of the episodes represented in the Renaissance cycle and their allegorical interpretion and adaptation in the Morantian poem support my intuition. A second reason is stylistic, based on the fact that both types of representation, the pictorial and the lyrical, are structured on a potent narrative architecture. My study finds evidence in some *figurae* that cointain a more convincing pattern between *Avventura* and some Carpaccian subjects. If we look at another of the seven panels, *St. George and the Dragon*,[11] we can see that it shows the first of the three episodes dedicated to St. George. In this painting, the main event in the saint's life is represented: while on his riding horse, he pierces the dragon's head in the presence of a praying princess. Apart from the fact that St. George is the patron saint of England and R. T. M./Richard was English, we also know how concerned Elsa's fictional counterpart Elisa was with the lives of saints (Morante, *Opere* 1, 16).

In this *teléro*, however, we have some concrete iconographic elements that can be associated with the verses with the invocation for some help: "(ah, San Michele e San Giorgio, datemi il vostro scudo!) / per notti occhiute, selve purpuree, / dove incontrare potrò centauri e ippogrifi (Morante, *Opere* 1, 1389–90; "[ah! Saint Michael and Saint George, give me your shield!] / for these many-eyed nights, for this purple forest, / where I could meet centaurs and hippogriffs"). The shield, the dragon, and the hippogriff are a comprehensive part of the attributes of the saint; nevertheless, in the following verses Morante also describes the walls of Sodoma, and in doing so she mentiones "sette torri merlate" (seven battlemented towers) that correspond to the ones Carpaccio depicted on the left side of the painting. Morante, indeed, does not only apply the strategy of ekphrasis for the landscape and the architectural elements but the pictorial diegesis as well, a choice that brings her to imitate the high linguistic register of Arthurian tradition of Carpaccio's version of the legend.

The second and perhaps most convincing proof of the role of Vittore Carpaccio as source of Morante's poetry is the painting now called *Two Venetian Ladies*,[12] originally a quarter of a greater work. In recent times, namely when Morante wrote her elegy, it was believed that it portrayed two courtesans waiting for the sun to complete the operation of bleaching their hair. Morante describes the scene in the piece of poetry entitled *Alibi*. It is quite a long text; written in 1955, it was first published in 1957 in "Tempo presente." Most likely, the poem was inspired by Luchino Visconti (with whom she had an affair), or, as Garboli suggests, it was dedicated to "an imaginary boy-child" ("Prefazione" 19) and, adds Bardini, of a Melvillian origin (182–83). These are the verses where Morante, according to my reading, orthodoxly employed the strategy of ekphrasis: "Tu eri la dogaressa che scioglie al sole i capelli / purpurei, sull'alto terrazzo, fra duomi e stendardi" (Morante, *Opere* 1, 1393; "You were the doge's wife who in the sun lets her purple / hair down, on the high terrace, among domes and banners"). In both cases, the picture and the poem, the main character is on a terrace overlooking the lagoon, and Morante makes sure we know that she is (intimately) related to Venice, naming the girl "the doge's wife." Morante's strategy in the ekphrasis features an intense use of stylistic patterns, such as the continous switch from the masculine to the feminine pronoun[13] when she compares her lover either to magnificent heroes, or to the most common personae. In doing so, Morante continues to adopt a strategy based on the teachings of realism, since she presents to us, on the same stage and the same hierarchy, the whole spectrum of humanity. This forms a perfect synecdoche, since her beloved boy, by turns, corresponds to a variety of literary, and yet actual, presences: the Dioscuri, King Arthur, Alexander, Nisus, a Chinese princess, or Juliet, but also an anonymous page, a sailor or even a "poor pickpocket." In fact, the recollection of Neapolitan streets and cats owes a large debt to Caravaggio and Murillo, artists easy to meet with in Rome and whose poetics are so very close to Morante's.

I have already mentioned how some of the poems of the *Alibi* collection had already been included in her published novels. Morante's use of the literary strategy of repetition relates to one of my last points, which I exemplify by concentrating on one paradigmatic verse: "Tu eri l'incarcerato a cui si fan servi gli sbirri" (Morante, *Opere* 1, 1393; "You were the imprisoned for whom the cops become servants"). The poem "Alibi" was written in the same years when Morante was working on her novel *L'isola di Arturo*, and in this period Michelangelo's work, both the plastic as well as the lyrical, was a source of fascination for her. I have previously documented my findings on this subject (Cascio, "La prima"); however, the verse quoted above can be useful also in this essay because, besides being a proof of the usage of the the strategy of repetition, it also recalls an image taken from Michelangelo. The line, indeed, reflects the personal situation between Wilhelm, Arturo's father, and Tonino Stella, Wilhelm's young lover who has been imprisoned and to whom he is submitted. The verse, thus, reflects in a very concise manner the episode narrated in the novel: but what is prescient to us now is to see how such a repetition gives form to a reinterpretation of the text and, really, re-creates it anew. I have identified the reference to Michelangelo (this time Garboli had seen it right, since Michelangelo is a strong, dramatic, and sublime artist) in the *Dying Slave*.[14]

Tonino in *L'isola di Arturo* and Luchino Visconti in *Alibi* are the very same character (literary, not biographically), and they embody the real personification of the Michelangelo-esque statue. In doing so, Morante, perhaps, even breaks the rules of the descriptive ekphrasis, since her portrait is not a mere account of the slave, but an appropriation of it into the living body of Tonino/Luchino:

> *M'ispirava odio la sagoma del suo corpo, alto, bene sviluppato, e nel quale la muscolatura, che non pareva aver sofferto della prigionia, risaltava ai movimenti. E le sue spalle. E il collo robusto, che portava fieramente il capo (modellato con una grazia intrepida, nella sua pallidezza di prigioniero). E i bei capelli mori, tagliati con cura e fanciulleschi, dall'attaccatura piuttosto bassa sulla fronte, come nelle sculture. . . . Non c'era nemmeno un tratto, un gesto, in lui, che potesse indurmi al perdono.*
>
> *I suoi occhi, in ombra sotto le orbite incavate, dagli incolti sopraccigli, avevano una maniera sdegnosa, tracotante e sorniona di non guardare l'interlocutore direttamente, ma di sbieco. La sua bocca, dura e bella, nel sorriso non dischiudeva i labbri, limitandosi a sollevarli un poco da una parte, in una specie di brutalità allusiva; come se un vero, gentile sorriso disdicesse con la sua virilità. E sul mento aveva, appena accennata, una fossetta, che aggiungeva ancora risolutezza e ardimento alla sua espressione.* (Morante, *Opere* 1, 1308–9)

> I remember my conversation with him in a haze of hatred. I hated the shape of his tall, well-developed body, of his muscles, which seemed quite unspoiled by imprisonment, and which showed when he moved. I hated his shoulders, and the strong neck that carried his head proudly, and the head itself, which, pale as it was from prison, was modeled with fearless beauty. I hated his splendid dark hair, which was carefully and childishly shaped to hang rather low on his forehead, as if sculpted. . . . There was not a single feature or movement that could make me forgive him.
>
> His deep-set, shadowed eyes looked scornfully, haughtily, and at the same time slyly out from under thick eyebrows; he never looked directly at the person talking to him, but sidelong, as it were. When he smiled, his hard, beautiful lips never parted; one corner of his mouth lifted slightly with a sort of suggestive coarseness, as if a proper, kindly smile would detract from his manhood. And his chin was very faintly cleft, which made his expression still tougher and harder. (Morante, *Arturo's Island* 300).

If these are the pragmatic epiphanies of the (re)use of Michelangelo's icon, the ontological question is: Why did Morante turn to ekphrasis, here in *Alibi* as elsewhere? My hypothesis is that she made this choice because ekphrasis is the perfect rhetorical device in order to carry out her humanistic consciousness. In doing so, I believe, she reinvigorates the Horatian manner of "Ut pictura poësis." Besides, her procedure is used to intertwine genres and disciplines, and becomes the reflection on the possibility of reinventing languages as well as linguistic registers, since her hidden icons form a "vintage" diegesis into the structure of the book. In other words, she has succeeded in performing an extraordinarily sophisticated exercise of inter-semiotic translation. Thus, Elsa Morante's intent of transporting Carpaccio's and Lega's pictures into her book is the concrete implementation of her alibi: not in the common meaning of *pretext*, but in its philologically correct sense of "elsewhere." The ambition of the lyrical expression, thus, based on the perception of idols (here in the Lucretian meaning of *eidola* as simulacra) who, actually, have residence somewhere else than in the existential hic et nunc, turns to an hermeneutic instrument for (re)composing the world, its shapes, and its reality: that is to say, the perpetual and intrinsic Chaos that everyone can perceive outside and within our flesh.

NOTES

1. I take the expression from Schifano's *Barbara e divina*.
2. Morantian studies have not developed toward interdisciplinary intertexuality. To my knowledge, on this subject the only available work is Vannocci's. I do hope that my study will encourage more research toward these matters.
3. English translations are my own, with the exception of the one from *Arturo's Island*.
4. Among these volumes, of particular interest are the binomial Michelangelo/Quasimodo (1966); Da Messina/Sciascia (1967); Masaccio/Volponi (1968); Toulouse-Lautrec/ Caproni (1977).
5. For a correspondence between ethics and style, see Rasy.
6. The same syntagm can be found in Eugenio Montale's "Non chiederci la parola" (29) and Penna's "Il treno tarderà di almeno un'ora" (168). For more in-depth references, see my study "Elsa Morante, poetessa."
7. Silvestro Lega, *First Pain*, 1863, Palazzo della Provincia, Genoa.
8. Lorenzo Lotto, *Recanati Annunciation*, c. 1534, Museo Civico di Villa Colloredo Mels, Recanati.
9. Vittore Carpaccio, *Meeting of the Betrothed Couple and the Departure of the Pilgrims*, 1495, Gallerie dell'Accademia, Venice.
10. *Vision of St. Augustin*, 1502, Scuola di San Giorgio degli Schiavoni, Venice.
11. *St. George and the Dragon*, 1502, Scuola di San Giorgio degli Schiavoni, Venice.
12. *Two Venetian Ladies*, c. 1490, Museo Correr, Venice.
13. A paraphrase that denotes a real operation of appropriation of Shakespeare's verses ("What's in a name? that which we call a rose | By any other name would smell as sweet": *Romeo and Juliet*, act II, scene 2) is apparent in Morante's lines, "What is your name? Alike the sun | it changes every hour. Are you Juliet? or are you Theodora?"
14. Michelangelo Buonarroti, *Dying Slave*, c. 1513, Louvre, Paris.

WORKS CITED

Agamben, Giorgio. "Il congedo della tragedia." *Reporter*, 7–8 (December 1985): 22.
Bardini, Marco. *Morante Elsa. Italiana. Di professione, poeta*. Pisa: Nistri-Lischi, 1999.
Cascio, Gandolfo. "Elsa Morante, poetessa." *Studi Cattolici* LVII, 623 (January 2013): 36–39.

————. "La prima perla e la prima rosa. Elsa Morante e la ricezione dei «sonetti della notte» di Michelangelo." *Un altro mondo. Omaggio a Elsa Morante (1912–2012)*. Ed. A. Motta. Foggia: Istituto d'istruzione secondaria superiore "Pietro Giannone," 2012. 209–28.

Dell'Orca, Alessia. "Le illustrazioni di copertina dei romanzi di Elsa Morante." Zagra and Buttò 87–100.

Desideri, Laura. "I libri di Elsa." Zagra and Buttò 77–85.

Garboli, Cesare. *La stanza separata*. Milan: Scheiwiller, 2008.

————. *Scritti servili*. Turin: Einaudi, 1989.

————. "Prefazione." Morante, *Alibi* 7–24. Milan: Garzanti, 1990.

Horace. *Ars Poetica*; i.e., *Epistula ad Pisones*. 361–65.

Larbaud, Valery. "Letter to Jean Paulhan, 2 September 1930." IMEC. Fonds Valery Larbaud.

Montale, Eugenio. *Tutte le poesie*. Milan: Mondadori, 1995.

Morante, Elsa. *Alibi*. Milan: Garzanti, 1990.

————. *L'amata. Lettere di e a Elsa Morante*. Ed. Daniele Morante. Turin: Einaudi, 2012.

————. *Arturo's Island*. Trans. Isabel Quigley. South Royalton: Steerforth Press, 2002.

————. *Le bellissime avventure di Caterì dalla Trecciolina*. Turin: Einaudi, 1942.

————. "Due sposi molto giovani." 1937. *I racconti dimenticati*. Ed. Irene Babboni and Carlo Cecchi. Turin: Einaudi, 2004. 107–13.

————. "Morte della pittura?" (Report on Art, ed. A. Perilli e F. Mauri). *Almanacco Letterario Bompiani 1961*. Ed. S. Morando. Milan: Bompiani, 1960. 277.

————. "Navona mia." *Illustrazione italiana* 89 (2 February 1962): 44–49.

————. *Opere*. Ed. Cesare Garboli and Carlo Cecchi. 2 vols. Milan: Mondadori, 1988 and 1990.

————. "Presentazione." 1965. *Bice Brichetto. Dipinti e disegni 1946–2010*. Bardini 725–27.

Nietzsche, Friedrich W. "Vermischte Meinungen und Sprüche." *Umano, troppo umano*. Ed. Sossio Giametta. Milan: Adelphi, 1979–1981.

Penna, Sandro. *Poesie*. Milan: Garzanti. 1989.

Rasy, Elisabetta. "Personaggi come maschere." *Il Sole 24 Ore. Domenica* (11 September 2011).

Russo, Luigi, ed. *Il genio. Storia di una idea estetica*. Palermo: Aesthetica, 2008.

Schifano, Jean-Noël. "Barbara e divina." *L'espresso* 30, 48 (2 December 1984): 22–133.

————. "La divina barbara." *Cahiers Elsa Morante*. Schifano, J.-N. and Tjuna Notarbartolo, eds. Naples: Edizioni scientifiche italiane, 1993. 5–13.

Vannocci, Claudia. "La pinacoteca di Elisa: per uno studio dell'ipotesto figurativo." *Per Elisa: studi su Menzogna e sortilegio*. Pisa: Nistri-Lischi, 1990. 409–38.

Zagra, Giuliana, and Simonetta Buttò, eds. *Le stanze di Elsa: dentro la scrittura di Elsa Morante*. Rome: Colombo, 2006.

Chapter Eleven

Senza i conforti della religione

An Interrupted Path between Cinema and Poetic Creation

Claude Cazalé Bérard

Elsa Morante attributed a particular relevance (one might even say a strategic one) to her unfinished novel, *Senza i conforti della religione* (Without the Comfort of Religion).[1] The tormented course of her writing, the evident problems at the editorial level, the complexity of the issues involved, all certainly contributed to hampering the composition of the novel, right up to its final interruption. Notwithstanding these issues, Morante would persist in calling this novel for many years a work in progress (Cazalé Bérard, "Il romanzo in-finito").

This unfinished draft of her novel raises diverse and important issues. It provides a reference/source for the characters and situations Morante would later draw on in *Il mondo salvato dai ragazzini*, *La Storia*, and *Aracoeli*, as well as the materials and the ethical and aesthetic considerations she further elaborated in her essays "Sul romanzo," "Pro o contro la bomba atomica," and "Il beato propagandista del Paradiso."[2]

In this chapter, I address the complex link between the issues of filmmaking and poetic creation embodied by the two main characters of *Senza i conforti della religione*, the brothers Alfio and Giuseppe. Their profound relationship of affection and friendship is the very foundation of the novel, both structurally and thematically. This relationship sheds light on the turbulent interactions between cinema workers, directors, and actors, and between wealthy stardom and the *vie de bohème*, in the via Veneto of the 1950s. In her unfinished novel draft, Morante begins to develop the character of the Andalusian Aracoeli, actress and prima donna; depicts the failure of ncorcalism and of an *engagé* movie project about the Bikini nuclear tests; and finally, articulates the conflict between commercial ambitions and ethical and political motivations.

To summarize *Senza i conforti della religione*: fascinated by the heroic deeds of his brother Alfio and encouraged by him to become an artist, the young Giuseppe discovers his poetic and religious vocation thanks to divine epiphanies, which bring him closer to the mysteries of creation and to the secret language of animals. However, the unexpected death of Alfio, his idol despite his irreligiosity, diminishes his faith in the divine and signals the end of art and poetry.

In fact, Morante mirrors herself as a young poet and writer-to-be in Giuseppe, and experiments with highly original and engaging literary and artistic poetics throughout this novel.

THE UNFINISHED NOVEL[3]

Elsa Morante started writing *Senza i conforti della religione* in 1958, according to handwritten papers dated from April 16 to December 30 of that year; that is, immediately upon the completion of her second novel, *L'isola di Arturo* (1952–1957). She seems to have abandoned *Senza i conforti della religione* when she started writing *Il mondo salvato dai ragazzini*. This was probably around 1964, as the latest dates found in the surviving drafts refer to that year, although on the back cover of the first edition of *Il mondo salvato dai ragazzini* she mentions her old project:

> *Come professione o mestiere, il suo ideale sarebbe di andare in giro per le strade a fare il cantastorie; ma siccome (fra le altre difficoltà) non è capace di niente fuori che scrivere, dopo il presente libro avrebbe intenzione di pubblicarne ancora due: uno (già pronto) intitolato* Pro o contro la bomba atomica; *e un altro (in preparazione da anni) intitolato:* Senza i conforti della religione. *E poi basterà.* (Cives 52)

> Her ideal profession, or craft, would be to roam the roads as a nomadic storyteller; but since (among other problems) she is capable of nothing except of writing, after this book she wanted to publish two other ones: one titled *In Favor of, or Against, the Atomic Bomb,* which was completed; and another one (which has been in progress for several years) titled *Without the Comfort of Religion.* And that will have to do.[4]

In fact, the history of her work on *Senza i conforti della religione*—in layers of drafts, partial or complete erasures, and new, almost unintelligible drafts—is much more complicated and troubled than the above description would indicate. Several factors, which we cannot describe in detail here due to space constraints, seem to suggest on the contrary that this project possibly did proceed—together with the writing of poems—at least up until the 1970s with *La Storia* (not to mention the many connections with *Aracoeli*). Perhaps the unfinished novel even cast its shadow onto the final heartbreaking days of her life.

I will not quote here the many statements of Morante on the genesis of her work in progress. However, the different stages of the project must be defined: from a short story about a gnostic intended to be included in the collection *Lo scialle andaluso*; to a novella already entitled *Senza i conforti della religione* dealing with the death of an exuberant, flighty young man enamoured of life, to a full-blown novel drafted between 1959 and 1960 (Bardini 580–87) in which the story is split between the two main characters, the atheist and the believer, bound together yet in conflict.

Meanwhile, Morante provided her definition of the genre of the novel, in her answer published in the survey "Sul romanzo." She continued to mention *Senza i conforti della religione* in her own bibliographical notes until 1969. Finally, in 1972, while she was writing *La Storia*, she explained to Enzo Siciliano that she could not tell a story that occurred in 1953, unless she first told about the events that led to that story.

The pursuit of happiness is the central thread that leads the adolescent Giuseppe to God, due to his boundless admiration for his brother Alfio: a pursuit that his enthusiasm (in the etymological sense of divine possession) allows for mystical contemplation and poetic creation, seen as inseparable entities. But Alfio, even with all his apparent strength and invulnerability, turns out to be merely the keeper of a fragile vocation that depends on the magic of the poetic game, on cryptograms and arabesques, on the phantasmagoria of an imagination attracted by the mystery of inanimate matter and of living beings. The mystery existing in *Senza i conforti* will in the end remain inaccessible, despite the clear reminder of some passages from future Morante novels to fragments from it: "TUS: 'Tutto Uno Scherzo'" (*La Storia* 853; "It's All A Joke" [*History* 573]) reoccurs like a refrain in the song of the birds, while—in the eyes of Giuseppe—memory turns out to be misleading (all is an "imbroglio" [trick]; and "omertà" [conspiracy of silence]) so that the words appear as irredeemably degraded and indecent. That complex theme regarding the failure of language, along with the issues concerning ethics and aesthetics, will actually find its development and raison d'être in *La Storia*, and its final and desperate outcry in *Aracoeli*. Instead, when working on *Senza i conforti*, Morante is still looking for an answer, the solution to crucial existential and religious questions that haunt her, namely, the death of the innocent, the call of the divine, the meaning of language, the reasons for art , this without finding any solution.

Afterward, Morante will never again touch upon the theme of *movie/poetry*—an exuberant and optimistic component of the plot—in other works (cf. *Senza i conforti*).

CINEMA WORKERS, DIRECTORS, AND ACTORS:
VIA VENETO IN THE 1950S

In *Senza i conforti della religione*, Alfio, who made his fortune as a *borsaro nero* (black market dealer), moves to Rome, where he settles in a fancy residential area, the Parioli. There he establishes his movie production company the *Miliardo Film* (Billion Movie), with the financial support of a wealthy businessman—an allusion to the famous film producer Stefano Pittaluga?—in sumptuous yet modern offices overlooking the Excelsior Hotel. Tellingly, in the manuscript the hotel is referred to as the "Palazzo bello" (beautiful palace) or "il Palazzo fatato" (fairy palace). Giuseppe, now a teenager (celebrated as the brother of the filmmaker, and as a writer-to-be), who often visits Alfio after school, is fascinated by that enchanted world. Among the odd characters who are being kept waiting for a meeting with Alfio—whose success has made him very arrogant—are figures similar to those of popular movies of that period and characteristic of the Roman scene Morante knew so well and was intimately involved with, especially during the years when she was writing her *Cronache del cinema* (Cinema Chronicles) for RAI, the Italian National Broadcasting Corporation, from 1949 to 1951. For example, waiting for Alfio are a girl with the same dress and the same hairdo as the young girl Maria in Luchino Visconti's *Bellissima* (1951); and a character who greatly resembles the famed comedian Totò.

Directors and actors are part of Alfio's court. Though caricatured, they can be identified with some famous figures: from the old movie director of fascist propaganda movies (perhaps Carmine Gallone) to the assistant director Raimondo (a young aristocrat, finely educated, a rich man who had spent time in Hollywood, always wearing a sweater around his waist: perhaps Luchino Visconti), who mentors a young actor, Spartaco (handsome like an ancient Roman: maybe Massimo Girotti). And the movie *Spartaco* by Freda, was produced in 1953. The set designer, a loquacious and hirsute man from the Marche, named Michael ("Mic"), suggests turning the Bikini bomb tests into a movie.

This portrayal of the Roman cinematic/artistic scene becomes increasingly detailed when dealing with the actress Aracoeli Sanchez, of Andalusian origin, promoted by Alfio to *primadonna*. Her name and profession are derived from Maria Zambrano's sister, whom Elsa met in Rome in 1949, when she struck up a close friendship with her. But it is more interesting to note that certain physical and psychological traits of this Aracoeli closely foreshadow the mother of the protagonist's of Morante's last novel, also named Aracoeli. Sensual and childlike, with her girlish little black curls, Aracoeli of *Senza i conforti della religione* is very religious, and so superstitious that she adorns herself with medals and tiny holy pictures, as if they were amulets. Still very young, she is eager for male attention and easily yields to her admirers. Insatiable yet jealous, she gains among her aquaintances the bad reputation of being a lascivious and morbid person, which Giuseppe never quite understands. In fact, the manuscript acknowledges in several passages how the young man often faces a puzzle he cannot piece together.

BIKINI: PRO O CONTRO LA BOMBA ATOMICA.
(FOR OR AGAINST THE ATOMIC BOMB)

The movie project proposed by Mic—Bikini—deals with the nuclear tests in progress at that time on the Bikini Atoll, in the Marshall Islands at the Pacific Ocean. The subject Mic entertains for the film is ridiculed by Alfio ("Bikini criticava Alfio. Già il titolo è la prima fesseria. Uno magari ci va di corsa con l'idea di trovarci le ragazze in costume. . . . Che ce ne frega a noi della campagna antibomba! A Micco ci hai preso per il Congresso/ i Congressisti della pace?," *Senza i conforti* 3/4, c.182/1; "Bikini—Alfio scorned him— Even the title is rubbish. It may attract people who hope to find girls in swimsuits. . . . What do we care about the anti-bomb campaign? Hey Micco, did you take us for a pacifist organization?") and mocked by his other colleagues. Mic makes the point that it's not a matter of propaganda, but of spreading a new genre that will catch the interest of moviegoers. Alfio silences Mic, then goes on mocking him. For Alfio, the only viable alternative to neorealism is simply the production of commercial movies, specifically conceived to make money. Mic still claims that there is a duty to meet the current needs of the masses after the débacle of neorealism—and in doing so he arouses the old director's irony. At that point, Spartaco—usually silent— cuts into the argument with a seemingly random, but actually relevant question, about the role by Aracoeli, as "the bomb."

This is not just a vulgar and misogynistic joke: we should remember that starting in 1958, Bikini—which had become a nuclear firing range in 1946 after the first deadly bombs on Hiroshima and Nagasaki—was the theater of ongoing nuclear experiments with the first hydrogen bombs. Moreover, female nicknames were given to those bombs: the Able bomb was called *Gilda*, in a coarse reference to Rita Hayworth; the second, Baker, bears the nickname of *Helen of Bikini*, in a subtle allusion to the Trojan war and to that explosive mixture of seduction and destruction that patriarchy attributes to women as a great privilege.

Morante pays attention to the current events determining her time, and she desperately cares about social issues just as much as oppressive powers around the world. Another interesting event that may have influenced her choice of the theme of *Bikini* is the 1959 release of Stanley Kramer's movie *On the Beach* in New York. At that time, Morante was in town for an extended stay. Starring Gregory Peck, Ava Gardner, Anthony Perkins, and

Fred Astaire, the movie depicts the end of the human race after a nuclear third world war, and the final journey of an American submarine hosting the few survivors. The cinematographer for *On the Beach*—a specialist in black and white—was the famous Giuseppe Rotunno (same name and initials of Giuseppe Ramundo) who also worked with the greatest film directors of Cinecittà: Vittorio De Sica, Federico Fellini, Luchino Visconti.

As the reader may know, Morante would return to the topic of the atomic bomb with the 1965 lecture she gave at the Teatro Carignano in Turin; the text of her lecture was published posthumously in *Pro o contro la bomba atomica*. Since we cannot devote enough time here to this fierce pamphlet, it should at least be noted that, for her, only art and poetry could prevent the self-destruction of mankind and its tragic and ultimate disintegration.

On the other hand, in *Senza i conforti della religione*, the producer Alfio opposes any innovative project that is not commercially profitable—he thus reflects the drift of Italian cinema during those years, due to a conservative turn in politics, an escalation of the Christian Democrat censorship, and the economic miracle: the so-called boom. Hence, in Alfio's hands, the Bikini project becomes a "bathing beauties" movie in which the *last* beach becomes assimilated to the then-in-vogue Ostia and Fregene. Giuseppe is absolutely taken aback and clearly shows his disapproval. By that time, nearly an adult, Giuseppe feels clearly that the mainstream mentality and the fashions of his time are progressively drifting away from his idea of art and poetry.

MOVIE PRODUCTION, POETRY CREATION

Even if his brother is gradually lapsing into vulgarity, endowed with "una grossezza maschia, da uomo arrivato, rivestiva ormai vistosamente la sua muscolatura" (*Senza i conforti* 3/4, c.185/1 "a manly coarseness—that of a successful man—now patently coated his muscles"), Giuseppe still feels a strong and lively affection for his brother. He often refers to Alfio as "il mio doppio luminoso" (my luminous double); "il mio riscatto contro la solitu-dine" (my redemption from loneliness); "la mia felicità" (my happiness), so much so as to consider his "vanti fraterni e terrestri" (brotherly and wordly qualities) as "un simbolo terreno" (a wordly sign) of his God.

In those very poetic pages, one cannot but think of the concurrent oriental phantasmagoria of *Alibi* (1958) and *La sera domenicale* in *Il mondo salvato dai ragazzini*—a later yet tragic work. The writer-to-be (but possibly also a budding journalist and film critic) proudly mentored by Alfio in order to promote the *Miliardo Film*, is a poet, "il poeta Ramundo Giuseppe," who jealously protects the secret of the divine epiphanies that mysteriously feed his mystical and pantheistic vein. On one occasion, managing to overcome his reluctance to confide in anybody—in a trip by car with Alfio—Giuseppe declaims some of his verses "con voce titubante dall'emozione" (his voice wavering with emotion). His naturalistic inspiration, in which nature becomes an epiphany of the sacred, cannot but evoke Saba. Especially if we take into account that Giuseppe not only finds the presence of the divine in the humblest animals—just as the Triestine poet did—but that he also interprets the language of the birds he meets in the little valley, an idyllic and meditative refuge, along the banks of the Tiber: "io facevo il poeta dalla mattina alla sera" (I was a poet from morning until evening).

But it is worthwhile to consider further the dialogue between the two brothers that clearly shows, besides their affectionate complicity, the distance that has grown between them (*Senza i conforti* 3/4, cc. 48–49/2). These were the years of the full-blown myth of Hollywood, of the fame of ambiguous figures in newspapers and cinema, like the billionaire and movie producer Howard Hughes, for American producers were relying on Cinecittà studios as an inexpensive and quite apt space for film production. Postwar Rome had two virtues for them: inexpensive labor and ideal locations for historical colossals. Actually, the dialogue between Alfio and Giuseppe underscores a marked disparity between two ideals of art and culture: the commercial and the one seeking eternal and universal truths (the latter defended by Morante in "Il poeta di tutta la vita," "Sul romanzo," and "Il beato propagandista del Paradiso"). Giuseppe's dream mirrors in part also Morante's. She was, in fact, also tempted by success and celebrity in her American adventure.

In truth, Giuseppe—who speaks for Elsa—embodies the very figure of a poet who transforms his existential and cognitive adventure, led by "una suprema attenzione—senza nessun giudizio—in un valore per il mondo" (Morante, "Sul romanzo" 44–45; "a supreme attention—without a judgment—in a value for the world"). In his poetic quest, Giuseppe succeeds in expressing his own experience of the divine as the very ground of any language.

THE END OF POETRY

When Alfio dies, Giuseppe renounces his secret religion and poetry, since both have lost their raison d'être, their source: the great love for his brother, and thus, any possible happiness. Giuseppe—finally alone and hopeless like Hamlet—says that perhaps alienation is the only remaining option. But—with these words—we suddenly find ourselves with desperate Davide Segre in *La Storia*, and with the tragically unsuccessful Manuele in *Aracoeli*.

The interrupted novel *Senza i conforti della religione* with its prophetic title anticipates clearly the tragic result Morante achieves in her last novel, as I concluded many years ago:

If the end of History is a tragic collapse of a world already condemned, after Hiroshima, to a perennial threat of atomic destruction, no less so is that of *Aracoeli*, in spite of the child Manuele's preference for stories with happy endings. By this point we know that heroes can die (Superman and Messia can fail), if the luminous Arturo has left for the war, if Davide Segre is reduced to a suicidal executioner, if Manuel Muñoz Muñoz is dead without glory and without redemption in spite of the "postcard from Heaven" and the promise of Christ on the cross ("Tomorrow you will be with me in Paradise"), after all of these signs have been revealed as bewitching and lying! [. . .] In reality Morante wants to denounce, with her last works—and above all with *Aracoeli*—in the most radical and atrocious manner, the absence and even the withdrawal of a God the Father. ("Morante and Weil" 158–59)

NOTES

1. Unless otherwise noted, all translations are mine.
2. This interrupted novel confirms the extraordinary continuity in Morante's entire production, beginning with the earliest youthful trials: a central thread—the religious *quête*—unites fables, stories, essays, and novels through *Aracoeli*. As I stated in a previous study, "[T]his last novel brings to maturation the themes, figures, narrative, and metanarrative procedures which appear in the first stirrings of the author's creative *iter*, thus offering a complete vision of life and of the world which integrates the painful stages of the quest for knowledge and love, never separated in Morante's oeuvre" (Cazalé Bérard, "Morante and Weil" 145).
3. The unpublished manuscript is held at Biblioteca Nazionale di Roma in the Fondo Morante. I'm grateful to Giuliana Zagra and Leonardo Lattarulo for their full support and help.
4. It should be noted how much *Pro o contro la bomba atomica* and *Senza i conforti* are linked and perhaps near to each other, not only in terms of time.

WORKS CITED

Bardini, Marco. *Morante Elsa. Italiana. Di professione, poeta.* Pisa: Nistri-Lischi, 1999.
Cazalé Bérard, Claude. "Il romanzo in-finito." *Testo e Senso* 13 (2012). Web.
———. "Morante and Weil: The Aporiae of History and the End of the Fairy Tale." *The Power of Disturbance. Elsa Morante's Aracoeli.* Manuele Gragnolati and Sara Fortuna, eds. London: Legenda, 2009. 145–60.
Cives, Simona. "Elsa Morante 'Senza i conforti della religione.'" *Le stanze di Elsa. Dentro la scrittura di Elsa Morante.* Giuliana Zagra and Simonetta Buttò, eds. Rome: Colombo, 2006. 49–65.
Morante, Elsa. *History: A Novel.* Trans William Weaver. South Royalton, VT: Steerforth Italia, 2000.
———. "Il beato propagandista del Paradiso." Morante, *Pro o contro* 119–38.
———. "Il poeta di tutta la vita." Morante, *Pro o contro* 31–40.
———. *La Storia: romanzo. Opere* 2. Cesare Garboli and Carlo Cecchi, eds. Milan: Meridiani Mondadori, 1990. 3–943.
———. *Pro o contro la bomba atomica e altri scritti.* Milan: Adelphi, 1987.
———. *Senza i conforti della religione.* Nd. MS. A.R.C. 52 I. 3/4, cc. 48–49/2; 182/1; 185/1, Biblioteca nazionale centrale di Roma, Rome.
———. "Sul romanzo." Morante, *Pro o contro* 41–73.

Chapter Twelve

Arturo in the World of the "Pharisee Fathers"

The Cinematic Adaptation of Arturo's Island

Hanna Serkowska

Damiano Damiani's cinematic adaptation (1962) of Elsa Morante's *Arturo's Island* invites a consideration of Morante's relationship with the world of cinema, sheds light on some aspects of her cultural elitism, and furthers our understanding of the role of Pier Paolo Pasolini, poet, writer, moviemaker, and friend at that time, in Morante's life and oeuvre. In his movie, Damiani tells a story of the loss of youthful illusions by telling about Arturo who frees himself from the enigmas of the past. This chapter suggests that Morante's utopian vision, her elitist demands on the world, society, art, movie industry, and even on her friends, emerge in part from her complex and unresolved relationship with cinema, transpiring also in her relationship to Pasolini (her most evident connection to the world of cinema), along with her contempt for realism as style in art and literature.

In his movie, on the other hand, Damiani seems to share none of Morante's reservations with respect to realism in art[1] and thereby would appear to be the least appropriate choice to direct a cinematic adaptation of a novel such as *Arturo's Island* with all its oneiric, fairy-tale, fantastic ambiguity. By transforming the novel into a petty bourgeois romance expressed in the idiom of realism, Damiani presents Morante's utopian claims in a realist garb. However, I believe Damiani's adaptation comes to embody in fact some of the statements Morante expressed in her essay "Sul romanzo":

Supremi esempi di non-realismo, *di* non-impegno, *e di* evasione, *a me sembra-
no certi prodotti del realismo socialista (così nominato), o del (così nominato)*
neo-realismo *contemporaneo.*

   *Un vero romanzo, dunque, è sempre realista: anche il più favoloso! E
tanto peggio per i mediocri che non sanno riconoscere la sua realtà."* (*Opere*
2: 1502; emphasis original)

Extreme examples of *non-realism*, of *disengagement*, and of *escapism*, seem
to me certain products of *socialist realism* (so called), or of (so called) *contemporary neo-realism*.

   A real novel, then, is always realist: even the most fantastic! So much for
the mediocre ones who do not recognize reality.[2]

Damiani makes an interesting contribution to Morante's oeuvre, and his film
remains today a valuable reading of her work. After discussing Morante's
involvement with Italian cinema, and with Pier Paolo Pasolini in particular, I
present a series of in-depth readings of some of Damiani's decisions in the
movie while comparing it to Morante's novel. They concern a discussion of
the protagonists' representation as well as the symbolism and metaphors in
the novel, the most notable deviation from the novel represented in the film's
happy ending.

   A brief catalog of Morante's encounters and confrontations with the tenth
Muse would contain at least the following items:

- Morante as extra, in Pasolini's *Accattone* (1961), where she is seated on
  the floor in a women's prison, playing the silent role of an inmate called
  Lina whose face wears a lost expression.
- Her brother Marcello (as Giuseppe) and her nephew Giacomo (as Giovanni) performing roles in yet another of Pasolini's movies, *Il Vangelo secondo Matteo* (1964).
- Morante as advisor and casting consultant for the early films of Pasolini—
  whom she accused of selling his soul to the movie industry—and as a
  member of the crew on the set.[3]
- Finally, and even after she expressed her deepest contempt for moviemak-
  ers and derided Pasolini's cowardice and submissiveness, Morante continued serving as his music advisor for *Medea* (1969/70). Among the possible reasons for this relentless collaboration, which continued despite the
  fading of their friendship, was a plausible appreciation on Morante's part
  for the fact that Pasolini turned to the "cinema di poesia" along with their
  shared passion for Greek tragedy (her interest was more ethical and political, his allegorical and formal, as Siti points out) (227).

Yet another, much earlier testimony appeared recently, thanks to Marco Bardini's investigations into the archives of the Fondo Morante at the National

Library in Rome. In all probability, the document dates to the late 1930s. Morante's early interest in the cinema is confirmed by a loose page she kept among other manuscript pages, in which a "Kafkian-Pirandellian" story is told (Bardini, "Appunti" 59), as well as by her scripts, cinema projects, and outlines ("treatments"): *Il diavolo*, *Miss Italia*, and *Verranno a te sull'aure*. All these texts were conceived explicitly for the cinema and, according to Bardini, are but modest demonstrations of the experience gathered by the young writer as a moviegoer (61).

The catalog of confrontations is a more fundamental one. Only by rubbing shoulders with filmmakers, with the cinema establishment, and most of all with the hated producers, those dictators of cultural politics, could Morante form her own opinion about cinema. For a short time at the turn of the 1940s and 1950s, she reviewed movies for the RAI-Radio Televisione. Morante's assignment at the *Cronache del cinema* ended abruptly on 1 December 1951 when she resigned following an attempt to induce her to write a positive review of Lionello De Felice's movie *Senza bandiera* (*Opere* LVIII). And from her friend Pasolini she expected and in fact demanded that he distance himself from the "Pharisees," to whom, in her opinion, he was too submissive. The very expression "l'adorazione ai padri farisei" ("the adoration for the Pharisee Fathers") appeared in *Madrigale in forma di gatto*, written in 1964.[4] The text of the poem was printed inside the outline of a cat, an important symbol in Morante's secret code with the filmmaker. Its title refers to Pasolini's *Poesia in forma di rosa*, but the true motive of the *Madrigale* was a conflict with Arco Film, the first production company for Pier Paolo Pasolini's films that had failed to pay the actors, who happened to be friends and family of Elsa and had been engaged for *Il Vangelo secondo Matteo*. Instead of pressing the producer to pay the money due, Pasolini offered to pay it out of his own pocket. Indignant at her friend's cowardice, Morante addresses him with her customary outrage.[5]

As these examples show, Morante moved away from her initial attraction to the business of moviemaking (script outlines, film reviews). She became weary of the cinema following her experience at the hands of the "Pharisee Fathers"—as she called the cinema producers from Arco Film—and the RAI people who tried to force her to write a positive review of a film she had no high opinion of.

It is at that point in Morante's development that Damiani makes a realist translation of her novel and inserts in it several references to Pasolini (a cat— a recurring figure and a sign of recognition between the two authors; the story of Wilhelm's love for Stella repeating Pasolini's infatuation with Ninetto Davoli, etc.). Toward this movie Morante shows a remarkable reserve. Her contribution to the making of the film based on her novel might appear close to nil, limited to the approval of the script, as was stipulated by the contract, without suggesting any changes.[6] She appeared on the set on only a handful of occasions (and only after Damiani called and invited her to come) where she sat discreetly, silently observing the making of the movie. She made no comments, voiced no objections, other than what Damiani himself remembers as a question related to the director's choice of the actress who interpreted the role of Nunziata.[7] All characters were very important for the writer, and as we might infer from an article by Andrea Barbato,[8] she found it difficult to accept the transformation that some of them underwent in Damiani's treatment.

On the one hand, we have an artist, complete and demanding, who considers herself an aristocrat way above the ordinary people. This artist wants to be understood only by those she dubbed the *felici pochi* (happy few) in her *Il mondo salvato dai ragazzini* (The World Saved by the Children). On the other hand, we have a popular medium, cinema, that chooses the *infelici molti* (unhappy many) as its audience. On one side stands Elsa Morante, at a later stage of her life decreeing her full outrage against the state and its institutions, with all its standardization of culture. On the other are the means of communication (the mass media, radio, press, cinema), a monstrous product—as she used to call it—of the social transformation and self-advancement of the bourgeois, the middle classes, "today's fascists." And there is the filmmaker, erstwhile director of documentaries, Damiano Damiani—making his first fiction movie,[9] and about to adapt Morante's best known novel, celebrated by the Strega literary prize in 1957. No small undertaking. Clearly it is impossible to register, to cut, and edit, and finally to distribute a movie without sponsors, finances, indeed without a producer, or a "Pharisee" in Morante's terms. How then did Damiani proceed?

The cinematographic techniques and means employed by Damiani are realist:[10] the movie is made in black and white, with minimal costs, amateur actors, long theatrical takes, static camera with a preference for close-ups with the effect of creating almost portraits of the protagonists. Moreover, several dreamlike scenes are translated in the movie into plain realism, as when the dream of the protagonist at the beginning of the film is acted out in every detail when he wakes up. Also extremely realistic is the rendering of psychological and emotional developments in the characters. Realistic are the movements, gestures, facial expressions, and grimaces of the characters. Finally, plot and time structure are linear.

Damiani's film is remarkably complete in that it leaves out little from the book; on the contrary, it supplements it with scenes and meanings that expand our perspective and allow us to recognize the writer's Weltanschauung. The movie script does not modify dialogues: from the book to the movie, the words remain the words and have not undergone a cinematic—regardless of which text whether visual or verbal—translation. Arturo must learn to live in a world without transcendence, in which the meaning of sacrifice has been lost. Damiani uses these same utterances for supporting his realist plot.

The interior monologue and the internal fixed focalization of the books are rendered in the movie by a non-diegetic voice. This use of voice-over helps to see the world through the eyes of Arturo, thus meeting Morante's aim at creating a protagonist who becomes both her alter ego and an alibi: "*Arturo c'est moi*," or "*Arturo sono io*," as she confided to her French translator, Jean-Noël Schifano ("Divina Barbara" 13). It is the nature of cinema to show, rather than to tell, and the voice-over is no longer used after it has helped to invoke the Morantian point of view and Arturo's introspective mode. This, one might argue, is the function of the brief appearance of the non-diegetic voice drawing our attention to the inter-semiotic transformation with which Damiani leaves his signature. The initial and final appearances of voice-over clearly stand out and call our attention to its redundant play on the frame structure of the book.

In Damiani's film, the plot advances chronologically with no flashbacks, almost projected only toward Arturo's departure from the island. The order of presentation has been changed, from retrospective as seen in the novel to linear in the movie. We learn about Arturo's shortcomings as intrinsic to the story line, while in the novel the return to the island of his youth as grown-up protagonist—a soldier in some unspecified war now—mystifies, idealizes, and de-realizes both island and youth. The chronological presentation in the movie reinvigorates the realistic dimension and accentuates the sensation of deprivation that becomes definitive and irreparable.

Synthesis and ellipsis are present, most clearly where there are many episodes in the novel that refer to the love of Arturo for his mother who died while giving birth. These episodes are reduced to one scenic image, the one with the cross at the coast, painted on the rocks, washed over by the waves beating against the coast. We see the cross twice, first indicating Arturo's suffering from unrequited love for his father, and second when he is struck by a fit of jealousy because of his new stepmother's withheld love, conversely given to his little half brother Carmine Arturo. Moreover, we have seen him before hankering for his stepmother, fearing for her life when giving birth to Carmine. Sea and water—symbols of the womb of the mother, from which he was freed or expelled, as the mother died, make him think of the senseless savage cycle of birth and death. Arturo is thrown into a world with no God and no redeeming love. The cross, in its turn, which is not present in the novel and is here painted "in the sea," is also Damiani's homage to Morante's love for the bay of Naples.[11] Something Damiani couldn't have yet known is the epilogue to this cinematic invention written by life: the ashes of Morante would be dispersed in the bay of Naples.

What remains missing in Damiani's translation is the irreconcilability of mythical and historical worlds. Wilhelm, no longer a conqueror, is received and comforted by Nunziata in a truly realistically petty bourgeois scene. She accepts Wilhelm's return and welcomes back a man who has no one else but her to love him. In the novel, the degradation of the fatherly myth and the blows of history are compensated for by a reiteration of the mythical situation. While leaving, Arturo knows that the island will be inhabited by another Carmine Arturo who will run free and happy on the beaches. The father remains as an ideal in the distance, his absence instrumental for the son's idealization. Morante, time and again, prefers the myth to the historical or the real world, to such an extent that Arturo can live his fairy-tale childhood in the way and to the extent we see in her text. In Damiani's movie the eclipse of the fatherly myth coincides with a change of roles. The father enters into the world of the island that for him represents a prison—from which he has always kept himself distant, and he submits to the power of the woman who, now a mother, brings him to accept this detested sacrifice. Arturo, in his turn, hurries away from the island, and sees it disappear together with all his illusions. This is an important addition or change made by Damiani who, by making the story more realistic,[12] turns it into an almost petty bourgeois tale.

In the film, Morante's fascination with the act of reading—as the "romantic lie" that plays such an important role in all her works—is almost completely absent. Arturo defines his own childhood as *leggendaria*—a legendary one, in which the term refers to his growing up by way of reading (*leggere*). The novel lists a catalog of books contained in the library of the house, and suggests the Bovarian influence that reading these books had on the young boy, creating false notions of the real world and inducing a young reader to misconceived acts. Even while the "romantic lie" could help the director to create another reference to the youthful illusions felt as a burden and eventually left behind, by calling the act of reading into play, Damiani could have mislead us about his assessment of the novel. For sure, we are here dealing with barely cinematic objects, and the books are left where they belong.

Let us look now at some examples of additions to the book made in the movie. We hear a shot, maybe an echo of the faraway war. And we remember from the beginning of the movie, the voice-over saying, almost literally repeating part of Morante's character's monologue, that Arturo would prefer to be a fish that never leaves the island, rather than a seagull that flies away.[13] After the shot, however, we see in the film a dead seagull that the protagonist collects and places in an imaginary coffin on the sand. Arturo draws with his finger the form of a rectangle in the sand—a reference to the motif of his solitude expressed in the phrases "he is alone, he is terribly alone" that Morante made the boy write in the sand. The seagull unfolds a complex role. It announces the end of Wilhelm's flight (and of his disappearance from the narrative: having lost everything, no longer being able to continue his adventures, he will be confined in the island-prison). The seagull also introduces the theme of death, feared and hated (almost by way of impersonation) and the secret that Arturo tries to unravel by attempting to commit suicide. Death, with all its nothingness (with which Morante herself was so preoccupied) and which is the lethal enemy of life, is banished from the island, and we remember the poem with which the novel opens:

> *L'insegna paurosa non varcherà mai la soglia*
> *di quella isoletta celeste.*
> *E tu non saprai la legge*
> *ch'io, come tanti, imparo,*
> *—e a me ha spezzato il cuore:*
> fuori del limbo non v'è eliso. (Morante, *L'isola* 947)

> The sign of fear shall never cross the threshold
> Of that small, celestial island.
> Nor will you ever know the law
> that I, with multitudes of others, learn:
> [that law that broke my heart] [14]
> *there is no paradise except in limbo.*

Death throws a shadow over Arturo's happy youth. The silence about death is part of the second law in Arturo's secret code.

> *Nessuna delle mie leggi, voglio dire, nominava la cosa da me più odiata: e cioè, la morte. Tale reticenza era, da parte mia, un segno di eleganza e di sprezzo verso questa cosa odiata; alla quale non rimaneva che insinuarsi fra le parole delle mie leggi in modo subdolo, come un paria o una spia.*
>
> *Io, nella mia felicità naturale, scansavo tutti i miei pensieri della morte, come da una impossibile figura di vizi orrendi: ibrida, astrusa, piena di male e di vergogna. Ma nello stesso tempo, quanto più odiavo la morte, tanto più mi divertivo e mi esaltavo a far prove di audacia: anzi, nessun gioco mi piaceva abbastanza, se non c'era il fascino del rischio. (980)*

> None of my laws, I mean, mentioned the thing I most hated: death. This reticence showed my sophisticated scorn of the thing I hated, which could only creep slyly in among the words of my laws, like a pariah, like a spy.
>
> In my own natural happiness, I chased all my thoughts away from death, as if there were something impossible—a dreadful amalgam of vices, hybrid, complex, full of evil and shame. But at the same time, the more I hated death the more I exaltedly enjoyed giving proofs of my own temerity: no game was enough fun if it lacked the fascination of risk. (Morante, *Arturo's Island* 25)

A further additional motif in the novel is the procession of the Holy Week, with the preparations and the sequence of the ceremonies, from the cutting of the white lamb's throat in a pitch-dark cellar over a container, then to be disemboweled and prepared like an element of the decorations of the stage set for Easter. The violence of the ritual that perpetuates the death of the innocent, a death—we must add—that for Morante was groundless and senseless, causes disgust. The lamb is unable to resurrect, and its death offers redemption to no one. These two last elements together, the seagull and the lamb, refer back to the search for some form of transcendence, still present in this phase of Morante's oeuvre, given her sensation of the paucity of a material world deprived of all spiritual elements.

The most hazardous change is the moralizing happy ending that Damiani added, risky precisely because it might have changed the sense of it all. Morante's novel is not a parable on the return of the prodigal son (or the father, for that matter), nor is it an account of the law of revenge (an eye for an eye). When Arturo finally leaves the island, the filmmaker has Nunziata say "Don't worry, he will write us a letter," trying to console Wilhelm who is visibly unhappy about his definitive return or disembarkation on the island. The door closing behind Arturo resembles prison bars, making Nunziata into the prison guard of Wilhelm. This sentence, which does not occur in the novel and indeed would be inconceivable, brings back to mind the frustrated hope of the boy and the stepmother waiting for Wilhelm's letters. Nunziata's phrase echoes Arturo's plea to his departing father. Damiani while making this risky point, seems to also suggests to have shown a completed and coherent rendition of how events will turn out in the near future. He consoles the viewer with a magical metamorphosis: the insensitive Wilhelm is finally humiliated and punished. Instead of an eternal return to the mythical island of his youth (dreamed, imagined, heartwarming, in the novel), in the movie there is a realistic return, a return forever, of Wilhelm, not Arturo. Crime and punishment, so to say.

Yielding to popular taste, the filmmaker also reworks and overexposes the love motif. The love or rather bliss for Assunta is in Morante's novel just a short theft of an exclusively maternal love that had been transferred to the stepmother, the sexual initiation with the young woman—possibly a prostitute—and the love for Nunziata in which he buried his jealousy enraged by the kisses imprinted on the face of the little Carmine. This is replaced in Damiani's film by an all-out realistic love of a young man for his stepmother. The languishing and melodramatic good-bye from Arturo to Nunziata is accompanied by a voice-over: the love of other women will always be a love that was stolen from her.

The movie also takes up the motif of homosexuality. The secret life of Wilhelm encounters a delicate understanding and acceptance by Nunziata who resolves to love the "unfortunate Wilhelm," who has no one else but her in the whole world (she says) and who suffers from unrequited love for the man called Stella. The latter is to marry shortly, but before that, for a considerable amount of money (Wilhelm sold his garden to that end), agrees to take a last trip with Arturo's father. Stella's decision prefigures the circumstances in which Ninetto Davoli, Pier Paolo Pasolini's beloved, will abandon him for a woman whom he will marry in 1972. Morante (who modeled her homosexual protagonists on Pasolini), and Damiani for that matter, could obviously not know how the friendship of Pier Paolo with Ninetto would end. Morante's attempt to console her friend after Ninetto's flight, and also to explain that to truly love is to expect nothing in return, brought about Pasolini's infamous (he accused her of taking the side of Ninetto) outburst. [15]

Above magical realism, the mythical and the oneiric, Damiani prefers realism *tout court*. This realistic mode makes the movie into an autonomous and self-reliant work, next to the novel. The movie is both a story about the delusion that accompanies coming of age, and about the loss of youthful illusions that go together with the entrance into the world and real history, as well as about the vicissitudes of a petty bourgeois family, with its ups and downs, cheats, forgiveness, returns. Reality itself punishes those whose wishes cannot be fulfilled: Arturo who wished to be a fish, in the end leaves the island and its waters; Wilhelm, on the contrary, is forced to settle definitively on the island as despised and feared as a prison.

In this way, the movie becomes a homage also to the writer herself, because of the autobiographical elements so important in all her novels in which most characters are, as Siti rightly observes (279) trans-textual, that is, placed between literature and life. Morante, like Gustave Flaubert, distances herself from the characters on whom so much of herself has been transferred, characters in whom she resolves her own conflicts. The protagonists become the author's alibis. Like Flaubert, she achieves the moral distance through a sadistic relationship, one might say, with her heroes. First she burdens them with her own concerns, obsessions, anguishes, in order to then free herself from them, betray them, and leave them to their own destiny. Aware of the powerful autobiographical load of Morante's works, Damiani dedicates the movie to the writer also by replacing the mongrel dog Immacolatella with a cat [16] that keeps Arturo company all the time, waiting for him at home, or sitting on his lap. Moreover, as Francesca Comencini rightly notices in her documentary *Elsa Morante* (1997), Damiani's Arturo (performed by Vanni De Maigret) bears a striking resemblance to the writer's beloved American painter Bill Morrow who would die from a drug-induced tragic death in 1962.

Finally, the scene of Wilhelm's return is compassionate and appears as an attempt to make up for Morante's unfortunate family affairs. [17] Elsa Morante had dedicated her first novel *Menzogna e sortilegio* to her natural father, Francesco Lo Monaco, shortly after his alleged suicide. [18]

The triumph of Nunziata and her pure and simple heart over the degenerate Stella, and the return home of the remorseful Wilhelm—all the brilliant invention of Damiani—can be read through the prism of the rapid social change of the 1950s and 1960s: dynamic industrialization and urbanization, society that rushes too fast, according to Pasolini and Morante, toward well-being. That particular cultural and social climate with its altogether repulsive habits was perfectly represented by Damiani in the very last scenes: he lets Stella talk and thereby unmasks his meanness, himself a symbol of the vulgarity of the times, and a *homo novus*, immoral and rogue, who counts on assuring himself a happy life with the money that he cheated out of Wilhelm. For a short moment, and for the last time, and only in the world of celluloid, the world of traditional values could prevail, the (southern) rural civility. The world of the mothers could triumph over the expansive urban sociability that was in fact winning out as represented by social parasites like Stella. An ingenious happy ending consoles us: the repentance of Wilhelm, the fall of Stella from the Eden of the island, and the victory of Nunziata. The *Isola di Arturo* of Damiani thus is in part a story about the loss of illusions and in part about the possibility of keeping them.

Damiani thus illustrates—in a way comprehensible to viewers—Morante's utopian nostalgia. His "rewriting" of the plot helps us to understand not only this specific novel of the writer but also her artistic endeavor at large, and is at the same time a notable attempt to reestablish a connection between poetry and cinema, which Morante dissected in the dismembered manuscript of *Without the Comfort of Religion*. Paradoxically, we encounter Morante's "poetry" in the world of cinema.

NOTES

1. Peter Bondanella in *A History of Italian Cinema* describes realism in Italian cinema as follows: "often progressive or leftist ideological content, its use of non professional actors or the documentary quality of its photography"; "reverence for everyday reality" "focus upon the actual 'duration' of real time" (62).

2. Unless otherwise noted, all translations are mine.

3. Morante's *Aracoeli* was thoroughly inspired by the cinema and informed by its techniques and structures—and was considered a homage to her then late friend Pasolini. In his contribution to *Festa per Elsa*, Ninetto Davoli recalls that Morante made frequent comments on Pasolini's film: "On the films of Pier Paolo she was equally objective; she told him explicitly: 'I like this, I don't like that'. . . . And Pier Paolo would then explain saying 'Consider that this is so for this and that reason.' But she was not convinced and repeated 'I like this, I don't like that'" (86).

4. The text of this poem was first published by Nico Naldini in *Pier Paolo Pasolini, Lettere 1955–75* (lxxxiv–xc). As Walter Siti explains, the text of Morante's poem, contained within the calligram of a cat and signed "a cat that doesn't die," makes an allusion to Pasolini defining him precisely as "un gatto che non crepa" in "A desperate vitality." "The partly fatuous, partly revealing, game of the reciprocal mirror images, of the elective brotherhood between the artist and Morante, begins in this period" (275).

5. "It is clearly utopian to expect a similar respect from those filthy morons of Arco Film, not to say stupid, because they only look up to shit (that is exactly those few miserable Lire that you mention). Therefore I had wanted you, with your authority, to make them put at least their beak into their own shit, at least for a moment, and make them ashamed at least of their own shit, etc. etc. [. . .] During the final days I myself began at a certain moment to smell, because I was drawing the big picture of the structures of Arco Film, and finally I couldn't stand it any longer. Perhaps I cannot any longer. And you know very well that paying out of your pocket (or out of mine for that matter) doesn't mean anything here, because those people at Arco Film do not want anything else, because in this way they turn all the better in their own shit. Even if you were a billionaire (which you unfortunately aren't) I couldn't accept your money either for William nor for Giacomo (and in fact I'm not taking it, and I'm returning it with this letter). The shadow that you bring over our friendship, as you know very well, is not your *debt*, which,

besides, does not even exist; but the 'adoration of the Pharisee Fathers' as I already wrote you in the poem. Neither is this the first time that there is this shadow" (Naldini clxxiii, n. 58; emphasis in original).

6. Marco Bardini, to whom goes my deepest gratitude for making available for me a fragment of *Approdare all'Isola d'Elsa. Il rapporto con il cinema*, notes: "Her contribution to the movie was almost inexistent; she limited herself to approving the script as contractually arranged, without modifications, and visiting the set a few times, always with the greatest discretion. From these infrequent visits remain only a few nice pictures in black and white in which the writer is seated with her back to the actors who in the background are interpreting her characters" (Bardini, conversation).

7. "On what I was doing she made only one remark, with some tact, that expressed maybe disapproval. Why had I picked as protagonist a young American actress?" (Damiani 41). Damiano Damiani also stated in *L'avventurosa storia del cinema* that "Morante did not interfere with the script, she read it and accepted, and I remember that she was not very happy with the protagonist, because she had an Anglo-Saxon appearance—and indeed she was American [Key Meersman, HS]—and would have preferred her to be more southern, also less beautiful. She was probably right" (Bondanella 160).

8. Barbato quotes Morante's answer to his question "Il cinema?" For Morante, "Damiani's movie of *Isola di Arturo* is beautiful, but the characters are changed. The father, e.g., is presented as a bad guy. For my part, however, I cannot think badly of my characters. I need to excuse them before I can describe them" (11).

9. About the same time, in the sixties, Morante was working on a novel that would never be published (*Senza i conforti della religione*). Instead it would be "disassembled" and used for writing *La Storia* and *Aracoeli* (Cives 57). The manuscript allows us, however, to see the missing relation between poetry and cinema, the realm of vice, corruption, and all evil.

10. Realism is not introduced here as a value or as a prescriptive term, but rather as description of style and techniques. (See O'Leary and Rawe 125.)

11. The nearby Procida and Capri were the preferred summer holiday resorts where Elsa loved to go with a Siamese cat on a leash and Alberto with an owl on his shoulder.

12. Damiani may have drawn iconographic inspiration for his movie from the image from the first 1957 Einaudi edition in the "Supercoralli" series of Morante's novel: *Ragazzo addormentato sulla barca* by Renato Guttuso. It is Arturo, in his movie, who appears in a boat on the beach, in a scene noticeably inspired by Guttuso's painting (Desideri 77; 92). The choice of this image and of the one for the cover of the later Oscar Mondadori, 1969 edition (*Fichidindia*, by Renato Guttuso), was determined by a wish to join the followers of realist art against the then (i.e., in the Fifties) advancing abstract art (Dell'Orca 92–95).

13. "Ah, io non chiederei d'essere un gabbiano, né un delfino; mi accontenterei d'essere uno scorfano, ch'è il pesce più brutto del mare, pur di ritrovarmi laggiù, a scherzare in quell'acqua!" (Morante, *L'isola* 954; "If I could only get back there to splash about in those waters, I'd gladly become any sort of creature: not a gull or a dolphin or anything beautiful, but the ugliest thing in the sea, which is the scorpion fish!" [Morante, *Arturo's* 4]).

14. Verse missing from English translation.

15. According to Siti, Pasolini's poem, "Hobby del sonetto" bears witness to the crisis of his relationship to Elsa: "She watches him suffering like a dog because Ninetto is getting married, and she stands by Ninetto's side" (28).

16. While cats recall Pasolini's and Morante's poetic exchange, they were also Morante's lifelong and faithful companions.

17. Damiani speaks of Morante gently and full of respect. As he remembers the author, among his "faults" he enumerates one perhaps of his most serious faults, not having visited Morante in the hospital, postponing the visit until it was too late. He was to consider this his "most serious vice, worse than all others, because it had turned against a being that [he] deeply admired and loved" (42).

18. According to Marcello Morante, Irma Poggibonzi, Morante's mother, had decided to start a new life with Ciccio, as she called Francesco Lo Monaco. Once in Sicily, she discovered that Lo Monaco, the natural father of her four children, had a family, and she returned full of

regret. The family of Ciccio (possibly to prevent economic claims, as Marcello Morante contends) informed her shortly after of the suicidal death of Lo Monaco (124).

WORKS CITED

Barbato, Andrea. "La mancanza di religione," *L'Espresso* 8.40 (7 October 1962): 11.

Bardini, Marco. "Appunti per un *treatment.*" *Santi, Sultani e Gran Capitani in camera mia. Inediti e ritrovati dell'Archivio di Elsa Morante.* Ed. Giuliana Zagra. Rome: Biblioteca nazionale di Roma, 2012. 59–70.

———. Personal conversation. 26 June 2012.

Bondanella, Peter. *A History of Italian Cinema.* New York: Continuum Italian Publishing Group, 2009.

Cives, Simona. "Elsa Morante 'senza i conforti della religione.'" Zagra and Buttò 49–65.

Damiani, Damiano. "Dal libro al film." Schifano and Notarbartolo, *Cahiers* 41–42.

Davoli, Ninetto. "Gente con orari suoi." *Festa per Elsa.* Goffredo Fofi and Adriano Sofri, eds. Palermo: Sellerio, 2011. 84–88.

Dell'Orca, Alessia. "Le illustrazioni di copertina dei romanzi di Elsa Morante." Zagra and Buttò 87–100.

Desideri, Laura. "I libri di Elsa." Zagra and Buttò 77–85.

Faldini, Franca, and Goffredo Fofi, eds. *L'avventurosa storia del cinema italiano raccontata dai suoi protagonisti 1960–69.* Milan: Feltrinelli, 1981.

Morante, Elsa. *Arturo's Island.* 1957. Trans. Isabel Quigly. South Royalton, VT: Steerforth Italia, 2002.

———. *L'isola di Arturo.* Morante, *Opere* 1. 945–1370.

———. *Opere.* Cesare Garboli and Carlo Cecchi, eds. 2 vols. Milan: Meridiani Mondadori, 1988 and 1990.

———. "Sul romanzo." Morante, *Opere* 2. 1497–520.

Morante, Marcello. *Maledetta benedetta. Elsa e sua madre.* Milan: Garzanti, 1986.

Naldini, Nico. *Pier Paolo Pasolini. Lettere 1955–75.* Turin: Einaudi, 1988.

O'Leary, Alan, and Catherine O'Rawe. "Against realism: on a 'certain tendency' in Italian film criticism." *Journal of Modern Italian Studies* 16.1 (2011): 107–28.

Schifano Jean-Noël. "La divina Barbara." Schifano and Notarbartolo, *Cahiers* 5–13.

———, and Tjuna Notarbartolo, eds. *Cahiers Elsa Morante.* Naples: Edizioni scientifiche italiane, 1993.

Siti, Walter. "Elsa Morante and Pier Paolo Pasolini." *Under Arturo's Star: The Cultural Legacies of Elsa Morante.* Stefania Lucamante and Sharon Wood, eds. West Lafayette, IN: Purdue University Press, 2006. 268–88.

Zagra, Giuliana and Simonetta Buttò, eds. *Le stanze di Elsa. Dentro la scrittura di Elsa Morante.* Rome: Colombo, 2006.

Chapter Thirteen

No Novel Is an Island

Damiano Damiani's L'isola di Arturo

Thomas Harrison

Not much has remained recorded about the events that led up to the cinematic adaptation of Elsa Morante's novel, *L'isola di Arturo*, in 1962, nor about the process of the film's production. According to the scholar who knows most about it, Marco Bardini, virtually all of the important filmic decisions were taken independently of the novelist, who still succeeded in maintaining a demeanor of cordial reserve with the director Damiano Damiani and his team of filmic adapters. (She seems to have been most perplexed by Damiani's choice of the stunningly blue-eyed beauty Key Meersman, an American, for the role of Nunziata: see Bardini.) The filmic result was a significantly different work than the one Morante originally conceived. Within just a few years of its publication in 1957, this novel about an island had lost its insularity. "Doubled" as it was in another medium, it became subjected to an identity crisis, even independently of the changes the film wrought. "Si duo idem faciunt non est idem" (If two are the same, it is not the same), writes the philosopher Carlo Michelstaedter (104). Fortunately for Morante the film by Damiano Damiani has not weathered time so well and has not indelibly affected the reception of the novel; few readers of Morante have seen it.

Nonetheless, works of narrative fiction rarely remain immune to their audiovisual conversion. Every adaptation influences our perception of the original. Damiani's filmic treatment of *L'isola di Arturo* underscores certain things that *are* in the book and paradoxically brings others into relief by *excluding* them, or by altering their essential features. It happens, for example, that the film stresses the emptiness of Arturo's daily life just as much as the book does. The young islander never does anything in either medium (except read and occasionally listen to people talk; he himself doesn't talk much). We are not made privy to what he typically does to pass his daily long eighteen hours, without friends or company, week after week, month after month. Morante—through the persona of her narrator, the adult Arturo—often tells us that he would go off to spend the day on his own on the island, but omits all details about what he was doing. The same is the case in the film. The "doubling" of this phenomenon (the doubling of an "absence") brings the lacuna into the foreground. Then there are things that the film calls to mind because of how it changes them. Morante gives strong and clear reasons for why Arturo finally abandons his natal island. The *divergent* reasons of the film put those original ones into relief. (Incidentally, neither set of reasons is all that cogent in terms of emotional logic; both are "melodramatic.") The radically different ending of the film reinforces the contrasting finale of the novel.

Perhaps the ultimate question posed by filmic adaptions involves the *effects* of the cinematic remake, a question reaching much further than any issue of mere fidelity.[1] Rather, it involves what we learn about the original source based on the treatment. Broadly, and ostensibly tautologically, speaking, a film brings out the "cinematicity" of the book (any book)—in and of itself a matter of perfectly legitimate interest, which gets invariably realized by the film, insofar as the film makes us see how much the book does or does not lend itself to visualization, staging, and dramatization. Damiani's film declines the novel's implicit invitation to illustrate a typical day in Arturo's island wanderings (one requiring little screen time but potentially of great cinematic effect). Ignoring this, it chooses rather to dramatize a different feature of the book: its interpersonal struggles, and in particular the melodramatic interactions of Arturo, his stepmother Nunziatella, and his father Wilhelm. This is a different kind of cinematicity that the book lends itself to—in lieu of a lyrical, poetic essay on the ostensibly natural harmonies of childhood (again, posited, but not described, by the book's narrator). I dare say that if the book contained more reflection on these harmonies, or more theoretical analysis of them, it could have lent itself more easily to a different kind of film, maybe something more in the style of Terrence Malick (the director of *Days of Heaven*, 1978, and *The Tree of Life*, 2011). But then again, a "Malick-like" treatment of coming of age would have downplayed the book's melodramatic plot, and the film would have had to be considerably more complex than it ended up being.

I bring up this issue of another, more lyrical cinematic treatment because so much critical tribute has been paid to the presumably Edenic, idyllic, paradisiacal picture of childhood given by this book, which very few specifics have ever been provided to illustrate. As best I can tell, this so-called elysian picture of childhood might be more of a fantasy in the mind of readers than a reality articulated in the pages of the novel—a fantasy furnished primarily by Morante's own acts of self-exegesis. It begins with the book's oft-quoted opening poem, on the limbo-Elysium of childhood:

> L'insegna paurosa non varcherà mai la soglia di quella isoletta celeste. E tu non saprai la legge ch'io, come tanti, imparo,- e a me ha spezzato il cuore: *fuori del limbo non v'è eliso.* (Morante, *L'isola* 947)

> The sign of fear shall never cross the thresholdOf that small, celestial island. And you will not know the lawthat I, like many others, am learning: *there is no paradise except in limbo.* (Morante, *Arturo's Island*)

The effect of this authorial invitation to read the novel as a tale of the loss of a limbo-Elysium was much strengthened by the early support of prestigious and authoritative readers of *L'isola di Arturo* like Giacomo Debenedetti, and foreclosed attentive examination of the novel's rhetoric.[2] Moreover, even the novel's self-exegetical rhetoric has generally been taken literally rather than met with suspicion and deconstructed. The narrator's claims (he is the grown Arturo, not anonymous or omniscient) have tended to be accorded perfect credence; he has not been studied as unreliable. As a matter of fact, despite the Proustian spirit of his autobiographical recall, brought to light by Franco Ferrucci in 1963 and by Stefania Lucamante in 1998, there is hardly any *critical distance* between this narrator in the present and the boy of the past that he talks about. It seems rather to me that readers should take up as much distance from him as an adult as from him as a boy (as much distance as he does not take from the boy he once was) and ask why he is presenting things the way that he does. Of course this issue about the general lack of critical distance in the reception of the work precedes the issue of how the cinematic treatment illuminates the original work; as a matter of fact, it *influences* that treatment, for it launches Damiani's film on a certain interpretation; it magnifies a tendency in the book that is not necessarily its most profound.

From the very start of the film—in the opening credits—another question is raised about this adaptation when the name Cesare Zavattini flashes up among the film's screenwriters. It involves what, if anything, this transposition from text to film might reveal about the critical tensions between Elsa Morante's work and the aesthetics of neorealism. And yet it becomes evident after just a few minutes that this film is no more neorealistic in style than is the novel. Assuming the great neorealist screenwriter Zavattini did have a hand in this work, what effect could he have had on its style? Morante's correspondence archived by her nephew Daniele Morante hasn't turned up anything that sheds light on this matter. The letters between her, Damiani, and Zavattini are short, courteous, and avoid questions of artistic interpretation. In the absence of further clarification, the Zavattini role remains a mystery. As a matter of fact, the official Cesare Zavattini website does not even list *L'isola* among his screenwriting credits, and this sends us back to the opening credits where, on a more attentive, second view, we find that Zavattini does not figure as one of the three screenwriters of the film. Rather, he is mentioned immediately following them, under the title, "Con la collaborazione di" (With the collaboration of). His participation in the conceptualization of this film was thus probably slight.

As I have suggested, the inherent cinematicity of a book is made explicit, or enhanced, by its filmic adaptation, while other aspects of the book become conspicuous by absence or transformation. There are numerous examples of such absence or transformation in Damiani's *L'isola di Arturo*, but not all are of the same importance. Aside from the casting, where Wilhelm becomes a fifty-year-old man and Nunziatina a transcendent beauty, the most glaring transformation may be of the story's ending. It also happens to be the most revealing change, opening up to view the unique intentions of the film and how it was asking to be received, both of which tell us much about the socioethical contexts of Italy in the late 1950s and early 1960s when both novel and film were created. That is to say, the fact that the filmmaker produced a dramatically different ending to Morante's narrative says much about his and his producers' view of the filmgoing public of Italy, making us keenly aware of how much is at stake in the two different "resolutions" of the plot, dictating two different purposes and morals.

The sequence concluding the film begins in a dark subterranean room where the boy Arturo confronts his father Wilhelm and Stella, the man it has been revealed his father loves, and proceeds to a scene in which Arturo divulges this scandalous relationship to the father's wife Nunziatella. Here Arturo lusciously seals the revelation with a second kiss on his stepmother's lips, even more fatal than the one he had given her earlier. The next scene shows the father Wilhelm renouncing his plan to leave Procida with his lover, and Nunziatella commanding that Arturo leave instead. None of this occurs in the book—not the confrontation with the father, not the second kiss, not the surprise decision of Wilhelm to relinquish his homosexual relationship, or even the eviction of Arturo. The overall effect of these different elements is to remind us of that context of moral and social expectations—in Italy in the late 1950s and early 1960s—to which the novel responded in quite different ways.

Many issues at the heart of both novel and film loom large in this sequence. The biggest is the film's *pudeur* about the homosexual thematic of the book. (In the novel, Arturo's father Wilhelm is even more clearly in love with Stella, a prisoner in the penitentiary of Procida, and eventually leaves the island with him, much to his son's chagrin. After an appropriate period of crisis, Arturo then leaves the island as well, abandoning his neglected young stepmother Nunziatella, with whom, in the meantime, he has himself fallen in love.) Damiani's film version of *L'isola di Arturo* does not just downplay this paternal homosexual motif; it actually has Arturo's father *renounce* the devious tie and return to the fold of the heterosexual family. Although nothing similar exists in the book, what is interesting is that the *pudeur* of the film mimics, elaborates, and culls the inevitable consequences of the *official readings* of the book. That is to say, the audiovisual adaptation manifests a latent dimension of the original artistic phenomenon that might otherwise have gone ignored, or been successfully repressed. This adaptation also draws attention to a symptomatic difference between the book itself—the words written in its pages—and traditional criticism *of* the book, and this seems to me to constitute a bigger problem for the comprehension of Morante than for most twentieth-century Italian writers. That is to say, early commentators, nearly one and all, sidestep the novel's strong issue of homosexuality and a consideration of how it and other gender and erotic issues might fundamentally affect the father-son relationship of Arturo and Wilhelm. In fact, even this father-son relationship is generally ignored, despite its markedly peculiar nature. Following the example of Debenedetti, Morante's critics tend to *deflect* these issues, I am not sure how deliberately, by foregrounding dimensions of the novel's rhetoric that do not foster psycho-sociological analysis (and, again, in subservience to Morante's own exegetical recommendations): the mythical atmosphere of Arturo's island, its fairy-tale quality, the affinity of the novel to fable, its almost allegorical account of coming of age.

The psychology of adolescence is also put aside.[3] Yet precisely here a strong position could be taken. Arturo's cathexes—his emotional investments—are clearly substitutions, or surrogate satisfactions, to fill a void of parental affection. In one sense, the book is a tale of child abuse, or at least paternal neglect, in which an unnatural withholding of respect and affection on the part of a father creates a desperate clutching on the part of the son—an infection and bloating of affective investment. Here lies a potential, embryonic case of the cataclysmic adult aberration known as the Stockholm syndrome—that paradoxical development of love and dependency of a victim on his or her victimizer, which some spectators most starkly encountered in Liliana Cavani's *The Night Porter* (1974). The syndrome was named after a bank robbery and hostage taking that occurred in the Swedish city a year before the film was released in which a hostage subjected to captivity, terror, and torture developed a deep and traumatic bond with her abuser. Psychologists have explained this psychological aberration as triggering a compulsive regression back to the condition of a young child's absolute dependence on parents for the fulfillment of even the most basic needs. More recently the Stockholm syndrome has been linked to child abuse in general. Clearly, in children the mechanism of idolizing someone who enslaves you is much easier to see than it is in adults: withholding parental approval and quashing a small person's independence is the simplest and most formulaic way to be held in mystically high respect, to the point where, as David Ziegler writes in

Traumatic Experience and the Brain, "the degree of loyalty from a child to an abusive parent seems to be in direct proportion to the seriousness of the abuse the child received. In this counter intuitive way, the stronger or more life-threatening the treatment, the stronger the loyalty from the child."[4]

The abusive, unwholesome relationship between Wilhelm and Arturo is connected to an Oedipal scenario that early critics—I can only imagine out of moral *pudeur*—failed to unfold, fearing perhaps that to do so would be to question certain *sacrosanct assumptions* in the Italian ethical fabric, including (a) the ostensibly "natural" nature of filial loyalty, rather than a condition that is socially produced, especially of son with regard to father; (b) the nonsexual nature of love for the mother, or, in this case, the maternal figure of Nunziatella; (c) the heterosexuality, not homosexuality, of erotic desire. All these assumptions are thrown into question by the Oedipal scenario. And it is important to recognize that these are precisely the assumptions that Morante herself is implicitly examining in *L'isola di Arturo* (with others of her time, especially Luchino Visconti in the film *Rocco e i suoi fratelli* of 1960). But they are assumptions that her critics were perfectly unwilling to acknowledge. No wonder Morante needed Pasolini, an artist who would give these themes less polite an exposition. The taboo subjects had to be faced more frontally to provoke true discussion—and even then!

The Stockholm syndrome stops the Oedipal from becoming visible, from playing out its normal course of development. The Oedipal explodes the "sacrosanct." In *L'isola di Arturo* the boy's abnormal, dystrophic attachment to his father interferes with his inevitable need to push back at the dad, to establish and assert his own autonomy as a male youth. Yes, Arturo finally does it, but only after traumatic events. Up until the moment when he falls in love with his stepmother, and witnesses the abjectness of his father, Arturo is pathologically overdependent on that authority figure. Interestingly enough, one of the revelations of the film vis-à-vis the novel is Arturo's subjugation to his father, suggested by the convict Stella's declaration that the boy is jealous: "Tu sei geloso di lui! [tuo padre]. Eh, me l'ha detto. . . ." (You are jealous of him! [your father] Yes, he told me. . .). The novel, instead, insists that Arturo is jealous of Nunziatina, who takes up too much of his father's attention, just as he is later jealous of his younger brother, who takes up the attention of Nunziata, and again he is jealous of Antonio Stella. But this is something different. To be jealous of one's own *father* is rather to be pathologically under his thumb, to be resentful of the *appeal* that he has, and to feel that he wields too much power. The film sets forth the conditions for a revolt, but that revolt never happens. Critics can ignore its threat.

Only *because of* this dystrophic attachment to his father does Arturo fall in love with Nunziatina to begin with. Arturo is the mimetic rival of his dad.[5] Just as his father waxes misogynist and mistreats the new woman of the house, so does his son. Just as that misogyny turns erotic in Wilhelm, so it does in Arturo. In fact, what attracts Arturo most to his mother-in-law is his knowledge that she is not happy making love with his father; that this seemingly ideal adult male is not doing her justice. Imitation and rivalry produce the fantasy, "I can be a better lover than he."

Most of this becomes clear in the final sequence of the film, the one that best illuminates clandestine workings of the novel even as it suppresses them. There Arturo explicitly bonds with Nunziatina in the spirit of two disenfranchised underlings; they are not getting the proper affection that they deserve from the patriarch Wilhelm. Unlike the film, the book does not let his two dependents (let us call them such) avow their common dependence. And that is as it should be, for their relationships to Wilhelm are completely different, despite their common victimization at his hands. More than the book, the film respects Wilhelm as a patriarch on whom the others patently depend. Indeed, that is why it will not let him leave the island with his beloved convict "Stella" as he does in the novel: he must prove equal to his patriarchal duty. Arturo's sense of being betrayed by his father combines with Wilhelm's humiliation at being called a "parody" in front of his son to produce an ethical conversion in the man, who redeems himself as both father and husband. When his wife Nunziatella sees that he has come to blows with his lover and will no longer leave the island with him, she sends *Arturo* away. Even though she had passionately embraced him just two minutes before, she now literally closes the door in Arturo's face, sending him away from the house and the island. She does this not *despite* the fact that she has embraced him, but *because* of it. The film's final scene portrays Arturo crying on a boat as he leaves Procida for good.

The film's plot resolution occurs precisely when it becomes clear, in Arturo's mind, that the problem with Wilhelm as a dad is that another man lies at the center of his affections. The scene is staged in the house cellar—a dark dungeon evoking the realm of the repressed and the animalistic, protected by bars. The revelation down here of the true object of his father's affection is accompanied by a recognition that Arturo's father is not omnipotent, but himself dependent and subordinate. Unfortunately the film does not exploit this twist for the true comprehension of human nature that it could provide in place of a facile moral condemnation (as it would have in the hands of Visconti, where a similar discovery about Rocco's brother Simone's failings proves absolute, Dostoevskian, irremediable—universally human in its implications). No, this revelation of Wilhelm's dependency (which mirrors the dependency of his son, in a potentially infinite series) serves simply as license to cast a subjugating aspersion upon him: "You are a traitor!" Arturo cries out, with deep conviction—a traitor to him and the family. And Wilhelm subscribes to this judgment, allowing himself to be manipulated by social opinion. The family here asserts its value as sacred.

This "pathological" rapport between father and son, suggesting an over-attachment of the younger to the older male, is hinted at often in Italian cinema and literature ever since *Pinnochio*. It is already present in *Rome Open City* (1945) and *Bicycle Thieves* (1948), where the mothers literally fall out of the picture, despite their fortitude and activism, ceding their place to the true (male) problematic, to say nothing of more romantic and recent popular films like *Cinema Paradiso* (1988), where again the story is most concerned with the great role of the father in the son's eyes—a father who is literally deceased, but who is symbolically replaced by a surrogate, the film projectionist, establishing the existential dreams. It achieves a point where one suspects the workings of compensatory rhetoric. One imagines that the Italian father-son bond must *not* be so deep if it is *talked about so much*, if it is avowed and asserted so often. The males protest too much. In a society where the greatest affections seem to lie rather *between mother and son*, the idealization of the father appears to belong to an ideological superstructure, to a teaching that the country *needed* in these years to insist upon. Does it involve the ordeal of Italians to unite beneath a ruler they could call their own, already in the nineteenth century, and legitimate a distant king from Piedmont? Could it involve the traumatic *disappointment* of fathers in World War II—Mussolini to begin with and then the king, ignominiously fleeing his responsibilities on September 8, 1943? Fascism and the war are a narrative backdrop for the happenings in the novel *L'isola di Arturo*, and it is made abundantly clear by allusions that this war bodes ill for the *patria*. Arturo's disappointment in his father, and the severe "coming of age" that results from it, is also the nation's. This association between Arturo and the nation, confronting Wilhelm and its dysfunctional patriarchal authority, is suggested by the explicit denunciation of Wilhelm by Arturo in the film (not the book—where Arturo keeps the love for his childhood myth intact). Wilhelm comes into line.

The new ending of the film recounts a tale altogether different from the coming of age, or loss of Eden, that Morante may have wanted to tell in her novel. Her ending, with Arturo leaving the island to join the war effort not long after his father has left with Stella, essentially closes the chapter of childhood for Arturo and signals the beginning of a difficult life of adulthood. Damiani's ending develops a deep latency in the melodrama revolving around the mutual attachment of Arturo to Nunziatella, exploring the nature of their attraction. It gives us a heavy-handed morality play endorsing a series of emotional sacrifices for the betterment of society: the sacrifice of the wife to her man, of the son to the father, and of romantic love to affective duty. Let us look at these one by one.

The film sees a truly romantic tie develop between Nunziatella and Arturo that is both acknowledged and accepted by both of them just before the end of the story. The "acceptance" is emotional (rather than intellectual or moral) and is sealed with a passionate kiss. In the book we also observe this romantic relationship begin between the two of them, but there it is Arturo who, wounded, resentful, and confused, chooses at a certain point not to follow through with it. The book even leads readers to question whether he did the right thing to leave the island, considering that—with his father gone—Arturo might have happily worked out a union with his stepmother, despite the taboos against it. In the film, the romance is intensified; it is reaffirmed right after Arturo denounces his father in the cellar. However, what follows this reaffirmation of their bond is the discovery that Wilhelm, thanks to the guilt laid on him by his son, has decided to stay behind on Procida and let his Stella depart. In effect he has broken his illicit, homosexual bond and shows the marks of the rupture in bruises on his face. Nunziata, seeing that her husband has resolved to return to the family fold, also resolves to serve him. She gives up Arturo for the abusive, "no good" husband. Her sacrifice, Dostoevskian in nature, is made the more dramatic by the sultry, Elizabeth Taylor look-alike American actress that Damiani has cast in the role, more dazzling by far than the awkwardly attractive Campanian peasant of the novel. The filmic Nunziatella appears perfectly suited to the romantic desires of the chivalric "knight of the round table," yet she makes her choice to stay with the older man, his father, who stands in great need of her emotional and physical nursing. This is the sacrifice of a wife for her man—a sacrifice not only of many life possibilities but of the leanings of her heart. In that respect, the film offers a moral lesson to young women to be prepared to give up such compelling alternatives.

At the eleventh hour Nunziata takes charge of the action. She sends Arturo packing, literally, telling him that she will stay with his father and that he must make a life for himself elsewhere. She closes the door on him in a close-up shot, where Damiani positions us spectators with him, outside the door that she closes, showing us how it feels to be shut out by the woman one wants, to see her reassign herself to a socially entitled older man. Arturo sacrifices himself for the very same person. The Oedipal "resolution" of the father-son conflict, if one can call it that, is more pronounced here than in the book, where it never reaches this breaking point. Arturo, like Nunziata, renounces his heart's desire out of deference to patriarchal authority and *despite* the undeserving nature of this father. Nothing could be so unsatisfyingly acquiescent.

Damiani's film associates the moral shortcomings of Wilhelm with his sexual orientation—his homosexual leanings. It condemns them, making them turpitudinous. It is imperative for the sake of the family (or more strictly speaking, for the heterosexual *foundation* of the family, for with Arturo's departure, the family itself is weakened by the Oedipal scenario) that this homosexual orientation be renounced. One had the impression in Morante's novel that Wilhelm's failings as a father were somewhat separate from his sexual leanings. One clearly recognizes that he neglects and mistreats both his wife and his son, but neither Arturo, the adult narrator, nor Morante, the implied author, places any conspicuous judgment on Wilhelm's erotic proclivities. On the contrary, Morante, the friend of Pasolini, seems rather accepting of these proclivities, allowing Wilhelm to maintain them, and treats them with respectful discretion. Damiani and his screenwriters instead force Wilhelm to renounce his "sin." They demand that the father be redeemed and returned to the family. Their coming-of-age story directs Arturo to let Papa have what is Papa's and to give up individual desire for assimilation and adaptation. To ensure that the picture be complete, Wilhelm is the third character to renounce his libidinal wishes, making the renunciation affect all members of the group. (Actually, in order of cause and effect, he is the first to engage in the renunciation; it is his original, "patriarchal," decision that necessitates that this wife and son follow suit.) Thus is *L'isola di Arturo* "rescued" as mythology, fable, and fairy tale, though with a very different moral than in the literary narrative. The values and perspectives of the work affirmed remain equally "infantile," but in an altogether different sense, for they firmly endorse the "law of the father" and give it a most traditional, moralistic, and melodramatic cast. It is certainly striking, on the threshold of such a liberal and socially transformative decade as the 1960s, that the message of this film should be so conservative, eliciting questions about how such strong partisanship arose at all and why it took over the quite different and rather permissive intentions of Morante's novel. Certainly these intentions would have been more constructively served by the direction of a Visconti or a Pasolini.

NOTES

1. Extensive, illuminating discussions of the hermeneutics of film adaptation can be found in Cahir, Corrigan, Cortellazzo and Tomasi, Costa, Desmond and Hawkes, Genette, Marcus, and Ross.

2. Morante's emphasis on Arturo's childhood as a "paradiso terrestre, prima dell'inferno" (*Opere*, vol. 1, 66; "earthly paradise, preceding hell") supported by Giacomo Debenedetti's discussion of the book's "solare paradiso degli amori infantili" of Arturo (1134; "sunny paradise of infantile loves"), inspires critics like Kalay to consider this novel's vision of childhood as "a blessed time of oneness with nature, a primal state of grace, innocence, and happiness" (54). Kalay characterizes Arturo's youth with the following words, as if they denoted a healthy and happy situation: The boy leads an existence "devoid of any of the influences associated with civilization: he is left to grow up entirely on his own with little or no parental or adult presence; he receives no formal education; he has no friends, no relative, and shuns the company of the other islanders; he has no use for money or material things; he knows no rules other than the dictates of his own body; his days are unstructured and spent outdoors in an unconscious communion with nature" (56).

3. Entire monographs devoted to childhood in Morante, like that of Kalay, do not reflect on how Arturo's childhood might be affected by his relation with his father, or even by the absence of his mother, despite how strongly her absence is noted in his narrative account.

4. Cited in www.understanding-child-abuse.com/what-is-stockholm-syndrome.html. Accessed October 18, 2013.

5. For a good study of mimetic rivalry in the novel, see Della Coletta.

WORKS CITED

Bardini, Marco. "Appunti per un *treatment.*" *Santi, Sultani e Gran Capitani in camera mia. Inediti e ritrovati dell'Archivio di Elsa Morante.* Ed. Giuliana Zagra. Rome: Biblioteca Nazionale di Roma, 2012. 59–70.

Cahir, Linda Costanzo. *Literature into Film: Theory and Practical Approaches.* Jefferson, NC: McFarland, 2006.

Cornish, Alison. "A King and a Star. The Cosmos of Morante's *L'isola di Arturo.*" *MLN* 109 (1994): 73–92.

Corrigan, Timothy. *Film and Literature: An Introduction and Reader.* Upper Saddle River, NJ: Prentice Hall, 1999.

Cortellazzo, Sara, and Dario Tomasi. *Letteratura e cinema.* Rome: Laterza, 1998.

Costa, Antonio. *Immagine di un'immagine: cinema e letteratura.* Turin: UTET, 1993.

Debenedetti, Giacomo. "Isola della Morante." *Saggi.* Ed. Alfonso Berardinelli. Milan: Mondadori, 1999. 1117–38.

Della Coletta, Cristina. "The Morphology of Desire in Elsa Morante's *L'isola di Arturo.*" Lucamante and Wood. 129–56.

Desmond, John M., and Peter Hawkes. *Adaptation: Studying Film and Literature.* Boston, MA: McGraw-Hill, 2005.

Ferrucci, Franco. "Elsa Morante's Limbo without Elysium." *Italian Quarterly* 7 (1963): 28–52.

Genette, Gérard. *Palimpsests: Literature in the Second Degree.* Lincoln: University of Nebraska Press, 1997.

Kalay, Grace Zlobnicki. *The Theme of Childhood in Elsa Morante.* University, MS: Romance Monographs, 1996.

Lucamante, Stefania. *Elsa Morante e l'eredità proustiana.* Fiesole: Edizioni Cadmo, 1998.

———, and Sharon Wood, eds. *Under Arturo's Star: The Cultural Legacies of Elsa Morante.* West Lafayette, IN: Purdue University Press, 2006.

Marcus, Millicent. *Filmmaking by the Book.* Baltimore, MD: Johns Hopkins University Press, 1992.

Michelstaedter, Carlo. *La persuasione e la rettorica.* Milan: Adelphi, 1982.

Morante, Elsa. *L'amata. Lettere di e a Elsa Morante.* Ed. Daniele Morante. Turin: Einaudi, 2012.

———. *Arturo's Island.* 1957. Trans. Isabel Quigly. South Royalton, VT· Steerforth Italia, 2002.

———. *L'isola di Arturo.* Morante, *Opere* 1. 945–1370.

———. *Opere.* Cesare Garboli and Carlo Cecchi, eds. 2 vols. Milan: Meridiani Mondadori, 1988 and 1990.

———. "Sul romanzo." Morante, *Opere* 2. 1497–520.

Ross, Harris. *Film as Literature, Literature as Film: An Introduction to and Bibliography of Film's Relationship to Literature.* New York: Greenwood Press, 1987.

"What Is Stockholm Syndrome and the Relationship with Child Abuse?" www.understanding-child-abuse.com/what-is-stockholm-syndrome.html.

Chapter Fourteen

The Myth of Childhood

Luigi Comencini's Adaptation of La Storia

Giovanna De Luca

"(H) ai nascosto queste cose ai dotti e ai savi e le hai rivelate ai piccoli
... perché così a te piacque."

—Luca X-21 [1]

"L'unica felicità possibile: non essere sé, ma tutti."
—Morante, *Cronologia* LXXVIII [2]

Luigi Comencini, the father of the cinema of childhood in Italy, emerged as a filmmaker in the late 1950s. In the multifaceted panorama of the *cinema des auteurs*, which characterized post-neorealist cinema, only Comencini took a systematic approach to the treatment of childhood. With his twelve films for cinema and television, he galvanized the subject and created an Italian standard for filmmakers who followed.

Comencini's style had its roots in both documentary and in Pink neorealism, the derivative neorealist cinema that included elements of comedy and melodrama designed for the rapidly changing Italian mass audience. The filmmaker's interest in portraying childhood derives from his belief that it is "the greatest moment of freedom of the individual" (Toubiana 64). In his films, children face adults' incomprehension, are confronted with inadequate mothers, and cope with loneliness. As the French film critic Robert Benayoun points out, grown-ups in Comencini's films are unable to understand the uncompromised sense of justice and morality in children who must fight for attention, understanding, and compassion (56).

It comes as no surprise, then, that Comencini chose to adapt Elsa Morante's popular 1974 novel *La Storia*, focusing on the young character of

Useppe. The main protagonist of *La Storia* is Ida Ramundo Mancuso, a half-Jewish mother who lived through the war and "never really grew up" (Mana-corda 202). Of a fragile personality, burdened by her family secrets as she was, she did not assert herself in life but, rather, let life happen to her. She has two children: the independent Nino who—after many trials—would die smuggling cigarettes after the war, and the sick Useppe, the product of a rape by Gunther, a seventeen-year-old German soldier from Dachau. Ida and her children are part of a working-class Roman landscape devastated by the war. At the end of the film, Useppe, too, will die after an epileptic attack, pushing his mother across the thin line into insanity.

The RAI-produced TV-film *La Storia*, made in 1986, was Comencini's first work after the great success of *Cuore*, a 1984 television series that adapted Edmondo De Amicis's famous book. Comencini's adaptation sparked national interest in the dry, realistic way in which he adapted what was perhaps the most-read Italian collection of stories for a young public. After *Cuore*, the director rested for a while due to problems related to Parkinson's disease; soon, however, he became very interested in Morante's novel. He couldn't stay away from the camera and decided to visit a very sick Elsa Morante to secure the television rights to *La Storia.* Comencini describes the meeting: "Il nostro incontro fu quasi muto. Io parlavo male, lei era molto debole. Mi disse solo che aveva amato il mio *Pinocchio* e che si fidava di me. Forse aveva anche bisogno di soldi" (45; "She was very sick. I could not speak. Our meeting was almost silent. She said she loved my *Pinocchio* and she trusted me. Perhaps she also needed money").

Interestingly, Comencini reports that Morante's decision to trust him with the cinematic adaptation of her novel was mostly based on the present circumstances of her life and her need for money. One is left to wonder whether Morante's interest in the subject of childhood and Comencini's ability to portray it cinematically might have impacted her decision; Comencini says nothing to this regard. Morante died one year before the release of the movie. In his autobiography, Comencini expresses his double disappointment: Morante couldn't see the final product and the film was broadcasted on one night only for what he said was a distracted TV audience (3). Unlike the popular novel, Comencini's *La Storia* was received initially with some enthusiasm but quickly became subject to intense criticism.

The two television products *La Storia* and *Cuore* share many elements: the same screenwriters, same producer, and a similar long-form format. However, as Antonio Costa has pointed out in his article "'Cuore,' La Storia," Comencini's understanding of the text did not translate into a film appropriate for TV; for some the film suffered from a disconnect between interpretation and format (226). Emblematic of a certain lack of clarity in its assessment—confusion of stilistical choices above all—is the review by *New York Times* critic Vincent Canby:

The material appears to have been utterly beyond the talents (and, perhaps, the interests) of Mr. Comencini, who has told much of this dark tale as if it were the sort of soap opera in which cataclysmic events are mere inconveniences. With the exception of black-and-white newsreel footage, which is used from time to time to set the private story in history, the film is shot in color that is functional but characterless, which is the way that Mr. Comencini directs it.

To make his point, Canby ignores Comencini's dramatic *Tutti a casa*, a powerful rendition of the bitter return home of soldiers and camp prisoners. He stresses, instead, the director's presence in only one trend, Pink neorealism. He criticizes the film's lack of both depth and a coherent narrative, which, in his opinion, makes it inadequate to render the tragic tone of Morante's book. Canby even states that Ida is not a detailed character, spectators know nothing about her, even that "[t]he movie is almost over before one learns that Ida is a schoolteacher." Anyone who has seen the film knows that the school scene in which Ida feels sick from her pregnancy occurs right in the first part in which the TV film is divided. He also attacks the acting quality and disapproves of Comencini's choice of color, arguing that black-and-white would have made the film closer to Roberto Rossellini's *Open City* instead of a "soap opera." Canby's biased expectations for a neorealist imitation of Rossellini's film do not take into consideration Comencini's adherence to the physical structure of *La Storia*. The very suggestive shift from black and white footage—showing the personalities and events involved in World War II (Mussolini, Hitler, their meetings and speeches)—to color sequences is used to render the shift occurring in every chapter of the novel from the official chronicle of the war years to the story of Morante's characters. Nino, the brother of the young protagonist Useppe, lives a tumultuous life that ends early and tragically, but, according to Canby, in the film none of that chaos or surprise is conveyed.

Initially, the major criticism of Morante's novel was focused on its anachronistic pathos and popular melodramatic effects, which placed the book closer in style and topic to nineteenth-century feuilleton than to the ideologically charged works of that highly politicized period. Why is the pathetic aspect of Morante's novel so condemned? Gabriella Contini suggests a possible understanding of contemporary critics' diffidence to the novel with her definition of the "pathetic": "Una forma di violenza o disonestà nei confronti del lettore, un'interferenza indebita nella sfera della sua emotività e della sua esperienza privata che ne riduce, con artificio facile, le capacità di difesa" (187; "A form of violence or dishonesty toward the reader, an undeserved interference in the sphere of his or her emotions and private experience, which reduces, with an easy artifice, his or her defense capacities").

Comencini and his cowriters, daughter Cristina Comencini and the famous Suso Cecchi D'Amico, addressed some of what were perceived as being the novel's flaws, namely, the melodramatic-pathetic narrative, and successfully moved the film adaptation closer to an understated style. Among their strategies was a considerable transformation in the point of view, which shifts from the omniscient female narrator to the young child Useppe. Comencini conveys Morante's understanding of history as an unjust social and temporal trajectory controlled by the powerful but experienced by the masses. By changing the narrative point of view, Comencini focuses on the way in which the spectators perceive the story; empathy is substituted with identification precisely because of the film's shift in the point of view. A conscious knowledge of the narrator's perspective gives way to an unconscious alignment with the young Useppe, recalling Stam, Burgoyne, and Flitterman-Lewis's work on empathy and identification, wherein "the formula 'empathy = I know how you feel' relies on knowledge and perception as structuring categories, 'identification = I see as you see, from your position' relies on vision and psychic displacement to organize its terms" (150–51). The presentation of the child in cinema lends itself to a psychic displacement and unconscious hyper-identification. The child is a liminal figure in term of time and space, an outsider of the preconstructed order of life created by adults who therefore see the world from a different perspective. Paradoxically, the figure of the child—particularly in a war film, such as *La Storia* can be considered—is constructed as witness of adult weakness or ineptitude. In the novel, the narrator solicits the reader to side with Ida, as well as with Useppe, against the oddities of the war imposed upon these subalterns, a (poor) woman and child. Ida comes with the inherited illnesses of her family, prompting the reader's empathy for her character, which needs to be understood, and her behavior, which needs to be justified in a number of occasions—particularly as when, faced with rape and unwanted pregnancy, Ida accepts this destiny in a kind of stupor. Useppe, however, prompts spectators' identification for he is curious, passionate, open to the world. Quite the opposite of his timid mother, Useppe charms the spectator who can then identify (and establish an emotional link) with this child. While Ida undergoes violence without resistance to her fate, Useppe views the reality of war without any baggage or preconceptions because of his propensity to embrace everything, from love to cruelty, that is part of the human experience. He is one of the "felici pochi" (happy few) as Morante calls the children in *Il mondo salvato dai ragazzini*. This is partly also Comencini's own take on childhood. But, while Comencini had until then depicted childhood devoid of a historical backdrop, in *La Storia* he faces the challenge offered to all of Morante's readers (and interpreters): understanding *her* understanding of Useppe and World War II.

For Morante, the aberration of history is unreal. Cesare Garboli uses the term *unreal* referring to Morante and Pasolini's notion of faceless power, which manifests itself as political or intellectual fascism (1). In this gap between history and unreality, Comencini presents Useppe's death, which functions to contextualize Romans among the absurd (of which they are part): sometimes knowing, sometimes blind. Even innocent common people take part in aberrations of history; they are no mere spectators, but collaborators, or at least participants, just like children can be.[3] Borrowing in part from Hannah Arendt's concept of the banality of evil, *La Storia* shows common people participating in evil without full awareness because fascism deprives them of subjectivity and critical thinking. They become both victims and accomplices to history. In this process, the masses are not only exploited; they identify, at least to a degree, with evil (Haslam and Reicher 615–22). In Morante's work, Ida's naïveté and folly and Useppe's symbiosis with the natural world and death, place the two characters outside human time, obviating their active participation in events. In the film, Useppe's death is a profound interruption that forces the characters of *La Storia*, so far disengaged from the force of events, to consider their position within history.

David Bordwell describes adaptation as the transformation of the written word into "plastic matter," wherein the spectator is the ultimate instrument that brings to life the narrative through his interpretation (2–3). Adaptation for film cannot be univocal; it is inherently subject to molding by director and audience alike. Both Morante and Comencini aimed to portray a history ("unreality") that carried political and metaphysical significance; they were both intensely uninterested in a naturalistic portrayal of Rome during, and immediately after, the war. The novel and the film are informed by historical and cultural facts that distance them from the apex of realistic filmmaking, when neorealism reigned. The book was published in the 1970s during the so-called lead years of Italian terrorism, and it is informed by a national anxiety and social unrest that do not correspond with postwar neorealism. The same can be said of Comencini's post-neorealist artistic training and, above all, the new historical-social context in which he operated. Comencini was active during the great social and cultural revolution of the 1960s, and these ideologies were reflected in his cinema, which emphasized his characters' psychological traits and insecurities.

In this context, the wider concept of the "loss of the father figure" or the loss of guidance in a child's life assumes an integral/pivotal role in Comencini's treatment of childhood in cinema. Notwithstanding the tragic effects on children of the loss of a father figure, Jean Gili rightly argues that Comencini highlights also the "deep duality" of his children: on one hand, they are reliant on their parents, on the other, they are independent from the adults; their intuition liberates them from preestablished structures to which parents and educators want to submit them (7). American movies starring children tend to be marketed at young audiences, but in Italian cinema the child protagonist is used specifically to address adult spectators, offering them a new perspective on the world. The figure of the child serves as a symbolic catalyst for events and social unrest that marks his growing up. As Karen Lury puts it, the child in cinema is "often represented and perceived like 'the other' to the supposedly rational, civilized, grownup human animal that is the adult" (1). Comencini, in addressing the dyad dependency-autonomy of Useppe, reveals also an important aspect of the child's "otherness"—that is, a duplicity that makes him both knowable (for we recognize ourselves in him) and unknowable (for he is an unpredictable work in progress).

Ida has three secrets: she is half Jewish, she suffers from epilepsy, and she has an illegitimate son, Useppe. Useppe has a close relationship with his insecure and protective mother Ida. To preserve her third secret, she leaves the child at home alone most of the time. Useppe's duality is t he result of a learned independence mixed with (inherited) vulnerability. Comencini presents Useppe's innocence—his complete trust of others—as the element triggering his exposure to danger. At the same time, his purity of heart serves to remind spectators of his strong, independent character. It is mostly through Useppe and the shift in the point of view that Comencini distances himself from Morante's overemotional narrative.

Useppe is portrayed, in both the book and the film, in mythical terms, a status he achieves with his death. In Morante's novel, Useppe's mythical dimension is suggested at the beginning with a narrative that foreshadows the young boy's death by emphasizing his "uniqueness," innocence, his symbiosis with the primitive natural and animal world, and his extreme sensitivity. These traits seal his fate: an early, predestined death. In Comencini's rendition of *La Storia*, Useppe is a conventional child. The director highlights Useppe's sensitivity and openness toward others. But his vivacious and curious behavior is not so different from that of other children. In the film, the metaphysical status is reached through his startling, realistic, sudden death, which shocks the spectator. We have Comencini achieving the metaphysical *through* "realistic" portrayal—not an exact refutation, but the essential understanding, instead, of Morante's idea of reality versus unreality. Comencini understood very well Morante's tenets. With his adaptation he returned to audiences the integrity of reality denied to them in their daily lives "nel [loro] quotidiano, e logorante, e *alienante* uso col mondo" ("Pro o contro la bomba atomica" 102; "in [their] daily, and exhausting, and *alienating* interaction with the world"). Useppe, portrayed by the director as lacking Ida's (and Morante's) sentimentality, represents the dispossessed everywhere who are victims of history, what Morante calls "a scandal that has been lasting for more than 10,000 years."[4] Notwithstanding Morante's message, Comencini had to make changes to allow his own image of childhood to fit into Useppe's *storia*. The most important change, aside from the point of view, is marked by the casting for the role of Useppe: the young actor Andrea Spada is a vivacious dark-eyed boy. Comencini ignores Morante's heavy-handed descriptions by presenting a regular-looking boy. For Morante: "[e]ra serio, con un sorrisino incerto. In testa aveva un berrettino uso ciclista [. . .] e addosso i soliti pantaloni alla Charlot, con gli stivali fantasia, e l'impermeabile, *lungo* fino ai piedi che gli si apriva nel salutare" (*La Storia* 279; "[h]e was grave with only a little, hesitant smile. On his head, he wore a cyclist's cap she herself had found for him, his Chaplin-esque pants, his two-tone boots, and a raincoat that reached to his feet" [*History* 320]). Comencini modifies Morante's mannerist approach, presenting a more dynamic, positive character and a crepuscular, realist style. Morante's Useppe had blue eyes (German inheritance, but also closeness to the angels), but Comencini avoids heavy ideological and political implications. In Morante's book, the boy is a symbol of innocence and victimization, his lamentations likened to "le voci di gattini buttati via, degli asini legati alla macina, dei caprettini legati al carro" (*La Storia* 500; "It recalled, in fact, the voices of abandoned kittens, of donkeys blindfolded at the mill, of lambs loaded on a wagon for Easter festivities" [*History* 424]). Comencini corrects excessive victimization of Useppe by giving us a realistic version of childhood, portraying a young boy who alternates between the world of the powerful (*la storia*—history) and the world of the ignorant and innocent (*la vita*—life). In the film, life during the war is portrayed with relative normalcy, even though the family lives at times in communal barracks like the one in Pietralata with the "Thousand." The children play together; the families eat together; human interaction continues. Useppe is happier in Pietralata than he is at home. But the relative normalcy is interrupted at the end of the film when the boy suffers a strong epileptic attack that leads to his death. At the moment, death elevates Useppe's character to a symbol of protest for all the victims of history. In this ending, we find a point of cohesion between writer and director. Although much has been modified in the television film, Comencini's ending (unlike Damiano Damiani's adaptation of *L'isola di Arturo*) remains faithful to what Morante had decreed for her characters.

Epilepsy has frequently been used in literature and film to signify madness, delinquency, violence, or possession by a divine or diabolical force. Useppe's condition strengthens his uniqueness. The epilepsy attacks are sometimes accompanied by visions, an experience akin to what ethnologist-anthropologist Ernesto De Martino calls a "crisis of presence": when the individual becomes disoriented from reality and the situation becomes so intolerable that in order to survive one must escape to a different dimension (89–97). Useppe suffers such a crisis when he is told that his brother Nino is dead and when he learns that his best friend, Scimò Pietro, is in prison. During his final epileptic attack, as death overwhelms him, he has a vision of his brother mocking him. Yet Comencini treats even this scene modestly. There is no melodrama, only a simple death. A panting Useppe is running after his dog Bella along the Tiber when he sees young kids pilfering objects in the abandoned tent of his friend Scimò. A medium shot shows a sweaty and enraged Useppe. His dog Bella tries to defend him while he yells at the children.

When they tell him that Scimò escaped prison and will never return, Useppe first struggles to stop them then grunts like an animal, clenches his fists and wets his pants, has a final vision of his brother teasing him for this, then screams, falling to the ground. The other children run away, afraid of the protective Bella. Later, Ida finds him lying on the ground, alone. There is no sound track accompanying the scene, only the diegetic sounds of summer, a choice made by Comencini, who was interested in connecting this death to the many others that go unnoticed each day as they do through the course of history. Useppe symbolizes the unconscious search of the dispossessed for meaning. According to Morante, he is one of the *felici pochi*, the happy few to whom God has revealed the Truth, as the novel's epitaph suggests. His death is the metaphysical revolt of the dispossessed. According to Reinhard Kuhn, the artistic representation of a modern child's death has three functions: a) to portray a social protest, b) to present a metaphysical revolt, and c) to provide a commentary on the precarious status of childhood (193). The representation of a child's death also serves an expiatory function. An innocent (think of Abraham's son Isaac) dies without sin and to redeem others for their sins. Useppe's death could be considered as part of that "metaphysical revolt" described by Kuhn, a form of "atonement" for a sin committed by the powerful makers of history. In actuality, Morante and Comencini demonstrate quite the opposite. Children—as any subaltern—do not need to become societal scapegoats for the glory of the powers: how vain the death of these children is; how completely casual his birth was during war times; yet, his life made the happiness of all those around him. But a kind of negative providence takes care of his case and snatches him away from his mother who, after Useppe's death, will never recover from her loss of conscience. Her madness will now finally have a reason to exist: it is not merely epilepsy, but a more profound, more radicated form of madness caused by her inability to understand the ills of the world.

The last sequence of the movie, shot in slow motion, shows Ida at home with her lifeless son. She has been there three days in a state of detached madness. Neighbors and police burst into Ida's home to check the status of the family. The dog Bella protects them from intrusion. We do not hear the voices of the characters but only the extra-diegetic sound of piano music and Bella's barking. To add to the cruelty of the six-year-old child's death, the police must also shoot Bella, Useppe's surrogate mother, to gain entrance into the apartment. The use of slow motion perhaps heightens Ida's madness. Alternatively, Comencini draws attention to the aberration of history's unreality. Ida and Useppe cannot participate in any form of history, for they are neither the representatives of the faceless power that creates it nor do they belong to unaware masses that help to maintain it. In the moment of death and insanity, this cinematic scream of rebellion, they stand apart, affected by the course of events but not manipulated by them, for they are history's dissidents.

NOTES

1. Biblical epigraph at the beginning of Morante's *La Storia.* "[T]hou hast hid these things from the wise and prudent, and hast revealed them unto babes . . . for so it seemed good in thy sight" (Luke 10:21).

2. "It is only possible to be happy when others are happy." Unless otherwise noted, all translations are mine.

3. The lesson of neorealism is quite present. One needs only to remember Edmund in Roberto Rossellini's *Germany Year Zero* to come to grips with the horror of war, daughter of history: How can a child change and come to do evil when placed in the wrong environment?

4. The novel's complete title is *La Storia: uno scandalo che dura da 10.000 anni* (History: A 10,000-year-long Scandal).

WORKS CITED

Arendt, Hannah. *Eichmann in Jerusalem: A Report on the Banality of Evil.* London: Penguin Twentieth Century Classics, 2006.

Benayoun, Robert. "Luigi Comencini." *Positif* 156 (1974): 56–58.

Bordwell, David. *Making Meaning: Inference and Rhetoric in the Interpretation of Cinema.* Cambridge: Harvard University Press, 1996.

Canby, Vincent. "*La Storia* (1985) One Woman's Fight against Atrocities of Nazism." *New York Times.* 3 June 1988. Web. 5 January 2013.

Comencini, Luigi. *Infanzia, vocazione, esperienze di un regista.* Milan: Baldini e Castoldi, 1999.

Contini, Gabriella. "Useppe." "Venti anni dopo 'La Storia': Omaggio a Elsa Morante." Concetta D'Angeli and Giacomo Magrini, eds. *Studi novecenteschi* XXI, 47–48. Pisa: Giardini Edition, 1994. 185–213.

Costa, Antonio. "'Cuore,' La Storia." *Luigi Comencini: Il cinema e i film.* Ed. Adriano Aprà. Venice: Marsilio, 2009. 222–30.

De Martino, Ernesto. *Sud e magia.* Milan: Feltrinelli, 2002.

Garboli, Cesare. *La stanza separata.* Milan: Mondadori, 1969.

Gili, Jean. *Luigi Comencini.* Paris: Edilig, 1980.

Haslam, S. Alexander and Stephen Reicher. "Beyond the banality of evil: three dynamics of an interactionst social psychology of tyranny." *Personality and Social Psychology Bulletin* 33 (2007): 615–22.

Kuhn, Reinhard. *Corruption in Paradise: The Child in Western Literature.* Boston: Boston University Press, 1982.

La Storia. Dir. Luigi Comencini. RAI, 1986. Film.

Lury, Karen. *The Child in Film: Tears, Films and Fairy Tales.* London: IB Tauris and Co. Ltd., 2010.

Manacorda, Giuliano, ed. *Storia della letteratura italiana contemporanea: 1940–1965* . Rome: Editori Riuniti, 1967.

Morante, Elsa. *History: A Novel.* Trans. William Weaver. New York: Aventura, 1984.

———. *Il mondo salvato dai ragazzini. Opere.* Cesare Garboli and Carlo Cecchi, eds. Vol. 2. Milan: Mondadori, 1990. 2–254.

———. *La Storia: Romanzo.* Turin: Einaudi, 1974.

———. "Pro o contro la bomba atomica." *Pro o contro la bomba atomica e altri scritti.* Ed. Cesare Garboli. Milan: Adelphi, 1987. 97–117.

Stam, Robert, Robert Burgoyne and Sandy Flitterman-Lewis. *New Vocabulary of Film Semiotics: Structuralism, Post-structuralism and Beyond.* London: Routledge, 1992.

Toubiana, Serge. "Les Enfants et nous." *Cahiérs du cinéma* 143 (1981): 60–61.

Chapter Fifteen

Staging a Writer's Journey

Elsa Morante *by Francesca Comencini*

Gaetana Marrone

THE CHALLENGE OF DOCUMENTARY FILMMAKING

"Documentary is a clumsy description, but let it stand," writes pioneering Scottish filmmaker John Grierson in 1932. "The French who first used the term only meant travelogue. [. . .] Meanwhile documentary has gone on its way. From shimmying exoticisms it has gone on to include dramatic films like *Moana, Earth,* and *Turksib.* And in time it will include other kinds as different in form and intention" (Hardy 35).[1] Grierson's definition of the term documentary as being "the creative treatment of actuality" first appears in his 1926 review of Robert Flaherty's *Moana,* a film of great pictorial beauty on the daily life of a Polynesian youth, a worthy successor to *Nanook of the North* (1922).[2] Flaherty's films showed how the camera could bring the beauty of the natural world to the screen, an approach that offered an escape from Hollywood's studio technique.

During the 1930s, documentary became a movement in Britain, and Grierson (1898–1972) and his group, with their experiments in editing and sound, were its driving force. Films for them were a means of reaching out to an audience and influencing public opinion. Grierson understood that style is as important in documentary as in fiction film, and there is no prescribed formula for making documentaries. Thirty years later, this radical approach was initiated in the United States, Canada, and France by Robert Drew, Fred Wiseman, Ricky Leacock, Don Pennebaker, Albert and David Maysles, and the anthropologist Jean Rouch, among others, developing their own ideas about *cinéma vérité.* Their experiments were abetted by new technical breakthroughs that altered the structure and approach to documentary filmmaking.

These pioneer documentarians are all masters of camera and of editing. Many came to see voice-over commentary as a limiting factor. Most important, they pointed to the futility of dividing the documentary tradition into high and low categories: *cinéma vérité*, news reels, documentary drama, historical documentaries, industrial and public relations films, and educational films. All existed on the same continuum.

In Italy, whatever the difference in style and subject matter, the relationship between fiction films and documentaries has been problematic. As though to demonstrate this point, film critic Gian Piero Brunetta titles the short section on the documentary in his *Storia del cinema italiano* as "Il gioco delle riserve," roughly translated as "not playing in the main stream" (484). Italian documentary film has remained surprisingly homogeneous, at the margins, both in terms of reception and availability:

> *In Italia, rispetto all'Inghilterra o agli Stati Uniti, non c'è un programma o una scuola di documentarismo—alla Grierson—che si proponga di esplorare la realtà del paese; non ci sono gruppi, teorici, o manifesti. Soprattutto il documentario non vuole essere (nelle intenzioni del governo, che farà cadere a pioggia i milioni di beneficenza nel settore) un servizio di promozione della coscienza civile e culturale.* [3] (485)

> Compared with England or the United States, Italy has no documentary program or school—à la Grierson—that explores the country's realities. Neither are there groups, theorists, or manifestoes. Most of all, the documentary is not meant as a promotional service to our civic and cultural conscience. This suits the intentions of the government, who pours out excessive amounts of money to the sector.

Brunetta touches upon some important issues regarding the Italian documentary tradition. He reminds us of the widespread notion that, in so many instances, Italian directors cultivate nonfiction filmmaking as an alternative to their feature film production (or as a way to break into making feature films); that postwar documentary-like fiction films (all showed the influence of war documentaries) created a hybrid genre;[4] and, most important, that their work lacked any overt social and industrial function à la Grierson. With the exception of a few auteurs (Antonioni, Olmi, and the like), the Italian documentarians were labeled as "i commessi viaggiatori più docili e efficienti della volontà governativa" (traveling salesmen subservient to government pressure), who targeted uneducated, naïve spectators (486). Their work shows no true creativity, then, since they do not experiment with visual and narrative language. In a 1998 provocative article, Adriano Aprà went as far as to declare that the Italian documentary film did not exist (Angelone and Clò 83).[5]

Learning from Television

Virtually every kind of documentary has been influenced by new technical developments. In particular, since the 1960s filmmakers have found a venue in television. Indeed, the European networks became more open to financing outside productions and coproductions, becoming their most powerful sponsors. But there have been worries and complaints that TV stations shabbily serve the great tradition of documentaries by demanding the familiar pattern of newsreels and shying away from those that show deep feelings for specifically cinematic values. In general, television as producer has largely failed documentary in its more aesthetically important aspects.

Francesca Comencini seems attuned to the idea of documentary as being a form of artistic and social expression. She describes it in an interview as, "un'ottima scuola, un'esperienza importante per un regista di fiction, perché ti porta a confronti con la realtà, ti obbliga ad entrare in contatto con delle situazioni che altrimenti, chiusi nelle nostre storie e nei nostri ambienti, non vedremmo" (Ugolini; "A perfect school, an essential experience for a fiction film director, because it brings you face-to-face with reality; it forces you to encounter situations that you would not normally see, since we are so self-absorbed in our stories, in our own backgrounds").

Throughout her career, Comencini has chosen the less-traveled path where the production of both dramas and documentaries coexists. Born in 1961, a child of art, she has always been conscious of the cultural and social divide in a country whose economic growth has not translated into progressive ideological and sexual politics. She made her debut in 1984 with *Pianoforte*, a sort of autobiographical story, asserting her own cinematic identity. The film won the Vittorio De Sica Prize at the Venice International Film Festival, and this recognition made it possible for her to develop projects that would address issues of widespread public concern. During the next decades, she would use the genre to advance specific ideas for social betterment. Her first documentary, *Elsa Morante*, was produced in 1997 by France 3 (with RAI participation). Five more have followed, disclosing a more direct generational link to global politics: from the death of Carlo Giuliani (a young man who was shot by a police officer during the 2001 G8 meeting in Genoa), the earthquake at L'Aquila, to the dynamic account of the trade unionists' factory unrest in 2007. She has increasingly focused à la Grierson on a specific social and political spectrum, capturing the reality of her subjects or, as Dziga Vertov might have called them, "fragments of actuality." Comencini's creative aim derives from that of the social documentarians, with a moral fervor issuing from leftist ideological beliefs.

Elsa Morante is her most intimate and poetic documentary, set within the format of a French television biographical series, "Un siècle d'ecrivains." These weekly programs, directed and introduced by journalist Bernard Rapp, aired nationally between 1995 and 2001. They totaled 257 documentaries on twentieth-century writers. Each episode was fifty-two minutes long.[6] Comencini's film offers a revealing picture of Morante's persona. In the original version, Morante's story is narrated in a voice-over by French actress Odile Roire, with a commentary that is in turn informative and captivating; Morante's lyrical work, however, is read by Laura Morante, her niece, and a talented film star. We get to know the person who writes directly through her writings, but this rather traditional approach is punctuated by interviews in probing, catalyst-film fashion. Four of Morante's closest friends fabricate an image of her that slowly forms in our mind through their impressionistic recollections. The testimony of writer Cesare Garboli, actor Carlo Cecchi, poet Patrizia Cavalli, and Tonino Ricchezza, a young man from Naples's *bassi* (poor quarters) whom Elsa befriended and brought to Rome, functions, above all, to link off-screen narration with materials that re-create Morante's private and literary journey. These witnesses collectively paint a portrait of an unfailing artist who had a strong personality, culture, and self-control. Each friend describes her literary moods, aloof temperament, and dispositions: small fragments of memory enshrined in everyday life. Perhaps even more compelling is how Garboli seeks "to assimilate Morante to a masculine perspective and to sever links between her 'masterful' work and any other women writers" (Lucamante and Wood 9). He perceives her role as that of a nurturing, unfulfilled mother. In the documentary, Garboli declares that even *La Storia* is "un parto in pubblico" (a public delivery) that makes her a "madre per partenogenesi" (a mother by parthenogenesis). Morante's voice, deeply personal and passionately engaged in the literary turmoil of her country, stands out polemical, self-assured, and intellectually totalizing. Despite the inclusion of Patrizia Cavalli, this documentary is notable for its lack of feminist perspectives; a lack in line with the author's contemporary Italian culture and society, a tradition quite skeptical of feminist approaches. Morante's opinions, their variety, their power to provoke, and her way of looking at the world are fashioned in this manner. But it should also be noted that no family members were interviewed. One cannot help but wonder about such visible absence among the interviewees. Comencini does not try to enhance the film with sound effects, nor does she try to manipulate the viewers' emotions with music, of which there is very little. In general, editing seems to be downplayed.

Fashioning a Writer's Space: Memory Paths

Comencini's portrait of Elsa Morante addresses the connections between experience and creative representation, with the impossibility of art's resolving the tension between the private sphere and the public persona, a tension so prominent in one of Elsa's most endearing friends and artistic collaborator, Pier Paolo Pasolini. The selection of people, vistas, topics, and citations from her own writing conveys something quintessential about Morante's style and her way of interpreting life. Similarly, the stock footage shows fleeting moments of raw and unposed life taken from the most ordinary circumstances, yet a poetic halo surrounds Elsa from beginning to end.

The documentary opens with a clip from Pasolini's 1961 film *Accattone*, where Elsa plays a silent character sharing a cell in the Rebibbia Roman prison with two young, lower-class women speaking in dialect. As stated in a voice-over, she does not acknowledge them, "è come tagliata fuori dalla realtà delle altre" (as if she is cut out from their reality). The story of Morante's aloofness is told over and over again, as if retelling could capture the essence of her vision of real life as well as her obsession with writing itself. In fact, Cavalli reports in Comencini's documentary that, during the drafting of her last novel *Aracoeli*, Elsa went into seclusion, abandoning all of her friends, even on major holidays. That was because she *had* to write every single day, "come se i personaggi la chiamassero a casa" (as if her characters would call her home). In her growing inwardness, Morante's characters perfectly emulated the social and ideological world of the author (Pasolini, *Heretical* 91).

The opening scene establishes the elusive and reflective temperament of Elsa Morante. It is followed by a poetic fragment dedicated to Useppe, the protagonist of *La Storia*, recited over images, shot with a handheld camera, from the point of view of a person walking on a seashore, as the waves move back and forth. Eventually the camera rests on land, evoking a perfect symbiosis of life and art: the first real image of Morante is at her desk working. At this point, the film chronologically follows a linear biography, beginning with her birth in the Roman district of Trastevere and proceeding to her childhood notebooks that provide dazzling early evidence of Elsa's literary talent, to her independence at eighteen, when she eventually leaves her family. Though Comencini does not experiment with narrative structure, these events establish an unmistakably Morantian mood, as do the subsequent encounters that would define her private and literary milieu. Her awareness of exclusion provokes a thirst for love: Alberto Moravia, Luchino Visconti, the American artist Bill Morrow, and her favorite cat Caruso. Each biographical clip beats to the rhythm of Elsa's artistic career, which reflects most of the formal and technical evolution of the twentieth-century novel. The explanatory voice-over is used with restraint, and, in a sense, Comencini's depiction of Morante's artistic persona becomes an exploration of the nature of writing per se. She grafts her own discourse mainly taken from preexisting stock images, down to specific icons. The most meaningful among them are the sea and the island of Procida. Even the carefully selected sentences have an air of poetry.

The documentary comes to an abrupt end with Pasolini's violent death at Ostia, near Rome, in November 1975. The event traumatized Elsa as much as the kidnapping and execution of premier Aldo Moro by the Red Brigades three years later. These dramatic happenings bring to a close Morante's biography. For Elsa, they signified the end of an epoch when one might still believe in the transformation of the world. The first sign of her demise is her neglecting her personal appearance, followed by an attempted suicide in 1983, and ultimately her illness and long agony after being diagnosed with hydroencephalitis. The last shot of the film bears witness to her physical decay: the photograph shows her emaciated body, suggesting a withdrawn life.

Comencini's style intercuts photographic archival images with exterior black-and-white cinematography of seascapes and urban locations, a distinct stylized repertoire of compositional strategies that give the illusion of simplicity. The camera moves along steps, walls, and exteriors of buildings. She takes advantage of wide-angle and telephoto lenses, and emphasizes contrast and grain. Such rawness plays up the difference between the texture of the past and the polished, sharp look of the present. Only the interviews and the author's manuscripts and writing studio are shot in color, which makes them more real. As noted earlier, the sound track is extremely sparse, without any audio enhancement, supported by atmospheric images. The black-and-white stock footage is carefully selected, so are the places where Elsa once inhabited and that Comencini chose to include in the film. The interviews are conducted in a casual and calm style. The subjects are composed near windows with a sense of natural light. The motif of the window repeats itself throughout the film.

Morante is often shown as a solitary figure, with sparing moments of minimal dialogue and gestures. These visual elements, more than any words spoken, encompass Elsa's experience. At the end, faced with her emaciated figure in a hospital room, we perceive not a modern fable of a generation in defeat (as Morante felt during her last years), but the elusive meaning of an extraordinary existence. I am reminded of a book, *Vita di Milarepa*, which Elsa admired and recommended to Liliana Cavani. In reviewing Cavani's film adaptation in 1973, Pasolini described it as a rare, beautiful experience, "che si ripresenta alla memoria come una cosa reale, anche se sognata" (Pasolini, "La pazzesca" 184; "that resurfaces in one's memory and becomes real, even though it may be only a dream"). Milarepa and Elsa were lonely figures who existed at the margins of their culture. They were like children, creative and selfless. Both chose not to renounce dream and poetry. I would like to close this brief introduction to Comencini's documentary by evoking the spirit of Elsa Morante, forever present through the entire film: it is a spirit represented by the ancient figure of the *puer*, the child who symbolizes a creative vision of the world. It is a spirit animated by the idea that "il gioco è divino perché non c'è nessuna promessa/o speranza di guadagno" (play is divine because there is no promise/no hope to gain) (Morante 141). As the novelist of life's dreams and adventures, Morante always envisioned new spiritual and social worlds, even when she existed in the historical world of everyday life.

Francesca Comencini reminds us of the power of film to instruct and inspire, and she shows how this power can be used in our own time. The images, the symbols, and the interviews are well chosen, and there is depth in every situation and sentiment. She shows a commitment to the subject matter that ranges from an intimate form of reporting to a heightened form of poetic transfiguration. Her style has a clarity and precision that make *Elsa Morante* a worthy and significant film to watch

NOTES

1. Grierson refers respectively to Robert Flaherty's 1926 lyrical study of primitive beings, Alexander Dovzhenko's 1930 documentary that takes peasants for its theme, and Victor Turin's 1929 feature-length film on the building of the Turkestan-Siberia railway.

2. The anonymous reviewer, who signed "Flaherty's Poetic *Moana*" for the *New York Sun* on 8 Feb. 1926, was John Grierson. See Jacobs 25–26.

3. All translations are mine, unless otherwise cited.

4. In his pioneer book on the genre, historian Erik Barnouw mentions, for example, Roberto Rossellini's *Roma, città aperta* (1945) and Vittorio De Sica's *Sciuscià* (1946), as prototypes of the documentary-like-fiction trend set in motion by the war experience (185).

5. Aprà's "Primi approcci al documentario italiano" was published in the special issue of *Annali I* entitled *A proposito del documentario* (40–67). Aprà has since modified his position, see "La rifondazione del documentario italiano" (187–92). Also Aldo Bernardini speaks of a "buco nero" (black hole) for the history of the Italian documentary, often viewed as a "minor" genre (15). On the subject, see the seminal study by Gianpaolo Bernagozzi and, most recently, Marco Bertozzi; Giulia Conte.

6. Italy was represented by Giuseppe Tomasi di Lampedusa, Primo Levi, Curzio Malaparte, Alberto Moravia, Cesare Pavese, and Leonardo Sciascia. France, where she primarily resides since 1982, exerts a special fascination on Comencini. The French cinematic movement and techno-culture have produced documentaries of compelling style and richness. Such is the case, for example, of Agnès Varda, with her sophisticated background in still photography, or Chris Marker's accomplished range as an essayist.

WORKS CITED

Accattone. Dir. Pier Paolo Pasolini. Arco Film, 1961. Film.

Angelone, Anita, and Clarissa Clò. "Other Visions: Contemporary Italian Documentary Cinema as Counter-discourse." *Studies in Documentary Film* 5 (2011): 2–3, 83–89.

Aprà, Adriano. "Primi approcci al documentario italiano." *A proposito del documentario*. Special issue *Annali I* (Archivio audiovisivo del movimento operario e democratico) (1998): 40–67.

———. "La rifondazione del documentario italiano." *L'idea documentaria: altri sguardi dal cinema italiano*. Marco Bertozzi and Gianfranco Pannone, eds. Turin: Lindau, 2003. 187–92.

Barnouw, Erik. *Documentary: A History of the Non-Fiction Film*. 1974. New York-Toronto-Melbourne: Oxford University Press, 1983.

Bernagozzi, Gianpaolo. *Il cinema corto: il documentario nella vita italiana 1945–1980.* Florence: La Casa Usher, 1980.

Bernardini, Aldo. "Presentazione." *La Sicilia della memoria: cento anni di cinema documentario nell'isola.* By Sebastiano Gesù. Catania: Giuseppe Maimone, 1999. 15.

Bertozzi, Marco. *Storia del documentario italiano: Immagini e culture dell'altro cinema.* Venice: Marsilio, 2008.

Brunetta, Gian Piero. *Storia del cinema italiano: dal neorealismo al miracolo economico 1945–1959.* 3rd ed. Rome: Editori Riuniti, 2000.

Conte, Giulia. "Il cinema del reale: il documentario di creazione in Italia." *Cinéma italien du 21 e siècle,* special issue *Chroniques italiennes* 85–86 (2010). 23–40.

Hardy, Forsyth, ed. *Grierson on Documentary.* 1946. London-Boston: Faber and Faber, 1979.

Jacobs, Lewis, ed. *The Documentary Tradition.* 2nd ed. New York: W. W. Norton & Co., 1979.

Lucamante, Stefania, and Sharon Wood, eds. *Under Arturo's Star: The Cultural Legacies of Elsa Morante.* West Lafayette, IN: Purdue University Press, 2006.

Morante, Elsa. *Il mondo salvato dai ragazzini. Opere* 2. Ed. Cesare Garboli and Carlo Cecchi. Milan: Meridiani Mondadori. 2–254.

Pasolini, Pier Paolo. "La pazzesca razionalità della geometria religiosa." *Cinema nuovo* 23.229 (May–June 1974): 184–85.

———. *Heretical Empiricism.* Trans. Ben Lawton and Louise K. Barnett. Bloomington-Indianapolis: Indiana University Press, 1988.

Ugolini, Chiara. "Di mobbing non si muore." *La repubblica* 10 February 2004. Web. 21 January 2013.

III

Queering Morante:
Bodies that Matter from
Diario 1938 to *Aracoeli*

Chapter Sixteen

"Tuo scandalo tuo splendore"

The Split Mother in Morante's Works from
Diario 1938 *to* Aracoeli

Katrin Wehling-Giorgi

The mother or the maternal figure is a central presence throughout Elsa Morante's works, ranging from the early *Diario 1938* to her last novel *Aracoeli*. While a considerable amount of criticism has focused on motherhood in her writings, it has often been based on the assumption of a contrast emerging between the nurturing, "ideal" maternal figure (e.g., Ida, Nunziatella), on the one hand, and the subversive, "scandalous" portrayal of motherhood in *Aracoeli*, on the other. Indeed, scholars such as Cesare Garboli have identified a profound break in Morante's representation of the mother after *La Storia*, arguing that with *Aracoeli* "il vecchio schema glorioso (madre/figlio; Nunziata/Arturo; Ida/Useppe) viene lapidato e dato in pasto ai cani perché ne facciano strazio" (174; "the glorious old scheme [mother/son; Nunziata/Arturo; Ida/Useppe] is torn to pieces and thrown to the wolves for them to mutilate it").[1]

In this chapter, I will instead identify a clear continuity in Morante's increasingly complex depiction of the maternal figure throughout her literary career, which will in turn provide us with some new insights into the trajectory of selfhood in her works. There are numerous earlier texts that anticipate and indeed foreshadow the intrinsic ambivalence that characterizes Aracoeli, portraying the mother as an object of intense desire, on the one hand, and as a stifling, transgressive, and at times even revolting figure, on the other. By adopting a critical framework that is chiefly inspired by Julia Kristeva's ideas on the fundamental role of the mother in the early formation of the self, I will further investigate the presence of these contrasting elements in the

Morantian portrayal of the mother from the earliest texts from the 1930s (*Qualcuno bussa alla porta, Diario 1938*) to *Lo scialle andaluso* (1953) and *Aracoeli* (1982). While in her earlier writings, as I will show, it is the tension between the characters' nostalgia for the pre-lapsarian unity with the mother and the efforts to free themselves from her that prevails, in her last novel the Morantian protagonist succeeds in *abjecting* the suffocating side of the mother, paving the way for an autonomous form of subjectivity that transcends the destructive thrust of the maternal realm.

DIARIO 1938

There is a clear focus on the mother figure at least as early as in Morante's *Diario 1938* where, *in nuce*, she already displays the characteristically ambiguous features of Aracoeli.[2] What emerges from the self-exploratory *Diario*, which was of course never destined for publication, is not only a perceived lack of love, even rejection on the part of the mother, but the maternal figure is also repeatedly associated with death and disintegration. In fact, the diary opens with Morante's oneiric self entering a room in which a former acquaintance's (referred to only as "E. C.") mother has died and, while the space is described as "incantevole" (*Diario*, 5; "enchanting"), she is overcome by the odour of death ("la stanza odora di morte" [5]; "the room smells of death"). The imagery of this dream episode is highly suggestive and permeated with references to desire and the maternal, while simultaneously emphasizing the impossibility of satiating that very longing. The female character sees herself as not only somewhat clandestinely irrupting into the room "come una ladra" (like a thief) but also as having "violated" the mother's space with her physical entrance ("la stanza violata" [6]; "the room violated"). This impression is further reinforced when her menstrual cycle begins and she sees herself caught by E. C. contaminating the house with "un peso liquido, molle, caldo, fra le [sue] gambe" (6; "a soft, hot liquid weight, between my legs"), "perdendo fiocchi di sangue" (6; "losing drops of blood").

At that point in the dream sequence Elsa's brother enters the scene, equally desiring to gain access to the room ("Anche lui forse vorrebbe questa camera" [6]; "Maybe he would also like this room"), suggesting a form of sibling rivalry competing for the mother's affection. In her hands, the narrating self is described as holding a container (6; "recipient") akin to those generally used by the milkman that contains "un'acqua biancastra, mista a latte" (6; "a whitish color, mixed with milk"), with the milky liquid clearly recalling the original maternal substance. While in the dream Morante quenches her thirst, she wakes up "con la bocca bruciata dalla sete" (6; "with her mouth burning with thirst"), suggesting that while some of her needs are habitually satisfied in the oneiric dimension, in reality "lo stesso bisogno [rimane] insoddisfatto" (6; "that same need remains unfulfilled").

Like numerous episodes in *Diario*, this passage is haunted by an elusive maternal presence. The focus on the defiling nature of bodily liquids such as menstrual blood, which invites associations with the disruptive potential of the Kristevan notion of *abjection*,[3] underscores the author's troubled sense of selfhood, which is directly reflected in the unresolved tensions of the relationship with the mother. Indeed, as Elisa Gambaro puts it, "Morante's quest for identity as a woman . . . is achieved through a series of painful confrontations with the mother" (26). This line of interpretation is further reinforced by a number of episodes in the diary in which Elsa seeks to connect with the mother, or to gain access to a maternal space, and where she is downright rejected or fails to establish the desired contact. On one occasion the protagonist finds herself in her mother's vegetable garden (*orto*), surrounded by "beautiful pink flowers, full and soft" (11; "bellissimi fiori rosa, pieni e molli"), with the adjectives evoking the physical attributes of the maternal body in a powerful synecdoche. Elsa's desire to actually hold these flowers and her mother's refusal to hand her any of them suggests yet another failed attempt to regain access to the maternal. This brusque act of rejection only further fuels the daughter's frustrated desire, and upon reawakening she nostalgically recalls the soft color and texture of the plant:

> *Con un desiderio enorme fissavo uno di quei vasi e supplicavo mia madre di darmelo. . . . Ma mia madre, con una piccola mossa di rincrescimento sulle labbra, diceva che no, non poteva levarsi una pianta. Il mio desiderio aumentava, tanto che ancora da sveglia mi è rimasto il senso della tenerezza molle, del dolce colore di quella pianta. Mia madre, avara, scuoteva il capo. . . . Mi prendeva un tormento acuto per questa mancanza d'amore, e del sogno per ora non ricordo altro.* (Morante, *Diario 1938*, 11)

> I was focusing on one of those vases with an enormous desire, and pleading with my mother to hand it to me. . . . But my mother, with a hint of remorse on her lips, said no, she could not give away the plant. My desire was increasing, so much so that even now I am awake I still feel that soft tenderness, the gentle color of that plant. But my mother, ungiving, was shaking her head. . . . I was profoundly tormented by that lack of love, and for now I don't remember anything else about the dream.

This time the oneiric episode leaves the protagonist not only with frustrated desire, but she also suffers the emotional torment caused by her mother's cruel rejection. In her self-analysis of the dream Morante manifests a level of psychoanalytical insight that clearly stems from her reading of Sigmund Freud's *Introduction to Psychoanalysis* during those months (Bardini 71). In fact, she acknowledges that her desire for the flowers must originate in some profound inner source: "Questo desiderio che mi era parso così superficiale ed esile, doveva invece avere radici profonde in me stessa, se il mio sogno ha rievocato quei fiori con tanta forza" (Morante, *Diario* 12; "This desire, which had seemed to me so superficial and weak, must have been profoundly rooted in me if I preserved such a vivid memory of those flowers").

In yet another diary entry, the mother assumes a physically abject appearance that is directly associated with death and a distinctly disintegrating force.

> *A un certo punto di questi sogni, vedendo nel riquadro di una finestra il corpo enfiato, il viso disfatto di mia madre, io, distesa a terra più in basso in una specie di cortile, avevo un terrore spaventoso della morte. . . . La morte mi appariva come un corpo squallido, gonfio e viscoso. Un affetto cupo mi attirava a mia madre, già possesso della bruttezza e del disfacimento che preparano per lunghi anni la fine della morte.* (Morante, *Diario 1938*, 48–49)

> At a certain point in these dreams, when I saw my mother's swollen body and her disheveled face at a window frame, with me lying on the floor below in some kind of courtyard, I had an overwhelming fear of death. . . . Death appeared to me like a wretched, swollen, and viscous body. A dark affection tied me to my mother, an affection already imbued with the ugliness and decay that for many years prepare us for the end of death.

What is striking in this passage is both the horror evoked by the mother's decaying body ("corpo enfiato" [swollen body]; "viso disfatto" [disheveled face]), and the near-oxymoronic "affetto cupo" (dark affection) that she inspires. Furthermore, her disintegrating appearance is clearly echoed in the physical, corporeal attributes associated with death ("corpo squallido, gonfio e viscoso" [wretched, swollen, and viscous body]), with both assuming a swollen, disjointed physical aspect. In fact, there are a striking number of episodes in the *Diario* focusing on the fragmented maternal body and its associations with death,[4] on the one hand, and the desire she evokes, on the other. And it is precisely this profoundly split maternal imago, simultaneously marked by affection and destruction, that forms the basis of the filial relationship portrayed in her last novel *Aracoeli*, which we will further discuss below.

Kristeva's ideas on the role of the maternal in the formation of the subject provide a very useful interpretative tool in this context. According to the post-Lacanian critic and psychoanalyst, the mother plays a central role in the earliest stages of infantile development, and hence both in the ontogenesis of the self and language. Indeed, the mother is located at the threshold of the preconceptual and the symbolic realm of language and selfhood, with the child's separation from her coinciding with the passage from what she terms the "semiotic," preconceptual, and pre-linguistic level to the "symbolic," the realm of structured language and social order. So in order to form an independent sense of selfhood and to enter into the symbolic realm, the individual has to "abject" or reject the mother, which is a necessary precondition for the autonomous self. In this process of separation and the simultaneous transition from the semiotic to the symbolic, the mother becomes the first instance of alterity or of "the other subject, an object that guarantees my being as subject" (Kristeva, *Powers* 32). If this split ("matricide") does not occur, the self remains anchored in the stage of pre-narcissistic symbiosis with the mother and hence fails to establish an independent sense of selfhood: "For man and for woman the loss of the mother is a biological and psychic necessity, the first step on the way to becoming autonomous. Matricide is our vital necessity, the sine-qua-non condition of our individuation." (Kristeva, *Black Sun* 27–28). As I will argue below, this act of *abjecting* the potentially destructive aspects of the maternal is only successfully completed toward the end of Morante's last novel *Aracoeli*. Her earlier writings, on the other hand, are marked by a profound struggle between desire and rejection of the maternal, an ambivalence that lies at the very basis of the split portrayal of the genetrix.

LO SCIALLE ANDALUSO

In *Lo scialle andaluso*, the male protagonist Andrea is engaged in a desperate attempt to reclaim and possess his mother Giuditta, who appears to be more dedicated to her career as a dancer than to motherhood. Andrea deeply resents her passion for the stage, developing an outright hatred for the theater. Oscillating between scenes of "brutal"[5] separation and utter dedication between mother and son, he spends his childhood torn between these two extreme emotions, repeatedly and unsuccessfully claiming ownership of his mother: "Alla vista di Giuditta, i suoi occhi spalancati si empivano di fulgida ingenua dedizione; ma, dopo un istante, egli ritorceva il viso da lei [. . .] come uno che deve assistere, senza poterlo impedire, al furto della sua proprietà" (Morante, *Lo scialle* 166; "At the sight of Giuditta, his gaping eyes filled with a dazzling and naïve devotion; after a moment, however, he turned away from her . . . like someone who reluctantly assists in the theft of his own property"). In fact, Andrea's feelings for his mother are marked by a profound sense of ambiguity: "Era il sentimento duplice di una possibilità felice, e di una negazione crudele: troppo noto a lui fin dai suoi primi anni perché lui potesse sbagliarsi" (196; "It was the twofold feeling of a happy possibility and a cruel rejection: he knew it only too well from his early years, there was no mistaking it").

Resigned to the fact that he will never possess his mother, Andrea retreats into a religious institution to train as a priest, abdicating all desire for her while violently rejecting all her attempts to preserve the relationship. It is only when he sees his mother's photograph ("effigie di sua madre" [183];

"effigy of his mother") in exotic dress on a poster announcing her theater company's performance in town that his desire is instantly reignited with a strong burst of emotion ("L'emozione fu così forte che il sangue gli montò al viso" [183]; "The feeling was so strong that blood rushed to his face"). He decides to flee the institution to attend her play, thereby violating the symbolic authority of the church to return to his mother.

What follows is a seemingly happy reunion that sees a series of dress changes marking the return to the maternal: Andrea takes off his tunic to be wrapped in Giuditta's symbolic Andalusian shawl of the novella's title sealing the partial but incomplete reunion between the two. As Elio Gioanola has argued, the shawl symbolizes the return to the uterine space of the maternal, a union that fails to produce the desired happiness ("lo scialle è quello con cui la madre avvolge il figlio denudato della tonaca da prete, come se lo chiudesse nella custodia primaria della placenta" [368]; "having taken off the priest's robe, the mother wraps the son into the shawl, as if to envelop him in the primary custody of the placenta"). In fact, despite Giuditta's promise to give up her profession, Andrea soon realizes that her decision was based on the fact that she had been rejected by the theater itself. Bitterly disappointed by his inability to earn his mother's love and dedication, his attitude toward her once again turns into one of indifference and melancholy, and the novella ends with him roaming the streets "*con una banda di giovani scamiciati, fanatici e sovversivi*" (213, italics in original; "*with a group of disheveled, fanatical, and subversive youngsters*"), struggling to define his own identity:

> *Ma il personaggio fra tutti misterioso, ancora sconosciuto a lui stesso, è uno: Andrea Campese! . . . Egli vorrebbe immaginare il futuro se stesso, e si compiace di prestare a questo Ignoto aspetti vittoriosi, abbaglianti, trionfi e disinvolture! Ma, per quanto la scacci, ritrova sempre là, come una statua, un'immagine, sempre la stessa, importuna:*
> un triste, protervo Eroe
> avvolto in uno scialle andaluso. (213)

> But the most mysterious character of all, still unknown to himself, is only one: Andrea Campese! . . . He would like to imagine his future self and is content to lend to this Unknown victorious, dazzling features, triumphs and nonchalance! But, however much he rejects it, he always finds there, like a statue, the same, always the same persistent image:
> *a sad, haughty Hero*
> *wrapped in an Andalusian shawl.*

The nostalgia to return to the maternal frames Andrea's identity-building process, ending upon the image of a highly disorientated young man whose simultaneously desired and rejected mother constitutes a distinctly destructive force in his trajectory of selfhood. The closing image of the novella suggests that a profoundly unhappy Andrea remains trapped in the pre-narcissistic maternal sphere, symbolized by the Andalusian shawl.

ARACOELI

Many critics see *Aracoeli*'s eponymous maternal figure not only as antithetical to the author's previous portrayals of the mother, but she is also often considered the "tragic conclusion of [Morante's] descent to the mothers," a trajectory that is seen as ending in "silence and death" (Gambaro 27) in her last novel.[6] On the basis of the forms of maternal deviance identified in her earlier works, I would like to challenge this view, arguing that what really sets *Aracoeli* apart is not so much its self-destructive tone or the transformation of the mother into a transgressive figure, but rather Manuele's *active* role in this process, as I will illustrate below.[7]

Similarly to previous Morantian mother-son relationships, the bond between Manuele and Aracoeli is characterized by an intrinsic form of ambivalence. On the one hand, the protagonist desires to reenter the maternal realm once the "biological" separation has occurred at birth, "Da allora in realtà io non ho mai smesso di cercarla, e fino da allora la mia scelta era questa: rientrare in lei. Rannicchiarmi dentro di lei, nell'unica mia tana, persa oramai chi sa dove, in quale strapiombo" (Morante, *Aracoeli* 18; "From then on, really, I have never stopped seeking her, and from then on, my determination was this: to reenter her. To curl up inside her, in my only haven, lost now who knows where, in what abyss" [Morante, *Aracoeli* (trans.) 17]).

On the other hand, Manuele profoundly resents his mother's act of abandonment. The early period spent in Monte Sacro preceding the legalization of his parents' relationship through marriage is characterized by a symbiotic form of fusion between mother and son, which is often recalled by Manuele as a time of blissful, pre-lapsarian happiness. While his mother is totally dedicated to her son in the early "Totetaco" (Manuele's infantile designation of Monte Sacro) phase, this changes with the move to the paternal realm of the *Quartieri Alti* and the subsequent sudden death of Aracoeli's baby daughter, which triggers her profound transformation and ultimately sees her abandon the family home to work in a brothel.

What significantly distinguishes *Aracoeli* from previous Morantian narratives, however, is what I see as the male protagonist's successful "abjection" of the destructive, suffocating effect of the maternal figure following her death. While previous characters fail to liberate themselves from the grip of the maternal,[8] Manuele does not just passively endure the act of rejection, but he embarks on a striking process of disfigurement and mutilation of the maternal imago, turning her into a figure inspiring horror ("orrenda Aracoeli" [Morante, *Aracoeli* 301]; "horrible Aracoeli" [Morante, *Aracoeli* (trans.)

285]) and disgust ("mi facevi schifo" [Morante, *Aracoeli* 303]; "you disgusted me" [Morante, *Aracoeli* (trans.) 287]; "repulsiva" [Morante, *Aracoeli*
301]; "repulsive" [Morante, *Aracoeli* (trans.) 285]) who is eventually expelled as part of a self-protective defence mechanism:

> *Avevo già cominciato, infatti, fino dal mio ritorno in Piemonte, a difendermi*
> *dalla sua morte* sfigurando e devastando *il nostro amore.* . . . *La mamita*
> *Aracoeli regina dei ricordi si strappava via da me, come una* mutilazione. *E*
> *questa mia presente Aracoeli* . . . *[era] la sola che mi riprendesse figura dopo*
> *la sua morte.* . . . *Se in lei si riconosceva una somiglianza, era solo con*
> *quell'altra—spudorata e smaniosa—che mi si portava dietro fino all'ultima*
> *estate. [E]ra lei,* . . . *ma ridotta a una vecchia laida, cascante e imbelletta-*
> *ta.* . . . *Tutti.* . . *accorrevano, di ritorno, a lapidare la brutta Aracoeli. Ma ero*
> *io l'ordinatore della strage, io l'esecutore volontario.* (Morante, *Aracoeli*
> 300–301, my emphasis)

> I had already begun defending myself against her death by *defacing and de-*
> *stroying* our love. . . . The mamita Aracoeli, queen of memories, was torn from
> me in *mutilation.* And this present Aracoeli of mine. . .[was] the only one that
> resumed a form for me after her death. . . . If I recognized a resemblance in
> her, it was only with that other, shameless and raving, who carried me back to
> the last summer. Indeed, it was she, . . .but reduced to a loathsome old woman,
> sagging and painted. . . . All . . . came running, returning, to stone the ugly
> Aracoeli. But I was the director of the massacre, I was the willing executant.
> (Morante, *Aracoeli* (trans.) 284–85, my emphasis)

Hence Aracoeli is not only transformed into a subversive and repulsive figure
after her death, but this specific side of her is then also metaphorically
"killed" by her son. In the final scene of the novel, in which Manuele confesses the love for his father, the protagonist reconfirms the abandonment of
his mother who, "lasciata indietro sola a decomporsi nell'orrido parco" (left
behind alone, to decompose in the horrid park), he claims to have both
rejected ("negazione," "ripudio"; "denial," "repudiation") and forgotten
("oblio"; "oblivion") (Morante, *Aracoeli* 327). So what is new is not so much
the bad mother in itself, but it is the protagonist's mental transformation and
disfigurement of her "monstrous" side, which eventually allow him to liberate himself from her.

   While Fortuna and Gragnolati have convincingly shown that the protagonist's recovery of the father suggests some "new possible intersections"
("Affection" 17) between the linguistic realms of the semiotic and symbolic,
I would suggest that the protagonist's *abjection* of the "monstrous mother"
enables him to overcome the threat of disintegration emanating from her. In
fact, Manuele's move beyond the maternal allows him to envisage a notion
of selfhood that neither confines him to the pre-oedipal realm nor to the
dead-ended pursuit of self-obliteration in death, both troubled forms of iden-

tity that characterize previous Morantian characters instead. Through her near-obsessive preoccupation with motherhood and its "disruptive" effects on the subject, which can be traced back to split maternal imago emerging from her very first writings from the 1930s, Morante provides us with a unique exploration of selfhood and identity that finds an unprecedented form of resolution in her last novel. Contrary to the tragic and essentially negative conclusions that many critics have seen in *Aracoeli*, the protagonist's eventual *abjection* of the deviant mother paves the path for a new, autonomous form of subjectivity that remains unprecedented in her previous depictions of the mother-child relationship.

NOTES

1. Unless otherwise noted, all translations are mine. See also Benedetti (79, 83) and Zlobnicki Kalay (93–94), who see a similarly radical break in Morante's representation of the maternal figure after *La Storia*.

2. An even earlier occurrence of a "deviant" mother is Mirtilla in *Qualcuno bussa alla porta*, a novel "invasa dal tema della maternità" (Nelsen 273; "occupied by the topic of maternity"), which Morante published in 29 installments in "I diritti della scuola" between September 1935 and August 1936. Mirtilla, who is presented as "strana e selvaggia" ("strange and savage"; "Qualcuno bussa alla porta," 25 September 1935, 8) right from the beginning of the narrative, leaves the family home at the age of sixteen and gets pregnant by an unknown man who disappears soon after. She abandons her daughter at birth and is unknowingly reunited with her only in the last scene of the novel, where she appears as a stray gypsy who has succumbed to madness. Dai Pra argues that Mirtilla's unsettling presence at the end of the narration foreshadows some of the later developments of Morante's writings: "l'apparizione di quell'inquietante Mirtilla, insieme zingara, madre cattiva e mater dolorosa, ci [dice] molto più del resto della trama sulle reali condizioni dell'autrice" (54; "the appearance of the unsettling Mirtilla, gypsy, bad mother, and mater dolorosa in one, tells us far more about the real conditions of the author than the rest of the plot"). Mirtilla is not only the first in a series of "natural" Morantian mothers (see Nelsen 271), but the abandonment of her daughter, her untamed nature and nomadic, gypsy existence clearly foreshadow some of the subversive elements of subsequent maternal characters such as Giuditta, Nunziatella, and Aracoeli.

3. In Kristevan terms, due to its in-between status with respect to the natural perimeter of the body, the physically abject, including bodily substances like urine, excrement, vomit, blood, sweat, and semen, epitomises "what disturbs identity, system, order," and "what does not respect borders, positions, rules" (*Powers* 3–5).

4. Morante's mother often appears as dressed in black. See, for example, the *Diario* entry from 2 February 1938: 'Mia madre ci viene incontro camminando sull'acqua: ha un abito nero, con maniche larghe e sventolanti indietro' (My mother is coming toward us walking on water: she is wearing a black dress with wide sleeves fluttering behind).

5. See, for example, p. 164: "spazientita, con brutalità si liberava di lui, e spariva, sbattendo la porta" (having lost patience, she brutally freed herself from him and disappeared, slamming the door).

6. See, for example, Patrucco Becchi: "Nell'ultimo libro di Elsa Morante, infine, la ricerca dell'amore materno ha un'amara conclusione: la madre, così a lungo cercata, è per sempre perduta, e con lei il suo amore, che come prostituta ella ha venduto ad altri" (450; "In Elsa Morante's final book, at last, the search for maternal love reaches a bitter conclusion: the long-searched-for mother is forever lost, together with her love, which she has sold on to others as a prostitute"); see also Benedetti (83) for a similarly negative interpretation of the maternal imago in *Aracoeli*.

7. My interpretation of a continuity subsisting between the topics fundamental to earlier Morantian texts and *Aracoeli* is in line with Fortuna and Gragnolati's groundbreaking volume on *Aracoeli, The Power of Disturbance*, to which I am much indebted.

8. A number of Morantian mothers play a determining, and often suffocating, role in the child's trajectory of selfhood. *Menzogna e sortilegio*'s (1948) female protagonist Elisa remains very close to her adoptive mother Rosaria, whose death triggers her search for identity. As Lazzaro argues, Elisa's psychic development does not follow the "normal" Freudian route of eventually turning the affection toward the father. Instead, the protagonist's continuing focus on the maternal figure leaves her trapped in the "fase pre-edipica, di fatto non 'entra' nel complesso edipico vero e proprio" (237; "pre-oedipal stage, in fact she does not 'enter' the actual Oedipus complex"), which in turn results in an incomplete state of individuation: "il suo sviluppo non ha luogo. Di conseguenza, la sua vita è caratterizzata dal rifiuto della sessualità" (237; "her development does not take place. As a consequence, her life is characterized by the rejection of sexuality"). Similarly, in *La Storia* (1974) Useppe remains anchored in the prever-bal sphere of the maternal until his untimely death at the age of five, with the narrator observing that his unawareness of all symbolic codes based on social, racial, and gender categories turn him into a "vivente smentita [. . .] alla scienza del Professor Freud" (405; "a living refutation of the science of Professor Freud"; *History*).

WORKS CITED

Bardini, Marco. "Poetry and Reality in 'The Aesthetics of Our Time.'" Lucamante and Wood 67–93.

Becchi Patrucco, Anna. "Stabat mater. Le madri di Elsa Morante." *Belfagor* 31 (July 1993): 436–51.

Benedetti, Laura. *The Tigress in the Snow: Motherhood and Literature in Twentieth-Century Italy.* Toronto: University of Toronto Press, 2007.

Dai Pra, Silvia. "La preistoria della Morante: 'Qualcuno bussa alla porta.'" *Allegoria* 54 (2006): 47–56.

Fortuna, Sara and Manuele Gragnolati. "Between Affection and Discipline: Exploring Linguis-tic Tensions from Dante to *Aracoeli.*" *The Power of Disturbance: Elsa Morante's* Aracoeli. Sara Fortuna and Manuele Gragnolati, eds. London: Legenda, 2009. 8–19.

Gambaro, Elisa. "Strategies of Affabulation in Elsa Morante's *Diario 1938.*" Lucamante and Wood 21–44.

Garboli, Cesare. *Il gioco segreto.* Milan: Adelphi, 1995.

Gioanola, Elio. "Elsa Morante e la storia." *Psicanalisi e interpretazione letteraria: Leopardi, Pascoli, D'Annunzio, Saba, Montale, Penna, Quasimodo, Caproni, Sanguineti, Mussapi, Viviani, Morante, Primo Levi, Soldati, Biamonti.* Milan: Jaca Book, 2005. 353–70.

Kristeva, Julia. *Black Sun: Depression and Melancholia.* Trans. Leon S. Roudiez. New York: Columbia University Press, 1989.

———. *Powers of Horror: An Essay on Abjection.* Trans. Leon S. Roudiez. New York: Columbia University Press, 1982.

———. *Revolution in Poetic Language.* Trans. Margaret Waller. New York: Columbia Uni-versity Press, 1984.

Lazzaro, Laura. "Le relazioni madre-figlia e madre-figlio in due romanzi di Elsa Morante: *La storia* e *Menzogna e sortilegio.*" *Versants: Revue Suisse des Littératures Romanes/Rivista Svizzera di Letterature Romanze/Schweizerische Zeitschrift für Romanische Literaturen* 59 (2006): 229–59.

Lucamante, Stefania, and Sharon Wood, eds. *Under Arturo's Star: The Cultural Legacies of Elsa Morante.* West Lafayette, IN: Purdue University Press, 2006.

Morante, Elsa. *Aracoeli.* Turin: Einaudi, 1982.

———. *Aracoeli.* Trans. William Weaver. Rochester: First Open Letter, 2009.

———. *Arturo's Island.* Trans. Isabel Quigly. New York: Alfred A. Knopf, 1959.

———. *Diario 1938.* Ed. Alba Andreini. Turin: Einaudi, 1989.

———. *History: A Novel.* Trans. William Weaver. London: Penguin, 1977.

————. *L'isola di Arturo*. Turin: Einaudi, 1957.

————. *Lo scialle andaluso*. Turin: Einaudi, 1963.

————. *La Storia: romanzo*.Turin: Einaudi, 1974.

————. *Menzogna e sortilegio*. Turin: Einaudi, 1948.

————. "Qualcuno bussa alla porta." *I diritti della scuola*. 25 September 1935–15 August 1936.

Nelsen, Elisabetta. "*Qualcuno bussa alla porta*. Analisi tematica del primo romanzo di Elsa Morante." *Forum Italicum* 28.2 (1994): 269–80.

Rosa, Giovanna. *Cattedrali di carta: Elsa Morante romanziere*. Milan: Il saggiatore, 1995.

Serkowska, Hanna. "The Maternal Boy: Manuele, or the last Portrait of Morante's Androgyny." Lucamante and Wood 157–87.

Zlobnicki Kalay, Grace. *The Theme of Childhood in Elsa Morante*. University, MS: Romance Monographs, 1996.

Chapter Seventeen

Differently Queer

Sexuality and Aesthetics in Pier Paolo Pasolini's
Petrolio *and Elsa Morante's* Aracoeli

Manuele Gragnolati

The ideas that I will discuss in this chapter stem from my book *"Amor che move": linguaggio del corpo e forma del desiderio in Dante, Pasolini e Morante*, which proposes a diffractive reading of Dante's works and some of their late-twentieth-century reappropriations, and explores the relationship between a type of proto-modern subjectivity, like that expressed by Dante's texts, and a postmodern one, like that expressed by Pier Paolo Pasolini's and Elsa Morante's. In this chapter I will leave Dante aside and ask some new questions on Pasolini and Morante, focusing on the relationship between the aesthetics of their novels *Petrolio* and *Aracoeli*. I will argue that both novels mobilize a form of temporality that resists a sense of linear and teleological development and that, instead, appears contorted, inverted, suspended, and thereby allows for the articulation of queer desires and pleasures that cannot be inscribed in a normative logics of progression or productivity. In particular I am interested in understanding how the queer sexuality staged in Pasolini's and Morante's novels is reflected in their textuality but differs from each other.

I will begin with *Petrolio*, Pasolini's unfinished magnum opus on which he had been working for some years when he was killed in November 1975. *Petrolio* was meant to be a two-thousand-page-long novel in the form of a critical edition of a text composed of fragments coming from several manuscripts and put together by an editor who would have filled the gaps with historical documents like interviews, newspaper excerpts, and documentary material. It should have also contained other materials, such as letters, songs, and even illustrations. What we have extant is a text of approximately five hundred pages that was published for the first time in 1992 and that has the form of a magmatic accumulation of fragments—called *Appunti* (Notes). It intertwines the vicissitudes of the protagonist—the engineer Carlo who since the beginning is split into two halves: Carlo di Polis and Carlo di Tetis—with, on the one hand, the political and economic history of Italy in the 1950s, 1960s, and 1970s and, on the other, a disparate series of digressions that are often meta-narrative and meta-literary.[1] As the novel itself indicates, the course of narration is chaotic and swirly (*a brulichio*), rather than linear and progressive (*a schidionata*) and aims at inducing a feeling of disorientation in the reader (Pasolini, *Petrolio* 1275), where the phrase "a brulichio" refers to the chaotic and irregular movement of bees and "a schidionata" refers instead to the progressive logics of cause and effect represented by the *schidione* (the long metal skewer used for the shish kebab).

In my book, I read the form of *Petrolio*, or, rather, the lack of it together with *La Divina Mimesis*, Pasolini's work most explicitly modeled upon Dante's *Comedy*, showing that *La Divina Mimesis* and *Petrolio* destroy the modern sense of authorship that arguably begins with Dante. In particular, I maintain that *La Divina Mimesis* does so by staging its own failure, while *Petrolio* does so through a type of textuality consistent with what Pasolini in the *Divina Mimesis* calls "dilatazione" and defines in the following way: "Asimmetria, sproporzione, legge dell'irregolarità programmata, irrisione della coesività, introduzione teppistica dell'arbitrario" (1090; "Asymmetry, disproportion, the law of planned irregularity, derision of cohesiveness, the thuggish introduction of the arbitrary").[2] In other words: *Divina Mimesis* performs failure, while *Petrolio* performs dilation.[3]

Here I will mention two episodes in which the double protagonist Carlo, transformed into a woman, has sexual intercourse with *lumpenproletariat* boys, because these episodes offer a meditation on a particular declination of queer sexuality. I agree with Rebecca West that the protagonist's transformation into a woman, which occurs twice, does not imply any real opening toward a sexed alterity (39–50), and I would rather take it as an allegory for homosexual relations.[4] Indeed, the protagonist is always referred to as grammatically male, and both episodes seem to remain bounded within an entirely male universe. In particular, the two long episodes insist on the details of Carlo's sexual relationships with his partners and describe a masochistic submission, which shatters subjectivity and is experienced as a liberation from consciousness and history.

The first episode ("Il pratone della Casilina") describes in detail Carlo's numerous sexual experiences with a series of boys from the outskirts of Rome to whom the obedient and humiliated protagonist repeatedly submits with "the desire for depravity, for obscenity, for excess" (Pasolini, *Petrolio* [trans.] 178; "voglia della bassezza, dell'oscenità, dell'eccesso" [Pasolini,

Petrolio 1415]). This veritable rhetorical and sexual tour de force conveys an almost sacral fascination for the subproletarian boys' sexual organs and for a world radically different from one's own, as is made clear in the following excerpt from the description of the last intercourse:

> *Non amava Pietro solo per quel gigantesco pezzo di carne che aveva in bocca, liscio e duro [. . .] con quel loro calore, quel loro odore, e quel tanto di livido, quasi abbietto—cioè di non innocentemente animalesco—che trasudavano. Egli amava quel ragazzo anche per quello che non gli dava e non poteva dargli [. . .]. [T]utto questo [. . .] era [. . .] simbolo di una profonda diversità sociale, il mondo dell'altra classe, che era quasi il mondo di un'altra vita.* (Pasolini, *Petrolio* 1435)

> He did not love Pietro only for that gigantic piece of flesh that he had in his mouth, smooth and hard [. . .] with their heat, their odour, and that lividness, almost abjectness—that is, something not innocently animal—which oozed out. He loved that boy also for what he did not give him and could not give him [. . .]. [A]ll this [. . .] was [. . .] the symbol of a profound social difference: the world of the other class, which was almost the world of another life. (Pasolini, *Petrolio* [trans.] 193–94)

The second of these episodes ("Carmelo: la sua disponibilità e la sua dissoluzione") describes the protagonist's relationship with the Sicilian waiter Carmelo. A short passage from it will suffice to give a sense of the dimension of sacred ritual with which the protagonist undertakes his masochistic submission, experienced as a possibility to have access to the reality of the "other" and to forget one's own history:

> *Se la pressione sulla mano era stata sconvolgente, quasi paralizzante—come quella di un padrone sulla bestia ammansita—la pressione sulla nuca fece quasi perdere i sensi a Carlo. Cosa voleva quella mano, larga e massiccia, posata sulla sua delicata nuca di borghese che era sempre stato debole e reso ridicolo davanti a se stesso dai suoi complessi e dai suoi doveri? Tutta la sua storia non esisteva più: la forza di un corpo esercitata con tanta prepotente delicatezza su di lui attraverso quel palmo di una mano callosa, riduceva anche lui a un corpo.* (Pasolini, *Petrolio, Appunto* 62, 1509)

> If the pressure on his hand had been disturbing, almost paralyzing—like that of a master on the domesticated animal—the pressure on his neck was nearly enough to make Carlo lose his sense. What did that broad, massive hand want, resting on the delicate neck of a man of the bourgeoisie who had always been weak, had always seemed absurd to himself because of his complexes and his obligations? It was as if his entire history no longer existed; the force of a body exerted on him with so much overpowering delicacy by that callused palm reduced him to a body as well. (Pasolini, *Petrolio* [trans.] 247)

As explained in *Appunto* 65 ("Confidenze col lettore"), the value of sexual experience consists in its passive form of obedience and degradation that also frees oneself from the feeling of possession and power. Indeed the *Appunto* establishes a link between sexuality, economics, and ethics, distinguishing between the act of possessing, symbolized by the penis, and that of being possessed, and also identifying possession with Power and Evil and being possessed with the only possibility of Good:

> *Chi è posseduto perde la coscienza della forma del pene, della sua compiutezza limitata, e lo sente come un mezzo infinito e informe, attraverso cui Qualcosa o Qualcuno si impadronisce di lui, lo riduce a possesso, a un nulla che non ha altra volontà che quella di perdersi in quella diversa Volontà che lo annulla.*
>
> *[. . .] D'altra parte è fuori discussione che il Possesso è un Male, anzi, per definizione, è IL Male: quindi l'essere posseduti è ciò che è più lontano dal Male, o meglio, è l'unica esperienza possibile del Bene, come Grazia, vita allo stato puro, cosmico.* (Pasolini, *Petrolio* 1552–53)

> The one who is possessed loses consciousness of the shape of the penis, of its limited wholeness, and feels it as an infinite and formless means by which Something or Someone takes possession of him, reduces him to a possession, to a nothing that has no will except to be lost in that different Will which annihilates him.
>
> [. . .] On the other hand, it is beyond dispute that the Possessor is an Evil, in fact is, by definition, the Evil; therefore, being possessed is what is farthest from Evil or, rather, is the only possible experience of the Good as Grace, life in its pure, cosmic state. (Pasolini, *Petrolio* [trans.] 278–79)

While, then, *Petrolio* makes explicit the fascination with a passive sexuality of a masochistic type that allows one to be liberated from the sense of power and possession that Pasolini loathed so much, it also clarifies the connection between sexuality, ethics and aesthetics.[5] As the *Appunto* 99 points out, the traditional construction of a novel around the function of the narrator corresponds to an organization of reality that implies an effort to take possession of it, and this desire for possession, although it takes place on the cognitive or expressive plain, is always an act of brutality and violence, as it necessarily occurs with every possession and conquest (Pasolini, *Petrolio* 1679).

These reflections suggest that *Petrolio*'s "openness" and anarchical opposition to traditional literary conventions are bound to a specific form of sexuality. In particular, my hypothesis, which draws on the concept of aesthetics that Leo Bersani has developed with respect to Sigmund Freud's seminal texts *The Three Essays on Sexuality* and *Beyond the Pleasure Principle*, is that *Petrolio* does not simply describe scenes of masochism but also replicates, through its aesthetic choices, a form of sexuality grounded in a paradoxical kind of pleasure. In this respect, I find particularly interesting Bersani's reformulation of the concept of "artistic sublimation" as the possibility not of purifying or transcending desire but, on the contrary, of extending it to the movement of the text, thereby expressing, enacting, and making the reader experience sexuality, which for Bersani is masochistic in its ontological state and not domesticated by the normative, teleological model of sexual reproduction usually considered as "normal" and non-pathological (47–50).

Both *La Divina Mimesis* and *Petrolio* undo the form of the traditional novel and, by undoing it, they open it up to the articulation of nonlinear and nondomesticated pleasures and replicate the longed-for shattering of a subjectivity with boundaries that are otherwise experienced as too well defined. In both *La Divina Mimesis* and *Petrolio* linearity and progress coincide with the monstrous form of bourgeois power and represent everything that these texts seek to resist, either by accumulating all the layers of the past without ever arriving at a synthesis (*La Divina Mimesis*) or by expanding temporality endlessly (*Petrolio*), and in both cases contesting any teleological idea of the future or futurity. *Petrolio* makes it indeed explicit that the idea itself of future has become ridiculous: "L'idea della speranza nel futuro diventa un'idea irresistibilmente comica" (Pasolini, *Petrolio* 1651; "The idea of hope for the future becomes irresistibly comic" [Pasolini, *Petrolio* (trans.) 343]).[6] In this respect, the novel resonates with the reformulation of queer given by Lee Edelman in his *No Future: Queer Theory and the Death Drive*, that is, a position resisting (hetero)normative and progressive linearity in favor of repetition, negativity, and the death drive.[7] One could advance the hypothesis that *Petrolio*, which claims not to have a beginning, does not end either. Indeed, it refutes any form of teleology and proceeds chaotically or *a brulichio*," mobilizing a textuality that replicates the dissolution of a subjectivity based on the hegemony of the ego and reproduces its transformation into a mobile surface without memory and without history.

If this is the position expressed in Pasolini's texts, that of Elsa Morante's last novel *Aracoeli* is in many regards quite similar, but also presents significant differences. It has been often acknowledged that Pasolini is an important reference in Morante's *Aracoeli*. Some traits of Manuele, the protagonist, are modeled upon those of Pasolini himself, such as the feeling of guilt for being bourgeois or his unrequited love of young, often heterosexual, men (Siti 2006, 286; Bazzocchi, *Pasolini* 129). Notwithstanding whether in constructing the figure of its protagonist the novel draws on Pasolini or not, Manuele's sexuality exhibits some peculiarities that resonate with those of Carlo, *Petrolio*'s protagonist, but they take on a different meaning. I am referring in particular to Manuele's masochistic fantasies of a humiliating relationship with younger boys who despise him:

Erano tutti adolescenti e, per lo più, amanti delle donne. [. . .] Da loro, non
potevo aspettarmi amore, né l'ultima, desiata piaga. La massima grazia che
potevano, essi, concedermi, era di lasciarsi succhiare da me. A pagamento.
Loro, simili a statue regali. Io, come fossero santi, in ginocchio ai loro piedi.
E la mia pupilla, al berli, si velava, nello sguardo adorante e assonnato che ha
l'infante allattato dalla madre. (Morante, *Aracoeli* 1159)

They were all adolescent and, for the most part, lovers of women. [. . .] From
them I could not expect love, nor the final, desired wound. The maximum
grace they could grant me was to let themselves be sucked by me. For money.
They, like regal statues. I kneeling at their feet as if they were saints. And my
eye, at their taunts, became veiled, in that adoring and sleepy gaze of an infant,
nursed by its mother. (Morante, *Aracoeli* [trans.] 91)[8]

While Carlo's sexual experiences aimed at dissolution of the self, Manuele's
fantasies point back to his relationship with his mother, and indeed much of
the novel revolves around the relationship between mother and child. In a
series of articles on *Aracoeli* that I have written with philosopher of language
Sara Fortuna, we relate the central image of the baby suckling at the mother's
breast to a particular concept of linguistic subjectivity. In particular, we read
the novel by focusing on the maternal and corporeal language learned at
Totetaco. (This is how the little Manuele calls Monte Sacro, the Roman
neighborhood where he spent the first four years of his life in a magical
symbiosis with his mother.) In the novel, this language appears always in
stark binary opposition with the disciplinary and patriarchal language of *I*
Quartieri Alti, the high-bourgeois district of Parioli where Manuele and his
mother Aracoeli move in order to live with the navy officer Eugenio, Aracoeli's husband and Manuele's father ("*Attaccando*" 85–123; "Affection" 8–19).
      Totetaco represents the Edenic and fluid world of early infancy, which
Aracoeli reconstructs with the same luminous intensity of Morante's previous novels, emphasizing in particular the linguistic freedom of the joyous
and enchanted relationship between mother and child:

Se un cane si affacciava col muso al nostro cancello, essa mi chiamava fes-
tante: "Mira! que bonito!" E quando passava un gregge di pecore, o un volo
di storni: "Mira! Mira! belli!" A tutte le ore, capitava sempre qualche bellez-
za di passaggio, da mirar. Ma le bellezze più belle, chi le teneva? Io! Dal naso
agli orecchi al culillo alle dita dei piedi, non c'era luogo del mio corpo che lei
non giudicasse perfetto. E tanto le piacevo, che a volte tra i suoi baci schioc-
canti mi dava dei morsetti innocui, dicendo che mi mangiava, e decantando i
miei vari sapori. Le guance: manzane. Le cosce: pane fresco. I capelli: grap-
poletti de uvas. A guardare i miei occhi, poi, s'insuperbiva, come a un segnale
gaudioso del suo grande sposalizio esotico:

> *los ojos azules*
> *la cara morena.* (Morante, *Aracoeli* 1189–90)

If a dog stuck his nose inside our gate, she would call me, festively: "Mira! Qué bonito!" And when a flock of sheep went by or a flight of starlings: "Mira! Mira! Beautiful!" At every hour, some passing beauty always turned up for us to mirar. But the most beautiful beauties—who was their possessor? I was! From nose to ears to little behind to toes, there was no part of my body that she didn't consider perfect. And I so pleased her that at times, between her smacking kisses, she would give me harmless little nips, saying she was eating me, and extolling my various tastes. My cheeks: manzanas. My thighs: fresh bread. Hair: little bunches of uvas. When she looked into my eyes, then she turned proud, as if a joyous signal of her exotic marriage:

> los ojos azules
> la cara morena. (Morante, *Aracoeli* [trans.] 114)

Totetaco represents a moment of corporeal fullness without divisions or rules that also manifests itself in little Manuele's androgyny:

> *Per me fra l'unità e i suoi multipli non esistevano confini precisi, così come ancora l'io non si distingueva ancora dal tu e dall'altro, né i sessi uno dall'altro. Per tutto il tempo di Totetaco, io non ebbi nozione di essere maschio, ossia uno che mai poteva diventare donna come Aracoeli.* (Morante, *Aracoeli* 1186)

> For me precise boundaries didn't exist between unity and its multiples, just as the form "I" was not yet clearly distinguished from the "you" or any other, nor were the sexes distinct. For the whole Totetaco period, I had no notion of being male, or one who could never become a woman, like Aracoeli. (Morante, *Aracoeli* [trans.] 112)

Gender categories are not yet activated at Totetaco and Manuele has not yet been inserted within an order that forces him to assume either one in a process of normativization acting above all on the body.[9]

Unlike Totetaco's maternal space, which is fluid, affective, and corporeal, the paternal space of *I Quartieri Alti* is characterized by a normative order of prohibitions and hierarchies, which is introduced in the novel by the notice placed in the elevator of the new elegant building:

> *PORTATA: PERSONE 4*
> *CHI SI SERVE DELL'ASCENSORE LO FA A SUO RISCHIO E PERICOLO.*
> *L'USO DELL'ASCENSORE È VIETATO AI CANI AL PERSONALE DI SERVIZIO AI FORNITORI AI BAMBINI NON ACCOMPAGNATI E A TUTTE LE PERSONE CHE NON CONOSCONO LA MANOVRA.* (Morante, *Aracoeli* 1070–71)

CAPACITY: 4 PERSONS
ANYONE USING THE ELEVATOR DOES SO AT HIS OWN RISK.
USE OF THE ELEVATOR IS FORBIDDEN TO DOGS, SERVANTS,
DELIVERY BOYS, CHILDREN NOT ACCOMPANIED BY ADULTS
AND TO ALL PERSONS UNFAMILIAR WITH ITS OPERATION. (Mo-
rante, *Aracoeli* [trans.] 26)

While Totetaco's unstructured mixture of Spanish and Italian, learned by
the child spontaneously and playfully through an affective and corporeal
relationship with the mother, is the symbol of Totetaco's fluidity, "pure"
Italian, in particular the Italian promulgated by fascism, which is the language that Manuele is now forced to speak (to the extent that he will completely forget any knowledge of Spanish), is the symbol of the new symbolic
order, according to which the paradigmatic subject is a male adult belonging
to the dominating class and to its norm. (Carlo, the protagonist of *Petrolio*, is
this kind of subject.)

Referring to Julia Kristeva's meditation on the relationship between lan-
guage-learning and the development of subjectivity, Sara Fortuna and I have
argued that the language of Totetaco can be thought of as a language that has
not lost the "semiotic *chora*" (which for Kristeva designates a pre- or proto-
linguistic mode of signification that takes place in the body and is connected
with the experience of the child suckling at the mother's breast), while the
language of *I Quartieri Alti* is presented as a fully symbolic language that has
followed what Kristeva calls the "thetic break"—which begins with the mirror stage and is fully realized with the threat of castration in the oedipal
phase—and has therefore lost any trace of the "semiotic" component (*The
Revolution* 19–106, especially 46–51).

Neither Aracoeli nor Manuele manage to adapt to the symbolic order of *I
Quartieri Alti*, and as the mother finally (and tragically) resists the discipline
that wants to transform her into a lady—"il tirocinio da signora" imposed by
Zia Monda (Giorgio 97–116)—so it is repeated several times that the son has
never developed a fully oedipal subjectivity. For instance, when during the
"trial" *a più voci* the hypothesis is made that Manuele's case is part of the
common oedipal scheme, the Defense replies that "Ricascare nei soliti sche-
mi d'obbligo sembra, qui, essere fuori luogo. Il nostro caso non si adatta a
nessuno schema prefisso" (Morante, *Aracoeli* 1181; "Recurring to the usual
cut-and-dried patterns seems to me out of place here. Our case does not fit
into any preestablished pattern" [Morante, *Aracoeli* (trans.) 108]). And,
while describing the unconditional love between Aracoeli and Eugenio, Manuele stresses that he has never known envy for his father:

*Nessuna minaccia per me, da lui. . . . Fra me e lui, corse subito—in luogo
dell'affetto carnale—una silenziosa concordanza: forse anche in virtù della
nostra comune passione per Aracoeli. È certo che il nostro amore grande,*

esclusivo per la stessa donna era fra noi due motivo di riconoscenza, piuttosto che di contesa. . . . Quanto a me, nella mia incompetenza riguardo ai titoli di padre e di sposo, a me bastava che questi titoli contassero per Aracoeli e che questo mio padre, e suo sposo, a lei portasse onori e felicità. Ripercorrendo del resto, il mio passato, io mi convinco di non aver mai conosciuto, fino in fondo, la vera tragedia della gelosia. (Morante, *Aracoeli* 134-35)[10]

No threat to me from him. . . . Between me and him there sprang up at once—instead of carnal affection—a silent accord, perhaps owing to our common passion for Aracoeli. It is certain that our great love for the same woman was a source of recognition between us rather than of rivalry. . . . As for me, in my lack of expertise regarding the categories of father and husband, I was content to know that those titles mattered to Aracoeli and that this father of mine, and husband of hers, brought her honors and happiness. For that matter, as I review my past, I am convinced I have never known, profoundly, the true tragedy of jealousy. (Morante, *Aracoeli* [trans.] 126)

In our reading of the novel, the protagonist's trip to Andalusia in search for his lost mother allows for the reemergence of a memorial substratum, which is explicitly deemed the only practicable form of a "carnal resurrection of the dead":

La tentazione del viaggio mi aveva invaso recentemente con la voce stessa di mia madre. Non è stata una trascrizione astratta della memoria a restituirmi le sue primissime canzoncine, già seppellite; ma proprio la voce fisica di lei, col suo sapore tenero di gola e di saliva. Ho riavuto sul palato la sensazione della sua pelle, che odorava di prugna fresca; e la notte in questo freddo milanese, ho avvertito il suo fiato ancora di bambina, come un velo di tepore ingenuo sulle mie palpebre invecchiate. Non so come gli scienziati spieghino l'esistenza, dentro la nostra materia corporale, di questi altri organi di senso occulti, senza corpo visibile, e segregati dagli oggetti; ma pur capaci di udire, di vedere e di ogni sensazione della natura, e anche di altre. Si direbbero forniti di antenne e scandagli. Agiscono in una zona esclusa dallo spazio, però di movimento illimitato. E là in quella zona si avvera (almeno finché noi viviamo) la resurrezione carnale dei morti. (Morante, *Aracoeli* 1047–48)

The temptation of the journey had possessed me of late with the very voice of my mother. It was not an abstract transcription of memory that brought me back her earliest little songs, formerly buried, but her real, bodily voice, with its tender savor of throat and saliva. I felt again on my palate the sensation of her skin, which smelled of fresh plum; and, at night, in this Milanese cold, I sensed her still-girlish breath, like a skim of ingenuous warmth on my aged eyelids. I don't know how scientists explain the existence, inside our corporeal matter, of these other, hidden organs of feeling, without visible body, segregated from objects, and yet capable of hearing, seeing, and every natural sensation, and others as well. You would say they are equipped with antennae and sounding-lines. They operate in a field cut off from space, but of unlimited

movement. And in that zone there takes place (at least as long as we live) the
carnal resurrection of the dead. (Morante, *Aracoeli* [trans.] 9)

Throughout the journey the protagonist recovers bodily memory and an ag-
gregate of sensations long since lost: the "semiotic" dimension of subjectivity is thereby retrieved and Manuele is granted the possibility of overcoming
his obsessive tendency to interpret reality through exclusively rational grids.

Contrary to Manuele's previous experiences, which are symptoms of his
condition as a melancholic subject, the journey enhances a veritable re-elab-
oration of the suffered loss and allows him to move to a further stage, which
coincides with the recovery of the Spanish language and the fluid categories
that it carries. This is how Fortuna and I read the protagonist's final encounter with the ghost of his dead mother, which represents both a retrieval of the
past and a transformation of the way to relate to this past, granting him the
possibility of getting rid of the inclination always to define (negatively) his
own life and to see it obsessively under the aspects of not being loved and of
being abandoned.

The sign that the protagonist's final encounter with the mother opens up
the possibility of change is represented by what follows in the novel, that is,
his retroactive discovery of the love for his father Eugenio and (arguably) for
himself, which has been described as a "queer happy end" (Deuber Mankowsky 73–83).[11]

This return to the father is indeed very different from a return to the
(hetero)normative world of *I Quartieri Alti* and can actually only take place
after Eugenio has deserted from the navy and is now in an abject position
symbolized by his addiction to alcohol. Moreover, Manuele's retroactive
discovery of his love for Eugenio is only possible after the reemergence of
the Spanish language which, in Manuele's specific case, means the possibility of thinking, and therefore experiencing, the world in a fluid manner, free
from the normative violence of the symbolic order. What I find especially
interesting is that the development staged in the novel does not correspond to
an overcoming of the non-oedipal position of which everybody, including
himself, has constantly accused the protagonist but, rather, to the proposal of
the possibility of further elaborating and developing a corporeal and fluid
non-oedipal—but not necessarily pre-linguistic—subjectivity.[12]

I would like to conclude by proposing that, as for *Petrolio*, so for *Aracoeli*
one could imagine a kind of "artistic sublimation" à la Bersani that replicates
the movement of sexuality: on the one hand, the multilingual texture of
Morante's novel can be thought of as corresponding to a sort of Kristevan
"revolution of poetic language" that allows the semiotic component of language to reemerge. With respect to this, Pier Vincenzo Mengaldo aptly states
that Spanish constantly emerges on the surface in *Aracoeli* and, with the
sound of its formulae and songs "quasi fiacca le strutture razionali

dell'italiano stesso, e lo rende invertebrato" (29–30; "almost weakens the rational structures of Italian and makes it invertebrate"), as though the reactivation of the semiotic *chora* shakes the rigidity and hierarchies of the symbolic order, reinterpreting it and re-creating it anew. [13]

On the other hand, to the linguistic operation corresponds that of the novel's narrative structure, and the definition of "forma senza forma" (Morante, *Aracoeli* 1427; "form without form" Morante, *Aracoeli* [trans.] 291), used to describe Aracoeli's final apparition, can be taken as an appropriate definition of the novel itself. In other terms: not only language but the whole novel is "invertebrate": a revolution of poetic language also occurs at the level of the narrative structure, which is fragmented, distorted, and destabilizing in its continual interruptions and inversions of genres, rhythms, and perspectives. The text continually repeats itself, transforms itself, turns into itself. All boundaries—generic, temporal, linguistic, subjective—are lost, and so are the norms and directions. It is a fluidifying and integrative operation that replicates the movement of a polymorphously perverse sexuality that is endorsed in its nonbinary, non-teleological, and nonnormative character (Holzhey 42–58).

Through its qualities of repetition, retrospection, and inversion, *Aracoeli*'s textuality also mobilizes a multifarious, twisted, and suspended temporality, which interrupts any sense of linear progression and instead often inverts its course and goes backward. However, unlike Pasolini's *La Divina Mimesis* and *Petrolio*, *Aracoeli*'s narrative holds together and even deploys a sort of conclusion, but it is—again—a queer conclusion: not only left open but also turned over and reversed. That of *Aracoeli* is a conclusion that occurs in a magmatic time, carefully suspended between present/past and past/present and in which the progress of time coexists with its suspension. If both Pasolini's texts and Morante's *Aracoeli*, therefore, perform an act of resistance through the nonlinear form of their textuality and propose a queer subjectivity, they do so indifferent ways and deploy different strategies pertaining to the genre of the novel. The fragmented movement of Pasolini's textuality corresponds to a post-oedipal and fully formed subject who wants to shatter and annihilate himself by replicating the paradoxical pleasure of nondomesticated sexuality. The position performed in *Aracoeli*, instead, is that of never adapting to the symbolic order. The poetic operation of the novel consists in the staging of an interior journey, backward through memory and the body, toward an acceptance of the partiality and fluidity of an inter-subjectivity that is always in the process of becoming.

NOTES

1. Although critics' opinion differs in this matter, I agree with Carla Benedetti and Maria Antonietta Grignani who think that the form given to *Petrolio*'s unfinished text corresponds to

the one originally planned by Pasolini (Benedetti 159; Grignani 137–38). Benedetti and Grignani refer to the first edition of *Petrolio* edited by Maria Careri, Graziella Chiarcossi, and Aurelio Roncaglia. On the differences between this edition and that by Walter Siti and Silvia De Laude that I use and from which I quote, see Siti and De Laude, "Note e notizie sui testi" 1993–1996. Translations are taken from Pasolini, *Petrolio*, trans. Ann Goldstein (New York: Pantheon, 1997), which is also based on the edition by Careri, Chiarcossi, and Roncaglia.

2. All translations are my own, unless otherwise noted.

3. Cf. chapters 2 ("Rifare e disfare Dante. Dalla *Mortaccia* alla *Divina Mimesis*") and 3 ("Una perfomance *queer*. *Petrolio* e l'orgoglio del fallimento") of Gragnolati, *Amor che move* 35–67, and Gragnolati, "Pier Paolo Pasolini's Queer Performance: *La Divina Mimesis* between Dante and *Petrolio*" 134–64.

4. See also the recent interesting analysis by Donnarumma 293–321.

5. On the connection between sexuality and writing in *Petrolio*, cf. especially Fusillo 90–95, but also Genovese 79–92, Ward 101–14; Amberson 374–94. On the relationship between homosexuality and deviation from the traditional form of the novel, see Parussa 51–65. On Pasolini's frequent assertion of his irreducible distance from power and hate for it, see Nicoli 112–15, and, also with respect to the relationship between politics and sexuality, Cadel 107–17.

6. On the significance of the comic register and of laughter in *Petrolio*, see Cadel 107–17; Bazzocchi, Baubò 13–28; and Gragnolati, *Amor che move* 64–65.

7. See chapter 3 of my "*Amor che move*" for a discussion of the new kind of *impegno* that such queer position entails.

8. Excerpts from *Aracoeli* by Elsa Morante, translated by William Weaver, translation copyright © 1985 by Random House. Used by permission of Random House, an imprint and division of Random House LLC. All rights reserved.

9. On the significance of androgyny in Elsa Morante's work and *Aracoeli* in particular, see Serkowska (*Uscire* 158–66; Maternal, 157–87).

10. For an interesting analysis of the pre-oedipal condition of many of Morante's characters, and of their marginal position within the symbolic order, see Re 363–67. Re indicates significant analogies between Morante's text and Kristeva's paradigm of the semiotic *chora*. On Freud's presence in Morante's works, see Bardini, *Morante Elsa* and "Dei 'fantastici Doppi,'" 173–299.

11. On the significance of the rediscovery of love at the end of the novel, see Stellardi 96–106, and Martínez Garrido 118–27.

12. I would add that it is here that Morante, intriguingly, seems to differ from Kristeva's model, which implies the necessity of the thetic break for a nonpsychotic development of subjectivity.

13. On *Aracoeli*'s language, see also the beautiful remarks in Bernabò 271–75.

WORKS CITED

Amberson, Deborah. "Masochism and Its Discontents: From Franciscan Orgies to Schreberian Unmannings of Putrescence in Pasolini's *Petrolio*." *The Italianist* 30.3 (2010): 374–94.

Bardini, Marco. "Dei 'fantastici Doppi' ovvero la mimesi narrativa dello spostamento psichico." *Per Elisa: Studi su "Menzogna e sortilegio."* Lucio Lugnani et al., eds. Pisa: Nistri-Lischi, 1990. 173–299.

———. *Morante Elsa. Italiana. Di professione poeta.* Pisa: Nistri-Lischi, 1999.

Bazzocchi, Marco Antonio. *Pier Paolo Pasolini.* Milan: Bruno Mondadori, 1998.

———. "Baubò: la scena comica dell'ultimo Pasolini." *Corpus xxx: Pasolini, Petrolio, Salò.* Ed. Davide Messina. Bologna: Clueb, 2012. 13–28.

Benedetti, Carla. *Pasolini contro Calvino. Per una letteratura impura.* Turin: Bollati Boringhieri, 1998.

———, and Maria Antonietta Grignani, eds. *A partire da Petrolio. Pasolini interroga la letteratura.* Ravenna: Longo, 1995.

Bernabò, Graziella. *La fiaba estrema. Elsa Morante tra vita e scrittura.* Rome: Carocci, 2012.

Bersani, Leo. *The Freudian Body: Psychoanalysis and Art*. New York: Columbia University Press, 1986.

Cadel, Francesca. "Politics and Sexuality in Pasolini's *Petrolio*." Fortuna and Gragnolati, *Attaccando* 107–17.

Deuber Mankowsky, Astrid. "Baubo—Another, Additional Name of Aracoeli: Morante's Queer Feminism." Gragnolati and Fortuna 73—83.

Donnarumma, Raffaele. "Metamorfosi e nascondimenti. Pasolini e l'omosessualità in *Petrolio*." *Inquietudini queer: desiderio, performance, scrittura*. Eds. Saveria Chemotti and Davide Susanetti. Padova: Il Poligrafo, 2012. 293–321.

Edelman, Lee. *No Future: Queer Theory and the Death Drive*. Durham, NC: Duke University Press, 2004.

Fortuna Sara, and Manuele Gragnolati. "*Attaccando al suo capezzolo le mie labbra ingorde*: corpo, linguaggio e soggettività da Dante ad *Aracoeli* di Elsa Morante." *Nuova Corrente* 55 (2008): 85–123.

———. "Between Affection and Discipline: Exploring Linguistic Tensions from Dante to *Aracoeli*." Gragnolati and Fortuna 8–19.

Fusillo, Massimo. "Il protagonista androgino: metamorfosi e ruoli sessuali in *Petrolio*." *Progetto Petrolio. Una giornata di studi sul romanzo incompiuto di Pier Paolo Pasolini*. Ed. Paolo Salerno. Bologna: Clueb, 2006. 89–102.

Genovese, Rino. "Manifesto per Petrolio." Benedetti and Grignani 79–92.

Giorgio, Adalgisa. "Nature vs Culture: Repression, Rebellion and Madness in Elsa Morante's *Aracoeli*." *Modern Language Notes* 109 (1994): 93–116.

Gragnolati, Manuele. *Amor che move: linguaggio del corpo e forma del desiderio in Dante, Pasolini e Morante*. Milan: Il Saggiatore, 2013.

———. "Pier Paolo Pasolini's Queer Performance: *La Divina Mimesis* between Dante and *Petrolio*." Messina 134–64.

———, and Sara Fortuna, eds. *The Power of Disturbance: Elsa Morante's "Aracoeli."* Oxford: Legenda, 2009.

Grignani, Maria Antonietta. "Questione di stile." Benedetti and Grignani 137–38.

Holzhey, Christoph. "'The Lover of a Hybrid': Memory and Fantasy in *Aracoeli*." Gragnolati and Fortuna 42–58.

Kristeva, Julia. *Revolution in Poetic Language*. Trans. Marguerite Waller. New York: Columbia University Press, 1984.

Lucamante, Stefania, and Sharon Wood, eds. *Under Arturo's Star: The Cultural Legacies of Elsa Morante*. West Lafayette: Purdue University Press, 2006.

Martínez Garrido, Elisa. "Between Italy and Spain: The Tragedy of History and the Salvific Power of Love in Elsa Morante and María Zambrano." Gragnolati and Fortuna 118–27.

Mengaldo, Pier Vincenzo. "Spunti per un'analisi linguistica dei romanzi di Elsa Morante." *Vent'anni dopo "La Storia." Omaggio a Elsa Morante*. Concetta D'Angeli and Giacomo Magrini, eds. *Studi novecenteschi* 21 (1994): 11–36.

Morante, Elsa. *Aracoeli. Opere*. Cesare Garboli and Carlo Cecchi, eds. Vol. 2. Milan: Meridiani Mondadori, 1990. 1039–454.

———. *Aracoeli*. Trans. William Weaver. New York: Random House, 1984.

Nicoli, Massimiliano. "L'innocenza del potere. Una riflessione su *Petrolio*." *aut aut* 345 (2010): 99–115.

Parussa, Sergio. *L'eros onnipotente. Erotismo, letteratura e impegno nell'opera di Pier Paolo Pasolini e Jean Jenet*. Turin: Tirrenia, 2003.

Pasolini, Pier Paolo. *Divina Mimesis. Romanzi e racconti*. Vol. 2. Walter Siti and Silvia De Laude, eds. Milan: Meridiani Mondadori, 1998.

———. *Petrolio. Romanzi e racconti*. Vol. 2. Walter Siti and Silvia De Laude, eds. Milan: Meridiani Mondadori, 1998. 1159–830.

———. *Petrolio*. Trans. Ann Goldstein. New York: Pantheon, 1997.

———. *Petrolio*. Maria Careri, Graziella Chiarcossi, and Aurelio Roncaglia, eds. Turin: Einaudi, 1992.

Re, Lucia. "Utopian Longing and the Constraints of Racial and Sexual Difference in Elsa Morante's *La Storia*." *Italica* 70, 3 (Autumn 1993): 361–75.

Serkowska, Hanna. "The Maternal Boy: Manuele, or The Last Portrait of Morante's Androgyny." Lucamante and Wood 157–87.

———. *Uscire da una camera delle favole. I romanzi di Elsa Morante.* Krakow: Rabid, 2002.

Siti, Walter. "Elsa Morante and Pasolini." Lucamante and Wood 268–89.

———, and Silvia De Laude. "Note e notizie sui testi." Pasolini, *Romanzi e racconti*, Vol. 2, 199.

Stellardi, Giuseppe. "*Aracoeli* and Gadda's *La cognizione del dolore*: Disturbed Sons, Disturbing Mother." Fortuna and Gragnolati, *Attaccando* 96–106.

Ward, David. *A Poetic of Resistance: Narrative and the Writings of Pier Paolo Pasolini,* Madison, NJ: Fairleigh Dickinson University Press, 1995.

West, Rebecca. "Da Petrolio a Celati." Benedetti and Grignani 39–50.

Chapter Eighteen

Kaleidoscopic Sexualities

Defying Normative Resistance and Maternal Melancholia in Aracoeli

Maria Morelli

Elsa Morante's last and most ambiguous literary work, *Aracoeli*, written in 1982, questions the stability of identity categories by staging hybrid, multifarious subjectivities that attest to the tenuousness of the Cartesian assumption of a stable, sovereign "self." As contemporary scholarship has revealed, the novel displays early traces of theoretical models that would be systematically tackled only some years later, and as such, it can be read as Morante's signature statement on the breakdown of the binary paradigm of gender and the subsequent proliferation of hybrid sexualities. Manuele Gragnolati and Sara Fortuna have devoted attention to the exploration of the semiotic dimension in *Aracoeli*, which they have linked to the concept of Julia Kristeva's formulation of the psycholinguistic development of the child in order to propose a reading of the text that accounts for a bodily relationship between language and identity ("Between Affection and Discipline" 8–19).[1] On the other hand, Morante's queer feminism as made manifest in the eponymous female character of her last novel has been examined by Astrid Deuber-Mankowsky through Nietzsche's reading of the figure of the obscene mythical Baubo, an analysis that is made even more convincing by the recourse to Judith Butler's notions of melancholic "*gender* identification" and bodily estrangement perceived as "unlivable life" (73–83).

Adalgisa Giorgio was the first to point out the dichotomy between Culture and Nature in *Aracoeli*, which she did by looking at the relationship between the (bourgeois) societal order and the Symbolic as staged in the novel (93–116). Her analysis has been taken up, although with a somewhat different angle, by Gragnolati and Fortuna's work mentioned above, set within a Kristevan frame that highlights the semiotic mother-son union as crucial in the child's psycholinguistic development and, in turn, subjectivity formation. Though approached from different perspectives, these scholars seem all to agree on "the power of the maternal to break through the symbolic and claim what it gave birth to" (Giorgio 108), thus coming to the conclusion that the Symbolic cannot ultimately win over the Semiotic and, more importantly still, its maternal dimension.

What interests me here is not so much the possibility of looking at the revolutionary potential of the maternal semiotic in *Aracoeli* nor at the novel as a textbook example of a symbiotic union with the (m)other, nor at the play between nature/semiotic and culture/symbolic. Instead, I propose a reading of *Aracoeli* that accounts for the notions of social and maternal abjection and, related to these, the relationship that is established between the "abjected" subject, on the one hand, and the "abjecting" social order, on the other, a relationship that inevitably affects the sphere of subjectivity. My analysis will be set within the framework of the Butlerian and Kristevan models on abjection and self-individuation. While exhibiting both theoretical paradigms, *Aracoeli* also reveals interesting points of departure from them (specifically, from the Kristevan thesis of "matricide") that are worth exploring.

I shall, thus, look at the novel's protagonist as a social being entrapped inside a societal order that risks annihilating him as a subject and whose self-acceptance will be achieved through a personal (but also physical) journey through his mother's, and his own, life memories. The narration ends on a positive note, with Manuele's cry for love (for his mother, his father, himself) that hints at the blurring of societal taboos and affirms the never accomplished, highly ambiguous, and yet deeply fascinating nature of subjectivity formation.

In *Gender Trouble*, Butler takes issue with Kristeva's notion of a pre-linguistic and pre-symbolic maternal corporeality, which she interprets as forever subordinate to the symbolic and, as such, doomed to remain outside of culture. This, Butler contends, would be complicit in reiterating Lévi Strauss's paradigm of the nature/culture division (*Gender* 116–17), that is, an irreparable fracture between a pre-social, pre-cultural maternal dimension and a domain founded on its very suppression (*Gender* 121). Butler's criticism of Kristeva, however, does not take into account her later writings, those of the 1980s—namely, the trilogy *Powers of Horror*, *Tales of Love*, and *Black Sun*—that, along the lines of her own theories, are equally suspicious of prevalent patriarchal discourses on gender. In a similar fashion to Butler's formulations, these later works by Kristeva also serve to illustrate the flimsy nature of identity formation and the impossibility of fully adhering to predetermined gender categories—as is staged in Morante's last work.[2]

The novel is the story of the Andalusian Aracoeli told by her forty-three-year-old son Manuele in the form of, in his own words, a "monologo *srego-lato*" (Morante, *Aracoeli* 24; "*incoherent* monologue" [Morante, *Aracoeli* (trans.) 23]; italics added), the etymology of the word hinting at what lies beyond *regole* (rules), and as such prefiguring the breakdown of gender constraints that will follow in the text. But it is also an attempt on the part of the narrator to recover a prelapsarian unity following a twofold loss that he experienced long ago but is nevertheless unable to overcome: first, his mother's inexorable descent into madness and consequent demise and, prior to this, his expulsion from the maternal realm—the latter being the result of the Fall into the corruption of the adult world and Aracoeli's rejection of him after the premature death of her eagerly desired, only daughter. It is nostalgia for the lost maternal womb that prompts him to embark on a journey *à rebous* to his mother's native village of El Almendral, in Spain. Manuele's is a desperate, contradictory endeavor that is aimed at both turning away from his mother and retrieving her past, which is also *his* own—the necessity of recovering his life story illustrating, in Adriana Cavarero's words, the "human being's desire for narration, in which uniqueness and unity coincide once again, after birth" (62). Manuele yearns for a final reunion with Aracoeli, even if this means his own death: "Ma tu, mamita, aiutami. Come fanno le gatte coi loro piccoli nati male, tu rimangiami. Accogli la mia deformità nella tua voragine pietosa" (Morante, *Aracoeli* 109; "But you, Mamita, help me. As mother cats do with their deformed ill-born kittens, eat me again. Receive my deformity in your pitying abyss" [Morante, *Aracoeli* (trans.) 102]. The longed-for return to his mother's womb is also a return to his childhood, a pre-oedipal, pre-gendered, blissful (con)fusion with the maternal realm where "ancora l'io non si distingueva chiaramente dal tu e dall'altro, né i sessi uno dall'altro" (Morante, *Aracoeli* 118; "the form 'I' was not yet clearly distinguished from the 'you' or any other, nor were the sexes distinct" [Morante, *Aracoeli* (trans.) 112]).

Consonant to the androgynous character of his childhood memories is his dream about metamorphosing into a beautiful Indian (female) dancer who in turn transforms herself into a phoenix.[3] This image of the shining phoenix deserves some attention. Having already appeared in the dedicatory poem to *Menzogna e sortilegio* (*House of Liars*), it returned repeatedly throughout the novel as, in the words of Sharon Wood, "a symbolic trope of fiery splendour and ashes, of death and resurrection, and, on the level of the enunciation and narration, of metamorphosis and transformation" (78). Just as in *Menzogna e sortilegio*, the phoenix is an implicit presence also in *Aracoeli*, here serving as a useful, metaphorical staging of the ambiguous gender relations portrayed within the novel. Traditionally symbolizing Christ's resurrection and, as such, immortality, in Christian mythology the phoenix is seen as a phenomenon of change and perennial overcoming. On the other hand though, precisely for its sitting at the threshold between life and death, it alludes also to division and split—a dichotomy that aptly illustrates Manuele's ambivalent sense of self.

Manuele perceives himself as a hybrid, and not only during the idyllic phase of his childhood. Toward the end of his journey, he engages in metaphysical considerations that incisively sum up the treatment of the body in the novel: "E alla fine, la nostra esperienza totale risulta un ibrido, di cui ci appare solo il tronco esposto e mutilato, mentre la parte confitta ci scompare nella foiba. Quest'ibrido è il mio stesso corpo, è il tuo: sei tu, sono io" (Morante, *Aracoeli* 291; "And in the end, all our experience proves to be a hybrid, of which only the exposed, maimed trunk appears to us, whereas the buried part disappears into the pit. This hybrid is my own body, yours; it's you, me" [Morante, *Aracoeli* (trans.) 276]).

In a 2012 presentation, Nadia Setti notes that, in *Aracoeli*, "the hybrid overcomes the subject." This phantasmagoric creature, she asserts, "holds together all the characteristics of Aracoeli: the young girl, the ill woman and the dead mother"; it is male and female at the same time. Within a queer reading of the novel, Setti's remarks offer an interpretative key and allow me to expand further on the elision of gender boundaries in the text by turning to the Butlerian concept of *performative* identity and the subsequent sense of the abjection that derives from nonconformity to socially prescribed normative identifications.

FROM SOCIAL TO MATERNAL "ABJECTION"
IN *ARACOELI*

Butler's theory explaining traditional gender roles as "a legacy of sedimented acts rather than a predetermined or foreclosed structure, essence or fact, whether natural, cultural, or linguistic" can prove helpful in illuminating the notion of slippery gender identities as emblematically played out in the novel, a notion which puts into question the arbitrary nature of "category" itself ("Performative Acts" 523). Stressing how, far from being a cause, the subject is rather an effect of a series of Foucauldian structures of power, her argument critically addresses the dynamics of relational identity. Indeed, if it is true that femininity and masculinity are culturally, socially, and discursively inculcated and only then performed, thus retroactively coming to constitute us as subjects, it is also true that any violation of the Norm entails severe, punitive consequences.

Similarly, in Morante's text, we are given an insight into what it means to be trapped inside a socially prescribed and predetermined corporeality, a psycho-physical malady that Deuber-Mankowsky has noted in the character of Aracoeli (75). But it would appear that, just like his mother, Manuele also experiences an "insurmountable alienation of the body'" (Deuber-Mankow-sky 75). Indeed, because of his (self-)abjection and in a similar way to the character of Elisa in *Menzogna e sortilegio* he, too, fails to recognize himself in the mirror. In this respect, the hotel scene where Manuele looks at the reflection of himself unclothed, provides an emblematic example of his ex-traneousness to his body, a disaffection that recurs repeatedly in the narra-tion:

> *Mi è sempre più difficile . . . riconoscermi nel mio corpo, voglio dire in quello esteriore. Nell'interno di me . . . Il mio mestesso s'incarna ostinatamente in una forma perenne di fanciullo. Questo ammasso di carne matura, che oggi mi ricopre all'esterno, deve essere una formazione aberrante, concresciuta per maleficio sopra al mio corpo reale.* (Morante, *Aracoeli* 106)

> It becomes harder and harder for me . . . to recognize myself in my own body—I mean in the exterior one. In my interior . . . my self is stubbornly incarnated in a perennial boyish form. This bulk of aging flesh, which today covers me on the outside, must be an aberrant formation, an excrescence that has grown, thanks to an evil spell, over my real body. (Morante, *Aracoeli* [trans.] 99)

Encapsulated in these words is the gnostic conception of an inherent duality between body and soul, between the mortality of the reprehensible flesh and the immortality of the spirit (an opposition that is here quite tellingly con-jured up by recourse to the terms, respectively, "exterior" and "interior"). This connection, first noticed by Hanna Serkowska in her analysis of the similarities between the treatment of corporeality in *Aracoeli* and a pre-Christian (Platonic) ideology that sees the human body as a sepulcher (184), proves particularly fruitful in the context of the mirror scene. Perhaps even more striking in the above quotation is the antithesis between the idea of a spotless, timeless childhood ("perennial boyish form") and the stark reality of an aging, perishable body ("bulk of aging flesh"), which is indeed a recurrent topos in Morante's literary production.[4]

In his childhood Manuele had wished to be a little girl, the "muñeca" that his beloved Aracoeli longed for, just as his counterpart Elisa would have liked to be the son that her mother Anna ardently desired to bear to her beloved cousin Edoardo. Instead, he has become part of what he considers the "razza triste" (Morante, *Aracoeli* 135; "sad race" [Morante, *Aracoeli* (trans.) 127]), in opposition to the semidivine nature of his father, the em-bodiment of "VIRILITÀ" (Morante, *Aracoeli* 184; "MANHOOD" [Morante, *Aracoeli* (trans.) 175]), written in capital letters in the text in a way that is exemplary of the violence that this regime of masculinity exercises over Manuele who, imprisoned as he is in a sexed body, will never come to terms with a clear-cut gender categorization. In this light, what is made explicit in the protagonist's journey to Spain is a return to a pre-gendered existence free from the yoke of oppression that society bestows upon the individual who fails to comply with societal expectations. After all, Butler observes, gender is not something that one can do alone inasmuch as "'relationality' becomes constitutive of who the self is" (*Undoing* 148).

The androgynous structure of Manuele's subjectivity recalled above is a subversive attempt at destabilizing, in Butler's own formulation, "the norm [that] governs intelligibility" (*Undoing* 42)—namely, the borders of a patriarchal and heterosexual libidinal economy—that in the novel is also carried out through the figure of Aracoeli herself. During the course of the narration we witness her inexorable fall into Aracoeli-the-Whore, a metamorphosis that stands as a rebellion to the strictures of the Symbolic order that demands that women adhere to predetermined social scripts, namely, that they be virgins *and* mothers (Giorgio 93–116). The loving, beautiful, and chaste Andalusian metamorphoses into a reckless nymphomaniac who, after leaving her husband and son, consumed by her illness and erotic drives, will spend her last few months in a brothel. Aracoeli's subversion as set out during her malaise is a rebellion to the Law-of-the-Father that was, however, always already there, fire smoldering under the ashes that, triggered by the tragic circumstances of her daughter Carina's untimely death, erupts in all its disruptive force. In so doing, though, one might argue that she (and the author with her) becomes complicit to well-known, ready-made stereotypes of women modeled according to a clear-cut binary demanding that they remain outside culture (namely, in Giorgio's reading of *Aracoeli*, bourgeois culture), which, interestingly, is the same issue that Butler takes with Kristeva's theories of gender formation. Giorgio provides an illuminating answer to this quandary when she claims that "trying to reduce Morante's discourse on women and motherhood in *Aracoeli* [. . .] to clear-cut categories or definitions proves to be an impossible task" (94). Read in this light, motherhood in Morante's works would be a product of a specific milieu, namely, of social-historical conditioning, rather than a biologically innate trait. This is not too far from saying, as Butler does, that cultural processes can lead to a naturalization of predetermined identity categories—of which motherhood and, synecdochally, femininity can be seen as illustrative examples. Both Manuele and Aracoeli's "gender insubordinations," as Butler might express it ("Imitation" 307–20), are then to be interpreted as a form of political struggle against the patriarchal system and the assignment of gender roles that it validates: gender in the novel is not only a site of oppression but also, and more importantly, of resistance.

In the same way as its counterpart in *La Storia*, the Aracoeli-Manuele/ mother-son pair, too, would initially seem to keep itself in what Kristeva identifies as the semiotic realm. However, contrary to both Ida and Useppe, forever relegated to "the margins of the dominant symbolic order, in the most dangerous of territories" (Re 364), Manuele will eventually manage to enter the paternal Symbolic without, at the same time, leaving the maternal irremediably behind (Gragnolati and Fortuna, "Affection" 16–17).[5] Because, in order for Manuele to become a subject, it is essential that he initially lose his mother, that is, that he recognizes her as "other" to himself, his path toward individuation can be read against Kristeva's treatment of the dilemma about the necessity of a symbolic matricide as postulated in *Black Sun* (first published in 1987), which in turn stems from, and develops, her own formulation of the "abject" as she introduced it in her earlier work *Powers of Horror* (first published in 1980).

Kristeva elaborates and reconceptualizes the Freudian theorization of melancholia as a linguistic malady that manifests itself through the failure of language and symbolic signification. Melancholia springs from the denial of "matricide": that is, the separation from the mother, which, for Kristeva, is the first step toward a non-pathological psychic development of the subject. When this does not happen, because the grief of separation is insurmountable and as such refused, incomplete mourning develops into a melancholic pathological state that manifests itself in the loss of language and meaning: "the child refuses separation and mourning . . . the refusal to speak" (Kristeva, *Black Sun* 63). While it is extremely unlikely that Morante had Kristeva's theories in mind while writing *Aracoeli*,[6] the fact remains, however, that her last novel bears uncanny similarities to the work of the French philosopher (with which it shares, for example, a weariness with certain Freudian formulations), although, if we consider the most singular, ambiguous nature of Manuele's linguistic and psychosexual development, with a twist.

Explicitly refuting Freud's formulation of the oedipal triangle, in the course of an imaginary process that he sets up with, and against, himself, Manuele fails to succumb to feelings of rivalry toward his father. In an adamant refusal of dominant psychoanalytical interpretations, he will remain immune from jealousy even after witnessing the primal scene of his parents having sexual intercourse, an image that nevertheless will not cease to haunt his unconscious. After Aracoeli has turned away from him, Manuele reproduces this trauma in his suicidal phase first, and in his masochistic masturbatory fantasies later on. His primal maternal identification would thus be consonant with that of the Kristevan melancholic *female* subject, a linguistic malady that we can assume manifests itself, in Manuele's case, in the rapid loss of the Spanish language that follows his mother's death. Such a loss accounts for, in Kristeva's own terminology, a form of "noncommunicable grief" (*Black Sun* 3), the inability to resort to language to counterbalance the irretrievable maternal object. At the same time though, if we consider the stutter that he develops after he has moved in with his paternal grandparents, upon Aracoeli's death, it could be argued that Manuele equally fails to identify with the Symbolic (Gragnolati and Fortuna, "Affection" 13), the realm of language and social dictates that in the novel is metaphorically embodied by the figure of the "Doppia Statua" (Morante, *Aracoeli* 286; "Double Statue" [Morante, *Aracoeli* (trans.) 271]) that his grandparents themselves come to represent in his eyes, namely, the strictness of bourgeois conventions. But, if it is true that Manuele at first resists his mother's language as the consequence of an insurmountable grief, thus following the path that Kristeva describes for her female melancholic,[7] it is also true that he will, eventually, commit the matricide that the philosopher advocates as a vital necessity for identity formation (*Black Sun* 27).

Central to Kristeva's analysis is the thesis that, because heterosexual society disavows women the possibility of retrieving a mother-substitute as love object, it takes for them a great deal of symbolic effort in order to eroticize the (m)other (Kristeva, *Black Sun* 28). What remains implicit in her analysis is that female sexuality is melancholic precisely because it is primarily of a homosexual nature and, as such, must be repressed. Returning to the staging of melancholia in *Aracoeli*, though identifying with the maternal figure and clearly displaying melancholic traits, Manuele will, eventually, be able to separate from the mother, thus achieving a sense of subjectivity. More importantly still, he will not surrender to heterosexuality, nor will he plummet into psychosis, the "prediscursive homosexuality" bound to remain outside of Culture, which, in Butler's account, constitutes the inevitable outcome for the Kristevan homosexual (*Gender Trouble* 114).

"A FANTASY OF WHOLENESS": A RETURN TO THE FATHER VIA THE MOTHER

When Manuele finally arrives at his mother's native village of El Almendral, he has a visionary encounter with Aracoeli, who materializes to him in the form of an empty sack only to then dissolve into dust after a brief, empty linguistic exchange. He is looking for answers from Aracoeli, but he will get none, being simply told that "non c'è niente da capire" (Morante, *Aracoeli* 308; "there is nothing to be understood" [Morante, *Aracoeli* (trans.) 292]). This is Aracoeli's farewell to her son, who had set out on a search for his mother in the hope of finding, through her, the idyllic time of a pre-gendered existence. What he has found, instead, is the rocky desert of El Almendral and an alcohol-induced maternal vision. Yet, the novel seems to open up a new possibility, for the subject, that stems from the merging of masculine and feminine, paternal *and* maternal, no longer seen as mutually excluding entities. The postulation of a new, androgynous, being is well exemplified by the author in the text through recourse to metamorphosis as a trope for the exploration of the different permutations that gender might take on and of which the image of the phoenix in Manuele's dream is but an emblematic example. After haunting his dreams in a multitude of different guises ("Pastora. Idalga. Santa. Meretrice. Morta. Immortale. Vittima. Tiranna. Bambola. Dea. Schiava. Madre. Figlia. Ballerina" [Morante, *Aracoeli* 124]; "Shepherdess. Hidalga. Saint. Prostitute. Corpse. Immortal. Victim. Tyrant. Slave. Mother. Daughter. Ballerina" [Morante, *Aracoeli* (trans.) 117]), Aracoeli takes the form, or rather the non-form, of a shapeless sack. Having melancholically *introjected* his mother, it is against her that Manuele's self-hatred is addressed.[8] But now, having severed the tie that anchored him to the maternal—in Kristevan terms, choosing matricide over suicide, that is, separating the "I" (self) from the "(m)other"—he is ready to see her dissolve into dust, just like the shadow of his vision. In doing so, Manuele has *abjected* his mother, abjection being the process by which "a body becomes separated from another body in order to be" (Kristeva, *Powers of Horror* 10). In such terms, he has finally renounced his symbiotic union with Aracoeli in order to become a distinct "self"; in order to become a subject.

It is generally acknowledged that in Morante's works fathers are absent or otherwise negatively portrayed. This pattern of paternal ineptitude notwithstanding, Laura Benedetti has noted that, in her last work, Morante shows an awareness of this narrative paradigm, which she would try to overcome in her last work (82). Benedetti moves on to consider the maternal figure in *Aracoeli* before coming to the conclusion that, in the novel, "the search for the mother is revealed to be an inadequate solution" (82). This is a position that can be read as bearing similarities with Cesare Garboli's, for whom in *Aracoeli* "il vecchio schema glorioso (madre/figlio; Nunziata/Arturo; Ida/Useppe) viene lapidato e dato in pasto ai cani perché ne facciano strazio" (Benedetti 140; "the old glorious pattern (mother/son; Nunziata/Arturo; Ida/Useppe) is lapidated and thrown to the dogs" [Benedetti 140]). The question remains, however, whether, as both Benedetti and Garboli would have it, the bid to recover the lost maternal body in Morante's last literary effort does indeed end in failure. The unfolding of events that follow, in the text, the final mother/son reunion would seem to hint at a negative answer.

It is following the encounter with Aracoeli, even though this is revealed to be only an imaginary one, that Manuele can finally recover the maternal language. After his mother's farewell, Manuele asks for directions to El Almendral from a passerby using his mother's native Spanish, and, much to his surprise, he is pleased to notice that "il vecchio non tarda affatto a capirmi" (Morante, *Aracoeli* 309; "the old man is quick to understand me" [Morante, *Aracoeli* (trans.) 293]).What is more, this return to the mother does not exclude, but rather fosters, the possibility of recovering also the paternal realm, in a "most 'queer' happy ending" (Deuber-Mankowsky 81). Indeed, Manuele's vision of his mother Aracoeli is followed by another visual reconstruction of the adult narrator, who finds himself recalling the time when, aged thirteen, he decides to call on his father. A navy deserter, Eugenio has become a drunkard left aimless after the insurmountable grief of his wife's death, his fall paralleling that of Aracoeli. It is while reminiscing on this episode that Manuele feels, or, rather, thinks he is feeling, the sting of a large wasp—a clear phallic metaphor here used as a literary ruse to anticipate Manuele's subsequent declaration of love for Eugenio (Deuber-Mankowsky 81). Although just another visionary experience on his part, it is through this that Manuele discovers the love that he fails to profess to his father on the occasion of his visit: "Amore di chi? . . . Di Eugenio Ottone Amedeo" (Morante, *Aracoeli* 327–28; "Love of whom? . . . Of Eugenio Odone Amedeo" [Morante, *Aracoeli* (trans.) 311]).

This unexpected turn of events allows the renegotiation, just a few lines before its ending, of the reading of the novel as a whole. The unuttered "Ti Amo," a tacit declaration of love that defies heterosexual and incest taboo norms alike, encapsulates Manuele's longing for an existence freed from gendered constraints, the chimera that has guided his quest for the maternal Eden. It exemplifies the attainment of a longed-for dimension, which is, precisely, the androgynous realm of Manuele's early childhood and whose retrieval, at this point of the narration, successfully concludes the parabola of the protagonist's journey through his life memories. What is more, Manuele's acceptance of the paternal figure is a process that only happens a posteriori, triggered by his recollections of the event. When he calls on Eugenio, he feels an "invincibile riluttanza" that prevents him from pronouncing "le due sillabe: *pa-pà*" (Morante, *Aracoeli* 321; "invincible reluctance . . . the two syllables: *Pa-pà*" [Morante, *Aracoeli* (trans.) 304–5]). The same hesitation to utter the word *father* had already marked the blissful time of his childhood memories: "nel suono stesso di queste due sillabe, mi si faceva sentire un che di ridicolo, quasi d'indecoroso" (Morante, *Aracoeli* 184; "the very sound of these two syllables gave me a sense of something ridiculous, almost indecorous" [Morante, *Aracoeli* (trans.) 174]). That this resistance repeats itself at the concluding stage of the novel, just before the reconciliation with the paternal figure takes place, is no coincidence. Because the return to the father in *Aracoeli* does not postulate the repression of the maternal in favor of the paternal, but would rather entail the insertion of the former into the latter, Manuele's speech inhibition stands as his refusal to subject himself to a signifying order (the Symbolic that is, the realm of language) entailing the abandonment of the maternal realm, which, as his final encounter with Aracoeli has shown, he has only recently retrieved.

Furthermore, if it is true that the recognition of love for his father arrives just a few pages later, it is also true that "father" here does not refer to the bearer of the paternal Law—and indeed, given his present state, Eugenio's aura of "manhood" has long vanished in Manuele's eyes. It alludes, I suggest, to the Kristevean "imaginary father" or "father-mother conglomerate" (*Tales of Love* 40), both feminine and masculine and of which the seemingly sexless turtlelike creature that Manuele sees on the stairs just when he is leaving Eugenio's flat would be but an emblematic metaphor. Kelly Oliver, a philosopher who has written extensively on Kristeva, reads the imaginary father as a recuperation of the maternal dimension attained through a separation from the semiotic body and subsequent identification with the mother's desire (for the father, or the Phallus, that which satisfies the mother's *jouissance*) that allows the child to enter language, in other words, the Symbolic, via the mother (79). This return to the father ought to be understood as less a substitution of the paternal for the maternal function than a dialectic between the two. As such it is, also, a non-phallocentric challenge to traditional psychoanalytical discourses based on oedipal rivalry and castration threats in favor of an intensification of the maternal dimension (Oliver 70). Far from foreclosing a reunion with the paternal realm, in her last novel, Morante has presented this search to be the epitome of "a fantasy of wholeness" (Oliver 81), thus refuting the Lacanian paradigm of a relentless Symbolic father threating the child with castration and espousing instead a negotiation between maternal *and* paternal, seen as equally indispensable for a healthy sense of subjectivity.

In *Aracoeli*, characters metamorphose themselves in a complex staging of unresolved gender relations, thus performing the multifarious, kaleidoscopic nature of gender formation—of which the image of the phoenix is but a paradigmatic textual reminder. If, as postulated by Kristeva, the separation from the semiotic maternal continuously threatens the borders of an already tenuous "I," it follows that the speaking being is not a stable subject, but rather a never-ending process where subjects, and their identities, are constantly put under trial ("Question" 19). This position finds corroboration in Manuele's wish to fall back into the blissful realm of the maternal womb and points at the fragility of subjectivity formation, a logic that also parallels the Butlerian dynamics of gender formation within the novel. To conclude, and returning to Butler, gender, seen as a "corporeal style" that preexists the subject, becomes "[t]he act that one does, the act that one performs [that] is, in a sense, an act that has been going on before one arrived on the scene" ("Performative Acts" 526).

The theatrical imagery here employed allows for a reconsideration of the ways gender may operate; reciting the norm, that is, the socially prescribed gender script that predates our existence and is assigned to us at birth, might also lead one to cage one's body within a prisonlike chamber, to recall the platonic container model that Manuele himself experience firsthand and that is for him the source of an ineluctable sense of self-abjection. This, however, does not imply that one's social script cannot be recited differently, because gender can also be undone, a position to which Morante's last literary work would attest. And indeed, the very same point can be made by borrowing Manuele's theatrical metaphor: "Il corpo di cui mi vergogno mi ascherà di dosso, come un travestimento di commedia" (Morante, *Aracoeli* 124; "The body of which I am ashamed will drop from me like a comedy costume" [Morante, *Aracoeli* (trans.) 117]); he concedes to himself, in what seems to be a declaration of poetics on Morante's part. After all, as Manuele further comments anticipating the maternal fullness awaiting him at the end of his journey: "Maschio o femmina non significa niente" (Morante, *Aracoeli* 124; "Male or female means nothing" [Morante, *Aracoeli* (trans.) 117]).

NOTES

1. For an analysis of the maternal semiotic in *Aracoeli* by Gragnolati and Fortuna, see also "Attaccando al suo capezzolo le mie labbra ingorde" 85–124.

2. For a defense of Kristeva's work from Butler's (but also Grosz's) accusations of perpetuating the heterosexual norm, see also Oliver, especially 141–44.

3. For an in-depth study on the theme of "androgyny" in *Aracoeli*, see Hanna Serkowska, who links what she sees as the myth of the "Androyne" in the novel to the Platonic formulation of an original hermaphroditism and, expanding her analysis even further, to the doctrine of angelology (157–87).

4. For a comprehensive, chronological study of the treatment of the theme of childhood in Morante's oeuvre and its connections to the author's idea of "utopia," see Kalay's dedicated volume.

5. On the theme of the alleged conformity of Morante's (female) characters to patriarchal stereotypes, see Lucia Re's reading of Morante's *La Storia* from a feminist perspective. Re highlights what she identifies as the pre-oedipal state of the characters of Ida and her son Useppe, stressing their marginality to the symbolic and patriarchal order—a thesis that might partially be applied also to *Aracoeli*.

6. This is a speculation, however, over which Daniele Morante (Elsa's dearest nephew, son of her brother Marcello) has expressed his doubts (Conversation with Daniele Morante).

7. What awaits the male subject being, in Kristeva's formulation, the sublimation of the lost pre-oedipal maternal into artistic expression.

8. On self-hatred as resulting from maternal introjection: ". . . since I am She, (sexually and narcissistically), She is I? Consequently, the hatred I bear her is not oriented toward the outside but is looked up within myself" (*Black Sun* 29).

WORKS CITED

Benedetti, Laura. *The Tigress in the Snow: Motherhood and Literature in Twentieth-Century Italy.* Toronto: University of Toronto Press, 2009.

Butler, Judith. *Gender Trouble: Feminism and the Subversion of Gender Identity.* 2nd ed. 1990. New York: Routledge, 2007.

———. "Imitation and Gender Insubordination." 1989. *The Lesbian and Gay Studies Reader.* Henry Abelove, Michèle Aina Barale, David M. Halperin, eds. New York: Routledge, 1993. 307–20.

———. "Performative Acts and Gender Constitution: An Essay in Phenomenology and Feminist Theory." *Theatre Journal* 40.4 (1988): 519–31. Web. 28 March 2013.

———. *Undoing Gender.* New York: Routledge, 2004.

Cavarero, Adriana. *Relating Narratives: Storytelling and Selfhood.* Trans. Paul A. Kottman. New York: Routledge, 2000.

Deuber-Mankowsky, Astrid. "Baubo—Another and Additional Name of Aracoeli: Morante's Queer Feminism." *The Power of Disturbance: Elsa Morante's Aracoeli.* Manuele Gragnolati and Sara Fortuna, eds. London: Legenda, 2009. 73–83.

Giorgio, Adalgisa. "Nature vs. Culture: Repression, Rebellion and Madness in Elsa Morante's Aracoeli." *MLN* 109, 1 (1994): 93–116. Web. 29 March 2013.

Gragnolati, Manuele and Sara Fortuna. "Attaccando al suo capezzolo le mie labbra ingorde." *Nuova Corrente* 55 (2008): 85–124. Web. 29 March 2013.

———. "Between Affection and Discipline." *The Power of Disturbance: Elsa Morante's Aracoeli*, Manuele Gragnolati and Sara Fortuna, eds. London: Legenda, 2009. 8–19.

Kalay, Grace Zlobnicki. *The Theme of Childhood in Elsa Morante*. Columbia, MO: University of Missouri: Romance Monographs, 1996.

Kristeva, Julia. *Powers of Horror: An Essay on Abjection*. Trans. Leon S. Roudiez. New York: Columbia University Press, 1982.

———. "A Question of Subjectivity. Interview with S. Sellers." *Women's Review* 12 (1986): 19–22. Web. 1 April 2013.

———. *Soleil Noir: Dépression et mélancolie*. Trans. Leon S. Roudiez. New York: New York University Press, 1989.

———. *Tales of Love*. Trans. Leon S. Roudiez. New York: Columbia University Press, 1987.

Morante, Daniele. Personal communication. 27 October 2013.

Morante, Elsa. *Aracoeli*. Turin: Einaudi, 1989.

———. *Aracoeli: A Novel*. Trans. William Weaver. University of Rochester: Open Letter, 2009.

Oliver, Kelly. *Reading Kristeva: Unraveling the Double-bind*. Bloomington: Indiana University Press, 1993.

Re, Lucia. "Utopian Longing and the Constraints of Racial and Sexual Difference in Elsa Morante's *La Storia*." *Italica* 70.3 (1993): 361–75. Web. 22 March 2013.

Serkowska, Hanna. "The Maternal Boy: Manuele, or The Last Portrait of Morante's Androgyny." *Under Arturo's Star*. Stefania Lucamante and Sharon Wood, eds. Indiana: Purdue Universtity Press, 2006. 157–87.

Setti, Nadia. "Androgynous, Hybrid or Queer? Gender Reveries in Morante's Writing." Davy Carozza International Conference, Elsa Morante and the Italian Arts. Catholic University of America, Washington, DC. 26 October 2012. Conference Presentation.

Wood, Sharon. "Re-Dressing the Balance: Gender and Genre in Elsa Morante." *Vested Voices II: Creating with Transvestism: From Bertolucci to Boccaccio*. Federica G. Pedrali and Rossella Riccobono, eds. Ravenna: Longo. 2007. 77–87. Web. 26 March 2013.

IV

Morante's Essays:
The Self, Society, and Art

Chapter Nineteen

Between Perception and Prophecy

Elsa Morante's Reflections for the Present

Flavia Cartoni

This chapter focuses on Morante's reflections about Italian contemporary society, as exemplified in her posthumously published collection of letters and essays *Piccolo Manifesto dei Comunisti (senza classe né partito)*, her unsent letter to the Red Brigades, and the letter she sent to the newspaper *Paese Sera* regarding the Aldo Braibanti case. *Pro o contro la bomba atomica*—another posthumously published collection of essays on art and aesthetics—is also an important component of the analysis, for it further illustrates the author's critical stance. Morante's views on society, such as those about the need for truth to guide us and provide us with a sense of consistency, are of extraordinary importance. Indeed, when contextualized to current society, Morante's ideas exhibit a strong topicality for twenty-first-century social and political issues.

IL PICCOLO MANIFESTO DEI COMUNISTI

Morante wrote *Il Piccolo Manifesto dei Comunisti (senza classe né partito)* "around 1970, give or take a year,"[1] as Goffredo Fofi explains in the 2004 Nottetempo edition of the writings (23). Although Fofi never received a copy of the manifesto while Morante was alive, the writer discussed it at length with her younger friend. The manifesto is composed of thirteen points in which Morante articulates a spirited critique of the state of the Left at that time; it was addressed to Fofi, a young, engaged intellectual of a newer generation whom Morante believed might be instrumental in obtaining some clarity on the position and values of the Left. These thirteen points are in essence summaries of the arguments Morante put forth in her talks and other writings addressing the ethical roles of art and literature:

1. *Un mostro percorre il mondo: la falsa rivoluzione.*
2. *La specie umana si distingue da quelle degli altri viventi per due qualità precipue. L'una costituisce il disonore dell'uomo; l'altra, l'onore dell'uomo.*
3. *Il disonore dell'uomo è il Potere. Il quale si configura immediatamente nella società umana, universalmente e da sempre fondata e fissa sul binomio: padroni e servi — fruttati e sfruttatori.* (*Piccolo* 7; emphasis original)

1. A monster walks the earth: the false revolution.
2. The human race distinguishes itself from the other living creatures for two particular qualities. One is the dishonor of Man, the other is the honor of Man.
3. The dishonor of Man is *Power*. This is immediately and universally established in human society and is firmly based on the binomial: *master and servant / exploited and exploiter.*

With these first three points one can understand Morante's contempt for Fofi's ideology, which tended to crystallize such power dualities for the Maoist group to which he belonged at that time. We can also see the writer's clear stance about her respect for those she considers "human beings"— people who remain free from and untainted by power. The fact that not all people are human is, in fact, a constant consideration in Morante's writings. Her concept of "human being" and the subsequent respect for others can exist only when individuals exercise no power. Morante believed that the main difference between Fofi and herself derived from the one existing between Tao/Mao or (T)ao/(M)ao, with the understanding that totalitarianism and power are requisite attributes of extremist Maoist ideology. I consider it relevant to note that Morante considered herself always close to Taoist philosophy and always took distance from Fofi and his group's rigid Maoism.

4. *L'onore dell'uomo è la libertà dello spirito. [. . .] [intesa come] la realtà integra, propria e naturale dell'uomo.* (*Piccolo* 7–8)

4. The honor of Man is the freedom of the spirit. [. . .] [understood as] the complete, true, and natural state of Man.

Man can only continue to be a complete and free being if free from coercion and conditioning, when his spirit is completely free to express itself. The clear position Morante took regarding a famous legal case in Italy reveals the truth and tenacity of her beliefs. Among her manuscripts we find her letter to the *Paese Sera* newspaper published on July 17 regarding the 1968 Braibanti case (A.R.C. 52 II 3/15). In order to justify her writing to the newspaper, Morante takes her cue from an article published on February 3, 1968, by a journalist with the pen name of "Benelux." In his article, Benelux discusses the outrage of some Italians, regarding the San Remo Music Festival. Benelux's claim is that whoever is outraged by such a festival would do better to be outraged by the Vietnam War. Although eventually discarded from the final version, one section of Morante's letter is particularly interesting:

Sul numero di sabato 3 febbraio u.s. Benelux, nel suo trafiletto di prima pagina, sotto il titolo Le solite cose? elargisce ai nostri lettori (se ho ben capito) la seguente morale: che il Festival di San Remo e altri simili generi televisivi di stato non meritano in sostanza né proteste né indignazione, né tantomeno vergogna; appartenendo a un tipo di questioni futili. Anzi, gli italiani possono goderseli in pace e in ottima coscienza, col pieno incoraggiamento di Benelux: PURCHÉ, d'altra parte, gli stessi italiani non tralascino di indignarsi contro la guerra nel Vietnam, lo scandalo politico e altri simili misfatti, cioè delle questioni serie. Se davvero nel primo caso si trattasse di questioni futili e nel secondo di questioni serie, non si capirebbe perché Benelux dovrebbe mischiarle nello stesso trafiletto.

Ma io credo di intendere (o piuttosto spero) che Benelux in fondo alla sua coscienza riconosce invece fra i due casi una parentela piuttosto stretta.

In the February 3rd edition in his front-page article, Benelux, under the headline *The usual things?* bequeaths his readers with the following moral. Basically we should not protest against, be indignant about, or even be ashamed of the San Remo Music Festival and similar television programs; these, it seems, are all *futile* problems. Indeed, Italians should sit back and enjoy these things with a clear conscience and with Benelux's full approval: AS LONG AS, on the other hand, these same Italians don't forget to protest against the Vietnam War, political scandals, and other similar misdeeds, that is, serious issues. But if we really are dealing with empty problems in the first case and with serious problems in the second, it is difficult to understand why Benelux has grouped them all together in the same article.

I think I can see (or at least I hope so) that deep down Benelux admits that there is in fact a pretty strong link between the two cases.

In a note added on the same page of the manuscript, we read:

e che se è vero—come afferma Benelux—che non si possono trascurare le seconde, non si possono trascurare neanche le prime e, anzi non ha senso superare/trascurare?? [. . .] quei personaggi d'America o di dovunque sia per i quali la guerra nel Vietnam è un ottimo affare [. . .] e l'Italia compare di quei personaggi d'Italia o di dovunque sia per i quali la miseria altrui, materiale o culturale, con le relative Provvidenze e i relativi vari festivals di San Remo, ecc. sono ottimi affari.

and if it is true, as Benelux claims, that the second problems cannot be ignored, then neither can the first and in fact there is no sense in ignoring [. . .] those characters from America, or wherever they are from, for whom the Vietnam War is a great business opportunity [. . .] and in Italy, an accomplice, those characters from Italy, or wherever they come from, for whom other people's material or cultural impoverishment, through its similar promises of Future Happiness or its San Remo Music Festivals, etc., are great business opportunities.

The position taken by Morante on the role of Italy in relation to the United States is clear: Italy is perceived as the "accomplice" of the United States' hegemonic leadership and of the great business opportunities created by the war, which in turn create material and cultural poverty. Strong criticism emerges also for everything that contributes to economic gain and cultural impoverishment through the sacrifice of human lives.

Again on page 3 of the manuscript, on the left side of the vertical column, another statement appears, "Fra il primo male e il secondo, onestamente, è difficile giudicare quale sia più brutto. Comunque in entrambi i casi il problema sarebbe sempre lo stesso, cioè per dirlo con le parole di Benelux—pro o contro l'uomo" (It is difficult to judge what is really worse: the first evil or the second. In both cases, however, the issue remains the same, that is, in the words of Benelux, being either for or against Man). Further down on the same page of the manuscript draft we read: "Se Carlo Marx non fosse a quest'ora per mia fortuna libero dal problema che l'ha tanto travagliato da vivo (e che si definisce proprio con le parole usate da Benelux: pro o contro l'uomo) ci è permesso supporre che certo non si rallegrerebbe alla lettura di certi trafiletti" (If Karl Marx wasn't thankfully now free of the problem that troubled him so much when alive [problem defined in the very terms Benelux uses: to be for or against Man] we might well conclude that he wouldn't have been too happy on reading this article).

These are some of the discarded parts of the letter, eventually sent to *Paese Sera*, which deals with the Braibanti case. The central issue in this case was the arrest and trial of Aldo Braibanti,[2] writer, poet, and philosopher. Morante strongly condemned the rigid morality of the judges and gave her total support to those intellectuals like Braibanti, who made their thoughts public and shared them more widely. Here again there is a clear denunciation of the morals of the period, of those values displayed and defended by the judges, not to mention a strong criticism of the society at the time. In these final sentences, included in the text of the published letter (Bardini 729), Morante understands society as a conglomeration of "cadaverous cells" (to be intended in my view, rather than alive, as *anti*-life) and with no connection whatsoever to the real, vital world. For her, the real essence of the world is the truth, and it should never be hidden away or, perhaps even worse, ignored.

Returning to Morante's statement of being "for or against Man" we can say that to be *for* Man means to stand for the respect of the "human person." This is not a case of mere tautology, but a necessary distinction. For Morante, not every person is human—as we have seen—and she relentlessly asks us readers to reflect upon this claim. Her condemnation of the trial judges and the questions that she herself raises regarding Braibanti's crime of "moral subjugation" are extremely forceful in the published letter, but they are even more so in the lines that we find in the rest of the manuscript draft, for they encourage us to consider the importance that media in general, and television in particular, has on society. So, why were these lines erased from the published version?

HONOR AND HUMAN BEINGS

5. *In quanto onore dell'uomo , per definizione la libertà dello spirito sia come espressione che come godimento, è dovuta a tutti gli uomini. Ogni uomo ha il diritto e il dovere di esigere per sé e per tutti gli altri la libertà dello spirito.* (*Piccolo* 9)

5. The *honor of Man*—by definition the freedom of the spirit, both as an expression and as something to be enjoyed—is due to *all* men. Every man has the right and the duty to demand freedom of spirit for himself and for everyone else.

Already in 1951, Morante had avoided an attempt made by RAI, the state broadcasting company, to force her into taking a particular stance after she had written an unenthusiastic review of the film *Senza bandiera*.[3] RAI executives wanted the producer and director of the film *Senza bandiera* to be praised clearly and unequivocally in the program *Cronache del Cinema* to which Morante was a weekly contributor. Things did not go according to plan: Morante did not like the film at all, and she stuck to her guns. The result was that this particular episode of the program was canceled. Morante reacted immediately, writing a letter of resignation to the Board of RAI, later published in the newspaper *Il Mondo* on December 1, 1951 (Bardini 701–3). Morante's actions were consistent with her opinions: she gave a resounding "no" to manipulation and coercion, thus maintaining a clear, consistent stance on both a personal and professional level. In her letter to the RAI directors, she reminded them that her work consisted of reviewing films, not praising them (Bardini 702).

Similarly, in 1965, three years before the Braibanti case, she read the famous speech entitled "Pro o contro la bomba atomica" (For or against the atomic bomb). The bomb stood as a symbol for an ethical stance that aligned individuals for or against barbarity. This talk, in itself another brief manifesto of Morante's thoughts and unwavering steadfastness, lays down the necessary foundations for her ideas on a valid society. Moreover, it contains fundamental concepts regarding the value of poetry, of writing, and of the role of the intellectual in the world.

It has already been noted that Elsa Morante was an avid reader of Simone Weil (D'Angeli; Cazalé Bérard). Weil's writings emanate a consistent and infectious ethical passion and aspiration toward the good, summed up in her words, "ce désir de bien absolu constitue le fond de mon être" (277; "this desire for absolute goodness constitutes the core of my being"). This search for goodness within ourselves represents a Weilian ideal that Morante shared completely. While we find similar beliefs and ideals in Cristina Campo's writings (as in Ingeborg Bachmann's), Claude Cazalé Bérard has pointed out the different ways in which each of them read Weil:

> Morante, Campo and Bachmann embarked on a quest—following the trail led by Simone Weil (but each according to her own original means and literary forms)—towards the invention of a "poet(h)ics" aimed at a re-foundation of writing and artistic creation based upon a recognition of differences, on the defense of universally shared values and truths, and on love as the greatest realization of the human calling and the divine plan, to the extent that we associate these writers with "utopian poetics" (33).

For Cristina Campo, poetry is born of four elements: memory, dream, landscape, and tradition. These elements are four sphinxlike sisters, all of equal importance and all fundamental in the creation of poetry. These are the utopian poetics of which Cazalé Bérard speaks; necessity to reach the light, the truth, unity, and thus beauty. For Elsa Morante, poetry and truth are beauty; the rest is barbarity.

Points 6, 7, 8, and 9 of the *Piccolo Manifesto* argue for a new idea of the honor of Man, which is achieved by protecting the free spirit "from the germs of Power" (*Piccolo* 9–11):

> *10. In una società fondata sul Potere (come TUTTE le società finora esistite e oggi esistenti) un rivoluzionario non può far altro che porsi (foss'anche solo) contro il Potere, affermando (coi mezzi e dentro i limiti personali, naturali e storici che gli sono concessi) la libertà dello spirito dovuta a tutti e a ciascuno (Piccolo 11)*

> 10. In a society founded upon Power (as in ALL the societies that have ever existed and that exist at present), a revolutionary can do nothing but oppose such Power (even if acting alone), affirming (with and within the limits of the natural and historical status they have been given) the freedom of the spirit that is a right of each and every one.

This isolation in the face of power is, as we have seen, the price that Morante paid with her letter of resignation to RAI. During that time, she discovered herself to be essentially alone in standing up to power. The decision to put an end to her work on the radio program was a true declaration of independence.

ESSAYS VERSUS NOVELISTIC WRITING

In stark contrast to her narrative style—rich, full of adjectives, and, in the case of her first novel, even baroque—Morante's essayistic style is strikingly essential. Morante prefers the use of brief sentences to express her thoughts and ideas. This reflects a clarity of position and style that allows for no embellishments or poetic variations, but rather the distilled synthesis of her annotations, notes, and letters in which she criticizes and declares her opposition to the decisions of Power. This economy of style is, *mutatis mutandis*, similar to the succinct introductions of the historical characters preceding each section of *La Storia*. Those long sequences of events, the terrors and the disaster of war (one after the other, like the exploding shells of a machine gun) tell of the horrors taking place in those times. This style is more suited to a war report and has little to do with the narrative style of a novel. In this respect, the writing of essays is, for Morante, a reflection of her steadfast and original beliefs, expressed concisely and never drawn out (whether the essays are speeches, replies to the nine questions on the novel in *Nuovi Argomenti*, comments on Umberto Saba's poetry, etc.).[4] The style of the essays, mirrored by that of her letters, is short, concise, and dense; every affirmation that we find in the essays also has a clear parallel in the literary works. In her fiction, as in the points made in the *Piccolo Manifesto*, there is an emphasis on the separation between a free man and power—just as in the essays in *Pro o contro la bomba atomica*, there is an emphasis on the idea of the liberating role of art, poetry, and the novel, as well as on the vocational role of the writer.

Turning to her fictional writing, if we consider the character of Davide in *La Storia*, and if we also take into consideration what has been written about him—that Davide Segre represents Elsa Morante's beliefs as affected by her reading of Simone Weil's *Cahiers* (D'Angeli 109)—we see that her stance regarding power is consistent. I am referring here to Davide's famous speech in the tavern that immediately turns into a monologue, for no one is paying attention or listening to him. The only innocently attentive listener is little Useppe, who does not understand anything of what the young man is saying, but who does understand intuitively and clearly (he "feels" things as a small sensitive animal feels them) that Davide is suffering. Because of this feeling, the child urges Davide to leave; more than once, Useppe pulls at his sleeve in an attempt to interrupt his painful speech (Morante, *La Storia* 571).

Earlier in *La Storia*, Davide had vented his opinions on power, and his words had fallen on deaf ears. In one of his meetings with Santina, having talked about Nino's black market exploits, Davide says, "Il Potere, spiegava a Santina, è degradante per chi lo subisce, per chi lo esercita e per chi lo amministra!" (359; "Power, he explained to Santina, is degrading for those who submit to it, for those who administer it, and for those who control it!" [Morante, *History* 342]). These literary extracts reveal noteworthy ideas that should be considered within the framework of the general beliefs of the character as well as the narrator's/writer's. Davide has been talking to Santina, and he becomes increasingly restless in bed, leaving the woman without blankets in the cold. She, however, does not protest—she accepts it and remains silent. The description of Santina's state of mind and the reflections on her needs and her life give us a comprehensive understanding of what Morante thought about the humble: "la fame che fa cadere i denti, la bruttezza, lo sfruttamento, la ricchezza e la povertà, l'ignoranza e la stupidità . . . per Santina non sono né giustizia né ingiustizia. Sono semplici necessità infallibili" (*La Storia* 359; "the hunger that makes her teeth fall out, the ugliness, the exploitation, wealth and poverty, ignorance and stupidity . . . for Santina are neither justice nor injustice. They are simple, unfailing necessities" [*History* 343]).

Such are Morante's opinions of the disenfranchised, of those who submit to history and can do nothing against power. Moreover, in addition to what has been said about Davide's speech in the tavern, we find a suggestion, a reflection on what the customers there are assorted on doing. As previously mentioned, the reason why no one is listening to Davide's speech is that they are all listening to what is being said on the radio. They are interested in the soccer program, quickly going over the day's games and giving the scores. While the customers in the tavern listen to the radio, Davide continues to expound his theories on power and anarchy. He has declared himself to be a Jew, revealed his real name and said where his family is: they are all "piled up"; all, literally, in a pile. It is a horrible term, which Davide, with his wide-eyed look of a startled deer, uses to say that his family, being Jewish, has been deported and killed in the gas chambers like all the others, like all the Jews who ended up "nel mucchio" (Morante, *La Storia* 583; "in the pile" [Morante, *History* 654]). In this section of *La Storia* there is a stark contrast between Davide's speech (which refers to his conflict with his father, the work he did, and his views on economics) and the indifference of those present in the tavern who are simply listening to the soccer program. There is history, life, and politics, on the one hand, and confusion, opium, and the flight from reality to unreality, on the other. History and politics are represented by Davide; the unreality and the opium offered by the radio and soccer make the other customers in the tavern numb to his speech. As media developed, the influence of TV gained power, and its role to distract the attention of the viewer from what is of value, from what should be seen, followed, and reflected upon became fully realized. There is a clear link between Morante's position regarding the Braibanti case (the San Remo Music Festival vs. the Vietnam War) and the discussion of her stance for freedom and independence, as she proved when she resigned from *Cronache del Cinema*, due to censorship. In the novel *La Storia*, there are numerous occasions for Morante to express her ideas and position in order to keep her spirit free "from the germs of Power," and these are also present in the *Piccolo Manifesto*.

> *11., 12., 13. [. . .] Servirsi ai fini di potere degli sfruttati (anche solo del loro nome) è la peggiore forma di sfruttamento possibile. Peggio per chi lo fa a proprio beneficio personale. Proclamare il proprio amore per gli operai può riuscire un comodo alibi per chi non ama nessun operaio, o nessun uomo. Una folla consapevole che afferma la libertà dello spirito è uno spettacolo sublime. E una folla accecata che esalta il Potere è uno spettacolo osceno. (Piccolo 12–14)*

> 11., 12., 13. [. . .] Taking advantage of the exploited (or even just making use of their name) is the worst possible form of exploitation. It is even worse when it is done for personal gain. Proclaiming your love for *the* workers can be a useful alibi for those who do not love *any* worker or *any* person. A group of knowledgeable people who affirm the freedom of the spirit is a sublime sight. And a blinded group of people exalting Power is an obscene sight.

Morante's considerations here can be compared with the idea of beauty and truth discussed in the 1965 lecture "Pro o contro la bomba atomica." Morante sees barbarity also in the 1978 kidnapping of Aldo Moro in that it represents "the total disdain for the human person," and those who disdain others naturally disdain themselves, too; society can never improve if people are not worthy of themselves (*Lettera* 19). There can be no improvement if we are led by individuals who have no respect for people. Morante's letter to the Red Brigades (dated March 20, 1978), unfinished and never sent, ends with an interesting reference to her latest novel at that time, *La Storia*: "Whoever has by chance read my latest books will have noticed the esteem in which I hold established societies. No matter how inept or corrupt certain societies are nowadays, I hope I do not live long enough to see new totalitarianisms" (21).

It is apparent that in these early years of the twenty-first century, Western societies do not deal with domestic forms of totalitarianisms in the sense of the typical dictatorship to which Morante was perhaps referring in the 1970s. However, it is also clear that we are beholden to economic power, and perhaps in this we can appreciate that there is a divide between those who exercise power and those who are subject to such economic power, between the powerful and the humble. Never before as in these early years of the twenty-first century have we seen such a reshuffling of the cards on a European (and not only European) scale, ensuring that the accounts are balanced, but at the expense of the "little people" and to the detriment of those who are victims of such games.

At the time of the publication of *La Storia*, I believe that much of the criticism raised was primarily by those who believed fervently in the validity of the two different economic systems of the time: communism and liberalism. Nowadays, given the defeat of these two systems that once upheld, divided, subdivided, and dominated the world, we can see beyond those criticisms and fully recognize the value of the ideas sustaining Morante's 1974 novel and which underscore the position she takes in her essays and letters as well as in her attitude toward various public controversies. Whether market capitalism has been defeated or not, rereading her essays is of increasing interest in an economically globalized world; recognizing their value today confers their status as a literary classic.

NOTES

1. Unless otherwise noted, all translations are mine.
2. Aldo Braibanti, writer, poet, and philosopher, was accused of plagiarism and sentenced to nine years of prison for expressing his ideas and openly criticizing the judicial system in Italy. Behind the sentence lay the judges' rejection of his homosexuality as well as the accusation of leading two young men toward homosexuality.
3. The plot of this 1951 film by Lionello De Felice with music by Renzo Rossellini deals with espionage during World War I. Italian spies are paid and receive orders from Switzerland. After an investigation, a navy officer becomes aware that the intelligence chief is the Austrian consul in Zurich. A plot is organized to open the consul's safe in his mansion. A famous burglar opens it, and precious documents are found to destroy enemy espionage networks. The Austrian consul, now unmasked, commits suicide.
4. Some of these texts can be found in *Pro o contro la bomba atomica*, but most are collected in Marco Bardini's *Morante Elsa* (671–731).

WORKS CITED

Agamben, Giorgio, et al. *Per Elsa Morante*. Milan: Linea d'ombra, 1993.
Bardini, Marco. *Morante Elsa. Italiana. Di professione, poeta*. Pisa: Nistri-Lischi, 1999.
Cazalé Bérard, Claude. *Donne tra memoria e scrittura. Fuller, Weil, Sachs, Morante*. Rome: Carocci, 2009.
D'Angeli, Concetta. "La presenza di Simone Weil ne *La Storia*." Agamben, et al. 109–35.
Morante, Elsa. *History: A Novel*. Trans. William Weaver. Philadelphia, PA: Franklin Library, Franklin Center, 1977.
———. *Il Piccolo Manifesto dei Comunisti (senza classe né partito)*. Rome: Nottetempo, 2004.
———. *La Storia: Romanzo*. Turin: Einaudi, 1974.
———. *Lettera alle Brigate Rosse*. Morante, *Piccolo Manifesto* 15–21.

———. *Pro o contro la bomba atomica*. Milan: Adelphi, 1987.

———. Untitled Fragment. Nd. MS. A.R.C. 52 II. 3/15. Biblioteca Nazionale Centrale di Roma, Rome.

Weil, Simone. *Oeuvres complètes VI*. Vol. 3. Paris: Gallimard, 2002.

Chapter Twenty

"Pro o Contro *La rabbia*"

Elsa Morante, Pier Paolo Pasolini, and the Work of Art in the Atomic Age

Kenise Lyons

The professional and personal lives of Elsa Morante and Pier Paolo Pasolini were closely connected. Morante was responsible for initiating the process leading to the publication of the filmmaker's 1957 collection of poems, *Le ceneri di Gramsci*. Pasolini included the Roman writer in the production of his films including *Accattone* (1960)—in which Morante had a small role—as well as *Il vangelo secondo Matteo* (1964) and *Medea* (1969) in which she assisted with the selection of music. In addition to collaborating professionally, the two artists dined together frequently and also went on a trip together to India with Alberto Moravia in 1961. Their close relationship, however, did not prevent the two from disagreeing with one another. This is especially true in the case of their attitudes regarding the *mestiere di scrivere* (the craft of writing)—to borrow the words of Cesare Pavese.

While Pasolini chose to use his reviews of Morante's novels to express his differences in opinion, the Roman novelist generally utilized more private means when disagreeing with the filmmaker.[1] These means included her personal letters. For instance in an undated letter from 1963, Morante chastises the filmmaker for what she perceived to be his narcissism referring to him as a "STELLA FISSA P.P.P (FISSA perchè pure se gira, altro non fa che ruotare intorno/al proprio fuoco" (D. Morante 450; "FIXED STAR P.P.P [FIXED because even if it moves, it does nothing other than turn around/ its own fire]").[2] Another illustration of her use of her letters to critique her friend and collaborator can be seen in a letter from 1965. In it, Morante reproaches Pasolini for what she perceived as his adulation of the Pharisee

Fathers when he fails to intervene in her dispute with Arco Film over their failure to return Morante's investment in Pasolini's unfinished film *Il padre selvaggio* (let alone compensate its actors for their work).[3] Letters, however, where not the only space in which Morante felt she could take issue with Pasolini. At times, she employed more public means of challenging the director. Taking part in what Walter Siti describes as a "game of reciprocal mirror images," Morante embedded within her critical writings a number of elements belonging to the artists' shared imaginary. These images provided her a means of commenting upon and critiquing the ideas of Pasolini.[4] The figures used by Morante include the cat, the rose, Rimbaud, and Narcissus. They also include the atomic bomb.

The goal of this article is to demonstrate how at the same time atomic imagery in Morante's "Pro o contro la bomba atomica" is vital to the author's reflection on the work of art, it also provides the novelist a means of engaging "certi affezionati [che] si adoperano a smerciare i [suoi] libri facendoli passare sotto una specie di fiabe!!!" ("Pro o contro" 101; "certain dear ones who do their best to cheapen [her] books, making them pass as a type of fable!!!"). One of these "certi affezionati" was Pier Paolo Pasolini who, in his review of her 1957 *L'isola di Arturo*, described the novel's fictional world as a marvelous one "privo di rapporto storico o attualità" (*L'isola* 687; "lacking any relationship to history or current events"). By way of the lecture-cum-essay, Morante takes aim at the filmmaker's mis-characterization of her novel, offering a detailed explanation of how her writings are anything but fables lacking a relationship to history or current events.[5] The novelist shows instead how her narratives are deeply enmeshed in their historical moment, the Atomic Age in particular. Pasolini is unable to recognize her work's ties to reality, Morante argues, because of his erroneous beliefs about reality and art like those animating the filmmaker's own deployment of atomic bomb imagery in his film-essay *La rabbia*.[6]

LA RABBIA

Two years prior to Morante's penning of "Pro o contro la bomba atomica," Pier Paolo Pasolini released his ingenious film-essay *La rabbia* (1963).[7] The originality of the film lies in the fact that it is primarily comprised of photographic images and stock footage culled in part from the archives of the cinematic news journals *Mondo libero* and *Italia-URSS*. The material foundations of *La rabbia* are tightly bound to the text's very intent. As Pasolini tells us via voice-over narration at the film's opening, the point of the film was to comment on these images—with the aid of words and music—in an effort to express his political views and poetic sentiment.[8] Pasolini held that the images selected by him—ranging from the revolutions in Hungary and

Cuba to unnamed mining disasters in Italy—were intentionally hidden from the collective gaze of Italian society. They were consciously veiled by a set of illusory images generated by a culture industry bent on creating the appearance of peace, security, and general well-being vital to maintaining the postwar hegemony of the masters over their slaves. Only when the slaves were aware of the master's tools used to oppress them could they awake from the sleep of normality into which they were intentionally lulled. Pasolini's role as an artist, he informs us in the film's *trattamento* (synopsis), was to aid in this process of awakening by calling attention to turbulent reality of inequity hidden beneath the illusory veil of postwar normality. Like the iconoclasts of Byzantium, Pasolini felt he could best do so through the destruction of what he believed to be the false image (*irrealtà*) masking reality's *vera icona* (true image) from the eyes of society.

Reality's true appearance was not to be found in the faces of Ava Gardner or Sofia Loren. Instead it was reflected in the fragmented body of the detonating atomic bomb. From its initial dropping at Hiroshima and Nagasaki to its serial detonation during testing, the atomic bomb "si fa monumento [alla volontà dei padroni] sulla sommità degli Oceani" (Chiesi, *La rabbia* 189; "makes a monument out of itself [to the will of the masters] over the top of the Oceans"). "Col suo funebre cappuccio che si allarga in cieli apocalittici" (*Le belle bandiere* 226; "with its funereal cap expanding itself in apocalyptic skies"), as Pasolini explains to us in the film's synopsis, the bomb is "il frutto di questa divisione [tra i padroni e i servi]" (226; "the fruit of this division [between masters and slaves]"). It is a division that propagates itself through the seeds of racism, colonialism, and neo-capitalism. Pasolini's choice to include only stock footage taken from Italian cinematic newsreels, then, is tied to his desire to render the reality of the bomb and its progeny visible to the eyes of his viewer. The director's emphasis on these images, however, was not enough to awaken contemporary man to his social situation. Rather, as he emphasized in the finished film, it was the ordering of these images, as well as the juxtaposition of music and words accompanying them, that would allow him to help free society's slaves from their Platonic prisons.

At the same time the bomb represents the reality Pasolini craves to reveal, the weapon also structures the language used by the filmmaker to aesthetically advance his arguments. The dropping of "Little Boy" and "Fat Man," in Pasolini's opinion, awakened the world to the power inequalities allowing human beings to exploit other human beings. Contemporary man, however, is no longer aware of these divisions as he has been lulled into a state of normality in which "l'uomo tende a addormentarsi nella propria normalità, [lui] si dimentica di riflettersi, perde l'abitudine di giudicarsi, non sa più chiedersi chi è" (Pasolini, *Le belle bandiere* 223; "mankind tends to fall asleep in his own normality, he forgets to reflect, loses the habit of judging himself, and does not know anymore how to ask himself who he is"). In creating *La rabbia*, Pasolini hoped that his film would, like the bomb, once again awaken his viewers to an awareness of the profound Hegelian division separating the people of the world into masters and slaves. As an expression of his anger at postwar "normalizzazione che è consacrazione della potenza e conformismo" (224; "normalization that is the consecration of power and conformity"), Pasolini hoped that the film would shatter reality's false image and go on to reveal its true countenance. Montage—at the level of both image and sound—was crucial to the film's ability to do so. It is an aspect of film language Pasolini believed best embodied the sensation of anger visually expressed at the film's opening by the images of the atomic bomb detonating over Japan. It is not until the sequence of *La rabbia* addressing the death of Marilyn Monroe, however, that the linkages Pasolini creates between anger, montage, and the atomic bomb are made explicitly clear. In it, the director has spliced glossy magazine images of the film star and childhood photos of her pre-fame persona, Norma Jean Baker, together with filmed footage depicting the devastating effects of the atomic bomb observed during testing. The three sets of images are joined together by footage of detonating atomic bombs. The images of the detonating bomb decimate the images of the corrupted Marilyn, going on to reveal the innocent reality of Norma Jean Baker. At the same time, the footage of the exploding atomic bomb also reveals the macabre reality of illusory beauty manufactured by the film industry's factory of dreams willing to sacrifice the life of young girl in exchange for wealth, fame, and power.

PRO O CONTRO *LA RABBIA*

In "Pro o contro la bomba atomica" Morante takes issue with the connection that Pasolini makes between the bomb and reality and, consequently, his belief that the bomb can be called into the service of art. Like Pasolini, Elsa Morante believes that "nessun argomento, oggi, interessa, come [la bomba atomica], da vicino, ogni scrittore" ("Pro o contro" 97; "no other argument today intimately interests, like [the atomic bomb], every writer").[9] Her rational for why the bomb is central to the work of every artist, however, is quite different from that of Pier Paolo Pasolini. For the filmmaker, the bomb is both the embodiment of truth and the inspiration for the aesthetic strategy Pasolini believed best enabled him to reveal reality.[10] On the other hand, Morante, as Stefania Lucamante reminds us in her study of *La Storia*, belongs to the category of those artists who "non trovano alcuno stimolo vitalistico dietro tale scoperta scientifica" (298; "find no vitalistic stimulus in such a scientific discovery"). Instead, the Roman author seeks to underline "il pericolo in senso etico e estetico, consapevol[e] della carica mortifera dell'atomica persino quando si dovesse intenderla in termini del tutto simbolici" (298; "its danger in an ethical and aesthetic sense, knowledgeable of the lethal charge of the atomic bomb even when one must understand it in entirely symbolic terms").[11] Though acknowledging the threat the bomb poses to readers' bodies, as the literal embodiment of the very "dragon of unreality" from which Morante believed the true artist must rescue his or her audience, the bomb also represented an imminent risk to readers' minds.

Generated out of humanity's scientific impulse, the bomb is also rooted, Morante claims, in contemporary man's "occulta tentazione di disintegrarsi" ("Pro o contro" 99; "occult temptation to disintegrate himself") born from bourgeoisie culture's corruption of the so-called Nirvana instinct. No longer desirous of integration with Divine consciousness, humanity now seeks after its *maligno surrogato* (99; "malign surrogate"), or the *dis*-integration of individual consciousness from that of God, others, and—worst of all—itself. At the same time the bomb represents the destruction of the human psyche, it also aids in exacerbating its fragmentation. The weapon is representative of the alienating forces of what Morante refers to as the "confusione irreale, e frammentaria, e usati dei rapporti esterni" (102; "fragmentary, secondhand, confusing unreality of external relationships"). These forces prevent individuals from recognizing "simboli di verità poetica nelle cose reali" (Morante, "Sul romanzo" 55; "symbols of poetic truth in real things"). By reducing the world to "la multiformità sterminata e cangiante (la chiamata 'relatività') dell'oggetto reale" (53; "the immense [yet] ever-changing multiformity [the so-called relativity] of objective reality"), the atomic bomb impacts man's ability to experience spiritual totality. The purpose of art, in Morante's estimation, is to return to audiences the integrity of reality denied to them in their daily lives "nel [loro] quotidiano, e logorante, e *alienante* uso col mondo" ("Pro o contro" 102; in [their] daily, and exhausting, and *alienating* interaction with the world").

The bomb is not a representation of reality primarily because injustice, or the "dominio di una persona su un'altra persona, se è stato sempre iniquo, ormai è pure, definitivamente, acquisto come irreale; giacché l'uguaglianza fondamentale delle persone è acquista nella coscienza" (114; "dominion of one person over another, if it has always been unjust, is too definitively, understood as unreal; since the fundamental equality of people is acquired in the consciousness"). Along with "demenze organizzate, [. . .] miti degradanti, [. . .] noia convulsa e feroce, e così di seguito" (100; "organized forgetting, [. . .] degrading myths, [. . .] convulsive, ferocious boredom, and the like"), injustice is nothing but the proof of man's alienation from himself and others. Not only does it shatter the social body, power also forces people to engage only one aspect of human existence: pleasure in the case of the dominator and horror in that of the dominated. For Morante, life is more than just misery or pleasure. Rather, it is a complicated mix of joy and pain. "Nessuna persona viva" (107; "no living person"), Morante announces in "Pro o contro," "rimane esclusa dall'esperienza del sesso, dell'angoscia, della contraddizione e della deformazione" (107–8; "remains excluded from the experiences of sex, of anxiety, of contradiction, and of deformation"). This is because "il movimento reale della vita è segnato dagli incontri e dalle opposizioni, dagli accoppiamenti e dalle stragi" (107; "the real movement of life is characterized by encounters and oppositions, by couplings and by massacres").

No work of art should focus only a singular aspect of human life (i.e., injustice) as art is charged with defending the consciousness of its audience from illusions, especially those of Thanatos who "fabbrica le sue visioni mostruose per atterrire le coscienze e imbrogliarle, snaturandole, dalla loro solo contentezza e deviandole dalla spiegazione reale" (103; "constructs its monstrous visions to terrify consciousnesses and to deceive them, perverting them from their only happiness, distracting them from the unfolding of reality"). Any work, then, that seeks to "scansare quei moti della natura che la legge sociale, per il suo torbido processo, censura come perverse o immondi" (108; "shun those impulses of nature that social law, because of its murky process, censure as perverse or dirty"), only further plunges audience's minds into the mire of unreality. The true artist returns his or her audience to reality, their "paradiso naturale [. . .] almeno finché non si siano ancora trasformate nella struttura stessa visibile dei loro corpi. Non siano diventate, cioè, dei *mutanti*, come si dice in gergo atomico" (110; "natural paradise [. . .] as long as they have not already been transformed in their visible bodily structures. As long as they have not become, in other words, *mutants*, as they say in atomic jargon").

By focusing primarily on the negative aspects of contemporary human existence (i.e., injustice), Pasolini only succeeded in reducing his audience "alla elementare paura dell'esistenza" (104; "to the elementary fear of existence") vital to Thanatos's factory of horror. Though the filmmaker held that the poetics and aesthetics of his film revealed reality and destroyed the mask of unreality covering it, in actuality *La rabbia* only encouraged viewers to flee

> *da se stessi e quindi dalla realtà, loro, come chi ricorre alla droga, si assuefanno dell'irrealtà, che è la degradazione più squallida, tale che in tutta la loro storia gli uomini non hanno conosciuto mai l'uguale. Alienati, poi, anche nel suo senso della negazione definitiva; poiché la via dell'irrealtà non si arriva al Nirvana dei sapienti, ma proprio al suo contrario il Caos, che è la regressione infima e la più angosciosa.* (104–5)

from themselves and therefore reality, like those who turn to drugs, they develop a tolerance for unreality that is the most squalid degradation, one that in all of their history mankind has never its equal. *Alienated*, then also in their sense of definitive negation; since the way of unreality does not lead to the Nirvana

of the wise, but rather to its opposite, Chaos, which is the lowest regression
and the most distressing.

What Pasolini did reveal in the film was that, in this instance, he is no
scrittore (writer), but merely a *scrivente* (one who writes).[12] Unlike the *scrittore* who worked to diminish the system of disintegration, Morante considers
a *scrivente* to be an individual who was so mutated by the system that he or
she carries out their work in service to it, even if only unconsciously. *La
Rabbia* cannot "fissare in faccia i mostri aberranti (edificanti o sinistri) generati da quella cieca paura" (106; "stare in the face the aberrant monsters
[uplifting or sinister] generated by that blind fear") in an effort to unmask "la
loro irrealtà, col paragone della realtà della quale appunto è venuto a portare
testimonianza" (106; "their unreality, with [their] comparison to reality, of
which [the artist] precisely came to bring testimony"). Made in the image of
the system of disintegration, *La rabbia* presents Thanatos's monstrous visions as reality.

By focusing on the negative aspects of human existence he believed to be
hidden, Pasolini ultimately believed he was being scandalous and subversive.
Yet, as Morante explains, an artist does not have to try to shock anyone as "la
presenza dello scrittore (cioè della realtà) è sempre uno scandalo, anche se
viene tollerata, durante i periodi di tregua sociale" (110; "the presence of the
writer [and therefore of reality] is always a scandal, even if it is tolerated,
during periods of social truce"). Nor does Pasolini, in Morante's estimation,
need to intentionally demonstrate his subversion of the status quo because,
"nella pratica della vita sociale e politica, si sente sempre attirato verso
movimenti rivoluzionari o sovversivi, i quali proclamano come fine la cessazione di ogni dominio di una persona su un'altra persona" (114; "in the
practice of social and political life, [an artist] always feels himself drawn
toward movements that are revolutionary or *subversive*, those that proclaim
as their end the cessation of every kind of domination of one person over
another"). Pasolini, Morante implies, only need to be honest, writing "onestamente, quello che gli pare" (116; "honestly, what he feels like writing"),
utilizing a language given to him by reality itself. Such a language for Morante is one that like that of Scheherazade, does not seek to "consolare degli
orrori, di illuminare il buio di spettacoli e artifici mutando la cecità in abbaglio" (Bettin 219; "console the horrors [or] to illuminate the darkness of
spectacles and artifice transforming blindness into astonishment"). Rather it
is a language that allows reality to be seen for what it is, "un leone con la
pelliccia d'oro" ("Pro o contro" 117; "a lion with golden fur").

CONCLUSION

The differences animating Morante's and Pasolini's deployment of the atom bomb would ultimately prove disastrous. The seeds of the annihilation of their relationship, as we have just seen, were sown by Pasolini himself in his review of Morante's 1957 *L'isola di Arturo* and watered in "Pro o contro la bomba atomica." It would take almost ten years for the seeds, lying dormant much like an atomic bomb in an armory, to burst open in Pasolini's review of Morante's *La Storia*.[13] Further contaminated by Pasolini's radioactive words—detonating like a figurative bomb—their friendship dies.[14]

NOTES

1. Pasolini's decision to publically air what he believed to be errors in Morante's poetics and aesthetic approach is rooted in patriarchal privilege and his bitterness. The latter is especially true in the cause of his critique of *La Storia*, which is rumored to be rooted in his anger over what he perceived to be her support of his beloved Nino Davoli's marriage to a woman. One explanation for Morante's decision to keep matters between them could be Morante's respect and affection for Pasolini, which led her to lovingly correct him like a mother, not publicly humiliate him.

2. All translations are mine, unless otherwise noted.

3. See D. Morante, *L'amata* 408–9.

4. For more on the dynamics of this game and its various fields of play, see Siti.

5. The 1965 essay was first published in the pages of the March/April edition of the journal *Europa Letteraria*. "Pro o contro la bomba atomica" began as a public lecture read by Morante in Milan, Rome, and Turin in February of that same year.

6. When introducing *La rabbia*'s synopsis in pages of *Vie Nuove*, Pasolini describes the work as a "film tratto da materiale di repertorio [. . .] un'opera giornalistica, dunque, più che creativa. Un saggio più che un racconto" (*Le belle* 222; "a film composed of stock footage [. . .] a journalistic work, then, more than a creative [one]. An essay more than a story"). My reference to *La rabbia* as a film-essay attempts to render the director's complex description of the work in an economic way.

7. Much of what we know about the making of *La rabbia* is thanks to the work of Roberto Chiesi, specifically his article titled "Il 'corpo' tormentato de *La rabbia*, la genesi del progetto, la 'normalizzazione' del 1963, l'ipotesi dei ricostruzione del 2008." In it, Chiesi writes that the film's producer, Gastone Ferranti, originally approached Pasolini to make an episodic film. Pasolini, however, was able to successfully convince Ferrante to allow him to make a stand-alone film. Unfortunately, after viewing Pasolini's feature-length film, the producer was so unhappy with what he saw, that he returned to the original idea of a *film a episodi*. Pasolini reluctantly agreed to cut his film and join it to a second film of the same name directed by Giovannino Guareschi, a man who was Pasolini's ideological and aesthetic opposite. Following the release, and poor reception, of the film, Pasolini was so angered by Guareschi's contribution to the film that he even went so far as to press to have his name removed from the film—an effort that was ultimately unsuccessful. Pasolini's anger, however, should not provide scholars a reason to remove the film from the filmmaker's larger body of work. Pasolini did not reject his film. Rather, as Chiesi reminds us, Pasolini only wanted to remove his name after seeing Guareschi's episode. Moreover, in an interview with Andrea Barbato published around the time of *La rabbia*'s release, Pasolini states that he agreed to the changes ultimately believing that each filmmaker "si rivolgeva al suo pubblico," going on to say that his film "era già fatto quando Guareschi è entrato nel giro" (Chiesi, "Il corpo" 19).

8. Voice-over narration is a vital aspect of the film's construction. Pasolini wrote the film script in both poetry and prose, which was read, respectively, by Renato Guttuso and Giorgio Bassani.

9. Intensified by the complexities of the Cuban Missile Crisis, Morante's exploration of the atomic bomb in "Pro o contro la bomba atomica" is rooted in her unfinished novel *Senza I conforti della religione.* Begun, according to Claude Cazalé Berard, around 1958 and left uncompleted around 1964, many of the themes, situations, and characters found in *Senza i conforti della religione* made their way into Morante's later works (such as *La Storia*). Issues explored in *Senza i conforti della religione* were also incorporated into the Roman novelist's critical works, including the 1965 essay. "Pro o contro la bomba atomica" appears to absorb the interrupted novel's reflection upon the nuclear bomb. At one point in the novel, one of the novel's protagonists (Alfio) works with a young filmmaker who, according to Morante, wants to "fare un film-documentario, di un genere nuovo, una intricata parabola filosofico-morale, su Bikini e la minaccia atomica" (Cazalé Berard 16; "make a film-documentary, a new genre, an intricate philosophical-moral parable, on Bikini [Island] and the atomic threat"). The director's efforts are resisted by Alfio who would rather make more commercially viable film full of bathing beauties.

10. For more on bombs and truth in Pasolini, see D'Elia. While D'Elia limits his analysis to the bombs of Bologna featured in Petrolio, I expand to explore the nature of bombs in Pasolini's earlier work.

11. For more on Morante's relationship to the atomic bomb as depicted in *La Storia*, see Pischedda.

12. Though appearing to refer to those who are solely involved in the literary arts, Morante encourages us to consider the term *writer* to apply more broadly to the act of artistic creation when she writes that the term *scrittore* "vuole dire prima di tutto, fra l'altro, poeta" ("Pro o contro" 97; "means above all, among others, poet").

13. For a more detailed discussion of his review and its impact on Morante, see Bernabò.

14. As Francesca Cadel has shown, even after the end of the pair's friendship, and Pasolini's own death, Morante and Pasolini continued to engage one another through their writings. See Cadel.

WORKS CITED

Bernabò, Graziella. *La fiaba estrema, Elsa Morante tra vita e scrittura.* Rome: Carocci editore, 2012.

Bettin, Gianfranco. "Il drago della notte." *Per Elsa Morante.* Ed. Giorgio Agamben. Milan: Linea D'ombra, 1993. 219–33.

Cadel, Francesca. "Politics and Sexuality in Pasolini's *Petrolio.*" *The Power of Disturbance: Elsa Morante's Aracoeli.* Manuele Gragnolati and Sara Fortuna, eds. London: Legenda, 2009. 107–17.

Cazalé Berard, Claude. "Il romanzo in-finito." *Testo & Senso* 13 (2012). Web. 21 June 2013.

Chiesi, Roberto. "Il 'corpo' tormentato de *La rabbia*, la genesi del progetto, la 'normalizzazi- one' del 1963, l'ipotesi della ricostruzione del 2008." *Studi Pasoliniani* 3 (2009): 13–26. *La torrossa.* Web. 10 May 2012.

———, ed. *La rabbia.* Bologna: Cineteca Bologna, 2009.

D'Elia, Gianni. "*Petrolio,* la bomba di Pasolini." *Il fatto quotidiano.* 2 April 2010. *La torrossa.* Web. 10 May 2012.

Lucamante, Stefania. *Quella difficile identità. Ebraismo e rappresentazioni letterarie della Shoah.* Rome: Iacobelli, 2012.

Morante, Daniele, ed. *L'amata.* Turin: Einaudi, 2012.

Morante, Elsa. *L'isola di Arturo.* 1957. Turin: Einaudi, 1995.

———. "Pro o contro la bomba atomica." *Pro o contro la bomba atomica e altri scritti.* Ed. Cesare Garboli. Milan: Adelphi, 1987. 97–117.

———. *La Storia.* 1974. Turin: Einaudi, 1995.

———. "Sul romanzo." *Pro o contro la bomba atomica e altri scritti.* Ed. Cesare Garboli. Milan: Adelphi, 1987. 43–73.

Pasolini, Pier Paolo. *Accattone.* 1961. Walter Bearer Films, 2003. DVD.

———. *Le belle bandiere, dialoghi 1960–65.* Ed. Gian Carlo Ferretti. Rome: Editori riuniti, 1977.

———. *Le ceneri di Gramsci.* 1957. Milan: Garzanti, 1976.

———. "Elsa Morante: *La storia.*" Siti and De Laude, Vol. 2, 2096–107.

———. "*L'isola di Arturo.*" Siti and De Laude, Vol. 1, 686–90.

———. *Medea.* 1969. Entertainment One, 2011. DVD.

———. *La rabbia.* 1963. Rarovideo, 2011. DVD.

———. *Il vangelo secondo Matteo.* 1963. Walter Bearer Films, 2003. DVD.

Pischedda, Bruno. *La grande sera del mondo: romanzi apocalittici nell'Italia del benessere.* Turin: Aragno, 2004.

Siti, Walter. "Elsa Morante and Pier Paolo Pasolini." *Under Arturo's Star: The Cultural Legacies of Elsa Morante.* Stefania Lucamante and Sharon Wood, eds. West Lafayette, IN: Purdue University Press, 2006. 268–88.

———, and Silvia De Laude, eds. *Saggi sulla letteratura e sull'arte.* 2 vols. Milan: A. Mondadori, 1999.

Chapter Twenty-One

Timely Anachronisms

Elsa Morante, Adriana Cavarero, and Roberto Esposito on Power, Violence, and Subjectivity

Claudia Karagoz

Although Elsa Morante's anachronism has puzzled critics in the past, new perspectives on her writings call for a reevaluation of their prophetic quality, exploring in particular their influence on later generations of Italian novelists.[1] However, both the relevance of her ideas in today's world, and their dialog with contemporary philosophy remain uncharted. This chapter considers a selection of Morante's critical writings on power, violence, and human freedom in relation to recent reflections on these same themes by contemporary Italian philosophers Adriana Cavarero and Roberto Esposito. I argue that Morante's views on these issues are timely insofar as they clearly foresee the escalation of social inequality, aggression, and conflict occurring in the world today. Moreover, her insights prefigure—but also complement—some post–September 11, 2001, philosophical critiques of violence, hypersubjectivism, and the "politics of death" (Esposito, "Unpolitical" 212). Specifically, Morante's pronouncements foreshadow some aspects of Esposito's thought on biopolitics, and the interest in vulnerability and the perspective of the *inermi* (defenseless) of Cavarero's work on "horrorism."[2] However, by affirming the social function of art, in her critical writings Morante also offers a clear model of individual and collective engagement with the world, which helps navigate the complexity of contemporary violence and wars.

Cavarero and Esposito share, like Morante, a deep commitment to rethinking subjectivity, power, and politics vis-à-vis the challenges posed by contemporary global conflict. Both philosophers have, in the last decade, redirected their research to focus on large-scale violence and aggression, thus engaging with themes at the core of Morante's writings. Through his work on the category of immunity, biopolitics, and the concept of the "impersonal," Esposito has moved away from his primarily deconstructive research on the Unpolitical and *communitas* to embrace "a more explicitly affirmative approach" ("Unpolitical" 210). Cavarero's analysis of "horrorism" has led her to develop a new theory of subjectivity—what she describes as "the inclined self" ("Inclining" 195).

To date, I have not found any references to Morante's critical texts in Cavarero's and Esposito's recent books.[3] Similarly, critics of Morante do not treat her work in consideration of these philosophers. In juxtaposing Morante to Cavarero and Esposito, my goal is twofold. First, I aim to show the farsightedness and enduring influence of Morante's pronouncements on the violence and oppression intrinsic to human history—notwithstanding the momentous changes that have taken place in the world since her death in 1985. Moreover, I propose that Morante's ideas add to contemporary philosophical debates on aggression and conflict by offering a road map to effecting change in the present historical moment. This chapter thus hopes to broaden the scholarship on Morante by investigating a neglected aspect of her work, but also to show how her views expand present conversations on issues of violence, power, and social justice.

In my analysis, I focus on three of Morante's commentaries on crucial questions of her time: "Pro o contro la bomba atomica" (1965 speech), "Piccolo Manifesto dei Comunisti (senza classe né partito)" (c. 1970), and "Lettera alle Brigate Rosse" (1978). These texts articulate—in the context of her notions of "reality" and "unreality"—Morante's condemnation of power, fascisms, and false revolutions, her plea to preserve the dignity of the "human person," and her view of art as the antidote to modern disintegration—hence the poet's task as agent of resistance and change. Although this "concretion" of themes (Bareil 11) is a vital facet of Morante's entire oeuvre, it is especially vivid in the works I discuss here.[4]

"Piccolo Manifesto dei Comunisti (senza classe né partito)" (c. 1970) and "Lettera alle Brigate Rosse" (1978) are short texts, never published during Morante's lifetime, which illustrate her views on the ideology and actions of the Italian leftist, extra-parliamentary, and "lotta armata" (armed struggle) groups of the 1960s and 1970s. For Morante, the task of a true revolution is to abolish power, which rests on class division, and restore "la libertà di spirito" ("*Piccolo*" 7–8; "the freedom of the spirit") to men and women.[5] Moreover, all human action must respect life. A revolution that uses violence in order to achieve its goals is false and can only lead to the establishment of a totalitarian society. For these reasons, Morante rejects both the ideology and the actions of the 1968 Italian protest movements, and, a decade later, the violent campaigns of the Red Brigades. However, the ideas she presents in these texts also illustrate her broader beliefs about history, power, and social justice, and thus transcend the specific sociohistorical context that generated them. Specifically, they presage current concerns on post–September 11, 2001, global violence, be it related to Islamic religious fundamentalism and the West's wars of retaliation, or to the struggle of populations seeking to overturn totalitarian rule.

According to the note by Goffredo Fofi that accompanies the 2004 edition of the text, Morante wrote "Piccolo Manifesto dei Comunisti" around 1970 to explain her views on history to those who, like Fofi, were actively engaged in the *Sessantotto* movement.[6] Their fundamental disagreement, explains Fofi, was that he, like his fellow *sessantottini*, still believed in history, whereas Morante did not.[7] In this thirteen-point manifesto, Morante indicts what she calls the monstrous "false revolution" that was moving across the world at the time, and outlines her beliefs on "Power," which she contrasts to the freedom of the spirit, the former representing men's dishonor, and the latter their honor (*Piccolo* 7). Spirit, Morante explains, does not correspond to an ethereal, metaphysical entity. Rather, it coincides with "la realtà integra, propria e naturale dell'uomo" (*Piccolo* 8; "the unbroken, true, and natural reality of man"), by which Morante means human life in its ever-changing, multifaceted, authentic, and undivided nature.[8] Spirit's freedom manifests itself in many forms, all equally—that is, nonhierarchically—signifying the same unity. Two of these manifestations of freedom, beauty, and ethics, for example, are one. Things that wish to enslave the spirit, that is, that affirm power, cannot be beautiful, and vice versa. For Morante, works such as Marx and Engels' *Manifesto* or Einstein's essays are beautiful, just like Rembrandt's self-portraits or Rimbaud's poems are ethical. Morante's reading of these works upholds a view of power as the enforcement of class divisions; accordingly, all of the works are beautiful and moral insofar as they affirm man's freedom from hierarchy and class.

For Morante, all human beings are entitled to express and enjoy the freedom of the spirit. Power, however, erases this freedom in both oppressed and oppressor—hence the necessity of a revolution aimed at freeing all humankind through "l'abolizione totale e definitiva del Potere" (*Piccolo* 10; "the total and permanent abolition of Power"). Therefore, a revolution that reaffirms power is false. True revolutionaries must stand against power at all costs, even in complete isolation from others, if necessary, in order to uphold the freedom to which all are entitled. Conversely, revolutionaries who embrace power in any form betray the very idea of revolution. Exploiting the oppressed for personal gain is the greatest offense of all:

> *Proclamare il proprio amore per* gli *operai può riuscire un comodo alibi per chi non ama* nessun *operaio o* nessun *uomo.*
> *Una folla consapevole che afferma la libertà dello spirito è uno spettacolo sublime. E una folla accecata che esalta il Potere è uno spettacolo osceno: chi*

si rende responsabile di una simile oscenità farebbe meglio ad impiccarsi.
(Morante, *Piccolo* 14; emphasis original)

To proclaim one's love for *the* laborers can prove to be a convenient alibi for
those who love not *any* laborer nor *any* man.
    An informed crowd that affirms spirit's freedom is a sublime sight. And an
ignorant crowd that hails Power is an obscene spectacle: he who is responsible
for such an obscenity should hang himself.

Morante's juxtaposition of power with human freedom, and her indictment of political action that disregards what she describes as the reality of
life, foreshadow Esposito's call to "rethink politics starting from the very
phenomenon of life" ("Unpolitical" 212). For Esposito, rather than being
reduced to mere biological essence, life needs to be considered "in its irreducible complexity . . . in its depth, stratification, and discontinuity, . . . in the
diversity of its manifestations, in the extremeness of its transformations"
("Unpolitical" 212). A reenvisioning of life will engender a politics that sees
life as its subject, no longer as its object. Moreover, with his notion of the
"impersonal," Esposito calls for a rethinking of human life as something that,
rather than belonging to the subject, is the subject:

be it divine property, or the property of the subject who inhabits it, the living
body is always conceived as a thing. Only a thing can belong to someone.
Only a human body that does not belong to a subject, but that is itself the
subject could be a non-property. In order to conceptualize this I believe it is
necessary to think of the person in the impersonal form. ("Politiche")

Thus, for Esposito life and the "human person" must be rethought as one: "it
is necessary to give back to subjectivity a more corporeal materiality" ("Politiche").
    Placing the complexity of life at the center of all human actions is a key
tenet of both Morante's and Esposito's thoughts. As Morante would put it,
the goal of all human action must be the liberation of the "realtà integra,
propria e naturale dell'uomo" (*Piccolo* 8; "the unbroken, true and natural
reality of man"), which manifests itself in infinite and diverse ways. Like
Morante, Esposito calls for a new approach to considering human life that
can inspire a new vision of the person and of social interactions. Moreover,
Morante shares in Esposito's notion of the "Unpolitical" the refusal to legiti-
mize the forces that bring about political conflict. Esposito's concept rejects
any ethical or theological legitimization of power, "every attempt to bestow
value to the bare fact of politics, namely, the contest for power" ("Unpolitical" 206). What Morante adds to Esposito's vision is an acute awareness of
the ethical potential—and power to effect change—of artistic and intellectual
endeavors that affirm life and freedom.

In the unfinished "Lettera alle Brigate Rosse," which Morante never sent, she indicts another, more deadly, false revolution, founded precisely on a complete disregard of human life.[9] Here the writer even hesitates to use the word *revolution*: "dato l'uso che ne è stato fatto nella storia . . . mi ripugna ormai di ripetere la parola *rivoluzione*" (*Piccolo* 18; emphasis original; "given the way it has been used throughout history . . . at this point repeating the word *revolution* sickens me"). Her tone in this text signals a deeper despair concerning contemporary society, and true horror at the violence perpetrated by the *brigatisti*. Rejecting their self-legitimizing notion that "*il fine giustifica i mezzi*" (*Piccolo* 18, emphasis original; "*the ends justify the means*"), Morante aligns the actions of the Red Brigades with those of the perpetrators of previous false revolutions. She maintains that, instead, "I mezzi denunciano il fine. Ora, i mezzi di cui voi vi servite . . . corrispondono a un modello riconoscibile e preciso: quello stesso che distrusse le più oscure 'rivoluzioni' del nostro secolo, e che si fonda su[l] . . . totale disprezzo per la persona umana" (*Piccolo* 18–19; "The means reveal the ends. Now, the means you use . . . correspond to a recognizable and precise model: the same that destroyed the most obscure 'revolutions' of our century, and which is founded on . . . the utmost contempt for the human person").

Morante's condemnation of the actions and ideology of the *brigatisti* is predicated on the idea that only a politics of life, that is, a politics founded on the respect of life—one's own, and the lives of others—can foster a just society. Disregarding the lives of others engenders a loss of self-respect, which makes this goal impossible to reach. Morante states that: "Le società instaurate sotto il disprezzo della persona umana, qualsiasi nome prendono, non possono essere che fasciste: ossia società dove vige la sopraffazione dell'uomo sull'uomo, e la repressione più atroce, e le torture" (*Piccolo* 19; "Societies established in contempt of the human person, regardless of their name, are inherently fascist: that is, they are societies where men's mutual aggression and the most atrocious repression and torture are the rule"). She underscores the fact that this violence is perpetrated against the defenseless: "È facile assalire o *giustiziare* gli indifesi, e poi scappare, sapendosi impuniti" (*Piccolo* 19, emphasis original; "It is easy to attack or *put to death* the defenseless, and then flee, knowing that one will not be punished").

Morante's theme prefigures a central motif of Cavarero's reflections on violence: the discourse on vulnerability, and the reorienting of the debate on violence on the position of the victim. In a recent article, Cavarero maintains that:

> Contemporary reflections on violence . . . examine the issue from a new and radical perspective, not only by calling into questions the global, geopolitical order . . . but above all by developing a theory that considers violence in the light of the "human question." . . . This theoretical effort . . . focuses on the

need to radically re-examine violence, connecting it to an ontology that demonstrates a vulnerability ingrained in humanity. ("Judith Butler" 163)

But many years earlier, in her critical and fictional writings, Morante had
already centered her reflection on violence on the perspective of the defenseless—the victims of history. The oppressed—not their oppressors—are the
protagonists of *La Storia* (*History*), Morante explains, precisely because they
represent "life," the "reality" of the human condition ("Nota *Storia*" lxxxiv).
Similarly, for Cavarero vulnerability coincides with the "human condition
itself" in the concrete sense of "the materiality of corporeal conditions" ("Beyond" 141–42). It is also, however, a potentiality in that the vulnerable body
exposes itself to the wound, but also to care: "Ethics happen when one finds
oneself singularly facing a decision to wound or not to wound, to care or not
to care" ("Beyond" 142).[10] The choice of care for others is central to Morante's vision of the social function of writers, as theorized in her critical
writings, and, importantly, as enacted in her literary works. As Morante puts
it, *La Storia* was meant to be, above all, "un atto di accusa, e una preghiera"
("Nota *Storia*" lxxxv; "an indictment, and a prayer").

In *Horrorism. Naming Contemporary Violence*, Cavarero, like Morante,
rejects the notion that any violence, be it, for example, at the hands of suicide
bombers in Iraq or resulting from the so-called war on terror, can be justified
as part of a strategy aimed to attain greater goals, that is, the idea that "the
massacre . . . forms part of a strategy or a means toward a higher end" (1). If
considered from the perspectives of the victims, the scene of the massacre
appears in a different light: "the end melts away, and the means become
substance. More than terror, what stands out is horror" (1). Cavarero thus
redirects the analysis of contemporary violence to examine horror, the perspective and emotional response of the victim, and accordingly coins the
word *horrorism* to describe this violence. Unlike terror, which causes one to
flee, horror has a paralyzing effect—it petrifies. Ultimately, horror annihi-
lates its victim both physically and ontologically: it destroys his or her
uniqueness of being. For Cavarero, "What is at stake is not the end of a
human life but the human condition itself, as incarnated in the singularity of
vulnerable bodies" (8).

But, how does literature fit into discourses on power, violence, and vulnerability? What can literature do for the world? In this respect, Enrico
Palandri has cautioned us on the danger of reading Morante's work "against
the backdrop of the planet's catastrophes," adding that her ideas on the function of poetry "have no possible uses in political struggle" ("Alcune notazioni" 88). According to Palandri, "If collective action and organization are
politics' essential elements, literature draws . . . away from this (otherwise it
is already propaganda) and towards a private, existential self-exam" ("Alcune notazioni" 88).[11] However, Morante's 1965 speech "Pro o contro la

bomba atomica" provides different answers to these questions; she opens by qualifying her views on literature, drawing a sharp distinction between "literature" and "literati" on one side, and "writer" on the other:

> *Ho sentito dire che qualcuno, al sapere in anticipo l'argomento da me scelto, ha mostrato una certa perplessità. . . . Invece, a me sembra evidente che nessun argomento, oggi, interessa, come questo, da vicino, ogni scrittore. A meno che non si vogliano confondere gli scrittori coi letterati: per i quali, come si sa, il solo argomento importante è, ed è sempre stata, la letteratura; ma allora devo avvertirvi subito che nel mio vocabolario abituale lo* scrittore *(che vuol dire prima di tutto . . .* poeta*), è il contrario del letterato. Anzi, una delle possibili definizioni giuste di scrittore, per me, sarebbe addirittura la seguente:* un uomo a cui sta a cuore tutto quanto accade, fuorché la letteratura. (1539; emphasis original)

> I heard that someone, having heard ahead of time the topic I picked, appeared perplexed. . . . However, it seems clear to me that no other topic, today, touches so closely every writer. Unless one confuses writers with the literati: for whom, as everyone knows, the only important topic is, and has always been, literature; but then I have to warn you right away that in my usual vocabulary, the *writer* (which means, first of all . . . *poet*) is the opposite of the intellectual. Moreover, one of the possible correct definitions of *writer*, for me, would be the following: *a man who cares for all that happens, except literature.*

In this text, Morante attributes to art a clear social function: "nella laida invasione dell'irrealtà, l'arte, che viene a rendere la realtà, può rappresentare quasi la sola speranza del mondo" (1545; "in the odious invasion of unreality, art, which expresses reality, might represent almost the sole hope for the world").[12] Art has the power to counter the disintegration of the human conscience typical of the contemporary world, of which the bomb is the natural manifestation, by representing the integrity of the real. Poets are thus particularly well poised to unmask deception. Moreover, their words cannot be arrested, and multiply endlessly. Even when representing tragedy and evil, "la qualità dell'arte è liberatoria, e quindi, nei suoi effetti, rivoluzionaria" (1547; "the nature of art is liberating and thus, in its effects, revolutionary"). Similarly, for a poet experiencing horror directly, if his or her conscience is still exempt from "irrealtà," "l'orrore stesso . . . diventerà una risposta reale (poesia), nel punto in cui segnerà le sue parole sulla carta, compierà un atto di ottimismo" (1547; "horror itself . . . will become a real answer [poetry], at the moment in which he will mark his words on paper, he will perform an act of optimism").[13]

Moreover, according to Morante, the practice of art, or poetry, is not possible in isolation from others. For her, art is not, as Palandri puts it "a private, existential self-exam" ("Alcune notazioni" 88). Rather, Morante maintains that the artist or writer, although tempted to "mandare tutti al diavolo" (to tell everyone off) from time to time, will ultimately reject isolation because, "per sua natura, ha bisogno degli altri, specie dei diversi da lui. . . . E così, rimarrà sul campo" ("Pro o contro" 1545; "by his very nature, he needs others, especially those who are different from himself. . . . Thus, he will stay in the game"). In Morante's view, artists see themselves as vital members of their societies, joined to others by an inescapable duty: "la funzione dei poeti, che è quella di aprire la propria e l'altrui coscienza alla realtà, è oggi più che mai urgente e necessaria. Nessun poeta, oggi, può ignorare la disperata domanda . . . degli altri esseri viventi" ("Nota *Mondo*" lxxxi; "the function of poets, which is to open to reality their own conscience, and the conscience of others, is today more urgent and necessary than ever before. No poet, today, can ignore the desperate plea . . . of other human beings").

Connection with, and responsibility toward, others are key tenets of Morante's ethical vision of her craft. For her, poets enact the model of *communitas* theorized, and auspicated, by Esposito, that is, a community based on the *munus*—"the law *of the* gift"—whose members are bound by a duty to give to others ("Unpolitical" 208; emphasis in the original). For Esposito, while *communitas* eliminates the boundaries of individuality, "immunity" reinstates them "defensively and offensively against any outside element threatening it" (209). Immunity, however, protects and simultaneously risks destroying us in that "we lose . . . the very sense of our individual and collective existence. . . , which I named *communitas*" (209).[14] The consonance between Esposito's notion of *communitas* and Morante's views on the social function of poetry can be traced to the profound influence of Simone Weil's thought on both thinkers. Esposito has often acknowledged his indebtedness to Weil's emphasis on duties toward others over individual rights, and to her deconstruction of the category of person in favor of the impersonal ("Il *munus*" 53–54; "Politiche"). As Filippo La Porta points out, Morante's concept of reality, that is, life in all its mutability and contradictions, as opposed to unreality and power—the use and manipulation of others—as evil, was inspired by Weil's *Cahiers*, which Morante studied intensely during the 1960s (291–93). Both Esposito and Morante have assimilated into their critiques of subjectivism and power Weil's "invitation to 'de-create' ourselves, to empty ourselves" (La Porta 293), so that others might manifest themselves. But Morante has also striven to enact the ethical commitment to others advocated by Weil throughout her life as a writer. *Il mondo salvato dai ragazzini*, Morante explains, is her "autobiography" insofar as it conveys "l'avventura disperata di una coscienza che tende, nel suo processo, a identificarsi con tutti gli altri viventi della terra" ("Nota *Mondo*" lxxxi; "the desperate adventure of a conscience that strives, in its process, to identify itself with all others living on earth").

Several decades separate Morante's texts from Cavarero's and Esposito's work. Momentous global events such as the end of the Cold War, among others, have produced a geo-political landscape vastly different from that of Morante's world. Yet, today, as foreseen by Morante, one after the other, many of our "contemporary tribes" are still embracing "unreality" and ignoring the pleas of the oppressed and the disenfranchised ("Nota *Mondo*" lxxxi). In response to the continued growth of global violence and injustice in the contemporary world, philosophers like Cavarero and Esposito are engaging with the same questions on history and the human condition raised by Morante half a century ago. Like Esposito, Morante has called for a rethinking of power, life, and the human condition that would foster an individual and collective commitment to serve the needs of others. With Cavarero, Morante shares a forceful critique of "strategic" violence, and a profound interest in vulnerability and the perspective of the defenseless. Morante's views, however, complement Cavarero's and Esposito's by affirming the ability of artists or poets—but also philosophers, some of whom Morante includes among the "*Felici Pochi*" (Happy Few) in *Il mondo salvato dai ragazzini*—to overcome the paralyzing effect of horror, and challenge the "dragon" of unreality with their art ("Pro o contro" 1546).[15] Only recently have philosophers such as Cavarero and Esposito reoriented their research to engage more directly with today's scenes of violence and war. As Esposito, explaining his shift from a deconstructive approach to a more affirmative inquiry, puts it: "philosophy's main task is that of fashioning concepts that are adequate to the events involving and changing us" ("Unpolitical" 210). In response to a particularly acute phase of the world's history of violence, these philosophers—like the poets described by Morante in "Pro o contro la bomba atomica"—have chosen to explore the most obscure and tragic facets of the contemporary world in order to enlighten others and advocate change.

NOTES

1. In the introduction of their edited volume on Morante, Lucamante and Wood argue that "the anachronistic quality of Morante's work places her not behind, but ahead of her time" (14).

2. See also Cavarero's dialogue with Judith Butler's discussion of "injurability," reactive aggression, and the censorship of dissent on war and retribution politics ("Judith Butler").

3. Cavarero, however, is fully conversant with Morante's oeuvre, which was the topic of a graduate seminar she taught at New York University in the fall of 2000. Most likely, Esposito has also read Morante's works.

4. Morante's "Sul romanzo" (1959) and *Il mondo salvato dai ragazzini* (1968) also foreground these themes.

5. Unless otherwise indicated, all translations are mine.

6. Carlo Cecchi and Cesare Garboli found the "Piccolo Manifesto dei Comunisti (senza classe né partito)" amid Morante's papers after her death and gave it to Fofi. It was first published in *Linea d'ombra* 30 (1988).

7. See also the "Carteggio Elsa Morante—Goffredo Fofi," a selection of the letters they exchanged between 1969 and 1985 (D. Morante 553–76).

8. For a lucid discussion of Morante's concepts of reality and unreality, see La Porta. He thus encapsulates Morante's, and Pasolini's, notion of reality: "'the real thing' is life itself, which is by definition not docile, which never lets itself be 'possessed' in any way . . . and which includes within itself its own opposite (death, the negative)." (307).

9. Dated March 20, 1978, the unfinished "Lettera alle Brigate Rosse" was first published in *Paragone* 456 (1988) and later included in the "Cronologia" of Morante's *Opere* (Vol. 1), and in *Piccolo Manifesto*.

10. According to Cavarero, the infant, as utterly dependent and vulnerable, embodies all human helplessness.

11. Palandri generally attributes little importance to Morante's essays, describing them as "a sort of doodle in between novels" that fail to open new paths in her journey as a writer ("Narrative" 263).

12. For Morante, art and poetry are synonyms. In "Pro o contro la bomba atomica," by "writer" she refers to all artists.

13. An example of this, for Morante, is the poems written by Hungarian poet Miklós Radnóti in a Nazi concentration camp up until the time of his death.

14. However, in his later works Esposito theorizes that the dynamics of immunization, by attacking itself (autoimmunity), contradicts itself, "opening up to a possible transformation." Societies can thus "reach a turning point" that makes possible the rebuilding of *communitas* ("Unpolitical" 212).

15. It is interesting to note that Cavarero's philosophical—and strongly political—work relies considerably on literature. For Cavarero, literature is "a polysemous language that undoes the arrogance of every system claiming stability." Philosophy, instead, "is constructed by removing from language the liveliness of the body, the communicative sense of its resonance and, consequently, the voice that invokes another voice before and beyond what is said" ("Beyond" 160).

WORKS CITED

Bareil, Jean-Philippe. "Ricomposizione e ridistribuzione nell'opera di Elsa Morante. Svolgimento e concrezione." *Elsa Morante: Narrativa* 17 (2000): 5–13.

Cavarero, Adriana. "Beyond Ontology and Sexual Difference: An Interview with the Italian Feminist Philosopher Adriana Cavarero." Trans. Elisabetta Bertolino. *differences: A Journal of Feminist Cultural Studies* 19:1 (2008): 128–67.

———. *Horrorism. Naming Contemporary Violence*. Trans. William McCuaig. New York: Columbia University Press, 2009.

———. "Inclining the Subject. Ethics, Alterity and Natality." *Theory after 'Theory.'* Jane Elliott and Derek Attridge, eds. London and New York: Routledge, 2010. 194–204.

———. "Judith Butler and the Belligerent Subject." Trans. Anne Tordi. *Annali d'Italianistica*, *Italian Critical Theory* 29 (2011): 163–70.

Esposito, Roberto. "From the Unpolitical to Biopolitics." Trans. Santo Pettinato. *Annali d'Italianistica, Italian Critical Theory* 29 (2011): 205–13.

———. "Il *munus* da cui non siamo esonerati: pensare il comune nell'ambito del bios." Saidel 49–64.

———. "Politiche della vita sul margine pericoloso dell'impersonale." *Centro per la Riforma dello Stato*, 21 June 2007. Web. 27 June 2013.

La Porta, Filippo. "The 'Dragon of Unreality' against the 'Dream of a Thing.' On Morante and Pasolini." Lucamante and Wood. 290–309.

Lucamante, Stefania, and Sharon Wood, eds. *Under Arturo's Star. The Cultural Legacies of Elsa Morante.* West Lafayette, IN: Purdue University Press, 2006.

Morante, Daniele, ed. *L'amata. Lettere di e a Elsa Morante*. Turin: Einaudi, 2012.

Morante, Elsa. *Il mondo salvato dai ragazzini*. Morante, *Opere* 2, 3–254.

———. "Nota introduttiva alla prima edizione Struzzi del *Mondo salvato dai ragazzini*." Morante, *Opere* 1, lxxx–lxxxi.

————. "Nota introduttiva all'edizione americana della *Storia*." Morante, *Opere* 1, lxxxiii–lxxxv.

————. *Opere*. Carlo Cecchi and Cesare Garboli, eds. 2 vols. Milan: Meridiani Mondadori, 1988 and 1990.

————. *Piccolo Manifesto dei Comunisti (senza classe né partito)*. Rome: Nottetempo, 2004.

————. "Pro o contro la bomba atomica." *Opere* 2, 1537–54.

Palandri, Enrico. "Alcune notazioni in margine a *Pro o contro la bomba atomica*." *Studi novecenteschi* 21, 47–48 (1994): 79–90.

————. "Narrative and Essays: The Ethical Commitment." Lucamante and Wood 257–67.

Saidel, Matías, L. *Roberto Esposito. Dall'impolitico all'impersonale: conversazioni filoso-fiche*. Matías L. Saidel and Gonzalo Velasco Arias, eds. Milan: Mimesis, 2012. 49–64.

Index

About the Authors

Sarah Carey holds a PhD in Italian from UCLA. Carey was an Andrew W. Mellon Fellow in the Humanities Department of French and Italian at Stanford University until 2013. She has published in *Quaderni d'Italianistica*, *Italian Culture*, *La Fusta*, and *Carte Italiane*. Her new book project is entitled *Envisioning Italy: Photography and the Portrait of a Nation*.

Flavia Cartoni is associate professor of Italian literature at the University of Castilla–La Mancha, Spain. Among her publications, she has authored essays on Dacia Maraini's plays, Sandro Penna's poetry, Marco Lodoli, Antonio Scurati, and Elsa Morante's novels. She is the editor and translator of Elsa Morante's short stories collection *Lo scialle andaluso* in the Spanish edition of *El chal andaluz* (2006), is responsible for the Spanish edition of *La Historia y Aracoeli* (2008), and coeditor of the book *El tema el viaje: un recorrido por la lengua y la literatura italiana* (2010).

Gandolfo Cascio is assistant professor of Italian literature and translation studies at Utrecht University. His main field of research is the sixteenth and twentieth-century poetry and particularly the production of artist-poets, poet-translators, and the so-called anti-Novecento writers. He is also a literary critic and translator. He is currently engaged in a monograph on Morante's *Alibi*.

Claude Cazalé Bérard is emeritus professor of Italian literature at the Université de Paris Ouest-Nanterre. Among her many publications on women and the intersection of history and literature is *Donne tra memoria e scrittura. Fuller, Weil, Sachs, Morante* (2009). Cazalé Bérard serves on the board of *Strumenti Critici, Testo and Senso, Studi Ambrosiani di Italianistica* Studi Ambrosiani di Italianistica, *Tsafon*.

Francesco Chillemi received his PhD in Italian Studies from Rutgers University in October 2014. His dissertation, "Arts in the Mirror: Paradoxes of Self-Reference in Twentieth-Century Italy," investigates the philosophical theme of the essence of language by examining seminal self-referential works across theater, literature, and cinema. Chillemi also holds an MA summa cum laude in cinema from the University of Bologna (2007) and a BA in drama studies from the University of Padua (2004).

Giovanna De Luca is associate professor of Italian at the College of Charleston. Her articles on Italian cinema, literary and film theory, and cultural studies have appeared in *Filmcritica, Film Comment, Quaderni d'Italianistica, Forum Italicum, Italica, La Tribune International des Langues Vivantes* and *Cineaction.* She has authored *Il punto di vista dell'infanzia nel cinema italiano e francese: rivisioni.* Currently, she is working on her new project, *Harsh Spectacle: The Mafia in Italian and American Cinema.*

Manuele Gragnolati is professor of Italian literature at the University of Oxford, where he is a Fellow of Somerville College, and associate director of the ICI-Berlin Institute for Cultural Inquiry. He has published extensively on Dante and medieval and modern Italian literature and culture, with a special interest on the entanglement of corporeality, language, and aesthetics. His latest book is *Amor che move. Linguaggio del corpo e forma del desiderio in Dante, Pasolini e Morante* (2013).

Thomas Harrison, chair of Italian at UCLA, has written *Essayism: Conrad, Musil and Pirandello and 1910: The Emancipation of Dissonance* (1995), a transdisciplinary study of expressionist aesthetics and ethics. Harrison has widely published on Carlo Michelstaedter, Lukács, Nietzsche, Italian film, Zanzotto, Triestine culture, Montale, the Adriatic, and theories of humor.

Claudia Karagoz is associate professor of Italian and women's and gender studies at Saint Louis University. She has published several articles and book chapters on Italian women writers and directors, and coedited a volume on Sicily and the Mediterranean. Her current book project examines the representation of motherhood in contemporary Italian women's writing and cinema.

Stefania Lucamante is professor of Italian at the Catholic University of America. Among other titles, she is the author of *Forging Shoah Memories:*

Italian Women Writers, Jewish Identity, and the Holocaust (2014), *A Multitude of Women: The Challenges of the Contemporary Italian Novel* (2008), and *Elsa Morante e l'eredità proustiana* (1998) She is also the coeditor (with Sharon Wood) of *Under Arturo's Star: the Cultural Legacies of Elsa Morante* (2005).

Kenise Lyons completed her graduate studies at Yale University with a dissertation entitled "The Art of Writing with Light: the Photographic Presence in Italian Film, 1948–1978." Her areas of interest are contemporary Italian film and narrative, Pier Paolo Pasolini, and Elsa Morante. She is currently an independent scholar.

Gaetana Marrone, professor of Italian at Princeton University, specializes in modern Italian literature and postwar Italian cinema. Her principal publications include articles in nineteenth- and twentieth-century literature, film, gender, and cultural studies. She is also the author of award-winning books, and is General Editor of the Routledge *Encyclopedia of Italian Literary Studies* (2007).

Daniele Morante earned a Laurea summa cum laude from the University of Rome in Philosophy, and a doctorate in Linguistics from the University of Grenoble. As a linguist, he is the author of *Le champ linguistique gravitationnel*, a new general model of language parametrization and language change. He worked as a consultant and translator from English, French, and Russian for several Italian publishers, and is the author of short stories and translations that have appeared on literary reviews like *Nuovi Argomenti*, *Paragone*, and *Ombre Rosse*, as well as in the collection of his short stories *Belin o l'Impostura*. With *L'amata* (2012), his critical edition of Elsa Morante's correspondence, Morante was awarded the Prize Elsa Morante and the Prize V. Aganoor Pamphili.

Maria Morelli is Fulbright Teaching Assistant in Italian at Wheaton College, MA. She is completing her PhD in Italian studies at the University of Leicester, United Kingdom. Her doctoral research project investigates how the works of Elsa Morante, Goliarda Sapienza, and Dacia Maraini foreshadow positions of feminism and gender theory that will later develop in international contexts. Forthcoming publications include a book chapter on the gender politics of Maraini and a comparative analysis between Maraini and Sapienza's queer writing.

Gabrielle Orsi works in academic technology at Colorado Mountain College. Her academic interests include Holocaust studies and modern Italian literature; she is a contributor to the University of Chicago's Italian Women

Writers Database. Currently she is studying Elsa Morante's manuscripts as a visiting scholar at the American Academy in Rome.

Lorenzo Salvagni is a writer-musician native of Rome, Italy. His writings have appeared on peer-reviewed journals like *altrelettere*, *Romance Notes*, and *Annali d'Italianistica*; he collaborates with the Italian music magazines *Amadeus* and *Suonare News*. He is the author of an essay on Marguerite Caetani published in the edited collection *Roffredo Caetani, un musicista aristocratico* (2014). He lives in Cleveland, Ohio.

Hanna Serkowska directs the Italian Department of the University of Warsaw. Among her publications are *Uscire da una camera delle favole* (2002; awarded Elsa Morante's Prize in 2004) and *Dopo il romanzo storico. La storia nella letteratura italiana del '900* (2012). Serkowska is editor of six volumes (*Finzione, cronaca, realtà, Scambi, intrecci e prospettive nella narrativa italiana contemporanea*, 2011) and is currently working on a new project: *Narratives of ageing, ageism and ableism across Europe*.

Katrin Wehling-Giorgi is lecturer in Italian at the University of Durham, United Kingdom. She is author of *Gadda and Beckett: Storytelling, Subjectivity and Fracture* (2014), and she has published various articles on Céline, Gadda, Morante, Joyce, and Beckett in *Forum for Modern Language Studies*, *Italian Studies*, *Samuel Beckett Today/Aujourd'hui*, and *The Edinburgh Journal of Gadda Studies*.

Sharon Wood is professor of Italian at the University of Leicester. She writes on gender and literature, women's cultural history, contemporary narrative and theater, and translation studies. Publications include books on the history of women's writing in Italy. With Stefania Lucamante she edited a volume of essays entitled *Under Arturo's Star: The Cultural Legacies of Elsa Morante* (2005). Wood has translated works by Primo Levi, Dacia Maraini, and Romana Petri. She is currently preparing a collection of essays on Annie Vivanti.

Giuliana Zagra is a librarian at the Biblioteca nazionale centrale of Rome. Zagra is director of the twentieth-century literary collections area and is responsible for the acquisition, cataloging, and valorization of the Elsa Morante Archive. She has organized several exhibits and published catalogs on Morante's work and life.

Saskia Ziolkowski is visiting assistant professor of Italian studies at Duke University. She has published on Italo Svevo, Franz Kafka, Primo Levi, Robert Musil, Tommaso Landolfi, Rainer Maria Rilke, and Scipio Slataper. Her current book project, *Kafka's Italian Progeny*, examines Kafka's presence in modern Italian literature.